The Modern Middle East and North Africa

A HISTORY IN DOCUMENTS

The Modern Middle East and North Africa

A HISTORY IN DOCUMENTS

Julia Clancy-Smith
Charles D. Smith

New York   Oxford
OXFORD UNIVERSITY PRESS

For our daughter, Elisabeth Anna, and grandson, Miles

General Editors:

Sarah Deutsch
Professor of History
Duke University

Carol K. Karlsen
Professor of History and Women's Studies
University of Michigan

Robert G. Moeller
Professor of History
University of California, Irvine

Jeffrey N. Wasserstrom
Professor of History
University of California, Irvine

Cover photo: "Palestine Delegation of Arab Ladies." This photograph shows a delegation of unnamed Palestinian women, both Muslim and Christian, on October 12, 1938 on the platform at the Lydda Junction of the train line linking Palestine with Egypt. They were traveling to Cairo to attend the "Levant Women's Conference," convened from October 1938 15–18 at the headquarters of the Egyptian Women's Federation, to publicize mounting sociopolitical problems in Palestine under the British Mandate. Chaired by the Egyptian leader of the women's rights movement, Mrs. Hoda Shaarawi, the conference issued a report, subsequently published as a book whose revenues were used to assist distressed Palestinian families. The image illustrates many of the themes of this volume.

Frontispiece: Moslems worshipping the shrines sacred to Islam, Mecca, Arabia.

Title Page: Tahrir Square, 9 February 2011.

Oxford University Press is a department of the University of Oxford. It furthers the University's objective of excellence in research, scholarship, and education by publishing worldwide.

Oxford New York
Auckland   Cape Town   Dar es Salaam   Hong Kong   Karachi
Kuala Lumpur   Madrid   Melbourne   Mexico City   Nairobi
New Delhi   Shanghai   Taipei   Toronto

With offices in
Argentina   Austria   Brazil   Chile   Czech Republic   France   Greece
Guatemala   Hungary   Italy   Japan   Poland   Portugal   Singapore
South Korea   Switzerland   Thailand   Turkey   Ukraine   Vietnam

© 2014 by Julia Clancy-Smith and Charles D. Smith

For titles covered by Section 112 of the US Higher Education Opportunity Act, please visit www.oup.com/us/he for the latest information about pricing and alternate formats.

Oxford is a registered trade mark of Oxford University Press in the UK and certain other countries.

Published in the United States of America by
Oxford University Press
198 Madison Avenue, New York, NY 10016

Library of Congress Cataloging-in-Publication Data on file

9780195338270

9 8 7 6 5 4

Printed in the United States of America on acid-free paper

Contents

Note on Transliteration

The modern Middle East and North Africa (MENA) includes the Arab lands of the Arabian Peninsula bordered by the Red Sea, Arabian Sea, and Persian Gulf, Iran, Turkey, Iraq, Syria, Lebanon, Israel [Palestine to 1948], and the countries of Northern Africa bordering the Mediterranean and, in the case of Morocco, the Atlantic Ocean. Consistent transliteration for the history of these regions poses a number of problems because there is no single agreed-on system among scholars. Proper names, place names, and terms come from a range of languages—classical Arabic, dialectal Arabic, Berber, Ottoman Turkish, modern Turkish, Persian, and, in some cases, French. To complicate matters, proper names and place names often came into English or other European languages through different kinds of transliteration, which was not consistent and frequently deformed the originals. Therefore, transliteration in this volume is the product of compromise as is true of all published work on MENA. For the most part, a modified version of the transliteration system in the *International Journal of Middle East Studies* for Arabic, Turkish, and Persian is employed. Standard transliteration symbols are used in documents and document captions only when such symbols are used in the original document in the text. For Arabic, only the ayn (') and hamza (') are used in such cases. Turkish words, such as *bey* or *dey*, which refer to Ottoman political offices or titles, are used instead of the more accurate Arabic transliteration, *bay*. If a term, such as the Arabic word for "city," *madina*, has entered the *Oxford English Dictionary* (OED) in another variant form, such as *medina*, then the OED spelling is employed.

What Is a Document?

To the historian, a document is, quite simply, any sort of historical evidence. It is a primary source, the raw material of history. A document may be more than the expected government paperwork, such as a treaty or passport. It is also a letter, diary, will, grocery list, newspaper article, recipe, memoir, oral history, school yearbook, map, chart, architectural plan, poster, musical score, play script, novel, political cartoon, painting, photograph—even an object.

Using primary sources allows us not just to read *about* history, but to read history itself. It allows us to immerse ourselves in the look and feel of an era gone by, to understand its people and their language, whether verbal or visual. And it allows us to take an active, hands-on role in (re)constructing history.

Using primary sources requires us to use our powers of detection to ferret out the relevant facts and to draw conclusions from them; just as Agatha Christie uses the scores in a bridge game to determine the identity of a murderer, the historian uses facts from a variety of sources—some, perhaps, seemingly inconsequential—to build a historical case.

The poet W. H. Auden wrote that history was the study of questions. Primary sources force us to ask questions—and then, by answering them, to construct a narrative or an argument that makes sense to us. Moreover, as we draw on the many sources from "the dust-bin of history," we can endow that narrative with character, personality, and texture—all the elements that make history so endlessly intriguing.

Cartoon

This political cartoon addresses the issue of church and state. It illustrates the Supreme Court's role in balancing the demands of the 1st Amendment of the Constitution and the desires of the religious population.

Illustration

Illustrations from children's books, such as this alphabet from the *New England Primer*, tell us how children were educated and also what the religious and moral values of the time were.

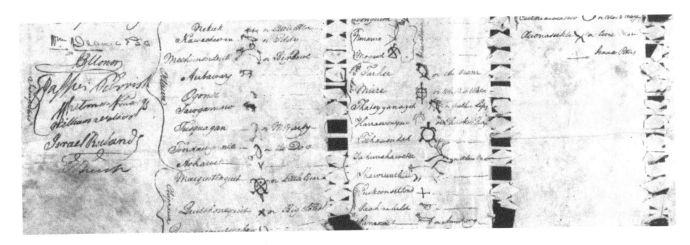

Treaty

A government document such as this 1805 treaty can reveal not only the details of government policy, but also information about the people who signed it. Here, the Indians' names were written in English transliteration by U.S. officials; the Indians added pictographs to the right of their names.

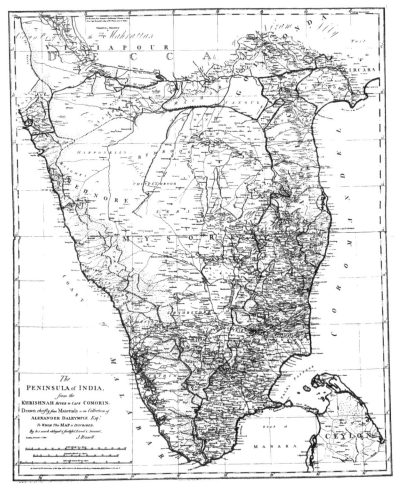

Map

A 1788 British map of India shows the region prior to British colonization, an indication of the kingdoms and provinces whose ethnic divisions would resurface later in India's history.

Object

In this fifteenth-century ewer, both the physical materials of brass and silver and the iconic depiction of heaven as a forest display the refinement of the owner, an Egyptian sultan's wife. Objects, along with manuscripts and printed materials, provide evidence about the past.

How to Read a Document

In the course of our daily lives, we all "leave crumbs behind"—bits and pieces of evidence regarding what we did or did not do—and ultimately clues about who we are as individuals and what kind of social universe we inhabit. When we use public transport, a purchased bus, train, or metro ticket indicates where we've been and/or where we were heading. An unfortunate encounter with a traffic officer while driving generates a fine and some paperwork registered with the DMV. Our favorite foods and drinks show up on grocery store receipts and often on our credit card bills as well. And what we throw away at night in the garbage or recycling bins divulges patterns of consumption. Records of checked-out books from the university library are revealing; they show the courses in which we enrolled, what our professors or instructors think is important for a specific discipline, and whether we prefer fiction or nonfiction or both. In the aggregate, societies, religions, cultures, states, and civilizations leave behind vast reservoirs of evidence from the past in many and complex forms. As is true for individuals, documentation for the history of larger social bodies or political entities is culled from a number of primary sources that historians generally categorize as written or unwritten. Recorded evidence ranges from population censuses; tax records; diaries; business ledgers; and scientific, religious, or literary works to monumental inscriptions on built structures. Written evidence can be personal, such as letters exchanged between family members, or public, such

as law codes or the proceedings of court cases. Some evidence is published, while much may remain in archival form, that is, unpublished. Nonwritten sources include works of art, photographs, posters, architecture, city space, clothing, and diverse objects of material culture. In addition to collecting and interpreting primary sources, historians consult available secondary sources to learn how other scholars have researched and reconstructed a particular historical topic or time period.

Nevertheless, primary sources constitute the raw materials of history writing. In their quest to understand, narrate, and interpret the past, the historian faces major problems and questions: who wrote, composed, or made the text or object under scrutiny and for what purposes or audiences? What was excised from a text or image and why? How was the text or image received or "read" by different audiences? Is the source "trustworthy," that is, does it approximate some social reality, or was it produced and used to mislead, for example, for propagandistic purposes? And how did a particular primary source, whatever its form, come down to us and why was it preserved?

Subject

This photograph of Constantinople (or Istanbul; opposite) in the late nineteenth century shows the newly rebuilt Galata Bridge, which connected two major urban quarters of the capital of the Ottoman Empire, the old imperial core and Islamic center, and newer neighborhoods on the other side of the Golden Horn. Together with written documentation, this image can be employed as a primary source for recreating daily life as well as investigating historical changes at the level of the state and society.

Interpretation

By analyzing the people, buildings, animals, and objects in the foreground, the historian sees that several modes of transportation existed: foot traffic, horse-drawn carriages, and small skiffs as well as larger vessels. In addition, we notice that bundles of goods are being transported and that a shop lines the bridge's left-hand corner, thus this is a place of commerce and trade. Clothing might yield clues about people's identity because Constantinople was a multireligious, multicultural, and polyglot city where dress betrayed communal belonging. Most of the human bridge traffic appears to be male and wearing some modified version of European costume together with the fez as headgear but one individual (in the left hand corner) has a turban, suggesting that he is a Muslim dignitary. But how did this photograph come to be and what meaning was it meant to convey? This question brings in the Ottoman state and modernization. We can see at the far end of Galata Bridge, a large mosque, the "New Mosque" (*Yeni Camii*) whose construction began the late sixteenth century, and other religious buildings. In proximity to these monumental Islamic structures, numerous Ottoman state or bureaucratic offices, connected to the exercise of power, whether local, regional, or imperial, were traditionally found. In the course

that broke out first in this North African nation in late December 2010 and subsequently spread across the Middle East. In contrast to the first image with city residents going about their daily business, here protesters shout slogans and display signs with political messages during a demonstration in the city center on January 19, 2011, five days after the dictator and president, Zine El Abidine Ben Ali resigned and fled the country.

Interpretation

As a piece of historical evidence, this image offers clues about the nature, strategies, and objectives of collective popular protest

of the nineteenth century, the construction of state-of-the-art bridges, such as this one completed in 1875, signified modernity and progress. Moreover, social progress was tied to new forms of urbanization, which Ottoman authorities initiated in the capital and provincial cities. Therefore, this image itself bridges the recording of daily-ness, people going about their business, and the state memorializing through photography a new symbol of the modern.

Subject

This photograph (below) captures a citizens' demonstration in Tunis, the capital of Tunisia, during the "Arab Revolution"

at a particular historical juncture. The young woman in the center carries in her arms the Tunisian flag, symbol of the nation. In addition, the hand-lettered sign in Arabic in the middle foreground says "No to al-Tajammuʿ." This means no to the official party of the president, Zine el-Abidine ben ʿAli (1936–). The party's full title was the "The constitutional, democratic Tajammuʿ [Assembly]," suggesting it was a fully inclusive party when in fact it represented a dictatorship. Moreover, the fact that the sign was "homemade" tells us that Tunisian citizens selected the kinds of messages and demands that they wanted to make public. The fact that Arabic was used meant that the intended audiences were speakers of Arabic, although some of the other placards in the background appear to be in other languages. By comparing images of the Tunisian Revolution from diverse sources, the historian finds that indeed a number of foreign languages were employed for political signage—notably French and English. This in turn reveals the kinds of media audiences the Tunisian protesters desired to reach and communicate with. However, this leads to an important question: why did these assembled people seek to internationalize their movement and its goals? Finally, the fact that this massive rally was held in the main streets of Tunis is significant because this "use" of capital city space concretized widely shared demands for true political change at the national level.

Cérémonie du Sélamlik de Vendredi à la Mosquée Hamidié

Introduction

The Hamidiye Mosque, near the Yıldız Palace, was commissioned by the Ottoman Sultan Abdul Hamid II and completed in 1886. Built on a rectangular plan, its architecture combines Neo-Gothic style and classical Ottoman motifs. It became the site of an elaborate Friday prayer ceremony and procession symbolizing the ruler's authority. The original photograph is captioned in both Ottoman Turkish and French.

The regions stretching from Northwest Africa to Southwest Asia and the Iranian Plateau, currently known as the Middle East and North Africa (MENA), have always been fundamental to humankind's history, in large measure due to geographical positioning at an international crossroads or series of interconnecting zones. Situated where Mediterranean, Atlantic, African, European, and Asian histories intersect, MENA was the birthplace of some of the world's greatest civilizations and has acted over the centuries as an important conduit between, and among, adjacent states, cultures, and economies. Aleppo in Syria is one of the oldest continuously inhabited cities in the world—in existence since the 6th millennium BC, according to excavations. Reputed to be consummate traders, the inhabitants of Aleppo have for millennia occupied a strategic commercial position in exchanges across Eurasia. There are few world regions that illustrate the complexities and currents of global history better than MENA, yet its borders and boundaries have never been fixed. The continual transregional movement of peoples, things, species, and religiopolitical ideas over millennia means that a neatly defined "outside world" did not, historically speaking, exist. As a 2011 work provocatively asked, *Is There a Middle East?* Thus, considerable scholarly debate has surrounded the notion of MENA whose geopolitical origins lie principally in European (and later American) imperial and strategic interests from circa 1800 until today. Moreover, the disintegration of the Soviet Union after 1989 and the emergence

1

"Aleppo, Khan el-Vezir." This image shows a *khan* or caravansaray in Aleppo, Syria's most densely populated city and one of the largest cities in the Levant. An ancient trading hub where routes converged from China, Mesopotamia, and Egypt, it attracted people of all races and religions because of its location at the terminus of the Silk Roads. However, when the Suez Canal opened in 1869, trans-Asian trade was diverted to maritime routes and Aleppo declined in commercial importance. Nevertheless, the city boasts the world's largest covered markets which extend for some eight miles.

of Turkish Muslim republics have effectively pushed out the already fluid eastern edges of "the Middle East." Former "Soviet" peoples, cultures, and places are now often subsumed under this rubric, which has lately grown bigger. If the term MENA now enjoys common currency, nevertheless the question remains—are there distinguishing historical, geographical, cultural, and political features and patterns that confer some sort of inner, central coherence or unity?

In addition, "human-induced environmental" transformations have marked the region long before the onset of what is known as modernity—indeed these kinds of changes can be detected much earlier in time. Environmentally, MENA has many faces in terms of ecological and resource structures that have shaped the long- and short-term evolution of human societies. One face is the Mediterranean and its shifting hinterlands, although the Inner Sea is fragmented by thousands of islands forming a complex of seas rather than a single body of water. The mention of the Mediterranean brings to mind olive groves, vineyards, and whitewashed villages standing starkly against deep blue waters. But the Sea forms an immense inland waterway surrounded by mountains and pierced by peninsulas, which constitute its "second face." A third subregion are the interior semiarid plains often located on the fluctuating margins of rain-fed agriculture where village economies and pastoralism comingle. Finally, deserts that approach the Mediterranean coastline in southern Tunisia, Libya, Egypt, and the Syrian littoral, also determine the geohistorical human and natural landscapes of the Arabian Peninsula, Iraq, Israel, Jordan, and Iran. Popular images in contemporary media and film present MENA as characterized mainly by oil rigs, oases, camels, and nomads (not to mention terrorists), but in fact the majority of its inhabitants have always been largely urban dwellers and peasants.

MENA has always maintained intense ties with adjacent areas—whether Europe, the central Asian steppes, South Asia and the Indian

Ocean, sub-Saharan Africa, and after 1500 with the emerging Atlantic worlds. "Strategic choke points," where land and maritime communication systems converge—Gibraltar, the Sicilian Channel, Dardanelles, and the Suez Canal and Gulf of Suez passages into the Red Sea—have facilitated multiple exchanges. Europe and Asia meet in Istanbul or Constantinople; the old Ottoman and Byzantine sectors of the city lie in Europe while the "newer" quarters are found across the Bosporus Strait in Asia Minor. And MENA served as redistribution hubs for trans-Asian goods and knowledge, long before and long after, European explorers, and subsequently navies and merchants, entered the Indian Ocean trade in force in the sixteenth century. For example, once among the world's largest cities, Isfahan was located on the main north-south and east-west trade routes crossing the Iranian Plateau. The capital of Persia in the sixteenth century under Shah Abbas I, the Great (r. 1587–1629), of the Safavid Dynasty (1502–1736), Isfahan's population may have reached half a million and boasted libraries, palaces, mosques, and pleasure gardens that bedazzled visitors, especially Europeans. Even today its sobriquet, "Isfahan is half of the world," persists.

If the Mediterranean has represented an expressway for invaders, migrants, enslaved persons, merchants, missionaries, and travelers, so too somewhat paradoxically has the desert. Advances in seafaring worked in tandem with changes in overland transportation. Caravan travel improved markedly between 600 and 300 BCE. By experimenting with camel breeding and transport techniques, some communities in the arid interiors of northern Africa and Southwest Asia became directly integrated into maritime circuits by employing camel power to move humans and goods within reach of ports. Pastoral-nomadic societies evolved into camel or horse specialists, middlemen in regional and long-distance commerce, or providers of transport. This proved crucial to the elaboration of the silk routes—the China to Mediterranean trade that flourished by the first century CE. Central Asian steppe peoples brought silk and other precious goods west via chains of oases and caravansaray;

"Mosque and street, Scutari, Constantinople, Turkey." Known in Turkish as Üsküdar, this large and densely populated municipality on the Anatolian or Asian shore of the Bosporus is now part of the greater Istanbul metropolitan region. Founded sometime in the seventh century BCE by Greek settlers, by the nineteenth century when this photo was taken, the suburb had grown into an important trading, religious, and residential area with a very mixed population of Greeks, Jews, Turks, and Armenians.

other trading intermediaries then oversaw the transport of highly prized commodities to MENA's sea and land emporia. Even more ancient routes channeled spices, dyes, and drugs from East African-Indian Ocean trade circuits into MENA via the Red Sea in exchange for textiles, luxury goods, and metals.

The Rise of Islam as Faith Community, State, and Empire

Rome's long hegemony over the entire Mediterranean Basin and Asia Minor ended in 246 CE, when the Emperor Diocletian divided the empire into western and eastern realms; the latter served as the seat of the Byzantine Empire (which endured in one form or another until 1453). This was the political world-system that the Arab-Muslim armies encountered when they moved out of northern Arabia and into the Fertile Crescent, Persia, and northern Africa after the Prophet Muhammad's death in 632 CE. Destabilized politically, religiously, and socially by the seventh century, the Byzantine and Sasanian Empires were no match for a new faith and movement, Islam. Arabian Muslim warriors embarked on extensive military campaigns beginning around 634 CE, first in Greater Syria and Palestine, where Byzantine-ruled Jerusalem fell in 638; the Sasanian capital, Ctesiphon, had capitulated a year earlier in 637. With the capture of Alexandria in 643, the conquest of the Byzantine province of Egypt was completed. This allowed Arab-Muslim armies to march west across North Africa, seizing Carthage by 698; soon thereafter the adjacent city of Tunis was revived and repopulated. In 711 these armies crossed the Strait of Gibraltar, the gateway to the Iberian Peninsula. The progressive sophistication of camel transport and saddle technology may have given the Arab-Muslims a certain military advantage over their Byzantine foes and thus directly or indirectly contributed to conquests and new waves of migrations. But the fierce fourth and fifth-century doctrinal and political conflicts within Christianity played a major role in the Muslim victories as did other historical forces. From the seventh century on, much of MENA, excluding Asia Minor, was under the rule of the Arab Umayyad Dynasty of Damascus (661–750), succeeded by the Arabo-Persian Abbasid Dynasty (750–1258) based in Baghdad. Eventually rival, but more localized, caliphates emerged in Muslim Spain, such as the

"Constantinople. St. Sophia, Interior of the Left Nave, circa 1860–1890." Dedicated in 360 CE, the basilica of Hagia Sophia ("Holy Wisdom") served as the Greek Orthodox patriarch's seat until 1453 when Constantinople fell to invading Turkish armies. The basilica was transformed into a mosque and remained thus until 1931. The huge suspended orb to the right has Muhammad written in Arabic. Under the Turkish republic, it was transformed into a secular museum in 1935.

Spanish Umayyad Dynasty and the Caliphate of Córdoba (929–1031).

Muslims became a majority population in most places in MENA by about the eleventh century. Under early Muslim rule, Christian, Jewish, and Zoroastrian communities were legally accorded the status of "Peoples of the Book" as adherents of earlier written revelations from the one true God. As inferior, yet protected groups or *dhimmi*-s, these fellow monotheists paid a special tax called the *jizya*; in return, they were generally permitted to practice their faith as well as maintain their own religious courts, places of worship, and schools. However, under some Islamic dynasties, the right to build or repair churches or synagogues required official permission; sumptuary laws requiring Christians and Jews to wear distinctive clothing existed, mainly in urban areas, but were not always strictly enforced. As a rule, *dhimmi* communal security reflected shifting historical relationships between Muslim and Christian states. The Crusades (1095–1291) and the later European economic and political penetration of the Muslim world, especially during the nineteenth century, created rising religious tensions and outbreaks of confessional conflict. Most Islamic dynasties (caliphates) in MENA, with the exclusion of Iran and the western Maghrib, were succeeded by the Ottoman Turkish dynasty based in Istanbul or Constantinople from 1453 until 1922.

Throughout the sixteenth century, titanic struggles for mastery over the Mediterranean Sea and North African littoral pitted the Spanish Hapsburgs against the Ottoman Turks, who by then claimed expanding domains in southeastern Europe or the Balkans. Nevertheless, political alliances did not match up with religion; Catholic France supported the Muslim Turks against its European rivals. By 1517, Syria, Palestine, and Egypt had submitted to Ottoman rule and by 1574, Algeria, Tunisia, and Tripolitania (as the Ottoman province in Libya was known) were formally incorporated into the empire. Never conquered by the Ottomans, Morocco was governed by a succession of local dynasties whose capital cities

"Muslim Worshippers leaving the Zaytuna Mosque-University, Tunis, c. 1899." Founded in the eighth century CE, and thus the oldest mosque in Tunis as well as one of the oldest Islamic structures in North Africa, the Zaytuna was (and still is) a place of worship as well as an institution of higher learning that has long attracted scholars from across the Maghrib and Africa. A very large congregational mosque, it is located in the heart of the old Tunis madina or souks adjacent to the "noble" professions, crafts, and trades, such as bookshops and perfume sellers.

"Sultan Selim III (reigned 1789–1807) holding an audience in front of the Gate of Felicity." A reform-minded ruler of the Ottoman Empire, Selim III attempted to undertake far-reaching military and other changes in statecraft. However, he had to deal with threats from Russia and Napoleon's unexpected invasion of Egypt and Syria in 1798 which dissolved the long-standing Franco-Ottoman alliance. Eventually, his own troops deposed and imprisoned Selim III, who had perhaps tried to modernize too quickly. This image depicts the Topkapı Palace, a large complex in Istanbul that had served as the primary residence of the sultans for over four hundred years. Note how the various grades of retainers and courtiers are not only dressed but are also lined up according to court protocol.

were generally inland—Fez or Meknes, for examples—due to threats from nearby Christian states, notably Spain. At the end of the sixteenth century, Istanbul boasted a population of nearly one million, but Muslims remained a minority until the nineteenth century. Greeks, Slavs, Iberian Jews, Armenians, Arabs, Circassians, Georgians, Africans, Turko-Mongol peoples, and a host of others resided in the city on the Bosporus whose soubriquet *alem penah* or "refuge of the universe" expressed its astonishing diversity—a diversity that only the fairly recent emergence of nation-states would undermine. In the same period, central Iran had become an inter-

"Monumental Gate of Semnan (or Simnan) Castle, Iran." Built by the Qajar Shahs in the city of Semnan in north central Iran, this monumental gateway was highly decorated with multi-colored tiles that illustrated scenes from ancient Persian epics as well as idealized portraits of the Qajar rulers. Birthplace of the Qajar Dynasty (1785 to 1925), Semnan dominated major trade routes to their new capital, Tehran, as well as to the Islamic holy city of Mashad. An important medical center for the royal family, Semnan was also graced by numerous Qajar palaces and pleasure gardens.

national cosmopolitan center of trade, learning, the arts, science, and pilgrimage.

In addition to military conquests and commercial displacements, religious travel must be considered because MENA contains many of the most sacrosanct and ancient pilgrimage sites of the Monotheistic world—Jerusalem, Mecca, and Medina—to name only the most important. Since pilgrimage functions as a huge intake for diverse peoples, pilgrims, like migrants, merchants, or invaders, disseminate new or different ideas, skills, commodities, and information. States and ruling elites have always sought to control religious travel as well as the objects, spaces, and places of pilgrimage. Profane motives often inspired the most pious pilgrims who might, under certain conditions, turn into holy combatants or warriors for the faith; sacred travel could also be manipulated for political or personal ends. And pilgrimage has always been very much about identity. Pilgrimages to the exemplary centers of Judaism, Christianity, and Islam represented "hemispheric" events since individuals and groups from across Afro-Eurasia made the journey. That pilgrimage, commerce, and trade have always been closely associated is well documented. Trade diasporas, often associated with religious minorities, such as

"A Persian Camp of Pilgrims to Mecca, Jaffa, Palestine, c. 1900." This group of Muslim pilgrims was on their way to Mecca in the Hijaz on the western side of the Arabian Peninsula. They must have come overland through Ottoman-ruled Mesopotamia to the port of Jaffa where sailing ships and steam ships would transport them through the Suez Canal and Red Sea and then to the holy cities of Mecca and Medina. The opening of the Canal in 1869 immensely facilitated not only the flow of commodities and goods but also people, including religious travelers. While its origins remain unknown, Mecca, located fifty miles inland near the Red Sea port of Jidda, has served as both a pilgrimage site and a caravan crossroads for millennia.

"Wailing Wall, Jerusalem, c. 1900." As a city sacred to Judaism, Christianity, and Islam, Jerusalem has welcomed countless pilgrims over the centuries. The "Wailing Wall" or place of weeping is located in the old city of Jerusalem at the foot of the western side of the Temple Mount, a remnant from an ancient wall surrounding the Temple's courtyard. For centuries, it has been one of the most sacred sites in Judaism for prayer and pilgrimage; the earliest Jewish source evoking the sacred importance of the site dates from the fourth century CE. From the mid-19th century onwards, European Jews sought to establish property rights over the wall but without success. The term "wailing wall" appears to be a European designation from the nineteenth century.

the Armenians or Jews, were connected to local and trans-local pilgrimages, often facilitating them.

Sacred and mundane journeys, warfare and traveling scholars, disseminated not only people, knowledge, and cult objects but also a wide range of new plants, crops, and agrarian techniques, many originally from eastern or tropical Asia. Because of this, by about 1500, MENA's landscapes and food-scapes had changed dramatically in many places, although the triad of olive oil, grain, and small livestock remained fundamental to basic daily diets.

Babel: Religion, Language, Ethnicity, and Race c. 1800

If a visitor from somewhere "outside" of MENA encountered a "typical" inhabitant (which did not exist, in any case) and inquired into the significant question of identity, what sort of response might be forthcoming? For most, religious affiliation and membership in a patriarchal family represented the primordial forms of identity, but language was also important. Moreover, allegiance to dynasties or ruling elites was not necessarily determined by religious affiliation; indeed, Muslim rulers frequently relied upon non-Muslim minorities as diplomatic envoys or administrators. And in villages, towns, or cities, loyalties, and therefore identities, were forged by places of residence and type of work; in large urban areas, ties to particular city quarters or neighborhoods proved strong and often gave rise to either cohesion or factions. However, the vast majority in 1800 were peasant-cultivators living in villages and townspeople, the latter involved in production, trade, and commerce. Nomads and/or pastoralists engaged in various forms of animal husbandry on the margins of settled agriculture either in cooperation, or in competition with, peasant-producers. In tribal areas, clan solidarities formed the core of communal and political organization. Thus religion and kinship were key features of social identity and integration.

"Ourmiah (Urmia), Persia: Awaiting the Shah, c. 1911." Iran has always encompassed religiously and ethnically diverse populations. Lake Urmia in northwestern Iran is home to Assyrian Christians, or Nestorians, as well as Azerbaijani, Kurdish, and Armenian minorities. Because native Christians made up nearly 40% of the city's population in the nineteenth century, American Christian missionaries set up a mission there in 1835, although most local Christians fled after World War I in 1918. This image shows city residents awaiting a royal visit by the Qajar ruler Ahmad Shah (r. 1909–1925).

By 1800, the majority of MENA's population had been Muslim for a long time, although wide variations within all three monotheistic traditions existed. Thus, the idea of religion as locally understood and lived helps to avoid essentialized views of complex historical and cultural phenomena. While the vast majority of Muslims were Sunni, large and diverse communities of Shii were found in Iran/Persia, Iraq, Bahrain, the Arabian Peninsula, including Yemen, and elsewhere. Other Shi'i groups, such as the Druze or Alevi, resided in parts of Lebanon, Syria, and southern Anatolia (and today in Israel).

Depending on social class, gender, ethnicity, and location, non-Muslims participated in many dimensions of sociopolitical and economic life in this "western branch" of global Islamic civilizations which by 1500 stretched to China and southeast Asia. In the eyes of the Ottoman state, the designated religious leaders of its minority subject populations were best suited to administer judicial, charitable, and educational institutions. Historically speaking, MENA has always had important Jewish communities of Arab, Berber, Iberian, and Persian origins who resided mainly in cities and towns but also in villages and oases in North Africa, notably in Morocco and Algeria. In Ottoman lands, Sephardic and Ashkenazi Jews generally had separate synagogues. Some minorities defined themselves as both religiously and ethnically distinct, such as Armenians, for whom there were Orthodox and Catholic branches. But the Armenian Church itself formed an administratively unified body that included not only Armenian speakers but also other Monophysites in Syria and Egypt. The Eastern Orthodox Church claimed Greek, Rumanian, Slavic, Bulgarian, and Arab believers. Among the Orthodox faithful, the largest in numbers were perhaps the Greeks who resided throughout MENA but were concentrated in the Balkans, the Black Sea, the Istanbul region, and in Mediterranean port cities.

In the eighteenth century, the Eastern Orthodox Church split into two branches; the Greek Catholic Church counted numerous Arab followers in Greater Syria. United with Rome in the sixteenth century, the Arab Maronite Church of the Mount Lebanon enjoyed

"Nestorian Archbishop, Iran, c. 1890." Liturgically part of the East Syrian Rite, the Nestorian Church was associated with a disputed theological position on the nature of Jesus Christ. Condemned by the First Council of Ephesus in 431, the Nestorian Church split with the Eastern Orthodox tradition and sought refuge in pre-Islamic Sassanid Persia where Nestorians flourished as they did later under Muslim rule. The Nestorian Church was active in evangelizing in Central and South Asia—India, Tibet, and China—and between the 9th and 14th CE centuries it was geographically the world's largest Christian church with dioceses from the Mediterranean Sea to East Asia. Over the centuries, and recently, the Church has split into branches; the patriarchate of the Assyrian Church of the East is currently in exile in Chicago. This image shows the Nestorian archbishop seated in the center surrounded by retainers and secretaries.

"A Sabean Silversmith, Baghdad, Iraq, c. 1932." Although in Iraq Shias are the majority Muslims, and Sunnis the second largest community, it has also counted numerous religious minorities whose origins and traditions date back millennia. The Sabeans or Mandeans are a sect that regards water is the essence of life and worship Adam as their prophet; they hold John the Baptist in particular veneration. Because of these beliefs, their sacred places were traditionally built adjacent to rivers in order to perform baptism and ablutions. A Semitic people, the Sabeans appear to have migrated in the first centuries CE from the southern Levant to Mesopotamia, where most of them resided until the recent 2003 invasion of Iraq which provoked a mass exodus from the country.

closer ties with Europe than other Ottoman Christian minorities, connections that would become entangled with imperialism in the nineteenth century. In Egypt, the Coptic Orthodox Church of Alexandria was the largest Christian Church; although part of the Oriental Orthodox body of churches, it had assumed a theologically different position on the nature of Christ since the fifth-century Council of Chalcedon. The Copts consider themselves to be descended from Pharaonic Egyptians but trace their church's establishment to the apostle, Saint Mark. In the past, and today, Copts reside in both urban areas as well as villages and represent about nine percent of Egypt's total population.

Religious pluralism was entwined with linguistic pluralism, but for many communities, religion, language/ethnicity, and race did not fall into tidy categories. The largest language families were Arabic, Turkish, Farsi (Persian), Greek, Berber (i.e., Amazigh), Armenian, and Kurdish, each with numerous dialects and spoken forms depending on social class, region, and time period. For example, the Kurds, a distinct ethnolinguistic grouping, inhabited key areas of Anatolia, Iran, Iraq, and Syria, but ethnicity did not always match up with religious affiliation; in the past, there were not only Sunni Muslim Kurds but also Jewish Kurds. In contrast, the diverse Berber speakers of northern Africa have principally been Sunni Muslims, but Berber Jews also existed in the south of Morocco. Moreover, many churches employed liturgical languages that differed from the language of daily life; for example, Syriac (Middle Aramaic) used to be the liturgical language of northern Mesopotamia and the Lebanese Maronite Church, although it was gradually replaced by Arabic.

Historically, most states and/or societies have exploited humans as coerced or servile labor—from military to domestic to plantation slavery. In MENA, race and slavery should not be confused because the former is historically and culturally determined; legal definitions of slave status and race diverged. The Afro-Eurasian slave trade is ancient and people of all racial and ethnic origins were trafficked against their will. Until abolition in the nineteenth century, the trade in enslaved persons and the forced appropriation of their labor were integral to MENA's social life and economy. As a legal, economic, and socioreligious institution, slavery channeled North Africans or sub-Saharans to Europe or Southwest Asia; "white" Circassians or Georgians to Ottoman domains; and Mediterranean folk, often from islands, to bagnios and households in MENA. In 1816, the traffic in Europeans was ended for the most part. As for the trade in sub-Saharan Africans, abolition decrees were passed in 1807 in England, in French and British colonies by 1848, in Tunisia by 1846, and in the Ottoman Empire starting in 1857. While these measures reduced the number of enslaved persons circulating around the Mediterranean, a clandestine traffic continued on the high seas. Because Islam does not prohibit miscegenation, high degrees of "interracial mixing" marked populations in specific regions and social classes.

In short, MENA has always represented a place where "worlds meet." As a result, its peoples, states, societies, and cultures have varied extraordinarily in languages, systems of belief, practices, and racial/ethnic composition. Because of this, the region has been characterized as a cultural mosaic, although this metaphor should not obscure the fact that the shifting components forming that mosaic have been in intense interaction, interpenetration, and exchange over millennia.

Encounters with Modernity

Even in the early twenty-first century, the Middle East is frequently portrayed as premodern, outside of current historical processes, or resistant to modernity. Nothing could be further from the truth. As lived in daily life or experienced as a set of ideas and world views, modernity assumed many guises and occurred in a number of social arenas—from new modes of knowledge production, communications and transportation, and urban organization to novel forms of leisure and entertainment, education and health, and above all, in ways of thinking about the natural world, the state, and religion as well as normative gender roles.

Mediterranean port cities, such as Istanbul, Beirut, Alexandria, Tunis, and Algiers, developed new consumer tastes, trading partners, and business practices that impacted local labor markets and the webs of social relations underlying them. Ruling classes and urban elites embraced, cautiously at first and then more eagerly, various forms of

"Armenian Patriarch, Palestine, Jerusalem, c. 1900." The Armenian Patriarchate of Jerusalem, or the Patriarchate of St. James, was (and still is) located in the Armenian quarter of Jerusalem. In the seventh century CE, the Armenian Church began appointing its own bishops to Jerusalem where they were later elevated to the position of patriarch in deference to the city's sacred status in Christianity. This image from before World War I shows the Armenian Patriarch, Harootiun Vehabedian, wearing a hooded vestment adorned with crosses, holding a strand of prayer beads. As a result of the persecution of Armenians by Turkey during World War I, the Armenian population of Jerusalem expanded to some 25,000 people, most of them refugees, although very few remain there today.

"Turkish Woman, Full-Length Portrait, c. 1880–1900." This studio photograph shows an unnamed Turkish woman whose dress and demeanor indicate that she is from the upper classes. By the late nineteenth century, gendered dress codes for men and women had changed in many, although not all, urban areas in MENA. The woman's diaphanous face veil and the style of her bonnet suggest that she came from a family with modern notions of appropriate female dress.

"The Obelisk horizontal position, Alexandria, Egypt." Founded near a small Pharaonic town in about 331 CE by Alexander the Great, the city had became Egypt's largest seaport by the nineteenth century and a major international shipping center after the opening of the Suez Canal. Its ties to British-ruled India increased also increased precipitously after 1869 and, with the lucrative commerce in prized Egyptian cotton, the port grew into a global commercial hub that mediated between the Mediterranean, North Africa, the Ottoman Empire, and the Indian Ocean. This image captures Alexandria's water front where an ancient obelisk is being crated up for shipment to New York in 1880.

modernity, although in varying tempos, from the nineteenth century on, if not before. Thus, different places were affected with varying degrees of intensity by modernity's global reach in large measure because the processes collectively known as modernity did not only arise in western Europe, as older scholarship held, but rather had more far-flung and diffuse origins. In general, those peoples and places that were somewhat remote from major communication hubs tended to retain "traditional" ways of life and modes of resource extraction, but even seemingly inaccessible areas, such as the interior of the Arabian Peninsula, were indirectly or directly touched. Finally, global capitalism, both cause and consequence of modernity, created unforeseen fluctuations in market prices, demands for labor, and access to resources as well as loss of autonomy or of independence, and above all, introduced more efficient deadly forms of warfare.

In 1798 a French fleet and army under Napoleon conquered Egypt in an ephemeral occupation that ended in 1801 after combined Ottoman-British armies expelled French forces from the Nile Valley and Palestine. While Egypt's conquest shocked Ottoman political elites, it did not necessarily introduced modernity into the empire because the reform-minded Ottoman ruler, Sultan Selim III (r. 1789–1807), was already attempting to initiate far-reaching changes in statecraft. What the French military campaign did was render the idea of radical change more urgent and acceptable to MENA's rulers and their subjects. In addition, Bonaparte's invasion of Egypt, while short-lived, utterly transformed relationships be-

tween the Ottoman Empire, North Africa, and the European Great Powers. It set the stage for bitter protracted European rivalries in the region, which lasted until after World War II, as well as for British and French cultural influences. In 1801 Great Britain seized the strategic Maltese islands from the French army, which made the British into a redoubtable sea power with increased interests in the Mediterranean. At the same time, Bonaparte's disastrous campaigns in Egypt and Syria, as well as the publication of the multivolume, lavishly illustrated *Description de l'Égypte*, sparked wider European interest in MENA, which gave birth to full-blown Orientalism in literature, art, and scholarship. The term *Orientalism* refers to the depiction of "Eastern" peoples and cultures whether in MENA, India, or East Asia by European artists, writers, and literati who portrayed them in print and visual media as innately exotic, different, and frequently inferior. Moreover, Orientalism was very much invested in modern imperialism.

Napoleon's invasion sparked state-led reforms and modernization projects from Istanbul to Cairo to Tunis and beyond to Iran and Morocco. In Iran, external threats came from two directions—Russia to the north and the expanding British Empire in India and Afghanistan. The Qajar Dynasty (1785 to 1925) fought a series of wars from 1804–1913 against the Russian Empire, which seized territories in the Caucasus that had traditionally been Iranian domains. As the nineteenth century progressed so did the threat of either direct foreign occupation or heightened European interference in MENA. In 1830, France invaded the Ottoman province of Algeria but European commerce, banking, transportation, and law increasingly became the "Trojan horse" of creeping imperialism in adjacent North African states, principally Egypt, Morocco, and Tunisia even prior to the imposition of formal colonial rule. In addition, the Crimean War (1853–1856) resulted in heightened Russian interference in the Ottoman Empire that was intimately related to the practice of religion. Christian and Jewish pilgrimage from Russia

"Jewish Wedding in Morocco." The French Orientalist painter Eugène Delacroix (1798–1863) accompanied a French diplomatic mission in 1832 to the court of the sultan of Morocco, Moulay Abd al-Rahman in 1832, to reassure the ruler that France's invasion of neighboring Algeria in 1830 posed no political threat. While in Morocco, Delacroix attempted to enter Muslim households to paint but was only permitted into Jewish homes. This portrayal of a Jewish wedding, executed from sketches and notes, was completed between 1837 and 1841. It is difficult to ascertain the exactness or veracity of the painting which sparked keen European interest in North Africa. (It is now in the Musée du Louvre in Paris).

and Eastern Europe to Jerusalem steadily increased with improved security and communications, including roads and steam lines to Jaffa, Haifa, and Acre. By 1914, the Ottoman Empire had lost most of its Balkan territories as well as former African provinces to European powers: Italy invaded Libya in 1911, Great Britain claimed Egypt, and France ruled Tunisia and Algeria as well as Morocco. By 1918 the empire was no more.

Generally speaking, the response of MENA's rulers and statesmen to imperialism during the long nineteenth century displayed degrees of uniformity—initial modernization of military institutions followed by deeper changes in ever-widening social spheres. But the attractions and dangers of modernity, often confused in the collective mind with "foreign" or "outside" influences, elicited resistance and counterarguments, particularly among religious bodies and leaders—whether Muslim, Jewish, or Christian. Some accepted the need for adopting European technologies but insisted on retaining the essence of sacred law and values. Other local social groups challenged state-imposed changes labeled as "modern," maintaining that the good and just order should continue be based on "traditional" religio-moral imperatives defining the structures and norms of family, women, faith, and community. In any case, for many peoples across the globe in the period, what we understand to be modernity represented an unknown destiny and unfamiliar destination.

Comparative research from a global perspective for the period around circa 1800 suggests that significant variations in living standards for Middle Eastern, South Asian, or European peasants or laborers had not yet emerged. Most nonelites or ordinary people lived more or less at subsistence levels and older bodies of knowledge governing, for examples, agriculture and medicine, had not diverged sharply. But by the 1870s, comparatively speaking, conditions had changed dramatically due to the confluence of numerous factors: industrialization in Europe and North America; global population movements, notably the trans-Atlantic migrations; continued European imperial expansion across Asia and Africa; pressures on non-Western economies or states to lower trade barriers and open markets; spectacular innovations in global transportation, such as the opening of the Suez Canal in 1869; new methods of mobilizing labor on a scale never before experienced; and the rapidly accelerating spread of ideas, institutions, and ways of doing things. However, all was not change by any means. Many transformations were uneven in scale and intensity, their causes and consequences only dimly grasped by many of those whose lives, livelihoods, and social worlds were profoundly affected; the old and new cohabitated.

This volume thus represents a compromise between conventional political and diplomatic approaches and social and cultural history. Diversity in the ways that MENA came to variant expressions of modernity weaves together the historical narrative, the chapters, the documents, and the images. This leitmotif encourages students to question portrayals of the region as undifferentiated, monolithic, or unchanging. In addition, we draw on world

"The Harbor and Admiralty, Algiers, Algeria, c. 1899." Captured by the French army and navy in 1830, Algiers became a showpiece of French imperialism by the end of the century. In this image, both older and newer urban elements are juxtaposed. The modernized port in the foreground linked Algiers and Algeria to France, especially to the port of Marseille. In the background is the pre-colonial Ottoman port, dating from the sixteenth century, as well as an architecturally typical North African mosque.

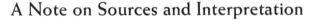

and comparative history to demonstrate that the peoples and places under consideration participated fully in modern global history and that many of the processes at play in the region reflected worldwide trends. By juxtaposing a wide range of political, social, economic, and cultural documents, a rich tapestry emerges, one that suggests the historical importance of webs as much as linear trajectories. The images in this chapter introduce some of the peoples and places found in MENA in the nineteenth century when our story opens. It is more of a collage than a mosaic, a short journey over a vast and varied landscape whose contours will come into focus more sharply in subsequent chapters.

A Note on Sources and Interpretation

This note surveys shifting interpretations of MENA's history and connects changes in scholarship to new fields of inquiry as well as sources of documentation on the past. To grasp the significance of these transformations, we must go back in time. Few world regions have been as closely involved in the broad sweep of global history as the Middle East. However, nineteenth-century European Orientalist literary and artistic representations of MENA portrayed it as a place of incorrigible cultural "otherness" and "exceptionalism." This older Eurocentric historical literature tended to "distance" MENA's history, despite—or perhaps because of—its proximity to "the West" and of the long-standing presence of Islamic states and societies on the fluid political and cultural boundaries of something called "Europe."

Moreover, from the nineteenth century on, most of the region was subjected to some form of European colonial and/or imperial control—although Turkey and Iran suffered from indirect or informal European rule. Thus until recently, MENA's history was largely written by "the winners"—the colonial powers seeking to reconcile their often self-serving high-minded ideals of the "civilizing mission" with the harsh realities of colonialism. With independence from the post-World War II era on, nationalist historians from the region began challenging and dismantling the colonial historiography. Nevertheless, the growth of area studies in the 1960s resulted in highly specialized, indeed fragmented, approaches to MENA's past. Largely, but not exclusively, a product of the Cold War, area studies tended to treat the region as distinct and different from those surrounding it—despite the fact that MENA links at least three continents, Asia, Africa, and Europe—and has been part of the Atlantic, Mediterranean, and Indian Ocean worlds for a very long time. In addition, some political commentators persisted in characterizing the region and its peoples as "premodern"—outside the complex historical processes that forged global modernity—or, at best, as passive recipients of the modern bequeathed by "the West." Current scholarship rejects older mythologies that cast European (or Euro-American) empires as the bearers of modernity to MENA as well as the notion of exceptionalism. What forces coalesced to bring this re-thinking and reevaluation about?

Political upheavals of the past decades together with disciplinary and intellectual shifts have produced a re-territorialization of MENA that might be conceptualized as a series of interconnecting zones bridging Afro-Eurasia. The disintegration of the Soviet Union and the emergence of Turkic republics in Central Asia have effectively pushed out the already fluid boundaries of "the Middle East." And new work in migration history, to provide one example, has relinked MENA's past not only to European and trans-Mediterranean history but also to Asian and trans-Atlantic histories. The prominence of critical subfields, such as women's history, and the reconceptualization of older units of analysis, for example "the Mediterranean world," has played a key role as well. World History with its comparative approach to humankind's long march across time has produced scholarship that now contrasts and compares not simply

"Ottoman ports" but instead port cities around the Mediterranean Basin and Indian Ocean. Recent work in environmental history provides a welcome corrective to older paradigms that see a Christian–Muslim divide marked only by hostility and not by exchange. A focus on changing ecologies and resources structures demonstrates similar, frequently identical, responses by both European and Muslim societies to new environmental conditions. The management of scarce resources, such as timber or water, by bureaucracies proved crucial to the rise of modern states—in MENA and globally.

The historical sciences have benefitted from new fields of inquiry, sources of evidence, and methodologies for rereading familiar primary sources. In the older tradition, many sources came from foreign diplomatic archives or the pens of European diplomats, businessmen, travelers, or colonial officers in imperial service in, for instance, British-ruled Egypt or French Algeria. Nevertheless, one of the largest repositories of data on MENA, the Mediterranean, and Europe is in Istanbul, former capital of the Ottoman Empire, whose imperial rule spanned three continents for over five centuries. Countless Ottoman bureaucrats, scribes, and tax collectors kept for many periods and regions precise records, generally neither destroying archival material generated by preexisting authorities, nor removing records from sites in the provinces. It is estimated that the "State Archives of Turkey" contain some 150 million records, which constitute at most 30% of what was produced by the vast bureaucratic machinery of the Ottoman state and empire since the sixteenth century, if not before. The record keepers detailed everything from road management, taxation, and regulating urban dress codes to supplying the armed forces, modernizing cities, and concluding treaties with foreign states. Until two decades ago, the central Ottoman archives in Istanbul were somewhat difficult to access. This was due to a lack of finding aids, inadequate staff, and insufficient funding to declassify, preserve, and organize this gargantuan amount of material. However, since the 1990s, these archives have been more widely available to researchers often interested in social and cultural history. Deploying new methods of primary source analysis, historians can now, for instance, reconstruct the social worlds of the urban poor based on a rereading of older cadastral surveys. The greater accessibility of these massive, diverse records has resulted not only in a critical rethinking of many aspects of MENA's history, including the issue of how the region and its peoples came to modernity, but also of European, African, and Asian histories.

CHAPTER 1

European Imperialism, c. 1750–1914

In the latter half of the eighteenth century, revolutions and European wars over empire overturned existing political systems around the world. In 1763, the Treaty of Paris that ended the Seven Years War in North America not only forced France to give Britain Canada and its possessions east of the Mississippi River; Britain also won exclusive imperial rights in India, forcing French withdrawal. Britain's position in India would have a lasting impact on central Middle Eastern developments. The Ottoman Empire's central Arab provinces (Syria, Mesopotamia, Egypt) provided swifter transit routes to India than the sea route around South Africa, either overland to the Euphrates River and down to the Persian Gulf or via Cairo to Suez for the Red Sea voyage. Hoping to avenge France's 1763 defeat by blocking British routes to India via the Middle East, Napoleon Bonaparte (1769–1821) led a French military expedition to occupy Egypt in 1798. And Britain invaded and occupied Egypt in 1882 to protect its sea route to India by way of the Suez Canal that had opened in 1869.

British concerns about the security of her route to India via the Mediterranean calls attention to another area of European expansion, Russia's move southward to the shores of the Black Sea by 1775. Russia absorbed lands the Ottomans had ruled directly or indirectly for over two centuries. London saw this Russian presence as a threat to its own imperial interests. If the Tsars could oust the Ottomans from Istanbul or gain navigation rights for warships through the Bosporus Strait to the Mediterranean, Britain's route to India through Arab lands could be endangered. The British concern, if not obsession, with Russia's goals

Ottoman Firman Permitting British Steam Vessels to Navigate the Euphrates River, December 29, 1834.

The Ambassador . . . of Great Britain, Lord Ponsonby, one of the most illustrious personages among Christian nations, has presented to our Sublime Porte a note . . . that the British Government requires permission . . . to navigate by turns two steam boats on the river Euphrates which flows at a small distance from . . . Baghdad for the purpose of facilitating commerce. We in consequence [asked] . . . our illustrious governor of Baghdad and Bussora [Basra] . . . to furnish [us] with information on the proposed navigation. Although [his] answer has not arrived, the ambassador . . . [informed] our Sublime Porte that the British Government awaited our reply. For this reason we . . . permit two steam boats to navigate the Euphrates by turns.

From Lord Palmerston to the Prime Minister on English support of the Ottoman Empire against Russia, October 7, 1853.

My dear Aberdeen. I wish to propose to the Cabinet today—'whereas it is deemed by England and France to be an object of general European interest and of special importance to them that the political independence and territorial integrity of the Ottoman Empire should be maintained inviolate against Russian aggression, the two Powers engage to furnish to the Sultan such naval assistance as may be necessary in existing circumstances for the defence of his empire.'

regarding the Ottomans created what was known during the nineteenth century as "The Eastern Question." Britain would prop up the Ottomans to prevent Russian access to the Mediterranean, both diplomatically and, if necessary, militarily. For example, the Crimean War (1853–1856) saw the British and French allied with the Ottomans to drive the Russians from the Black Sea's shores. Still, continued Ottoman loss of territories to Austria-Hungary as well as Russia ultimately led Britain in 1878 to abandon Istanbul and focus its imperial concern elsewhere. The opening of the Suez Canal in 1869 offered a swifter passage to India, making Egypt the crucial transit point for access to India and British dominions in Australia and New Zealand. And it was during the latter half of the nineteenth century that the European "scramble for empire" exploded in a competition for territories in Africa and Southeast Asia. By 1914, only two regions of the African continent were not occupied by a European power: Ethiopia in the east and Liberia in the west. Likewise, the Ottomans then held only a sliver of land in Eastern Europe, battered by Russo-Austrian competition for these regions, which progressively rebelled against Ottoman control and sought independence. In Asia, the Ottomans retained Greater Syria (including Palestine), Mesopotamia, and the Hijaz region of the Arabian Peninsula that included the Muslim holy places of Mecca and Medina, along with parts of Yemen.

Europe's takeover of these regions was sparked in part by power politics, but as much if not more by a desire to gain access to minerals and goods that fed its industrial expansion. In addition, many European merchants and industrialists invested in modernization projects in non-Western regions whose profits were threatened in the financial crisis of the mid-1870s when Egypt's rulers and the Ottoman sultans went bankrupt. Unable to repay the debts they had incurred to finance these ventures, they were forced to submit to European oversight of their finances, a step that triggered Egyptian nationalist resentment and encouraged Britain to invade Egypt in 1882.

Imperialism could take various forms: outright conquest and occupation, interference in economic and political affairs, or, in its most extreme form, settler colonization, as occurred in Algeria beginning with the French invasion of 1830. France went on to take Tunisia in 1881 and in 1912 much of Morocco along with large parts of the Sahara; Italy occupied Libya in 1911. Settler colonialism occurred mostly in French or Italian possessions as opposed to British-ruled Egypt, although much of Egypt's wealth was controlled by European interests. North Africa's geographical proximity to southern Europe and the generally favorable climatic conditions for agriculture along the Mediterranean coast attracted colonial settlers. By 1900, hundreds of thousands of Europeans considered areas of northern Africa as their home. Beginning with Algeria, France encouraged its own citizens and other Europeans to settle, dispossessing Algerians of their lands and integrating their production into the French economy.

Given this variety of pressures, local economies in the Middle East and North Africa were increasingly, if unevenly, drawn into world market networks centered primarily in Western Europe and North America. Male and female producers, whether in cities or the countryside, were often subject to the fluctuations of economic and commercial forces over which they had little, if any, control. These processes ultimately unleashed transformations deeply affecting all levels of social organization—from a redistribution of wealth and power to the emergence of new kinds of classes, from basic alterations in the gendered division of labor to the appearance of novel consumer tastes—and fed into the growing nationalist movements demanding freedom from colonial rule. Given the enormous diversity of peoples, states, economies, and methods of resource extraction, these changes affected states or geographic areas at different times and in different ways.

In Algeria, fierce resistance arose to French military forces and to the settlers; the country was not fully subdued until the late 1870s, nearly fifty years after the invasion. In Morocco, rebellions against foreign occupation had scarcely been suppressed when the Moroccan nationalist movement emerged in the post-World War I era. In other cases, confronted by superior force, North African responses ranged from emigration to evasion, refusing to have any contact with the foreigners, to calculated accommodation or in some cases outright collaboration with the colonizers, although collective or individual resistance did not have to be military in nature; people refused to pay taxes or to work for the colonizers on the lands taken from native owners.

A major point of resentment for indigenous peoples throughout MENA, and elsewhere, was that their rulers were forced to grant legal immunity, "capitulations," to resident Europeans who were not subject to local laws, jurisdictions, or authorities. Originally granted by the Ottomans from a position of power in the sixteenth century to permit non-Muslim foreigners treatment under their own laws, this right of extraterritoriality came to be granted to foreigners of all classes in MENA, an immense privilege that could be exploited for economic, commercial, political, or social gain. Even states that were not occupied, such as Iran, had to grant such immunities.

In addition, as European powers expanded their reach, Christian missionary activity in the region increased sharply. Efforts to convert Muslims and Jews were rarely successful, but missionaries played a crucial role by introducing modern education and health measures.

Lord Cromer [Evelyn Baring] (1841–1917): The Influence of Racial Theories and Darwinian thought on British imperial attitudes.

The theory of existence terminating in the survival of the fittest . . . still applies to people as to plants. And I know of no instances in history of a nation being educated by another nation into self-government and independence; every nation has fought its way up in the world as the English have done, testifying freely for the great principle, and putting out its blood when needed.

What energy can be expected of a people with no heels to their shoes.

—Lord Palmerston's caustic personal view of the Turks, c. 1862

The immense canvas painted by the French artist Baron Antoine-Jean Gros, entitled "The Battle of the Pyramids," shows a decisive military clash between the invading French army under Napoleon Bonaparte and local Egyptian forces in July 1798. The defeat of the Mamluks allowed France's army to march to Cairo.

Secondary schools established by missionaries would later become universities, such as the American University of Beirut; elite Muslim families, as well as Christians, began to send their sons to these schools. European women also engaged in missionary or other kinds of work; most European women in the period subscribed to the notion of the "Civilizing Mission," and did not question imperialism's principal ideology regarding "inferior" African and Asian peoples. However, some women undermined aspects of imperialism through modern education, especially for girls, in ways that challenged not only the dominant imperial ideology but traditional ideas on whether women should be educated.

As important, the notion of inherent racial superiority held by the vast majority of Westerners toward non-Western peoples and societies justified imperial expansion and conquest. Directly related was a complicated set of attitudes toward MENA in particular that portrayed its peoples and customs as "exotic," particularly Middle Eastern women. These collective attitudes and ways of thinking about others, known today as "Orientalism," was found in art, literature, and photography. Orientalism reflected European (or Western) ideas regarding the inherent cultural, social, and spiritual differences between "us" and "them." Yet, as some of the documents following indicate, the inhabitants of MENA often viewed their culture as equal to, if not superior to, the cultures of their European colonial masters.

Napoleon in Egypt

Egypt was absorbed into the Ottoman Empire in 1517, ending the rule of the Mamluks, a series of Turkish military dynasties. In the second half of the eighteenth century, direct Ottoman control over the Nile Valley weakened and as a result the local Mamluk princes in Egypt exerted increased political power as they vied for control of land, labor, and trade between the Mediterranean and Red Sea. As the Directory (the Governing Council in Paris after the Revolution) noted in ordering Napoleon Bonaparte's (1769–1821) 1798 Egypt expedition, Egyptian merchant trade with England was a major French concern.

The French sought to control the eastern Mediterranean coast from Egypt north to Syria, thus blocking British access to the Persian Gulf and India. Egypt would become a French possession, of value for its strategic location and its agricultural fertility, and serve as a potential base for reaching India. Napoleon's venture failed. By 1801 France had agreed to withdraw its troops, leaving the way open for Ottoman reassertion of its control over the area with British military assistance.

Decree of the Directory

The Executive Directory, considering that the beys [Mamluks] who, having seized the government of Egypt, have established intimate ties with the English and have [resorted to] . . . absolute dependence [on Britain]; that in consequence they have engaged in open hostilities and most horrible cruelties against the French, whom they vex, pillage, and assassinate daily;

Considering that it is its [the Directory's] duty to pursue the enemies of the Republic wherever they may be and in any place where they engage in Hostile activities . . . Considering, in addition, that the infamous treason which enabled Britain to become mistress of the Cape of Good Hope [in South Africa] has rendered access to India very difficult to the vessels of the Republic, it is important to open to the Republican forces another route, to combat the satellites of the English government and dry up the source of its corruptive riches;

Decrees as follows:

Article 1. The General-in-Chief of the Army of the Orient [Napoleon] shall direct the land and sea forces under his command to Egypt and shall take over that country.

Article 2. He shall expel the English from all their possessions in the Orient which he can reach and shall in particular destroy all their factories [trading posts] on the Red Sea.

Article 3. He shall have the Isthmus of Suez cut and shall take all necessary measures to insure to the French Republic the free and exclusive possession of the Red Sea.

Article 4. He shall improve by all the means at his disposal the conditions of the natives of Egypt.

Article 5. He shall maintain, as much as this depends on him, good understanding with the Grand Seigneur [the Ottoman Sultan] and his immediate subjects.

Article 6. The present decree shall not be printed.

As the French prepared to land at Alexandria in 1798, Napoleon addressed his troops about their mission and its hoped-for impact on

England and presented himself as inheriting the mantle of Rome and Alexander the Great.

Headquarters on Board the Orient, the 4th Messidor, Year VI (June 22, 1798)

Bonaparte, Member of the National Institute, General-in Chief

"Soldiers—You are about to undertake a conquest the effects of which on civilisation and commerce will be incalculable. The blow you are about to give to England will be the best aimed, and the most sensibly felt, she can receive until the time arrives when you can give her her death blow. We must make some fatiguing marches; we must fight several battles; we shall succeed in all we undertake. The destinies are with us. The Mameluke [Mamluk] Beys, who favour exclusively English commerce, whose extortions oppress our merchants, and who tyrannise over the unfortunate inhabitants of the Nile, a few days after our arrival will no longer exist.

The people amongst whom we are going to live are Mahometans. The first article of their faith is this: 'There is no god but God and Mahomet is His prophet.' Do not contradict them. Behave to them as you have behaved to the Jews—to the Italians. Pay respect to their muftis, and their Imaums [Imams], as you did to the rabbis and the bishops. Extend to the ceremonies prescribed by the Koran and to the mosques the same toleration which you showed to the synagogues, to the religion of Moses and of Jesus Christ.

The Roman legions protected all religions. You will find here customs different from those of Europe. You must accommodate yourselves to them. The people amongst whom we are to mix differ from us in the treatment of women; but in all countries, he who violates is a monster. Pillage enriches only a small number of men; it dishonours us; it destroys our resources; it converts into enemies the people whom it is in our interest to have for friends.

The first town we shall come to [Alexandria] was built by Alexander [the Great]. At every step we shall meet with grand recollections, worthy of exciting the emulation of Frenchmen."

In the camp at Alexandria, Napoleon also drew up an Arabic-language proclamation to persuade Egyptians that he and his army had come to liberate them from Mamluk rule (the French would in fact rout most of the Mamluks' military forces in 1798). He couched his proclamation so as to appeal to Muslims, including the suggestion that the French expedition was sympathetic to Islam due to recent French attacks upon the Papacy.

Appeal in Arabic to Egyptians

In the name of God, the Merciful, the Compassionate. There is no god but God. He has no son, nor has he an associate in His Dominion.

On behalf of the French Republic which is based on the foundation of liberty and equality, General Bonaparte, Commander-in-Chief of the French armies, makes known to all the Egyptian people that for a long time the *Sanjaqs* [Ottoman officials] who lorded it over Egypt have treated the French community basely and contemptuously and have persecuted its merchants in all manner of extortion and violence. Therefore the hour of punishment has now come. . . .

O ye Egyptians, they may say to you that I have not made an expedition hither for any other object than that of abolishing your religion; but this is a pure falsehood and you must not give credit to it, but tell the slanderers that I have not come to you except for the purpose of restoring your rights from the hands of the oppressors and that I more than the Mamluks serve God—may He be praised and exalted—and revere His Prophet Muhammad and the glorious Qur'an . . .

[T]ell your nation that the French are also faithful Muslims, and in confirmation of this they invaded Rome and destroyed there the Papal See, which was always exhorting the Christians to make war with Islam. And then they went to the island of Malta, from where they expelled the Knights who claimed that God the Exalted required them to fight the Muslims. Furthermore the French at all times have declared themselves to be the most sincere friends of the Ottoman Sultan and the enemy of his enemies, may god perpetuate his empire! And on the contrary the Mamluks have withheld their obeisance from the Sultan, and have not followed his orders. Indeed they have never obeyed anything but their own greed!

"Part of the Grand Harbor, Malta." The strategic Maltese islands, located dead center in the Mediterranean, were seized by the British in 1801 from Napoleon's occupying forces. The port of Valletta became Great Britain's chief Mediterranean naval station as well as a key maritime commercial hub.

Blessing on blessing to the Egyptians who will act in concert with us, without any delay, for their condition will be rightly adjusted, and their rank raised. Blessing also upon those who will abide in their habitations, not siding with either of the two hostile parties. . . . But woe upon woe to those who unite with the Mamluks and assist them in the war against us, for they will not find the way of escape and no trace of them shall remain.

First Article:

All the villages situated within three hours' distance from the places through which the French army passes are required to send to the Commander-in-Chief some persons, deputed by them, to announce to the aforesaid that they submit and that they have hoisted the French flag, which is white, blue, and red.

Second Article:

Every village that shall rise against the French army shall be burnt down.

Third Article:

Every village that submits to the French army must hoist the French flag and also the flag of our friend the Ottoman sultan, may he continue forever.

Fourth Article:

The *Shaykh* [village head] of each village must immediately seal all property, houses and possessions belonging to Mamluks, making the most strenuous effort that not the least thing be lost.

Fifth Article:

The *Shaykhs, Qadis* [judges], and *Imams* [prayer leaders] must remain at their posts and every countryman shall remain peaceably in his dwelling, . . . Prayers shall be performed in the mosques as customary and the Egyptians, all of them, shall render thanks for God's graciousness, praise be to Him, and may He be exalted in extirpating the power of the Mamluks, saying with a loud voice, May God perpetuate the glory of the Ottoman Sultan! May God perpetuate the glory of the French army! May God curse the Mamluks and rightly adjust the condition of the Egyptian people!

Written in the Camp at Alexandria on the 13th of the month Messidor [the sixth year] of the founding of the French Republic, that is to say toward the end of the month Muharram in the year [1213] of the Hijra [July 2, 1798].

Abd al-Rahman al-Jabarti (c. 1754–1822), a member of the *ulama* [scholars of Islamic law] at al-Azhar in Cairo, reacted to Napoleon's Arabic-language appeal by writing a treatise that criticized Napoleon's message and revealed al-Jabarti's negative opinion of the French Revolution and French customs generally. He rejected Napoleon's claim that the French expedition was sympathetic to Islam due to its attacks upon the Papacy. However, he expressed great interest in the library the French established for their scholars to investigate Egypt's resources, geography, and past history. His appreciation of French scholarship and the spirit of investigation was consistent with that of other Muslims who encountered European rule, even as they condemned them politically or for their immoral personal behavior.

Here is an explanation of the incoherent words [in Arabic of Napoleon's proclamation] and vulgar constructions which he put into this miserable letter.

His [Napoleon's] statement 'In the name of God the Merciful, the Compassionate. There is no god but God. He has no son, nor has he an associate in His Dominion.' In mentioning these three sentences there is an indication that the French agree with the three [monotheistic] religions but at the same time they do not agree with them, nor with any religion. . . .

[B]ecause they have no chief or sultan with whom they all agree, like others, whose function it is to speak on their behalf. For when they rebelled against their sultan [Emperor] six years ago and killed him, the people agreed unanimously that there was not to be a single ruler, but that their state, territories, laws and administration of their affairs should be in the hands of the wise men among them. They appointed persons chosen by them and made them heads of the army, and below them generals and commanders . . . on condition that they were all to be equal and none superior to any other in view of the equality of creation and nature. They made this the foundation . . . of their system. . . . Their officials are distinguished by the cleanliness of their garments. They wear emblems on their uniforms and on their heads. . . . They follow this rule: great and

The Anglo-Dutch Bombardment of the Ottoman port of Algiers, August 1816, painted by the Dutch artist, Martinus Schouman, completed in 1823. The joint expedition led by the British admiral Lord Exmouth to the Barbary Coast in 1816 was a postscript to the Napoleonic expedition to Egypt and a harbinger of the French invasion of Algeria in 1830.

small, high and low, male and female are all equal. Sometimes they break this rule. . . . Their women do not veil themselves and have no modesty; they do not care whether they uncover their private parts. Whenever a Frenchman has to perform an act of nature, he does so wherever he happens to be, even in full view of people, and he goes away as he is, without washing his private parts after defecation. . . .

The administrators, astronomers, and some of the physicians lived in this house in which they placed a great number of books and with a keeper taking care of them and arranging them. Whoever wishes to look something up in a book asks for whatever volumes he wants and the librarian brings them to him. . . . All the while they are quiet and no one disturbs his neighbor. When some Muslims would come to look around, they would not prevent them from entering. Indeed they would bring them all kinds of printed books in which there were all sorts of illustrations and *cartes* [maps] of the countries and regions, animals, birds, plants. . . . I have gone to them many times and they have shown me all these things and among the things I saw there was a large book containing the Biography of the Prophet, upon whom be mercy and peace. . . . The Glorious Qur'an is translated into their language. . . . I saw some of them who know chapters of the Qur'an by heart. They have a great interest in the sciences, mainly in mathematics and the knowledge of languages. . . . [and] they possess extraordinary astronomical instruments of perfect construction. . . .

[During the occupation, the French] printed a number of papers and posted them up in the marketplaces. They read: "On Friday . . . we intend to make a ship fly through the air . . . by a French trick." As usual people gossiped a lot about it. When the day came many people and many Frenchmen assembled in the early afternoon to see this miracle. I was there, too, and saw a piece of cloth round in shape and resting on props. It was colored white, red, and blue and the props were arranged in a circle. In the center was a bucket with a wick standing in some kind of fat. This bucket was tied to the circular cloth with wires. The cloth itself was extended with ropes and pulleys and the end of the ropes were held by men standing on the roofs of the surrounding houses. About one hour after the afternoon prayer they lit the wick and the fumes arose into the cloth and filled it. It swelled up and became a sphere. The fumes wanted to rise inside it and, finding no way out, carried it up in the air. They pulled it together with the ropes until it rose above the ground and when they cut the ropes the wind carried the cloth up into the air. It moved quite prettily for a while, then the bucket with the wick fell off and down came the cloth. When it fell one could see what it was and it was clear that what they had asserted was not correct, namely, that people could travel with it to distant lands to discover new things and such fantastic illusions. Moreover, it was clear that the balloon was something like the kites the carpenters make at the time of festivals.

Algeria: French Colonization and the Algerian Response

Three decades after Napoleon's Egyptian expedition, French forces took Algiers in July 1830, beginning an occupation that endured until 1962. This was a classic case of colonization. The French encouraged European settlement, ousting Algerians from their lands, but they encountered fierce resistance and did not pacify all of Algeria until the 1870s. In 1848 France made northern Algeria into three African *départements* (administrative districts) of France, incorporating them, and later all of Algeria, into the French state. This official pronouncement declared that land, houses, and businesses belonging to the inhabitants of Algiers were subject to seizure and encouraged Algerians to inform on each other with the promise of reward.

Algiers: September 8, 1830

Art. 1. All houses, stores, shops, gardens, lands, places, and establishments whatsoever formerly occupied by the Dey, the beys, or Turks who have left the territory of the Regency of Algiers, or which are

"Attack of Algiers by Sea, June 1830." On May 25, 1830, an enormous French fleet of some 600 ships bearing over 40,000 military and support personnel left Toulon, eventually landing in June at a small bay known as Sidi Ferruch, some twenty miles to the west of Algiers. After a series of battles with Algerian-Turkish forces that were overwhelmed by superior French weapons and manpower, the army reached Algiers on July 4. The next day, the ruler Husayn Dey capitulated and agreed to the terms imposed by the French commander.

managed for their accounts, as well as those belonging in any way whatsoever to Mecca or Medina, revert to the public domain and shall be managed for its profit.

Art. 2. Persons of any nation who are holders or tenants on the said properties are obliged within three days to file declarations indicating the nature, location, and consistency of the domains of which they enjoy the use of management, together with the amount of the income or rent and the time of the last payment.

Art. 3. This declaration shall be transcribed onto registers opened for this purpose by the municipality.

Art. 4. Any person subject to this declaration who fails to file it within the time prescribed shall be condemned to a fine that shall not be less than one year's revenue or rent of the undeclared property, and he shall be constrained to the payment of this fine by the severest penalties.

Art. 5. Any individual who reveals to the French government the existence of an undeclared domain property shall be entitled to half the fine incurred by the delinquent party.

Proclaimed by Clauzel, General in Chief, French Army in Algeria.

This poem by an unknown poet of Algiers (no relation to the Algerian resistance leader of the same name) serves as a tragic lament upon the French attack and occupation of Algiers. The poet makes caustic reference to the country's former rulers, the Ottoman military government, which failed to oppose the invading French army and save Algeria. Part of the Ottoman Empire since the sixteenth century, Algerians looked in vain to Istanbul for military assistance in 1830 in expelling the French army.

"Abd al-Qadir (1808–83)." Emir Abd al-Qadir led armed resistance to the invading French army in Algeria between 1832 and 1847. Proclaimed "sultan of the Arabs" for mobilizing tribesmen under his green-and-white flag, Abd al-Qadir faced better equipped and numerically superior French forces. After 1847, militant resistance came to be centered in the Sahara and mountains, such as the Kabylia.

O regret times gone by!
I am grieved, oh world, about Algiers,
The French march on her
With troops whose number (only) God knows.
They have come in vessels which cleave the sea;
It is not a matter of a hundred vessels, or two hundred,
Mathematics does not understand.
Those who counted wore themselves out;
O Muslim, you would have said they were a forest!
They swam ashore; but, the dogs, as soon as they faced the port,
Saw the cannons aiming at them,
And they went toward Sidi-Farruj [west of Algiers]

Burj al-Fanar [lighthouse tower] had terrified them!

Soon the sea and the waves became swollen,

In order to vomit on our shores the French, sons of Ilja. [sons of European slave women]

From all sides they were seen stomping about;

Time called them and they came:

It is known that everything has its time.

The Agha Brahim [Ottoman military commander] hastened to mount his horse

with his flags, his music, and his foul-mouthed Turks.

Arabs and Kabyles joined in,

Horsemen and foot soldiers charged,

The battle became hot, Oh my brothers!

Its fire raged through Sundays and Mondays,

And the volley fell on our warriors.

Death is worth much more than shame:

If the mother of the cities is taken,

What will you have left, Oh Muslim?

Be patient, do not be frightened,

Death is our share,

We are all its prey.

Death in holy war (*jihad*)

Is life in the other world.

To the east of Algiers is a rugged mountainous region, the Kabylia, whose loftiest peak is named after a holy woman, Lalla Khadija. The Berber-speaking inhabitants have always been known for their spirit of independence as well as for the veneration they accord to local Muslim saints, male and female; Berber women were renowned for their courage in battle. Fatima N'Soumer, a Berber holy woman born in 1830, the year of the French invasion of Algeria, led armed resistance to the French military assaults on the Kabyle Mountains from 1854 to 1857. Fatima's political and religious influence stretched all over the Kabylia where her disciples believed that, clad in her red cloak, she wielded miraculous powers from God to cure the sick, ward off evil, and foretell the future in oracles. Captured by the French army in July of 1857, Fatima died in prison in 1863 at the age of 33 years. Her memory, however, has persisted to this day in oral traditions. This report, written by a French military officer, Antoine Carette, who traveled through the Kabylia, provides an eyewitness account of the region's traditions regarding women and war.

Almost all [Kabyle] women follow their brothers and husbands [into battle]. They are even seen in the midst of the battle, encouraging the combatants with their cries, caring for the wounded, helping

The Anglo-Turkish Commercial Treaty of 1838

On the Anglo-Turkish Commercial Treaty of 1838, which opened the door for a massive influx of European manufactured goods into the Ottoman Empire, the Austrian consul to Istanbul noted:

The Treaty of 1838 is ... hostile to Ottoman industry. . . . Now a Belgian merchant pays 5% on goods sold in Turkey; a Turkish merchant pays 12% for exports or even for transport from one of the Ottoman states to another.

to carry the dead off the battlefield, sharing in the dangers of the struggle—in the pain of defeat or the joy of victory. Bloody examples prove the part that these women play in holy war [against the French army]. In December 1834, a Kabyle woman served as a foot soldier in an attack against a [French military] cavalry charge; her body was discovered among the dead afterwards. In a military confrontation in 1835, fourteen women were killed or wounded. Finally in June 1836, I saw the widow of a Kabyle religious leader, who had been killed the day before in combat, arrive at the head of a column of Berber warriors. She remained at the site of her husband's death weeping and wailing despite the fact that bullets [from French rifles] rained about her for an hour.

American-Ottoman Relations in an Imperial Age

In the midst of the American Civil War, President Abraham Lincoln (1809–1865) ratified this commercial treaty with the Ottoman Empire. It guaranteed the same rights of legal immunity [capitulations given to other Western countries] and granted the United States the same low tariff rates given to Britain in the 1838 treaty of Balta Liman. As Article XX noted, this treaty thus applied to all Ottoman possessions, including Egypt, Tunisia, and Tripolitania (modern-day Libya).

Whereas a treaty of commerce and navigation between the United States of America and the Ottoman Empire was concluded and signed by their respective plenipotentiaries at Constantinople on the twenty-fifth day of February last, which treaty, in the English language, is word for word as follows:

Treaty of Commerce and Navigation between the United States of America and the Ottoman Empire.

The United States of America on the one part, and His Imperial Majesty the Sultan of the Ottoman empire on the other part, being equally animated by the desire of extending the commercial relations between their respective countries, have agreed, for this purpose, to conclude a treaty of commerce and navigation, and have named . . . their respective plenipotentiaries . . . who, after having communicated to each other their respective full powers, found in good and due form, have agreed upon the following articles:

ARTICLE II. The citizens of the United States of America, or their agents, shall be permitted to purchase, at all places in the Ottoman empire and its possessions, (whether for the purposes of internal trade or of exportation,) all articles, without any exception whatsoever, the produce or manufacture of the said empire and possessions; and the Sublime Porte having, in virtue of the second article of the [Balta Liman] convention of commerce, of the 16th of August, 1838, with Great Britain, formally engaged to abolish all monopolies of agricultural produce, or of every other articles whatsoever, as well as all "permits" (tezkerehs) from the local governors, either for the purchase of any article, or for its removal from one place to another when purchased, any attempt to compel the citizens of the United States of America to receive such "permits" from the local governors shall be considered as an infraction of this treaty, and the Sublime Porte shall immediately punish with severity any viziers, or other officers, who shall have been guilty of such misconduct, and shall render full justice to citizens of the United States of America for all losses or injuries which they may duly prove themselves to have suffered thereby.

ARTICLE III. If any articles of Ottoman produce or manufacture be purchased by citizens of the United States of America, or their agents, for the purpose of selling the same for internal consumption in Turkey, the said citizens, or their agents, shall pay at the purchase and sale of such articles, and in any manner of trade therein, the same duties that are paid in similar circumstances by the most favored class of Ottoman subjects, or of foreigners in the internal trade of the Ottoman empire.

ARTICLE IV. . . . No charge or duty whatsoever will be demanded on any article of Ottoman produce or manufacture purchased by citizens of the United States of America, or their agents, either at the place where such article is purchased or in its transit from that place to the place whence it is exported, at which it will be subject to an export duty not exceeding eight per cent, which shall once have paid this duty shall not again be liable to the same duty, however they may have changed hands within any part of the Ottoman empire. . . .

ARTICLE XIII. Citizens of the United States of America, or their agents, trading in goods the produce or manufacture of foreign countries, shall be subject to the same taxes, and enjoy the same rights, privileges, and immunities, as foreign subjects dealing in goods the produce or manufacture of their own country. . . .

ARTICLE XVIII. Contraband goods will be liable to confiscation by the Ottoman treasury; but a report, or *procès verbal*, of the alleged act of contraband, must, so soon as the said goods are seized by the authorities, be drawn up and communicated to the consular authority of the citizen or subject to whom the goods said to be contraband shall belong; and no goods can be confiscated as contraband, unless the fraud with regard to them shall be duly and legally proved . . .

Article XX. The present treaty shall receive its execution in all and every one of the provinces of the Ottoman empire; that is to say, in all the possessions of His Imperial Majesty the Sultan, situated in Europe or in Asia, in Egypt, and in the other parts of Africa belonging to the Sublime Porte, in Servia [Serbia], and in the united principalities of Moldavia and Wallachia [modern Rumania]. . . .

Done at Constantinople, on the twenty-fifth day of February, 1862. . . . And whereas the said Treaty has been duly ratified on both parts, and the respective ratifications of the same were exchanged at Constantinople, on the fifth ultimo, by Edward Joy Morris, Minister Resident of the United States at the Sublime Porte, and by his Highness Mehemed Emin Aali Pacha, Minister of Foreign Affairs of His Imperial Majesty the Sultan of the Ottoman Empire, on the part of their respective Governments:

Now, therefore, be it known that I, ABRAHAM LINCOLN, President of the United States of America, have caused the said Treaty to be made public, to the end that the same, and every clause and article thereof, may be observed and fulfilled with good faith by the United States and the citizens thereof. In witness whereof, I have hereunto set my hand and caused the seal of the United States to be affixed. Done at the City of Washington, this second day of July, in the year of our Lord one thousand eight hundred and sixty-two, and of the Independence of the United States the eighty sixth.

ABRAHAM LINCOLN.

By the President:

F. W. SEWARD, Acting Secretary of State.

Anglo-French Justifications of Imperialism: Racial Superiority and Commercial Investments in Egypt and Tunisia

The idea of a canal linking the Mediterranean with the Red Sea dates back to ancient Egypt when, as early as 1380 BCE, an attempt was made to construct such a waterway. Napoleon also considered building a canal but, upon hearing that the Red Sea was over thirty feet higher than the Mediterranean, he gave up the plan. The French consul in Cairo, Ferdinand de Lesseps (1805–1894), renewed the project in the 1850s and the Suez Canal Company was formed, a venture contracted by a French company with the Egyptian ruler, Muhammad Said Pasha (r. 1854–1863). Work on the Canal demanded the forced labor of thousands of conscripted Egyptians, mainly peasants. The Canal was opened to great pomp in 1869. It immediately changed the nature of Mediterranean trade, transport, and communications with Asia. By linking the Mediterranean and Red Seas, it halved the time required for travel to India, thus making the Canal Zone and Egypt of major concern to Great Britain. This report on the abuse of laborers for constructing the Canal was written by a chaplain who was attached to the British consulate in Alexandria.

A large body of *corvée* [forced] labourers are at work a little to the south of Lake Timsah . . . the fresh water from Ismailia to Port Said flows in large iron tubes along the side of the Canal. . . . Only half of the distance (to Kantara) is yet finished . . . a small side canal (salt) leads from Ismailia to the Canal Maritime; the latter enters Timsah at its north-east corner. About an hour from Ismailia we reached El Guisr, an enormous cutting in the sand some four miles long and very deep; the canal in the cutting was but a mere thread of water and very shallow. . . . Beyond Kantara all through Lake Menzaleh the Canal is of full breadth but nowhere at present is there a depth of more than 2 metres and in most places much less. Near Kantara there were some 7,000 *corvée* labourers at work and, according to our estimates, there were altogether 13,000 employed. When they had reached water level it was intended to execute the rest by dredging machines which could not be employed till the earth had been removed by manual labour to water level. . . . Their appearance [that of the *corvée* laborers] was very pitiable. All told us that they did not come of their own free will; they came by force '*b'il nabut*' [driven by clubs].

In 1872, a worldwide financial crisis triggered Egyptian and Ottoman bankruptcy. The British Prime Minister, Benjamin Disraeli (1804–1881), took advantage of the crisis to buy the Egyptian-held shares of the Suez Canal Company in November 1875 from the financially desperate Egyptian ruler, Khedive Ismail (r. 1863–1879). By acquiring Egypt's shares,

"Ceremonies for the Opening of the Suez Canal, 1869." The canal opened to shipping on November 17, 1869. While numerous technical, political, and financial problems had been overcome, the final cost was more than double the original estimate. The opening was presided over by Khedive Ismail of Egypt and Sudan, who invited the French Empress and wife of Napoleon III, Eugénie, to pass first through the canal in the imperial yacht. Significantly, the next ship to follow the empresses' vessel was the British P&O liner Delta bound for India. In the image, we see Empress Eugénie seated on a camel with her retinue.

Great Britain became a major partner in the canal's operations, defended by Disraeli as a victory for the British Empire. The Egyptian financial crisis and Egyptian resentment at European control of Egypt's finances ultimately led to nationalist opposition and the British invasion and occupation of Egypt in 1882.

The Parliamentary debate on approving the purchase of the shares occurred on February 21, 1876, with Disraeli defending himself against his arch-rival, William Gladstone (1809–1898), who, as prime minister in 1882, ordered the British attack on Egypt to secure British communications through the canal. Gladstone argued here that Disraeli should not have borrowed the funds to purchase Egypt's shares in the canal from the Rothschild banking family and that the canal was of little value to Britain.

Sir . . . it cannot be denied that the discussion of this evening at least has proved one result. It has shown, in a manner about which neither the House of Commons nor the country can make any mistake, that had the right honourable Gentleman the Member for Greenwich (Mr. Gladstone) been the Prime Minister of this country, the shares in the Suez Canal would not have been purchased. . . . What is this question of the Suez Canal? . . . the House must be tolerably aware that during the whole period of the existence of the present Parliament the question of the Suez Canal has more or less been before us. . . . Why, my right honourable Friend the Chancellor of the Exchequer was intimately acquainted with the subject, and was himself present at the opening of the Suez Canal. . . .

"The Lion's Share." This cartoon from the British satirical paper, *Punch*, was published in February 1876 just after the ruler of Egypt, portrayed in a fez, sold the country's shares in the Suez Canal Company to the British government at great loss. The caption under the lion, who symbolized Great Britain, reads: "The acquisition of the Suez Canal Shares was accepted by the country [i.e., the British] as securing the safety of the 'Key to India.'"

We are here to guard the country against complications, and to guide it in the event of complications; and the argument that we are to do nothing—never dare to move, never try to increase our strength and improve our position, because we are afraid of complications—is certainly a new view of English policy. . . . We believe, on the contrary, that, instead of leading to complications with other nations, the step which we have taken is one which will avert complications. . . . I feel that at this moment our position is much stronger, and for the reason that we are possessors of a great portion of the capital invested in the Canal.

. . . [But] I have never recommended, and I do not now recommend this purchase as a financial investment. . . . [or] as a commercial speculation although I believe that many of those who have looked upon it with little favour will probably be surprised with the pecuniary results of the purchase. I have always, and do now recommend it to the country as a political transaction, and one which I believe is calculated to strengthen the Empire. That is the spirit in which it has been accepted by the country, which understands it though the two right honourable critics may not. They [the country] are really seasick of the "Silver Streak." (The English Channel) They want the Empire to be maintained, to be strengthened; they will not be alarmed even it be increased. Because they think we are obtaining a great hold and interest in this important portion of Africa—because they believe that it secures to us a highway to our Indian Empire and our other dependencies, the people of England have from the first recognized the propriety and the wisdom of the step which we shall sanction tonight.

Egypt's Khedive Ismail on the Benefits of Contacts with Europe, 1867

For thirty years, the European influence has transformed Egypt; now . . . we are civilized.

France had long sought to take Tunisia, which bordered Algeria. During the Congress of Berlin in 1878 ratifying British claims to the island of Cyprus, which was part of the Ottoman Empire, Great Britain agreed that France could occupy Tunisia. France justified its 1881 military occupation by claiming that Tunisian tribes had crossed into Algeria to aid Algerian resistance to the French occupation; it also declared that Tunisian financial instability stemming from the worldwide financial crisis of 1872 that had also affected the Ottoman Empire, and Egypt required European intervention. The Treaty of Bardo was imposed on the Bey [ruler] of Tunisia. France claimed full authority over Tunisian affairs and would have the right (Art. 6) to represent Tunisia and individual Tunisians in other countries. For a blunter assessment of why France took Tunisia, see the speech of Jules Ferry that follows. France ruled Tunisia as a Protectorate until 1956.

Art. 1. All treaties of peace, friendship and commerce and all other agreements currently existing between the French Republic and H.M. the Bey of Tunis are expressly renewed and confirmed.

Art. 2. In order to facilitate for the government of the French Republic the accomplishment of the measures which it must take in order to attain the goals proposed by the high contracting parties, H.M. the Bey of Tunis consents to the occupation by the French military authority of such points as it shall deem necessary to assure the re-establishment of order and the security of the frontiers and the coast.

This occupation will cease as soon as the French and Tunisian military authorities have together agreed that the local administration is able to guarantee the maintenance of order.

Art. 3. The Government of the French Republic pledges to give constant support to H.M. the Bey of Tunis against any danger which menaces the person or the dynasty of His Highness or which compromises the tranquility of his States.

Art. 4. The Government of the French Republic guarantees the execution of treaties currently existing between the Regency Government and the various European powers.

Art. 5. The government of the French Republic will be represented before H.M. the Bey of Tunis by a resident minister, who will observe the execution of the present act and who will be the intermediary for communications between the French Government and the Tunisian authorities for all affairs commonly concerning the two countries.

Art. 6. The diplomatic and consular agents of France in foreign countries will be charged with the protection of Tunisian and national interests of the Regency. In return, H.M. the Bey pledges to draw up no act of an international character without having notified and previously come to an agreement with the Government of the French Republic.

Art. 7. The Government of the French Republic and the Government of H.M. the Bey of Tunis will agree together on a basis for a

"The Sea Gate and Entrance to the Tunis Madina, 1860–1890." The Sea Gate, renamed Porte de France with the 1881 establishment of the Protectorate, mediated between the new city boasting European businesses and laid out in grid-like fashion, and the old city, which remained relatively untouched during the colonial period. Similar urban transformations occurred throughout MENA in this period.

financial organization of the Regency which will assure the service of the public debt and guarantee the rights of Tunisian creditors.

Jules Ferry (1832–1893) was twice prime minister of France (1880–1881, 1883–1885). He is especially remembered for championing laws that removed Catholic influence from most educational institutions in France and for promoting a vast extension of the French colonial empire, including France's invasion and occupation of Tunisia in 1881. Here, addressing the Chamber of Deputies in 1884, he presents a classic justification of European imperial expansion.

The policy of colonial expansion is a political and economic system . . . that can be connected to three sets of ideas: economic ideas; the most far-reaching ideas of civilization; and ideas of a political and patriotic sort . . .

In the area of economics, I am placing before you, with the support of some statistics, the considerations that justify the policy of colonial expansion, as seen from the perspective of a need, felt more and more urgently by the industrialized population of Europe and especially the people of our rich and hardworking country of France: the need for outlets [for exports]. Is this a fantasy? Is this a concern [that can wait] for the future? Or is this not a pressing need, one may say a crying need, of our industrial population? I merely express in a general way what each one of you can see for himself in the various parts of France. Yes, what our major industries [textiles, etc.], irrevocably steered by the treaties of 1860 into exports, lack more and more are outlets. Why? Because next door Germany is setting up trade barriers; because across the ocean the United States of America have become protectionists, and extreme protectionists at that; because not only are these great markets . . . shrinking, becoming more and more difficult of access, but these great states are beginning to pour into our own markets products not seen there before. This is true not only for our agriculture, which has been so sorely tried . . . and for which competition is no longer limited to the circle of large European states. . . . Today, as you know, competition, the law of supply and demand, freedom of trade, the effects of speculation, all radiate in a circle that reaches to the ends of the earth. . . .

That is a great complication, a great economic difficulty; . . . an extremely serious problem. It is so serious, gentlemen, so acute, that the least informed persons must already glimpse, foresee, and take precautions against the time when the great South American market that has, in a manner of speaking, belonged to us forever will be disputed and perhaps taken away from us by North American products. Nothing is more serious; there can be no graver social problem; and these matters are linked intimately to colonial policy. Gentlemen, we must speak more loudly and more honestly! We must say openly that indeed the higher races have a right over the lower races. . . . I repeat, that the superior races have a right because they have a duty. They have the duty to civilize the inferior races. . . . In the history of earlier centuries these duties, gentlemen, have often been misunderstood; and certainly when the Spanish soldiers and explorers introduced slavery into Central America, they did not fulfill their duty as men of a higher race. . . . But, in our time, I maintain that European nations acquit themselves with generosity, with grandeur, and with sincerity of this superior civilizing duty.

I say that French colonial policy, the policy of colonial expansion, the policy that has taken us under the Empire [the Second Empire, of Napoleon III], to Saigon, to Indochina [Vietnam, Cambodia, Laos], that has led us to Tunisia, to Madagascar—I say that this policy of colonial expansion was inspired by . . . the fact that a navy such as ours cannot do without safe harbors, defenses, supply centers on the high seas. . . . Are you unaware of this? Look at a map of the world.

Gentlemen, these are considerations that merit the full attention of patriots. The conditions of naval warfare have greatly changed. . . . At present, as you know, a warship, however perfect its design, cannot carry more than two weeks' supply of coal; and a vessel without coal is a wreck on the high seas, abandoned to the first occupier. Hence the need to have places of supply, shelters, ports for defense and provisioning. . . . And that is why we needed Tunisia; that is why we needed Saigon and Indochina; that is why we need Madagascar . . . and why we shall never leave them! . . . Gentlemen, in Europe such as it is today, in this competition of the many rivals we see rising up around us, some by military or naval improvements, others by the prodigious development of a constantly growing population; in a Europe, or rather in a universe thus constituted, a policy of withdrawal or abstention is simply the high road to decadence! In our time nations are great only through the activity they deploy; it is not by spreading the peaceable light of their institutions . . . that they are great, in the present day.

Spreading light without acting, without taking part in the affairs of the world, keeping out of all European alliances and seeing as a trap, an adventure, all expansion into Africa or the Orient—for a great nation to live this way, believe me, is to abdicate and, in less time than you may think, to sink from the first rank to the third and fourth.

In 1882, Lord Cromer [Evelyn Baring], (1841–1917), began a quarter century as British Consul-General in Egypt. This account, taken from his two-volume work *Modern Egypt* (1908), serves to justify the British takeover in 1882, based on supposed Egyptian inability to govern themselves, Great Britain's need to control the Suez Canal, blocking interference by another European power, and the threat to European capital investments in Egypt. His remarks illustrate his conviction in the superiority of Englishmen in ruling "Orientals."

Egypt may now almost be said to form part of Europe. It is on the high road to the Far East [via the Suez Canal]. It can never cease to be an object of interest to all the powers of Europe, and especially to England. A numerous and intelligent body of Europeans and of non-Egyptian Orientals have made Egypt their home. European capital to a large extent has been sunk in the country. The rights and privileges of Europeans are jealously guarded, and, moreover, give rise to complicated questions, which it requires no small amount of ingenuity and technical knowledge to solve. Exotic institutions have sprung up and have taken root in the country. The capitulations impair those rights of internal sovereignty which are enjoyed by the rulers or legislatures of most states. The population is heterogeneous and cosmopolitan to a degree almost unknown elsewhere. Although the prevailing faith is that of Islam, in no country in the world is a greater variety of religious creeds to be found amongst important sections of the community.

. . . . It has to be borne in mind that in 1882 the [Egyptian] army was in a state of mutiny; the treasury was bankrupt; every branch of the administration had been dislocated . . . whilst, at the same time, no more orderly and law-abiding form of government had been inaugurated to take its place. Is it probable that a government composed of the rude elements described above, and led by men of such poor ability as Arabi (Ahmad Urabi 1841–1911) and his coadjutators, would have been able to control a complicated machine of this nature? Were the sheikhs of the El-Azhar mosque likely to succeed where Tewfik Pasha (r. 1880–1892) and his ministers, who were men of comparative education and enlightenment, acting under the guidance and inspiration of a first-class European power, only met with a modified success after years of patient labor? There can be but one answer to these questions. . . . The

The Influence of Economic Interests on British Expansion and Occupation. Lord Alfred Lyall (1835–1911), letter to Lord Cromer, 1908.
With regard to the events and transactions that preceded the establishment of the English Protectorate in Egypt [1882], it is . . . wonderful that [Prime Minister William] Gladstone's incapacity or unwillingness to comprehend and face the situation did not turn the whole business into confusion and failure. . . . Material interests, the heavy money stake of the European financiers in Egypt, the pluck and tact of the men on the spot prevailed. Just as they will always prevail in India, where the immense investments of English capitalists will always have a sobering effect on Liberal theories [of increasing self-government] for that country.

full and immediate execution of a policy of "Egypt for the Egyptians," as it was conceived by the Arabists in 1882, was, and still is, impossible.

History, indeed, records some very radical changes in the forms of government to which a state has been subjected without its interests being absolutely and permanently shipwrecked. But it may be doubted whether any instance can be quoted of a sudden transfer of power in any civilized or semi-civilized community to a class so ignorant as the pure Egyptians, such as they were in the year 1882. These latter have, for centuries past, been a subject race. Persians, Greeks, Romans, Arabs from Arabia and Baghdad, Circassians, and finally, Ottoman Turks, have successively ruled over Egypt, but we have to go back to the doubtful and obscure precedents of Pharaonic times to find an epoch when, possibly, Egypt was ruled by Egyptians. Neither, for the present, do they appear to possess the qualities which would render it desirable, either in their own interests, or in those of the civilized world in general, to raise them at a bound to the category of autonomous rulers with full rights of internal sovereignty.

If, however, a foreign occupation was inevitable or nearly inevitable, it remains to be considered whether a British occupation was preferable to any other. From the purely Egyptian point of view, the answer to this question cannot be doubtful. . . . The special aptitude shown by Englishmen in the government of Oriental races pointed to England as the most effective and beneficent instrument for the gradual introduction of European civilization into Egypt. An Anglo-French, or an Anglo-Italian occupation, from both of which we narrowly and also accidentally escaped, would have been detrimental to Egyptian interests and would ultimately have caused friction, if not serious dissension, between England on the one side and France or Italy on the other. The only thing to be said in favor of Turkish intervention is that it would have relieved England from the responsibility of intervening.

By the process of exhausting all other expedients, we arrive at the conclusion that . . . it was impossible for Great Britain to allow the troops of any other power to occupy Egypt. When it became apparent that some foreign occupation was necessary, that the Sultan would not act save under conditions which were impossible of acceptance, and that neither French nor Italian cooperation could be secured, the British government acted with promptitude and vigor. A great nation cannot throw off the responsibilities which its past history and its position in the world have imposed upon it. English history affords other examples of the government and people of

England drifting by accident into doing what was not only right, but was also most in accordance with British interests.

Zionism: Its Origins and Objectives

Zionism originated in Eastern Europe in the 1870s and 1880s as a Jewish national movement seeking a homeland, preferably in Palestine, formerly Ancient Israel. Zionism gained momentum with the 1896 publication of Theodor Herzl's *The Jewish State*, which argued that Jews could never be truly free in Europe because of European anti-Semitism. Following the foundation of the World Zionist Organization in 1897 with Herzl (1860–1904) its first president, Zionists sought great power recognition for their demands while also encouraging settlement in Palestine. As a result, Zionism was both a national movement for people seeking to escape discrimination and, as Herzl noted (see sidebar), a settler movement, seeking a state where others lived; Palestinian Muslims and Christians were 90 percent of the population in 1900.

The idea that I have developed in this pamphlet is an ancient one. It is the restoration of the Jewish state. . . . The Jewish question still exists. . . . It is a misplaced piece of medievalism which civilized nations do not yet seem to shake off, try as they will. . . . The Jewish question exists wherever Jews live in appreciable numbers. . . . We are naturally drawn to those places where we are not persecuted and our appearance there gives rise to persecution. This is the case, and will inevitably be so, everywhere . . . so long as the Jewish question is not solved on the political level.

Anti-Semitism is a highly complex movement, which I think I understand. . . . [Jewish] equality before the law, granted by statute, has become practically a dead letter. [Jews] are debarred from filling even moderately high offices. . . . Modern anti-Semitism is not to be confused with the persecution of Jews in former times, though it still does have a religious aspect in some countries. . . . In the principal centers of anti-Semitism, it is an outgrowth of the emancipation of the Jews . . . the very impossibility of getting at the Jews nourishes and deepens hatred of them. . . .

The whole plan is essentially quite simple. . . . Let sovereignty be granted us over a portion of the globe adequate to meet our rightful national requirements; we will attend to the rest. . . . Is Palestine or Argentina preferable? The society [to be founded] will take whatever is granted and whatever Jewish public opinion

Many European Jews rejected Zionism. They feared that attaining a Jewish state would mean that Europeans would force them to lose their citizenship and move to the new state. In his 1898 article, "Who Fears a State?," published in Berlin, Zionist Theodor Herzl countered these fears.

I cannot see how an attempt to create a homeland for a part of a people that feels superfluous . . . could have a harmful effect on the rights of those who want to remain where they are. Don't you know what a colonial age we are living in? As a consequence of overpopulation, and of the resultant ever more acute social question, many nations are endeavouring to found overseas colonies in order to channel the flow of emigration there. This is the policy that England has been pursuing for decades, and which has been regarded as exemplary by many nations. I believe that Germany too has taken steps to become a Greater Germany, since it has looked across the seas and has striven to found colonies everywhere. . . . Both speakers seem to recoil from the word "state." Well, what is a state? A big colony. What is a colony? A small state. Mankind seems never to have found anything terrible in that. . . .

favors. Palestine is our unforgettable national homeland. . . . If his Majesty, the [Ottoman] sultan were to give us Palestine, we could in return undertake the complete management of the finances of Turkey. We should then form part of a wall of defense for Europe in Asia, an outpost of civilization against barbarism. We should as a neutral state, remain in contact with all of Europe which would have to guarantee our existence. . . .

Missionary Ventures and Educational Experiments: European and Middle Eastern Feminine Interactions

European and American Christian missionary activity in MENA initially focused on Palestine and conversion of Jews there and elsewhere to hasten Judgment Day. Failing in that effort and hostile to Islam, they sought to convert Muslims to Christianity, but many missions found only local Christians interested in their message. However, their medical services and educational institutions began to be frequented by Muslims as well as Christians. This document illustrates the more militant side of American missionary views during and at the end of the nineteenth century, including Samuel Zwemer's (1867–1952) and Arthur J. Brown's (1856–1963) ignorance of the local inhabitants after they had spent decades unsuccessfully seeking to convert Muslims to Christianity. The idea that Kabyles, as Berbers with blue eyes, would be more open to Christianity contradicts the French military officer Antoine Carette's account of their bravery in resisting the French in Document 5. Despite his years among Arabs, Zwemer remained unaware that traditional Muslim societies participated in religious festivities celebrated by non-Muslims, since Jesus is revered as a prophet in Islam, and that peasant women in many Muslim societies such as Egypt did not wear the veil. As shown in the following sidebar, Muslim-Christian celebrations of each other's festivals annoyed Catholic priests in Lebanon who sought to make local Christians and Muslims separate themselves from each other

"Hotel du Parc, Jaffa, Palestine, 1902." Religious migrants were part and parcel of growing Western involvement in MENA but maintained complex relations with the local representatives of imperial powers. Originally from Chicago, the Spafford family led an American contingent in 1881 to Jerusalem to organize a Christian utopian society; they were later joined by Swedish Christians. Originally believing that their presence in Jerusalem would hasten the Second Coming of Christ, the American Colony engaged in extensive philanthropic work among Jerusalem's inhabitants, regardless of religion. In the image, members of the society pose in one of Jaffa's European hotels.

for religious reasons and also to serve imperial goals. The denigration of Islam found in Ion Keith Falconer's (1856–1887) c.1885 statement below is similar to that found in American evangelical attacks on Islam today; Falconer was a missionary to Egypt and then to Aden.

    1. "There are weak points in Islam which, if persistently attacked, must lead to its eventual overthrow, while Christianity has forces which make it more than a match for Mohammadanism or any other religion. From its birth Islam had been steeped in blood and lust, blood spilt and lust sated by the sanctions of religion. The Koran is doomed. (**c. 1885**)

    2. 'The Gospel in North Africa.' The unbroken phalanx lines of Moslem countries along the Mediterranean were once the centres of Christian teaching. Origen, Tertullian, Athanasius, Cyprian, and Augustine were all from North Africa. But Islam swept across this region like a desert sinoon and withered the garden of God. Yet there exists to the present day among those Berber or Kabyle tribes of North Africa various customs which have come down to them through twelve long centuries of Mohammadanism and which speak of the time when they were a Christian people. For example, the Kabyle women refuse to wear the veil and certain of these Kabyle tribes, although . . . Mohammadans, observe the Christian Sabbath as a day of feasting. The mark of a cross is tattooed on the foreheads of many of the boys and men at Biskra. . . .

From the middle of the 19th century on, European women settled in colonial empires in Asia and Africa in greater numbers. Some attempted to effect changes for the good of colonized women. One example from French Algeria was Hubertine Auclert, (1848–1914) the radical Parisian feminist writer and women's suffrage activist. Auclert lived in Algeria from 1888 to 1892 and published an important work in 1900 on Algerian women, *Les femmes arabes* (Arab Women). She devoted numerous articles to the cause of Algerian women's emancipation through modern education, access to work, and transformations in a colonial legal system that disenfranchised the colonized, reducing many to misery. Traditional female crafts—such as pottery, embroidery, textile weaving, and carpet production—had suffered greatly in Algeria due to competition from imported, machine-made products. Losing their status as artisans and producers, women also lost economic independence in their own society. In addition, Auclert critiqued the French colonial regime in Algeria for refusing to establish sufficient schools for girls and even closing some academic institutions to replace them with native handicraft workshops. On the 28th of May 1892, Auclert published an article in the French journal, *La Petite Republique Française*, entitled "Women's Work and Handicraft Production."

In nineteenth-century Mt. Lebanon, civil strife erupted in 1840 and 1860, principally over issues of lands ownership between Maronite Catholics and the Druze, an offshoot of Shii Islam. But these issues were exacerbated by rival missionary efforts pursued by Catholic Jesuits linked to France and Protestant missionaries from the United States or Britain. Given Ottoman lack of interest in improving educational facilities at the time, Maronites went to Catholic schools, Druze to Protestant schools sponsored initially by British missionaries. But many in Lebanon, as elsewhere, observed the traditional feast days of their neighbors of other religions, angering missionaries such as the Jesuit quoted here.

We are sorry to say that there was a sort of coexistence [fusion] between the Christians and Muslims of Sayda. They visited each other frequently, which resulted in intimate relations between them and which introduced, bit by bit, a community of ideas and habits all of which was at the expense of the Christians. These latter joined in the important Muslim feasts and the Muslims [in turn] joined in the important Christian feasts; this kind of activity passed for good manners, sociability, while in truth it resulted in nothing more than the weakening of religious sentiments.

"Disembarking from a ship, Algiers, c. 1899." This shows labor immigrants and travelers arriving in French Algeria's major port. By this period, European settlers were in the majority in Algerian coastal cities due to immigration. The social diversity of the crowd on the dock indicates that ports and ships attracted a wide range of people—from native porters, French military, and ordinary folks to bourgeois travelers whose class is apparent from their wearing apparel.

In Algiers after Madame Luce was forced to transform her school [for native girls] into a workshop [by the French colonial regime], she taught young Algerian girls how to embroider with creative motifs, some simple, others sculpted like lace, and how to achieve stitchery whose evenness makes it look as if it were machine made. . . . Winter tourists come and purchase Algerian women's handicrafts; English and American exhibitions like to show them to their visitors. Some pieces of embroidery were bought for the Chicago Exposition [then being organized for the next year, 1893]. However, the French in Algeria, and even some Algerians themselves, appear to be unaware of the existence of this artistic embroidery whose inspiration is Arab. Clearly the French colonial administration does little to promote feminine handicrafts. For example, when in 1878, Madame Ben-Aben, the grand-daughter of Madame Luce and her administrative successor at the women's craft school, asked permission to exhibit her pupils' best pieces, colonial authorities promised her a place in the Algerian section of the Paris Exposition. However, when she arrived in Paris with the very finest handicraft pieces produced by two young Algerian Muslim girls, she [was] not accorded any exhibition space. . . . We would not have to denounce the colonial administration in French Algeria—which is responsible for ruining native women's crafts because of its policies—if women, who are better able to appreciate beautiful needle work than men, had been allowed to serve as adjuncts to the male-dominated organizing committee for the Paris Exposition.

Instead of encouraging education for Arab girls in Algeria, the French administration has closed the schools that existed prior to the conquest [1830], allowed conservative Muslim men to shut down those schools for girls that were established after the conquest, and thus the capital of Algeria has not had a single [academic] school for native girls for thirty-five years. When the rector of the Academy of Algiers, Monsieur Jeanmarie, opened a class where young Arab girls could receive education, these girls proved so prodigiously intelligent that the French became alarmed. The French said that these young girls when they graduate from school would no longer want to stay at home in seclusion.

North Africa has long been home to ancient, diverse communities of Jews. Traditionally Morocco boasted a large Jewish community whose numbers reached in the hundreds of thousands. As the notion of the civilizing mission spread throughout the French Empire during the nineteenth century, French Jews from Paris embraced this idea to promote the cultural regeneration of non-European Jews, mainly in North Africa and the Middle East, by introducing modern education. In 1860 a new, private Jewish organization was founded in Paris, the Alliance Israélite Universelle, whose goal was to teach modern French ideas in the realms of social, political, and cultural life, above all, in primary education, to Jews outside of Europe. To that end, French or European Jewish teachers trained in modern pedagogy, books, and curricula were dispatched as "missionaries" to places like Morocco. The kind of education and social organization advocated by the Paris-based Alliance Israélite constituted a revolutionary break with the past for North African Jews. At first schools were only for boys, but by the late nineteenth century, girls schools had also been created in Algeria, Tunisia, and Morocco.

Despite their good intentions, French Jews attempting to modernize their fellow Arab Jews encountered resistance, particularly when it came to changes in gender relations, women's legal status, and girls' upbringing. In Mrs. M. Coriat's 1902 report, "A Sympathetic Account of the Condition of the Women of Marakesh," submitted to the Alliance headquarters in Paris, we see some of the same attitudes that Christian missionaries held toward non-Christian peoples in Asia and Africa or, indeed, middle-class social reformers in the United States or Europe toward working class peoples in American or European cities.

Education. What most surprises the parents of your girls is the cleanliness and the polite manners acquired by the children at the school. All of our efforts in this direction have been crowned with success. Prior to the foundation of our school the young girls one would see in the streets were dirty, unkempt, and barefoot; now they are unrecognizable, as they come to school every day perfectly presentable. Even today, at the end of the school day, a good number of women stand in their doorways to watch the "girls from the school" pass by. There is whispering and chattering. "Look over there. So-and-so's daughter is wearing stockings and shoes; see that other one with the hat?" These little scenes are played out day after day. At present our girls laugh about it and are amazed that, not long ago, they could have gone out of the house without stockings, sometimes even without shoes. In my first letters to the Central

Committee, I found many occasions to discuss the character of our girls: dishonest, sly, selfish. Those were the principal faults against which we had to fight. They would not hesitate an instant to accuse one of their friends, even their best friends, or to try and fool the teacher. Some progress has been made in this direction also. I am not saying that the girls are models of solidarity, cooperation, and kindness. But I have noted with satisfaction that there is no longer the same spirit of cunning and deceit among my students. Before, it was always a question of who could find the best ruse to get out of a difficult situation. There was joy on their faces when one of their classmates was being punished. Now they have stopped trying to trick their teacher, and when they have done something wrong, I am able to get at the truth of the matter, something that was impossible in the beginning.

World Fairs and Tourism: Imperial Portraits of the Oriental and the Oriental Response

One of the most important arenas for shaping Western attitudes toward "non-Western" peoples, cultures, and societies was the world fair, or exhibition, an invention of the nineteenth century. World Fairs were held in Paris, London, Vienna, and in Chicago in 1893, among many places,

"People on 'a street in Cairo' in front of Moroccan café, Paris Exposition, 1889." The World Fairs, which emerged in nineteenth-century Europe and then North America, were directly linked to imperialism since the exhibits displayed "subjugated natives" from the colonies or from regions under foreign imperial influence. In this image, we see reconstructions or architectural caricatures of an Egyptian street and a North African café, which the Parisian crowd could visit in a sort of simulated voyage to Africa.

and invariably sought to offer up to viewers the most exotic and bizarre aspects of foreign lands and peoples, Orientals.

The 1893 World's Fair—From the *Chicago Tribune*

It will be a unique procession, one which cannot be seen elsewhere, and one which may never be seen here again after the Fair closes. Headed by the United States regulars, there will follow in picturesque array Turks with Far-Away Moses leading them, Bedouins, sedan bearers, Algerians, Soudanese, the grotesque population of the Cairo street, with its wrestlers, fencers, jugglers, donkey boys, dancing girls, eunuchs, and camel drivers, Swiss guards, Moors and Persians, the little Javanese, South Sea islanders, Amazons, Dahomians, etc.... The march of this heterogeneous conglomeration of strange peoples, brilliant in color and picturesque in attire, will be enlivened by music of all kinds.... It will be a picture in miniature of the World of the Orient in this newest city of the Occident, and a day's diversion in the routine of sight-seeing which will be of an agreeable if not exciting character to witness the queer and strange spectacle."

In the nineteenth century, European and North American tourism to the Middle East and North Africa took off thanks to an awakened interest in antiquities, the expansion of the European middle class with time and money to travel, and the advent of steam ship transportation across the Mediterranean, which greatly reduced the time required to reach the region. One of the most popular and widely read travel guides was put out by Karl Baedeker (1801–1859). Here is fairly typical advice for the European traveler to Egypt in 1908 found in nearly all such travel books.

Intercourse with Orientals. Dragomans [translators/guides]

The average Oriental regards the European traveller as a Crœsus, and sometimes too as a madman,—so unintelligible to him are the objects and pleasures of travelling. He therefore looks upon him as fair game, and feels justified in pressing upon him with a perpetual demand for *bakshish* which simply means 'a gift'. Travelers are often tempted to give for the sake of affording temporary pleasure at trifling cost, forgetting that the seeds of insatiable cupidity are thereby sown, in the infinite annoyance of their successors and the demoralization of the recipients themselves. Bakshish should never be given except for services rendered, or to the aged and crippled; and the

An Egyptian's View of Tourists: Muhammad al-Muwaylihi (1864–1930)
They're tourists from Western countries.... They're used to civilized living and regard Oriental people with utter contempt.... They posture and show off, and keep bringing in innovations. Their activities are evil and their knowledge is pernicious. They're the people who rob others of their wages.... When they travel to the East, they can be divided into two categories. The first consists of the leisure class with modern ideas who are besotted by their own wealth and amused by novelties of civilization. As far as they're concerned, there's nothing left to do.... They're beset by the twin diseases of listlessness and boredom. They wander around on their own from one area and country to another.... The second group consists of scholars, politicians, imperialists and spies, who use their knowledge and ideas to occupy and control countries ... and crowd folk out of their land and homes. They're the precursors of destruction, even more deadly to people at peace than the vanguards of armies in wartime.

"Experts purchasing silk cacoons [i.e. cocoons], for export to France, Antioch, Syria, c. 1913." Economic imperialism came in many forms to MENA. One early manifestation was the French silk industry established first in Maronite villages in the Mount Lebanon area during the nineteenth century and later throughout Greater Syria. Local women and young girls were often employed in the laborious process of growing silkworms because they could be paid lower wages and were believed to be more docile. The cocoons in this image were exported to Lyon where the thread was reeled; the finished silk cloth, manufactured in France, was sold to importers in New York and the Middle East.

Government appeals to the tourist by public placards not to encourage the habit of begging. . . .

While much caution and firmness are desirable in dealing with the people, it need hardly be added that the traveller should avoid being too exacting or suspicious. He should bear in mind that many of the natives with whom he comes in contact are mere children, whose demands should excite amusement rather than anger, and who often display a touching simplicity and kindliness of disposition. The native communities hold together with remarkable faithfulness, and the bond of a common religion, which takes the place of 'party' in other countries, and requires its adherents to address each other as '*yâ akhûya*' (my brother), is far more than a mere name. On the other hand, intimate acquaintance with Orientals is to be avoided, disinterested friendship being still rarer in the East than elsewhere. This caution is especially necessary in reference to the Dragomans [interpreters], who sometimes presume on their opportunities of social intercourse. . . .

The Ascent of the Pyramid

"The ascent of the pyramid, though fatiguing, is perfectly safe. The traveller selects two of the importunate Beduins . . . and proceeds to the N.E. corner of the pyramid where the ascent usually begins. Assisted by the two Beduins, one holding each hand, and, if desired, by a third (no extra payment) who pushes behind, the traveller begins the ascent of the steps, which are each about 3 feet high. The strong and active attendants assist the traveller to mount by pushing, pulling, and supporting him, and will scarcely allow him a moment's rest until the top is reached. As, however, the unwanted exertion is fatiguing, the traveller should insist on resting as often as he feels inclined. '*Uskut willa mâ fîsh baḳshîsh* (be quiet or you will have no fee) is a sentence which may often be employed with advantage."

Egypt: British and Egyptian Critiques of Imperialism

Formerly in the British diplomatic service, Wilfred Scawen Blunt (1840–1922) traveled widely in the Middle East and India during the 1870s and settled with his wife in Egypt in 1880 where he ran an Arabian horse stud farm and became engaged in Egyptian politics. An ardent critic of British imperialism and imperialism generally, he defended Colonel Ahmad Urabi (1841–1911) and the Egyptian national movement in 1882 and condemned the subsequent British occupation. These diary entries present his views as well as those of members of the British government on imperialism and British views of what constituted international law—especially the entry of October 17th, 1898.

9th Jan. 1896. The German Emperor has telegraphed his congratulations to Kruger [head of the Afrikaaner (Boer) resistance to British control of South Africa], and this seems to have produced great anger in England. We have now managed in the last six months to quarrel violently with China, Turkey, Belgium, Ashanti, France, Venezuela, America, and Germany. This is a record performance, and if it does not break up the British Empire nothing will. For myself I am glad of it all, for the British Empire is the greatest engine of evil for the weak races now existing in the world—not that we are worse than the French or Italians or Americans—indeed, we are less actively destructive—but we do it over a far wider area and more successfully. I should be delighted to see England stripped of her whole foreign possessions. We were better off and more respected in Queen Elizabeth's time, the "spacious days," when we had not a stick of territory outside the British Islands, than now, and infinitely more respectable. The gangrene of colonial rowdyism is infecting us, and the habit of repressing liberty in weak nations is endangering our own. I should be glad to see the end. . . .

17th Oct. 1898. I have had it out with George [Wyndham (1863–1913), parliamentary undersecretary in the War Office] about Fashoda [a dispute with France following British occupation of Sudan in 1898]. He states the English case with brutal frankness. 'The day of talking,' he says, 'about legality in Africa is over, all the international law there is there consists of interest and understandings.' It is generally agreed by all the powers that the end of African operations is to 'civilize' it in the interests of Europe, and that to gain that end all means are good. The only difference between England and France is which of them is to do it in which particular districts. England intends to do it on the Nile, and it makes no difference what the precise legal position is. We may put forward the Khedive's rights if it is convenient or we may put forward a right of conquest, or a right of simply declaring our intentions. One is as good as another to get our end, which is the railway from Cairo to the Cape [South Africa]. We don't care whether the Nile is called English or Egyptian or what it is called, but we mean to have it and we don't mean the French to have it. The Khedive [Egyptian ruler] may be kept on for some years as a sort of Indian maharajah, but it will end in a partition of the Ottoman Empire between England, Germany, and Russia. France will be allowed Northwestern Africa. It is not worth while drawing distinctions of right and wrong in the matter, it is a matter entirely of interest. . . .

22nd Dec., 1900. The old century is very nearly out, and leaves the world in a pretty pass, and the British Empire is playing the devil in it as never an empire before on so large a scale. We may live to see its fall. All the nations of Europe are making the same hell upon earth in China, massacring and pillaging and raping in the captured cities as outrageously as in the Middle Ages. The Emperor of Germany gives the word for slaughter and the Pope looks on and approves. In South Africa our troops are burning farms under Kitchener's command, and the Queen and the two houses of Parliament, and the bench of bishops thank God publicly and vote money for the work. The Americans are spending fifty millions [sic] a year on slaughtering the Filipinos; the King of the Belgians has invested his whole fortune on the Congo, where he is brutalizing the Negroes to fill his pockets. The French and Italians for the moment are playing a less prominent part in the slaughter, but their inactivity grieves them. The whole white race is reveling openly in violence, as though it had never pretended to be Christian. God's equal curse be on them all! So ends the famous nineteenth century into which we were so proud to have been born. . . .

31st Dec., 1900. I bid good-bye to the old century, may it rest in peace as it has lived in war. Of the new century I prophesy nothing except that it will see the decline of the British Empire. Other worse empires will rise perhaps in its place, but I shall not live to see the day. It all seems a very little matter here in Egypt, with the pyramids watching us as they watched Joseph, when, as a young man four thousand years ago, perhaps in this very garden, he walked and gazed at the sunset behind them, wondering about the future just as I did this evening. And so, poor wicked nineteenth century, farewell!

In 1906, British officers hunting pigeons for sport near the Egyptian village of Dinshawai northeast of Cairo were accosted by peasants who relied on the birds for food. After an altercation, a British officer collapsed and died while running to get help. Lord Cromer decided to use the incident to quell Egyptian opposition to British rule. After a show trial, four Egyptian peasants were hung, others were imprisoned for long sentences, including life, and some were brutally whipped. Following bad international press and Egyptian nationalist outrage, Cromer was forced out of office in 1907 due to repercussions of the Dinshawai affair. Blunt recorded his impression of the Dinshawai incident in his diary.

21st June 1906. It is an abominable case. As far as one can learn . . . the officers were part of a English military force making a promenade through the Delta . . . [to demonstrate] for political purposes the military power of Great Britain. Finding themselves encamped . . . they could think of nothing better to do than to shoot the tame pigeons in a village hard by . . . but when they got there the villagers objected and as none of them [the officers] knew Arabic they got frightened; a gun then went off in the hands of one of [the officers] . . . and the officers were belaboured with *nabuts* [clubs]. Two ran away . . . to bring help and one of them was found dead four miles from the village. This is exactly like all these cases, except that it is the first time an officer has been killed. . . . All treat it as a case of murder with prearrangement, not on the part of the officers but of the *fallahin* [Egyptian peasants].

This Egyptian nationalist satire in Arabic appeared as Cromer announced he was leaving Egypt in 1907; it refers to those peasants hung after the Dinshawai trial.

> Hey lord! Go ahead and leave/and don't let the door hit you on the way out!
> Those who were hanged are greeting you/saying their hearts will always be with you.

Playwright George Bernard Shaw (1856–1950), encouraged by Scawen Blunt, wrote this sympathetic commentary explaining the Egyptian peasant reaction in "The Dinshawai Horror," excerpted from his 1907 play "John Bull's Other Island."

Try to imagine the feelings of an English village if a party of Chinese officers suddenly appeared and began shooting the ducks, the geese, the hens and the turkeys, and carried them off, asserting that they were wild birds as everybody in China knew, and that the pretended indignation of the farmers was a cloak for hatred of the Chinese, and perhaps a plot to overthrow the religion of Confucius and establish the Church of England in its place.

Those who were flogged or orphaned/ they declare their
eternal love for you.

Those who were imprisoned or had their houses demolished/
hold you in great favor

Truly all your good works speak for themselves/ and all are
covetous of you

But Lord!/ Please leave/ and don't let the door hit you on
your way out!

Iran and The European Powers: Oil Concessions and Territorial Partitioning

By the early twentieth century, some Middle Eastern rulers, especially in Iran (Persia), had begun the practice of granting concessions to foreign companies for the development of a variety of enterprises, from banking, insurance, and postal service to railroads, processing of commodities, and mineral and oil exploration and exploitation. The concessions represented monopolies over enterprises or exclusive access to valuable resources in return for investment as well as the supply of technology and expertise by the concessionaire. Often the payment for the concession was pocketed by the grantee, the shah or a powerful official, with nothing going to the state treasury.

William Knox D'Arcy (1849–1917), an Australian entrepreneur, received in 1901 the drilling rights to nearly all of Iran for 60 years. In 1908 he discovered oil in southwest Iran, and formed the Anglo-Persian Oil Company, with mostly British capital, to exploit the concession. On the eve of World War I, the British government became the major investor in the oil company to ensure a steady flow of petroleum for the British navy.

Between the Government of His Imperial Majesty the Shah of Persia, of the one part, and William Knox d'Arcy, of independent means, residing in London at No. 42, Grosvenor Square (hereinafter called "the Concessionnaire"), of the other part. . . . The following has by these presents been agreed on and arranged—viz.:

ART. 1. The Government of His Imperial Majesty the Shah grants to the concessionnaire by these presents a special and exclusive privilege to search for, obtain, exploit, develop, render suitable for trade, carry away and sell natural gas petroleum, asphalt and ozokerite throughout the whole extent of the Persian Empire for a term of sixty years as from the date of these presents.

ART. 2. This privilege shall comprise the exclusive right of laying the pipe-lines necessary from the deposits where there may be found one or several of the said products up to the Persian Gulf, as also the necessary distributing branches. It shall also comprise the right of constructing and maintaining all and any wells, reservoirs, stations and pump services, accumulation services and distribution services, factories and other works and arrangements that may be deemed necessary.

ART. 3. The Imperial Persian Government grants gratuitously to the concessionnaire all uncultivated lands belonging to the State which the concessionnaire's engineers may deem necessary for the construction of the whole or any part of the above-mentioned works. As for cultivated lands belonging to the State, the concessionnaire must purchase them at the fair and current price of the province. . . .

ART. 7. All lands granted by these presents to the concessionnaire or that may be acquired by him in the manner provided for in Articles 3 and 4 of these presents, as also all products exported, shall be free of all imposts and taxes during the term of the present concession. All material and apparatuses necessary for the exploration, working and development of the deposits, and for the construction and development of the pipe-lines, shall enter Persia free of all taxes and Custom-House duties.

ART. 8. The concessionnaire shall immediately send out to Persia and at his own cost one or several experts with a view to their exploring the region in which there exist, as he believes, the said products, and, in the event of the report of the expert being in the opinion of the concessionnaire of a satisfactory nature, the latter shall immediately send to Persia and at his own cost all the technical staff necessary, with the working plant and machinery required for boring and sinking wells and ascertaining the value of the property. . . .

ART. 10. It shall be stipulated in the contract between the concessionnaire, of the one part, and the company, of the other part, that the latter is, within the term of one month as from the date of the formation of the first exploitation company, to pay the Imperial Persian Government the sum of 20,000 sterling in cash, and an additional sum of 20,000 sterling in paid-up shares of the first company founded by virtue of the foregoing article. It shall also pay the said Government annually a sum equal to 16 per cent of the annual net profits of any company or companies that may be formed in accordance with the said article. . . .

After the discovery of large oil fields in southwestern Iran in 1908, such as the one this oil well is situated on, the Anglo-Persian Oil Company (APOC) was formed, the first company to extract petroleum from the Middle East.

ART. 12. The workmen employed in the service of the company shall be subject to His Imperial Majesty the Shah, except the technical staff, such as the managers, engineers, borers and foremen. . . .

ART. 15. On the expiration of the term of the present concession, all materials, buildings and apparatuses then used by the company for the exploitation of its industry shall become the property of the said Government, and the company shall have no right to any indemnity in this connection. . . .

A constitutional movement emerged in Iran during 1906 that sought to restrict growing foreign influence in the country by limiting the powers of the shah. In the view of the constitutionalists, he and his father, Nasir al-Din Shah (r. 1848–1896), had granted far too many concessions to foreigners who were immune from Iranian law because of the capitulations. The 1906 constitution [Chapter 2] sought to limit royal authority and required all sales of land or rights to enterprise in Iran to be approved by the new parliament [*majlis*]. The constitutional movement alarmed both Russia and Great Britain, because it decreased their ability to influence prominent government personages to their advantage. Former rivals for influence in Iran, Russia and Britain now agreed to divide the country into spheres of influence, a move also intended to block possible German inroads into the country. While professing concern for Iranian stability and territorial integrity, the agreement served to undermine parliamentary restraints on the Shah.

The Governments of Great Britain and Russia having mutually engaged to respect the integrity and independence of Persia, and sincerely desiring the preservation of order throughout that country and its peaceful development, as well as the permanent establishment of equal advantages for the trade and industry of all other nations;

Considering that each of them has, for geographical and economic reasons, a special interest in the maintenance of peace and order in certain provinces of Persia adjoining, or in the neighborhood of, the Russian frontier on the one hand, and the frontiers of Afghanistan and Baluchistan on the other hand; and being desirous of avoiding all cause of conflict between their respective interests in the above-mentioned provinces of Persia;

Have agreed on the following terms:—

I. Great Britain engages not to seek for herself, and not to support in favour of British subjects, or in favour of the subjects of third Powers, any Concessions of a political or commercial nature such as Concessions for railways, banks, telegraphs, roads, transport, insurance, etc.—beyond a line starting from Kasr-i-Shirin, pass-

"Nasser al-Din Shah (r. 1848–1896) in front of the Peacock Throne." The first Iranian ruler to visit Europe in 1873, 1878, and again in 1899, Nasser al-Din was astonished by the display of European might and military technology. At first a reformist, the shah granted a number of concessions to European financial and economic interests within Iran; for example, he ceded control of Iranian customs income to the German-born Paul Julius Reuter, founder of Reuters news agency. These concessions enraged the Iranian people and in 1896 Nasser al-Din was assassinated. In this image, the shah is seated before the opulent Peacock Throne that the Persians had seized from the Mughal capital at Delhi in 1739; the throne came to symbolize the monarchy in Persia/Iran.

ing through Isfahan, Yezd, Kakhk, and ending at a point on the Persian frontier at the intersection of the Russian and Afghan frontiers, and not to oppose, directly or indirectly, demands for similar Concessions in this region which are supported by the Russian Government. It is understood that the above-mentioned places are included in the region in which Great Britain engages not to seek the Concessions referred to.

II. Russia, on her part, engages not to seek for herself and not to support, in favour of Russian subjects, or in favour of the subjects of third Powers, any Concessions of a political or commercial nature—such as Concessions for railways , banks, telegraphs, roads, transport, insurance, etc.—beyond a line going from the Afghan frontier by way of Gazik, Birjand, Kerman, and ending at Bunder Abbas, and not to oppose, directly or indirectly, demands for similar Concessions in this region which are supported by the British Government. It is understood that the above-mentioned places are included in the region in which Russia engages not to seek the Concessions referred to. . . .

All concessions existing at present in the regions indicated in Articles I and II are maintained.

"The Selamlik (Sultan's procession to the mosque) at the Hamidiye Camii (mosque) on Friday, c. 1880–1893." Under increasing European political, military, and economic pressure, the Ottoman Sultan Abdul Hamid II (r. 1876–1909) was the last Ottoman ruler to exercise fairly unrestrained royal authority. Reacting negatively to growing foreign intervention, the sultan suspended the Ottoman constitution in 1878, emphasized his role as caliph, and catered to religious authorities. Note in this image that the sultan's guard is wearing European-style military uniforms.

Al-Afghani and Azoury: Muslim and Arab Christian Rejections of Indigenous Accommodation to Western Inroads

Jamal al-Din al-Afghani (1838–1897), whose name suggests he was born in Afghanistan, was a Shiʻi Muslim from Iran. He and his followers sought to defend Muslim countries from foreign control while calling for reform of Islam to make it more amenable to modern scientific developments. In this essay, al-Afghani attacks British rule in India and the Islamic reform movement headed by Sayyid Ahmad Khan (1817–1898) that, he argues, strayed from basic Muslim principles in the interest of accommodating itself to imperialism. His position was consistent because he defended the independence of Muslim territories and accused Ahmad Khan of collaborating with the British and thus sacrificing Indian independence. Al-Afghani's ideas greatly influenced nationalist movements in the Middle East.

The Awakening of the Arab Nation

Neguib Azoury (c.1870–1916), a Maronite Catholic from Beirut and former Ottoman bureaucrat in Jerusalem, formed the League of the Arab Fatherland and promoted a total separation of the Arab lands from Ottoman rule in his 1905 book *Le Réveil de la Nation Arabe dans l'Asie Turque*. Azoury also warned of the forthcoming clash between Arab nationalism and Zionism.

I. . . . The league wants . . . to separate the civil and religious power in the interests of Islam and the Arab nation, and to form an Arab empire stretching from the Tigris and Euphrates to the Suez Isthmus, and from the Mediterranean to the Arabian Sea. . . .

II. . . . Two important phenomena of the same nature but opposed . . . are emerging at this moment in Asiatic Turkey. They are the awakening of the Arab nation and the latent effort of the Jews to reconstitute on a very large scale the ancient kingdom of Israel. Both of these movements are destined to fight each other continually until one of them wins. The fate of the entire world will depend on the final result of the struggle between these two peoples representing two contrary principles.

The English entered India and toyed with the minds of her princes and kings in a way that makes intelligent men both laugh and cry. They penetrated deeply into India's interior, and seized her lands piece by piece. Whenever they became lords of the land they took liberties with its inhabitants, and showed anger and contempt regarding their stay among them, saying that the English were occupied only with commercial affairs. As for tending to administration and politics, that is not their business. However, what calls them to bear the burdens [of administration and politics] is pity for the kings and the princes who are incapable of governing their dominions. When the kings or princes are able to control their land, no Englishman will remain there [they said], because they have other important affairs that they have abandoned out of sheer compassion. With this, the English stole property from every owner on the pretext that work on property is oppressive to a person and fatiguing for mind and body. It is better for the owner of the property to relax and to die poor and humble, free of the pains of management. [The English] declare that when the opportunity presents itself, and the time comes when the affairs of this world and the hereafter will not influence bodies and thoughts, they are prepared to leave the country (on the Day of Resurrection!). And today they are saying the very same words in Egypt!!

When [the English] entrenched themselves in India, and effaced the traces of Mogul rule, they gave the land a second look, and found within it fifty million Muslims, each of whom was wounded in heart by the extinction of their great kingdom. They were connected with many millions of Muslims in the East and West, North and South. [The English] perceived that as long as the Muslims persisted in their religion, and as long as the Qur'an was read among them, it would be impossible for them to be sincere in their submission to foreign rule, especially if that foreigner had wrested the realm from them through treachery and cunning, under the veil of affection and friendship. So they set out to try to weaken belief in the Islamic faith in every way. They encouraged their clergymen and religious leaders to write books and publish tracts filled with defamation of the Islamic religion, and replete with abuse and vilification for the Founder of Islam (may God free him of what they said!). . . .

With that they aimed only, on the one hand, to weaken the beliefs of the Muslims, and to induce them to profess the English religion. On the other hand, they began to restrict the means of livelihood available to the Muslims, and to intensify their oppression and disadvantages in every respect. They hurt their interests regarding public works, and plundered *waqfs* [charitable endowments] set aside for mosques and *madrasahs* [theological seminaries] and exiled their ulema and leaders . . . hoping to use this means, if the first one did not work, to alienate the Muslims from their religion, and to reduce them to the depths of ignorance concerning their faith. . . . It happened that a man named Ahmad Khan Bahadur [an honorary title in India] was hovering around the English in order to obtain some advantage from them. . . . He appeared in the guise of the naturalists [materialists], and proclaimed that nothing exists but blind nature, and that this universe does not have a wise God (this is a clear error), and that all the prophets were naturalists who did not believe in the God taught by the revealed religions, (we take refuge in God!). . . . His doctrine pleased the English rulers and they saw in it the best means to corrupt the hearts of the Muslims. They began to support him, to honor him, and to help him to build a college in Aligarh, called the Mohammadan College, to be a trap in which to catch the sons of the believers. . . . Ahmad Khan wrote a commentary on the Qur'an [where]. . . . He called openly for the abandonment of all religions (but he addressed only the Muslims), and cried, "Nature, Nature," in order to convince people that Europe only progressed in civilization, advanced in science and industry, and excelled in power and strength by rejecting religions and returning to the goal aimed at by all religions (according to his claim), which is the explanation of the ways of nature. ("He invented a lie against God.")

When we were in India. . . . We wrote a treatise exposing their corrupt doctrine and the ruin that arose from it. We established that religion is the foundation of civilization and the pillar of culture. . . . Those materialists are not like the materialists of Europe; for whoever abandons religion in Western countries retains love for his country, and his zeal to guard his country from the attacks of foreigners is not diminished. . . . But Ahmad Khan and his companions, just as they invited people to reject religion, [also] disparaged to them the interests of their fatherland, and made people consider foreign domination over them a slight thing, and strove to erase the traces of religious and patriotic zeal. . . .

Traditional Palestinian agriculture continued to rely on camels and donkeys as well as cattle, along with the one-handled wooden plow used by this Palestinian peasant in the Jezreel Plain. European Zionists, aided by funding from the Rothschild banking family in Paris, introduced a heavy horse-drawn metal plow in the 1890s and imported tractors by 1910. Their use illustrates Zionist ability to import advanced European devices.

CHAPTER 2

Between Old and New

Reforming State and Society,

c. 1750–1914

This image features the newly constructed Galata Bridge completed in 1875 that spanned the Golden Horn as part of urban reform in Istanbul, the Ottoman capital. In the course of the nineteenth century, urban renewal transformed certain sectors of cities such as Istanbul, Cairo, and Tunis, often employing European urban planning as models; ports and harbors in places like Alexandria or Beirut were endowed with modern infrastructure to encourage trans-Mediterranean shipping.

In response to dramatically changed geopolitical and economic conditions, whether experienced through direct foreign occupation or indirect military or diplomatic pressures, MENA's governing elites embarked on ambitious modernization programs seeking to fortify their states and thus lessen foreign threats. These programs invariably began with the reform of the military establishment along European lines, which entailed reorganizing armies, restructuring officer education, obtaining new technologies, and somewhat paradoxically, hiring European military specialists, especially French and British, to assist in training modern armies. Concurrently, the huge expense of overhauling military institutions dictated that Middle Eastern states secure greater tax revenues from producers, mainly the peasantry but also merchants, traders, and urban productive sectors. In addition, since conscription of ordinary subjects for the army represented an entirely new idea—military service had traditionally been limited to specific socio-ethnic groups—another challenge arose: how to find enough manpower to field the new modern armies. Finally, European ideas of popular representation forced many MENA rulers threatened by European expansion to confront the dilemma: how could they adopt new technologies, forms of statecraft, and bodies of knowledge without upsetting prevailing political and social hierarchies?

Although historians have often seen Napoleon's 1798 invasion of Egypt as the catalyst for the region's modernization efforts, MENA

• over the next century, Ottomans attempt to modernize, Europize update their military & tech.

leaders had previously initiated important projects. In 1793, the Ottoman Sultan Selim III (r. 1787–1807) instituted military reforms called the "The New Order" following Ottoman defeats by Austrian and Russian armies. He sought to reduce reliance on the once-fabled Janissary Corps, the Ottoman infantry whose training and weaponry had become ineffective against European forces. Faced with severe opposition, Selim focused reform efforts on creating a new officer class trained in European methods of warfare and relied on French officers to oversee the project. Ottoman officers dressed in uniforms that distinguished them from traditional military attire. Changes in clothing would become a significant index of change not only for military forces but for a new class of Ottoman bureaucrats as well. Selim also appointed ambassadors to London, Paris, and Vienna.

Selim did not initiate modernizing reforms; his father had previously founded a school of naval engineering. But his efforts were more focused and sought to rely on new systems of taxation that threatened traditional landholding classes. They in turn eventually joined with others who opposed Selim's reform efforts, centered in the Janissary Corps and the Muslim religious leadership. Forced to step down in 1807, he was assassinated a year later, but his initiatives had a lasting impact on subsequent reform movements, including Egypt, where Muhammad Ali, an Ottoman officer appointed governor of the region following the departure of French forces, emulated Selim's efforts.

Faced with a Greek revolt that gained independence for half of Greece by 1830, Selim's successor, Sultan Mahmud II (r. 1808–1839), ordered the destruction of the Janissary barracks and corps in Istanbul in 1826, setting the stage for more intensive reforms based on European models that were taken up by his successor, Abdul Mejid (r. 1839–1861) in 1839. And Mahmud copied European practices by organizing the Ottoman military band along Western lines, advised by an Italian composer, Giuseppe Donizetti (1788–1856) who in 1844 composed a march for the sultan that became the Ottoman national anthem.

Abdul Mejid is better known for legislating reforms known as the Tanzimat [reform period of 1839–1876] which meant "re-ordering" or "restructuring" the older relationship

In this lavish audience chamber, the Tunisian Husaynid Dynasty (r. 1705–1956) formally received foreign diplomats and local government officials. The eclectic ornamentation of this throne room—with its enormous Venetian chandeliers, Parisian clocks, and Louis XV furniture—reveals the growing importance of esthetic and artistic elements from Europe, although North Africa and Ottoman art and architecture are also in evidence.

between the state and the disparate social bodies or communities, non-Muslim as well as Muslim, regarded as subjects. Other ruling elites in the region followed the Ottoman example, with varying degrees of success. But as all reforming political elites soon found, state-imposed change in one sphere often had unforeseen consequences in another. Moreover, since the accumulated knowledge of modern militaries, including engineering and other related fields, was chiefly written in European languages, translations from French or English into Turkish, Arabic, or Persian had to be undertaken. In turn, this required reforms in education as well as the introduction of government printing presses and modern bureaucracies. Mahmud II initiated this process in Istanbul by creating the nucleus of a modern bureaucracy whose members wore European clothing.

Many of these changes were imposed from the top down, principally by rulers who saw no conflict between modernization of the state structure and strengthening of their own powers. The Tanzimat promised that non-Muslim religious minorities [dhimmis], for example, the Greek Orthodox and Jewish communities, would become citizens of the empire enjoying equal rights under the law; they would no longer have to pay the jizya, the tax required of non-Muslims. But equal status also meant new state taxes and liability for military service; dhimmis had not served in the military previously. Ultimately government councils would appear on which non-Muslim members served with Muslims, but these councils were advisory rather than possessing legislative authority.

Still, as more people from the region traveled to Europe, mainly for education, although later to attend worlds' fairs and expositions, they became exposed to European political, scientific, social, and educational institutions, which conferred a growing awareness of the weakness of traditional ways of organizing state and society. Often, this exposure—at first limited mainly to upper classes from the Middle East or North Africa—led to calls for greater political participation, including the creation of constitutions and parliaments. But these initial experiments in parliamentary life were frequently aborted owing to pressures from imperial powers as occurred in Egypt and Tunisia, or because, as seen in Istanbul and Tehran, rulers, on occasion with great-power encouragement, sought to crush the limits on their authority they had initially accepted under popular pressure.

On the other hand, reformers created new bureaucracies open to men outside the traditional elites whose advancement was tied to the expansion of the new systems. As a result, a new class of government employees emerged who, like their rulers, were often attracted to aspects of European culture, as seen in their adopting the manners, clothing, and household furnishings of middle-class Europeans, even if they retained traditional religious beliefs. Some sent their sons to schools in Europe or those institutions organized on European models in the Middle East. Cities were transformed with urban renewal projects in Istanbul and Cairo, where beginning in the 1860s, entire neighborhoods were demolished to make way for broad boulevards and buildings imitating Paris. Moreover, the architecture and arrangement of state buildings or domestic spaces began to change in aesthetic, function, and organization. In 1871, Giuseppe Verdi's (1813–1901) opera Aida opened to its world premiere at Cairo's Khedivial or Royal Opera House, built by Khedive Ismail and designed by Italian architects in 1869 to celebrate the opening of the Suez Canal.

Modernity, however, could be a double-edged sword. Though authorized by local rulers, projects such as the Suez Canal, opened in 1869, could serve as an excuse for imperial intervention as happened when the British occupied Egypt in 1882 to protect this new route to India. In addition, modernity created growing cultural differences between elites and the majority of their own populations who often suffered from state-imposed development and European commercial inroads. In Egypt, the peasantry throughout the nineteenth century was forcibly conscripted to build major projects, including the Suez Canal.

The question of women's status and rights was often at the center of debates about the legitimacy and morality of adopting new laws, customs, and ways of doing things. In Istanbul, a teacher training school for girls was established in 1870, based on the Regulations for Public Education of 1869 that mandated compulsory primary education for boys and girls. In 1871 the Ottoman capital saw the graduation of seventeen women teachers who were assigned to posts at girls' schools in the city. Then in 1873, the wife of the Egyptian ruler, Khedive Ismail (r. 1863–1879), established a girls school, a private endowment lacking the government sponsorship seen in Istanbul. The British did not encourage state spending for education during their period of full control of the government down to 1922, but many private schools, including some for girls, were founded.

These efforts were accompanied by calls for reform in the legal and social status of women, by elite women as well as men during the 1890s. In general, urban middle classes were more open to the need to educate girls; women had begun to publish journals in Istanbul and Cairo by the late nineteenth century. But the influx of new ideas, and mores, and the implicit and at times explicit criticism of Muslim clerics as hindering progress, created severe tensions, especially since the multiple, often disorienting forces for change were based on a Western civilization whose nations were occupying Muslim countries.

Cairo vs. Istanbul: Egyptian and Turkish Reforms and Their Implications

Muhammad Ali (r. 1805–1848), a former officer in the Ottoman military, emulated the reform efforts of Ottoman Sultan Selim III who had appointed him governor of Egypt in 1805 once Ottoman and British forces evacuated the country. Supposedly loyal to Istanbul, Muhammad Ali set about centralizing his own political and military authority, instituting a program of modernization intended to ensure his ultimate independence from Ottoman authority and form his own dynasty based in Cairo. He established a state monopoly over the land and its crops, inflicting great hardship on the peasants. He also taxed *waqfs*, Muslim charitable endowments, traditionally not subject to taxation since their revenues maintained religious institutions and provided public assistance to the poor. Writing in his chronicle of Egyptian history, al-Jabarti was as critical of Muhammad Ali as he had earlier been of the French army occupying Egypt. Indeed, he notes that Napoleon's army, unlike Muhammad Ali, left the *waqfs* alone and recounts how officials ignored petitions from cultivators protesting vastly increased taxes, leaving them at the mercy of the state.

↗ guy writing this source

And in [1224 AH/1809 AH] [**AH:** denotes the Islamic calendar that began in 622 CE] they began to prepare a register for the taking of half the yield from the *multazims* [tax farm overseers] and another for the imposition of taxes on produce of waqf devoted to mosques, foundations, alms, and charitable works. . . . Proclamations were dispatched to the villages and countryside and officials were sent by the various provincial governors with power to investigate the property belonging to mosques or used for charitable works. Each person controlling such land was ordered to present his title deed to the central government office and replace it with a new one; a delay of forty days was allowed for this, after which the title of the property could be taken away and given to another person. The pretext used in the proclamation was one which had never been advanced before, that

David Roberts RA (1796–1864), a Scottish painter known for his prolific and detailed lithograph prints of Egypt and the Holy Land, traveled to the region in 1838. This painting executed between 1846 and 1849 shows Egypt's Muhammad Ali Pasha surrounded by his retainers as he receives a visiting delegation of British naval officers whose ships in port can be espied through the window.

when a sultan died or was deposed his orders and decrees ceased to be valid, and that the same applied to the sultan's deputies, and that therefore they had to be renewed by the new governor—and other such statements!

It should be remembered that these endowments dated back to Saladin's time—in the fifth century AH [*sic*; read sixth, i.e., twelfth century AD]—who paid for them out of the central treasury to facilitate matters for those who were entitled to receive allowances from the treasury. His example was followed by kings, sultans, and princes until our day: they built mosques, hospices, asylums, and fountains, endowing them with land taken from their own private property, and the taxes or revenues which were used for that purpose. Similarly they would make endowments in favour of scholars or poor people, as a charity, enabling them to live and pursue learning; and when the beneficiary died the judge or the supervisor would appoint some deserving person in his place. The beneficiary's name would then be put down in the record of the judge and also in the register of the sultan's office, which were kept by a special official known as the clerk of the waqf property. This official would deliver a title deed, under the terms of the decree, and would put on it his seal and that of the Pasha and the chancellor. . . . And thus the office of the waqf property remained preserved in perfect order in all the lands of Egypt, generation after generation. . . .

The French occupied Egypt but did not touch this institution. But Sharif Effendi, the [Ottoman] chancellor, who came shortly after the arrival of Yusif Pasha, the wazir [in 1801], ordered all multazims to pay to the government again. . . . Their pretext was that the French occupation had rendered Egypt a war area . . . which had been reconquered and whose lands had therefore become the property of the government; therefore anyone who desired to take possession of a piece of land or other property had to buy it from the sultan's deputy by payment of the prescribed amount. . . .

In [1227 AH/1812 AD] Ibrahim Bey (1789–1848), the son of the Pasha [Muhammad Ali] went to Upper Egypt, followed by Ahmad Agha Laz, the governor of Qina and Qus and the other sub-governors; they carried out a cadastral survey of the lands of Upper Egypt and imposed on them a tax of 7 riyals per faddan [One faddan = a quarter of an acre], a very high rate. They also made a survey of all the waqfs devoted to mosques, alms and charity in Upper and Lower Egypt; the total amounted to 6,000,000 faddans. They then proclaimed that mosque waqfs would pay half the assessed rate, i.e., 3 ½ riyals. The beneficiaries of the waqfs were greatly disturbed and many of them appealed to the sheikhs, who went off to speak to the Pasha on this subject. They said to him that that would lead to the ruin of the mosques, whereupon he replied: 'Where are the flourishing mosques? If anyone is not satisfied with this arrangement let him raise his hand and I will restore the ruined mosques and provide them with the necessary means.' Their protests were of no avail and they returned to their homes. . . .

And he [Muhammad Ali] seized all the iltizams [tax farms], leaving something to their former owners only in exceptional cases, and even so only in very small amounts. . . . And all the excess land resulting from the new cadastral survey . . . was taken over by the ruler.

As for the waqf property devoted to alms and charity, and to the upkeep of mosques, fountains, libraries, and other philanthropic works, they too were measured in the new unit and all the resulting excess was taken over by the government. The remaining part was registered in the name of the actual beneficiary and the original maker of the endowment and the actual cultivator. . . . Such land was subjected to the same tax as village land. [I]f the beneficiary could show satisfactory title, or had a new deed dating from the time of the Wazir and Sharif Effendi or later, half the rental value of the land would be registered in his name, the other half going to the government. . . .

Joseph Hekekyan (1807–1875) was an Armenian Christian born in Istanbul. His father worked for Muhammad 'Ali in Egypt as a civil servant. His parents sent him to England at the age of ten for his education. On his father's death, Muhammad Ali assumed responsibility for young Joseph's education with the understanding Hekekyan would return to Egypt to assist in the ruler's modernizing reforms. Hekekyan fully understood English life but was always an outsider to some extent because he was from the Middle East; in Egypt he was a Christian working for a Muslim ruler whose practices he often criticized in private.

Many cultivators or *fallahs* [*fallah/fallahin* pl. peasants], ruined by the exactions of the government, had taken refuge in the towns, in particular Cairo, where acting as servants or artisans they gained a pittance for their families and themselves. The Government, . . . making great efforts to restore cultivation, adopted the arbitrary measures of seizing and conveying to the provinces all individuals of the above description their agents could lay their hands on. But many of them contrived to . . . secrete themselves in their masters' houses;

Taken around 1928, this stereograph portrays Egyptian peasants employing an age-old device [shadduf] for irrigating fields and crops with Nile water with skin buckets and wooden lifts. Most of MENA remained overwhelmingly agrarian until well into the twentieth century.

several . . . emigrated to Syria and many . . . , putting on bedouin garb, entered the service of the independent sons of the desert. Hence the edict of the government . . . [that] whoever was found to connive or abet the secretion of a fallah should be decapitated, and all fallahs away from their villages after a certain time fixed, I believe, at forty days, should be immediately executed. It is the property of a weak and barbarous government to proclaim laws which it cannot put into execution. . . . [B]ut if the government actually sent back to their own villages the unhappy individuals who fell into its hands in order to assist their fellow villagers to pay the land tax which is fixed and not diminished on account of drafts into the army or epidemics, then emigration and some part of the odium would be palliated; instead of which all men who are caught are chained by the neck, put into boats and sent to the Pasha's farms. When a boat full is collected, an endless chain is passed around their necks so they have to march in a body . . . ; two or three men are sufficient to manage two hundred or so shackled. They are crammed into a boat and, as they descend the Nile, their wives and children follow them along the bank. The fallah wife never abandons her husband. . . .

In the nineteenth century, Middle Eastern political elites in the Ottoman Empire and Iran realized that the secret of Europe's military lay in modern forms of education. Muhammad Ali had begun sending student missions to Europe in 1825. In addition to their studies, each student had to translate a book from the foreign language he had studied, usually

English or French, into Arabic. In this manner, Egyptians would rapidly be able to study modern sciences in Arabic. Here Hekekyan describes the following discussion that occurred in 1843 among Egyptians, often products of the student missions, who had overseen translation efforts. By then Muhammad Ali's political fortunes had declined and unfavorable trade treaties, such as the Balta Liman convention of 1838, undermined the high tariffs he had imposed to protect his state industrialization efforts. With loss of funds, debates arose as to the fate of the translation program and of books already translated and printed in Arabic.

January 1843: Meeting of the Translation Committee of the Department of Schools, Cairo.

During the discussion I perceived three distinct parties—the first party was composed of such persons as had already given in translations and whose translations had been printed. Their argument was that they had already given out works of which hundreds of copies had been printed and nobody read them and they were in heaps in the Central Magazine [storehouse] of books . . . —that they had recommended their publication—that the government had incurred a great deal of expense—and they were liable to be called to account on some future day—and consequently they opposed the publication of such works as were not absolutely of immediate necessity in the schools. . . . The arguments of the second party were that the more books we had the better chance there would be of people reading them, that we should look not merely to the present—but more particularly to the future—that there was a great demand in Constantinople, the Hedjaz, and other parts—and that by proper measure some might be disposed of in India and Persia. The third party insisted on the publication as were especially wanted in their respective establishments. The most complete work we shall have shall be that of the Polytechnic School, the entire course of studies of which is based on that adopted in the French School. The themes and exercises are first translated by the Professors and taught for the first year—the second year the same are lithographed in the school—and the third year the same are improved and revised with a view to ulterior printing: by which means we shall possess a complete course of the Theoretical Branches of Mathematics and Natural Philosophy, Chemistry and Astronomy &c.

The modern census represented a powerful tool in the hands of states because it inventoried people and resources. The census could be used for taxation purposes and for military recruitment of young males. Here Hekekyan describes a conversation he had with Muhammad Ali who

This nineteenth-century lithographic print shows eleventh-century Fatimid gates forming a grand entrance to Cairo's al-Mitwalli district, with fifteenth-century minarets in the background. A crowded neighborhood for centuries, it was known for its vibrant, bustling bazaars and markets, and, during the first half of the twentieth century, also housed the office of the commander of the Cairo police force.

bemoaned Egyptian fear of his efforts to undertake any survey, while displaying his anger at those who opposed him.

We have no men . . . —everybody hides his money. They will not believe they are safe—their children will. Egypt is small but is there a finer country? How rich it might be! What think you we have, five million of inhabitants? The highest number estimated was three millions and it was only supposed to be two millions and a half. I told the Shaykhs at Mansourah [a town northeast of Cairo] that they must assist me in the census. They understood what it means—but as they wish to escape the just burden of service and taxes they are induced to give indirect opposition. I have determined to effect the entire establishment of the European system. I told the Shaykhs that I would surround some of their villages and if I found they had deceived me I would put them to death. I think the true number must be more than five millions—but the census must be repeated and we shall have a correct one.

Familiar with England from his studies there, Joseph Hekekyan here compares the security of English life and state maintenance of public roads with conditions in Ottoman lands, but also critiques the harsh life of the English working classes.

In Turkey I should deem a journey of 205 miles to be quite a journey—in the first place requiring a previous arrangement of affairs and of making one's will—in the next arming from head to foot. In England, on the contrary, we appoint the very place and time when, for instance from London to Edinburgh, 400 miles or more, we are to dine with a friend—and the business is done as quietly as if we were only going for a short walk to take the fresh air. . . .

The greatest care is taken of the [English] roads . . . and in all directions there are commodious conveyances for the service of the public. . . . for as knowledge and good laws together with their strict observance comprehend in great measure civilization, it is evident that the facility of intercourse [travel] promotes the collection of the former and the easy administration of the latter. . . . A country cannot be rich without being well governed and no great improvement in learning can be made in a country where there are no good laws. . . . I have one point to insist on—unless these laws be made by the people themselves, they will never be enforced without many coercive measures on the part of the despots being had recourse to;

and this circumstance tends more to the debasement of a people than their subversion by foreign arms. . . .

The English workmen come and leave whenever they please . . . whenever they get any money they run and spend it on drinking—and for a day or two after . . . their drunkenness they are unwilling to come to their work. Hence it is an ordinary circumstance that on Mondays few men can be mustered in the Manufacturies . . . for having abused the day of rest with debauchery, they are not fit to exert themselves on the following day, and they find themselves obliged to drink a little more to reanimate themselves.

In 1839, Egyptian forces in Syria, led by Ibrahim Pasha, crushed the Ottoman army and seemed about to march on Istanbul. British intervention forced the Egyptian army back into Egypt, but the crisis also served to create an opportunity for the British to encourage Ottoman reform. Thus, Sultan Abdul Mejid issued the Hatti Sherif (Noble Rescript), a public declaration that marked the official beginning of the Tanzimat era of reforms in the Ottoman Empire.

The Hatti Sherif was partly an attempt to solicit aid from the British government by proposing equal citizenship rights for all Ottoman subjects. This challenged traditional Muslim practice where Christians and Jews were of second rank to Muslims, but free to practice their religions on payment of a poll tax [*jizya*], and subject to their own religious laws. This idea of equal standing under the law would not to be put into effect until the later 1850s following the more far-reaching official decree, the *Hatti Humayun* of 1856. In return, non-Muslims would now be subject to conscription into the Ottoman army from which they had formerly been exempt. It should be noted that the sultan demanded a return to obedience to Islamic law, the *sheriat*, [*shari'a* in Arabic] when he addressed Muslims, before he proceeded to introduce the idea of equal rights. He thus appealed to traditional Muslim ideas about strengthening the Ottoman dynasty to set the tone for introducing changes that would turn upside down traditional conceptions of the right and just social order.

Hatti Sherif of Gülhane: The Rose Garden Decree

All the world knows that in the first days of the Ottoman monarchy, the glorious precepts of the Koran [Quran] and the laws of the empire were always honored. The empire in consequence increased in strength and greatness and all its subjects, without exception, had risen in the highest degree of ease and prosperity. In the last one hundred and fifty years, a succession of accidents and diverse causes have arisen which have brought about a disregard for the sacred code of laws and the regulations flowing therefrom, and the former strength and prosperity have changed into weakness and poverty;

Omer [an officer in the Egyptian army] was, happily for me, at home [in London]. I found him in his study surrounded by huge volumes, maps, sabers, and enveloped in tobacco smoke. On the sofa sat four young Turks who had just arrived from Liverpool. They were dressed in the English costume. They recollected having seen me whilst in quarantine. . . . We spent the day in reading Shakespeare and smoking cigars.

—Joseph Hekekyan

an empire . . . loses all its stability as soon as it ceases to observe its laws. . . . Ever since the day of our advent to the throne, the thought of the public weal [welfare], of the improvement of the state of the provinces, and of relief to the [subject] people have not ceased to engage [our mind]. If, therefore, the geographical position of the Ottoman provinces, the fertility of the soil, and the aptitude and intelligence of the inhabitants are considered, the conviction will remain that by striving to find efficacious means, the result . . . can be attained in a few years. Full of confidence, therefore, in the help of the Most High and certain of the support of our Prophet, we deem it right to seek by new institutions to give to the provinces composing the Ottoman Empire the benefit of a good administration.

These institutions must be principally carried out under three heads, which are:

1. The guarantees insuring to our subjects perfect security for life, honor, and property.
2. A regular system of assessing and levying taxes.
3. An equally regular system for the levying of troops and the duration of their service.

Indeed there is nothing more precious in this world than life and honor.

. . . Are not life and honor the most precious gifts to mankind? What man . . . can prevent himself from having recourse to [violence], and thereby injure the government and the country, if his life and honor are endangered? If, on the contrary, he enjoys . . . perfect security, he will not depart from ways of loyalty and all his actions will contribute to the good of the government and of his brothers. If there is an absence of security as to one's fortune, everyone remains insensible to the voice of the Prince and his country; no one interests himself in the progress of public good, absorbed as he is in his own troubles. If, on the contrary, the citizen keeps possession of all confidence of all his good, then . . . he feels daily growing . . . in his heart not only his love for the Prince and country, but also his devotion to his native land. . . .

As to the regular and fixed assessment of taxes it is very important that it be regulated; for the state, which is forced to incur many expenses for the defense of its territory, cannot obtain the money necessary for its armies and other services except by means of contributions levied on its subjects. Although, thanks be to God, our Empire has . . . been relieved of the scourge of monopolies, falsely considered in time of war as a source of revenue, a fatal custom still exists . . . known under the name of iltizam.

Under that name, the civil and financial administration of a locality is delivered over to . . . a single man; that is to say sometimes to the iron grip of the most violent and avaricious passions, for if that contractor is not a good man he will only look to his own advantage. . . . It is therefore necessary that henceforth each member of Ottoman society should be taxed for a quota of a fixed tax according to his fortune and means, and that it is impossible that anything more could be exacted from him.

. . . As we have said, the defense of the country is an important matter and . . . [as] all the inhabitants . . . [must] furnish soldiers for that object, it has become necessary to establish laws to regulate the contingent to be furnished by each locality, and to reduce the term of military service to four or five years. For it is . . . an injustice and . . . a mortal blow to agriculture and industry to take, without consideration to the . . . population of the localities, in the one more, in the other less, men that they can furnish; it is also reducing the soldiers to despair and contributing to the depopulation of the country by keeping them all their lives in the service.

In short, without [these] several laws . . . there can be neither strength, nor riches, nor happiness nor tranquility for the empire; it must on the contrary look for them in the existence of these new laws. . . . From henceforth . . . the cause of every accused person shall be publicly judged as the divine law requires, after inquiry and examination, and so long as a regular judgment shall not have been pronounced, no one can secretly or publicly put to death another by poison or in any other manner.

No one shall be allowed to attack the honor of any other person whatever. Every one shall possess his property of every kind and may dispose of it in all freedom, without let or hindrance from any person whatsoever; . . . [and] the innocent heirs of a criminal shall not be deprived of their legal rights, and the property of the criminal shall not be confiscated. These imperial concessions shall extend to all our subjects of whatever religion or sect they may be. . . .

As for the other points, as they must be settled with the assistance of enlightened opinions, our council of justice (increased by new members as shall be found necessary) to whom shall be joined, on certain days which we shall determine, our ministers and the notabilities of the empire, shall assemble in order to frame laws regulating the security of life and fortune and assessment of taxes.

Each one in these assemblies shall freely express his ideas and give his advice.

Visits across the Mediterranean: MENA and European Impressions of Each Other

In 1845, the Moroccan sultan sent a diplomatic mission to France headed by Muhammad al-Saffar (c. 1810–1881) a leading notable. Lasting over two months, it was one of the first such missions from a North African state to Europe. Upon his return to Morocco, al-Saffar composed a travel account for the sultan of the envoys' experience while in France. Here al-Saffar records his first encounter with Paris late in December 1845. Frequently official missions such as these resulted in calls for reforming the state along modern lines in North Africa or the Middle East.

You should know that this city is the seat of government of the land of the French, the mother of its cities, the throne of its kingdom, the abode of great men, the source of its laws, the home of its learning and sciences. The [French] glory in its name and aspire to live there, while imitating its inhabitants in their behavior, refined manners, and cultured way of life. It is an enormous city, one of the greatest cities in those parts, just as Constantinople is for Muslims, to which it may be compared; some say its distance around is forty-eight miles. Others among its inhabitants told me [i.e., Saffar] that its circumference is twenty-one miles. . . . It is a city overflowing with people. Compared to the other cities of France, it is like a market day in our country [i.e., Morocco] compared with days on which there is no market. Alongside it, you would consider other places empty, even though they may be filled with people. We heard from the lips of more than one of them that it has a million [inhabitants] and that accounting does not seem strange to one who has been there. Anyone who is born or dies there, or comes there or departs, is recorded in a register—a ceaseless and perpetual task that is practiced everywhere in the land of Rum [i.e., the Christians]. . . . The taxes that they collect on goods entering the city do not go into the coffers of the state, but are destined for municipal improvements such as repairing the roadways and lighting the street-lamps, which are found in every town but most of all in Paris. . . . There is a vast number of carts and carriages in this city. They say that there are 13,000 of them, with 8,000 for hire and the rest privately owned. . . . We did not see car-

"Tangier, Morocco, c. 1907." Fez represented the traditional religious and principal political center for the Moroccan Alawi Dynasty (r.1672–present) while Tangier, strategically situated on the Strait of Gibraltar, was the kingdom's main port and point of contact for European and general Mediterranean trade. An American consulate was established there in the 1790s because Morocco was the first MENA country to establish diplomatic relations with the newly created United States. By 1900, Tangier, as shown here, possessed a cosmopolitan aura as its foreign residents, the most of any Moroccan city, included European merchants, traders, and missionaries as well as labor migrants.

riages or horses like those [of Paris] in any other place. To sum up, in comparison with the rest of what we say in the land of the French, Paris is like a center of civilization compared with the countryside, and other cities seem rustic beside her.

Just as more people from the region traveled to Europe for diplomacy or education, increasing numbers of European travelers toured the Middle East and North Africa. Many became intrigued, indeed obsessed, by elite households in the Middle East and North Africa, especially the harem, the secluded female quarters in urban elite households. The harem was imagined and depicted by Western, largely male, writers and painters as places of deviance and oppression. For North African or Middle Eastern people of ordinary station, the harem was as exotic a notion as it was for Europeans. Few women, aside from the upper ranks of urban elites, ever lived in harems. Among families of whatever social class in "traditional" North African society, monogamy appears to have been more prevalent than polygamy.

What did the harem represent for those women who lived within its confines? It was a private social space within a large household where elite women from an extended family lived, worked, and interacted with their children and servants on a daily basis. While off limits to men from outside the immediate kinship circle, the female quarters were more or less accessible to male family members as well as to women visitors, whether North African or from Europe.

This account was provided by a young English woman, Miss Smith, who resided in the 1840s with the family of the British counsel general in Tunis, Sir Thomas Reade (1785–1849). Miss Smith accompanied Mrs. Reade and some other English ladies to the harem or household of the family of Prince Muhammad, brother of the ruler of Tunisia, Ahmad Bey (r. 1837–1855), and heir to the throne.

The ladies of the harem generally reside at the Bardo [palace in Tunis], except two or three months in the summer when Prince Mohammed takes his family to his country-house, situated near the sea at Marsa, from whence they have beautiful views of the sea, the coast, Cape Bon, the isle of Zembra, etc., for although the ladies' windows or jalousies are so constructed, that it is impossible for them to be seen by people outside, yet they can themselves see from within very tolerably all that passes. And this "privilege" I think forms their chief employment and pleasure. It was at this marine villa that we saw the Lillah [a prince's principal wife]. We entered by a great arched door . . . into a square courtyard, in which we were pleased with the sight of peacocks, turkeys, Barbary doves and other birds . . . we entered a marble patio, or upper court open to both the serene face of the dark court and the blue heavens, in which played refreshingly two or three marble fountains, the noise of the falling water gracefully enchanting the ear, and the scattered spray diffusing a delightful coolness through the place. The arcades and corridors supported by marble pillars, rendered this part of the building highly ornamental. When the heat is very great this place is covered with an awning of silk and other stuff. . . . I observed at a window, on one side of the patio, several women apparently embroidering and making clothes for the family. As they looked up from their windows with curious gaze at us, a whimsical thought passed my mind of the animals in the zoological gardens whose cages very much resembled their grated windows.

From an apartment opposite to this window, at the door of which hung a curtain, the Lillah met us, and, kissing us on each cheek, ushered us into the room, where we found several ladies, relatives and visitors sitting in the Oriental fashion, on a couch or divan, placed around the room, and its only furniture. This seat we found very uncomfortable, being higher than our sofas and chairs, and having no place to rest our feet upon, which hung a short distance from the ground. The apartment was paved with the common Dutch glazed tiles, as were also all the stairs, this pavement being common throughout Barbary. All the Lillahs behaved in a quiet lady-like manner, a sister of Prince Mohammed particularly so, although of course they were very inquisitive, examining our dresses and asking us a thousand questions—more particularly on the articles of marriage.

Official and Popular Calls for Reform: Tunisia, Iran, Ottoman Turks

Reforming the state was a preoccupation shared by Muslim reformers. One of the greatest political treatises on just government was written by a statesman in Tunis, Khayr al-Din (c. 1822–1890) with the title *The Surest Path to Knowledge Concerning the Condition of States* (1867). In it, Khayr al-Din advocated the modernization of Muslim states and their institutions, including in his discussion topics such as education and the establishment of libraries, always with the justification that Islamic principles supported these ideas. Khayr al-Din had the pamphlet translated into French and Ottoman Turkish and later served briefly as Grand Vizier to the Ottoman sultan. He also established one of the earliest institutions of advanced modern education in North Africa, the Sadiqi College, founded in Tunis in 1875.

In the name of God, the Merciful, the Compassionate. . . . After I had long contemplated the causes of the progress and backwardness

Originally from the Caucasus, Khayr al-Din was brought to Tunis around 1839 from Istanbul as a *mamluk*. He was one of the principal architects of the 1857 *Ahd al-Aman* (Fundamental Pact), the Tunisian version of Ottoman Tanzimat that attempted to reorder society, state, and law, largely in response to immigration and creeping imperialism. A former servant of a Tunisian government official, Khayr al-Din's uniform and regalia illustrate the status that could be achieved in the Tunisian court by persons of humble origin.

of nations generation after generation, relying on the Islamic and European histories I was able to examine and on what the authors of both groups have written concerning the Islamic *umma* [Islamic community], its attributes and its future according to evidence which experience has decreed should be accepted, I decided to assert what I believe no intelligent Muslim will contradict and no one who has been shown the evidence will oppose: If we consider the competition of nations in the fields of civilization and the keen rivalry of even the greatest among them to achieve what is most beneficial and helpful, it becomes clear that we can properly distinguish what is most suitable for us only by having knowledge of those outside our own group, and especially of those who surround us and live close to us.

Further, if we consider the many ways which have been created in these times to bring men and ideas closer together, we will not hesitate to visualize the world as a single, united country peopled by various nations who surely need one another. The general benefit to be derived from the experience of each nation, even when it is pursuing its own personal interests, suffices to make it sought after by the rest of mankind. . . . Thus, the object of this book is to remind the learned *'ulama* [scholars of Islam] of their responsibility to know the important events of these days and to awaken the heedless both among the politicians and all the classes of the people by demonstrating what would be a proper domestic and foreign conduct. It is also to call attention to these aspects of the Frankish [European] nations—especially those having close contacts or attachments with us—which ought to be known. This includes their own eagerness to learn about other nations. The folding-in of the globe whose farthest distance is now connected with its nearest [distance] makes this easier.

In the latter quarter of the 19th century, Iran, though never occupied, experienced great turmoil due to European imperial pressures and state attempts to reform. The ruler, Nasir al-Din Shah (r. 1848–1896), and members of the court issued concessions to European entrepreneurs ostensibly to modernize the country by introducing electricity, modern banks, and the like. But many Iranians, including merchants, saw these concessions as exploiting their resources for the profit of the court and the foreign concessionaires. The latter were exempt from Iranian law and reaped most of the profits while the fees paid for the concessions went to individuals, not to the state treasury. Nasir al-Din was assassinated in 1896, and a decade of lackluster rule by his son led a coalition of Shi'i clerics and modernizers to demand that the ruler institute a constitution and parliament based on the British model that restricted royal power.

Praise Poem

This 1867 poem by Hasan Ben Brihmat of Algiers, educated according to Islamic tradition but familiar with French colonial rule, praises Khayr al-Din's *The Surest Path*, for treading a fine line between innovation or "improvising," frowned upon by Islam and possibly causing mutiny, and renovation according to Muslim principles. Ben Brihmat's reference to Khayr al-Din creating "customs" uses the word *sunan*, the plural of *sunna*, the tradition of the Prophet Muhammad. Thus, Khayr al-Din has followed the proper path shown by the Prophet while also calling for a new direction for Muslim rulers.

You pursued the right road no matter how narrow
    To the paths which preserve us from mutiny.
You explained the best way and the surest,
    And stood victorious for religion and country.

You legislate in a way not misguided, nor merely improvised;
    Rather, you create customs, fine ones indeed.
How lofty the law built from this precept!
    The time and the popular mood, of these you take heed.

The basic laws passed in 1906 established electoral and voting qualifications and stressed checks on royal privilege to issue concessions. A supplementary law of October 1907, never implemented, created a special committee of Shii ulema [specialists in Islamic law] to review all legislation to ensure it did not contravene Islamic regulations, along with defining more clearly the constitutional rights of the population.

This popular movement, which aimed at introducing parliamentary practices, ironically led Britain to enter into its 1907 pact with Russia dividing Iran into two spheres of influence. One goal of the agreement, particularly for Russia, was to work through the Shah to bolster his authority against the parliament. Another purpose was to give Britain and Russia mutual assurance that they essentially divided Iranian affairs and territory between them, blocking any effort for Germany to gain a foothold in Iran. The property and literacy criteria disqualified most peasants from voting despite their eligibility according to class; compare Article 1 with Articles 2 and 4.

2. THE ELECTORAL LAW OF SEPTEMBER 9, 1906

Regulations for the Elections to the National Assembly, dated Monday, Rajab 20, AH 1324 (= Sept. 9, AD 1906).

The Regulations for the Elections to the National Consultative Assembly [to be convened] in accordance with the August Rescript of His Imperial Majesty [Muzaffaru'd-Dín Sháh r. 1896–1907], may God immortalize his reign, issued on the 14th of Jumáda ii, AH 1324 (= August 5, 1906) are as follows.

FIRST SECTION. Rules governing the Elections.

ART. 1. The electors of the nation in the well-protected realms of Persia in the Provinces and Departments shall be of the following classes: (i) Princes and the Qájár tribe: (ii) Doctors of Divinity and Students: (iii) Nobles and Notables: (iv) Merchants: (v) Landed proprietors and peasants: (vi) Trade-guilds. Note 1. The tribes in each province are reckoned as forming part of the inhabitants of that province, and have the right to elect, subject to the established conditions. Note 2. By "landed proprietor" is meant the owner of an estate, and by "peasant" the tiller of the soil.

ART. 2. The electors shall possess the following qualifications: (i) their age must not fall short of 25 years: (ii) they must be Persian subjects: (iii) they must be known in the locality: (iv) the landed proprietors and peasants amongst them must possess property of the value of at least one thousand túmáns (= about £ 200): (v) the merchants amongst them must have a definite office and business: (vi) the

Ahmad Shah (1898–1930) came to the Persian throne at the age of eleven during profound political upheavals, notably the Constitutional Revolution, dated from 1905–1911 that led to civil strife that undermined social stability and trade. He was the titular ruler of Iran (Persia) from 1909 until 1925 when the Qajar dynasty was abolished by Mohamed Reza Pahlavi.

members of trade-guilds amongst them must belong to a recognized guild, must be engaged in a definite craft or trade, and must be in possession of a shop of which the rent corresponds with the average rents of the locality.

ART. 3. The persons who are entirely deprived of electoral rights are as follows: (i) women: (ii) persons not within years of discretion, and those who stand in need of a legal guardian: (iii) foreigners: (iv) persons whose age falls short of twenty-five years: (v) persons notorious for mischievous opinions: (vi) bankrupts who have failed to prove that they were not culpable: (vii) murderers, thieves, criminals, and persons who have undergone punishment according to the Islamic Law, as well as persons suspected of murder or theft, and the like, who have not legally exculpated themselves: (viii) persons actually serving in the land or sea forces. The persons who are conditionally deprived of electoral rights are as follows: (i) governors, and assistant governors, within the area of their governments: (ii) those employed in the military or police within the area of their appointments.

ART. 4. Those elected must possess the following qualifications: (i) they must know Persian: (ii) they must be able to read and write Persian: (iii) they must be Persian subjects of Persian extraction: (iv) they must be locally known: (v) they must not be in government employment: (vi) their age must be not less than thirty or more than seventy: (vii) they must have some insight into affairs of State. . . .

3. THE FUNDAMENTAL LAWS OF DECEMBER 30, 1906

The Fundamental Law of Persia, promulgated in the reign of the late Muzaffaru'd-Dín Sháh, and ratified by him on Dhu'l-Qa'da 14, AH 1324 (= December 30, 1906).

"In the Name of God the Merciful, the Forgiving. WHEREAS in accordance with the Imperial Farmán dated the fourteenth of Jumáda the Second, AH 1324 (= August 5, 1906), a command was issued for the establishment of a National Council, to promote the progress and happiness of our Kingdom and people, strengthen the foundations of our Government, and give effect to the enactments of the Sacred Law of His Holiness the Prophet, . . . THEREFORE the National Consultative Assembly is now opened, in accordance with our Sacred Command; and we do define as follows the principles and articles of the Fundamental Law regulating the aforesaid

National Council, which Law comprises the duties and functions of the above-mentioned Assembly, its limitations, and its relations with the various departments of the State.

On the Constitution of the Assembly. . . .

ART. 22. Any proposal to transfer or sell any portion of the [national] resources, or of the control exercised by the Government or the Throne, or to effect any change in the boundaries and frontiers of the Kingdom, shall be subject to the approval of the National Consultative Assembly.

ART. 23. Without the approval of the National Council, no concession for the formation of any public Company of any sort shall, under any plea so ever, be granted by the State.

ART. 24. The conclusion of treaties and covenants, the granting of commercial, industrial, agricultural and other concessions, irrespective of whether they be to Persian or foreign subjects, shall be subject to the approval of the National Consultative Assembly, with the exception of treaties which, for reasons of State and the public advantage, must be kept secret.

ART. 25. State loans, under whatever title, whether internal or external, must be contracted only with the cognizance and approval of the National Consultative Assembly.

ART. 26. The construction of railroads or chaussées, at the expense of the Government, or of any Company, whether Persian or foreign, depends on the approval of the National Consultative Assembly. . . .

4. THE SUPPLEMENTARY FUNDAMENTAL LAWS OF OCTOBER 7, 1907

The original Fundamental Law, containing 51 Articles, was promulgated on Dhu'l-Qa'da 14, AH 1324 (= Dec. 30, 1906) by the late Muzaffaru'd-Dín Sháh. The following supplementary laws were ratified by his successor, the now deposed Sháh, Muhammad 'Ali (r. 1907–1909), on Sha'bán 29, AH 1325 (= Oct. 7, 1907).

"In the Name of God the Merciful, the Forgiving. The Articles added to complete the Fundamental Laws of the Persian Constitution ratified by the late Sháhinsháh of blessed memory, Muzaffaru'd-Dín Sháh Qájár (may God illuminate his resting-place!) are as follows.

General Dispositions.

ART. 1. The official religion of Persia is Islám, according to the orthodox Já'farí doctrine of the Ithna 'Ashari-yya (Church of the Twelve Imáms), which faith the Sháh of Persia must profess and promote.

ART. 2. At no time must any legal enactment of the Sacred National Consultative Assembly, established by the favor and assistance of His Holiness the Imám of the Age (may God hasten his glad Advent!) the favor of His Majesty the Sháhinsháh of Islám (may God immortalize his reign!), the care of the Proofs of Is-

The 1905–1911 Revolution in Iran sought to curb the Qajar dynasty's authority by demanding the promulgation of a constitution. Tabriz in northwestern Iran was the core of various constitutional movements that led to the establishment of a parliament in Tehran. This school for boys in Tabriz served as a mobilizing center for anti-Qajar forces. Modern forms of education nurtured nationalism as well as movements to limit the power of monarchs.

lám (may God multiply the like of them!), and the whole people of the Persian nation, be at variance with the sacred principles of Islám or the laws established by His Holiness the Best of Mankind (on whom and on whose household be the Blessings of God and His Peace!).

It is hereby declared that it is for the learned doctors of theology (the *'ulama*)—may God prolong the blessing of their existence!— to determine whether such laws as may be proposed are or are not conformable to the principles of Islám; and it is therefore officially enacted that there shall at all times exist a Committee composed of not less than five *mujtahids* or other devout theologians, cogni-zant also of the requirements of the age, [which committee shall be elected] in this manner. The *'ulamá* and Proofs of Islám shall present to the National Consultative Assembly the names of Twenty of the *'ulamá* possessing the attributes mentioned above; and the Members of the National Consultative Assembly shall, either by unanimous acclamation, or by vote, designate five or more of these, according to the exigencies of the time, and recognize these as Members, so that they may carefully discuss and consider all matters proposed in the Assembly, and reject and repudiate, wholly or in part, any such proposal which is at variance with the Sacred Laws of Islam, so that it shall not obtain the title of legality. In such matters the decision of this Ecclesiastical Committee shall be followed and obeyed, and this article shall continue unchanged until the appearance of His Holi-ness the Proof of the Age (may God hasten his glad Advent !). . . .

ART. 8. The people of the Persian Empire are to enjoy equal rights before the Law....

ART. 19. The foundation of schools at the expense of the government and the nation, and compulsory instruction, must be regulated by the Ministry of Sciences and Arts, and all schools and colleges must be under the supreme control and supervision of that Ministry.

ART. 20. All publications, except heretical books and matters hurtful to the perspicuous religion [of Islam] are free, and are exempt from the censorship. If, however, anything should be discovered in them contrary to the Press law, the publisher or writer is liable to punishment according to that law. If the writer be known, and be resident in Persia, then the publisher, printer and distributor shall not be liable to prosecution....

ART. 26. The powers of the realm are all derived from the people; and the Fundamental Law regulates the employment of those powers.

In 1908, the Young Turk political movement forced Sultan Abdul Hamid (r. 1876–1909) to reconvene the Ottoman parliament that he had suspended in 1878, and to restore the 1876 constitution. These principles of equal rights for all Ottoman subjects regardless of religion reaffirmed the principles stated in the Hatti Sherif of Gulhane and Hatti Humayun. On the other hand, the stress on Turkish as the official state language would encourage disaffection among some Arab subjects for whom Arabic had been the language of instruction. Compare these clauses to Document 2.10, the Persian constitution. Sharif Hussein of Mecca, guardian of the Holy Places, condemned this 1908 Proclamation for the Ottoman Empire and subsequent policies of the Young Turk/Committee of Union and Progress government as against Islam when he declared his revolt against the Ottomans in 1916.

All the general rights accorded by the Constitution of 1293 (1876) and confirmed by the Imperial Hatti communicated to the Sublime Porte the 4th of *redjeb* 1326 (1908) ... will be respected and preserved intact, as long as they are not abolished by the Parliament.

Patients rest in a tuberculosis ward organized according to modern standards of the day at the Hasköy Hospital for Women. Tuberculosis was rampant in Europe and MENA in the nineteenth century. Hasköy is a neighborhood on the northern side of the Golden Horn in Beyoğlu, Istanbul, which boasted an ethnically and religiously diverse population. One of the first modern orphanages was established there as well.

1. The basis for the Constitution will be respect for the predominance of the national will. One of the consequences of this principle will be to require without delay the responsibility of the minister before the Chamber, and, consequently, to consider the minister as having resigned, when he does not have a majority of the votes of the Chamber.

2. Provided that the number of senators does not exceed one-third the number of deputies, the Senate will be named as follows: one-third by the Sultan and two-thirds by the nation, and the term of senators will be of limited duration.

In this school portrait (c. 1890), students and physician-instructors pose before an Ottoman military hospital whose architecture betrays the influence of similar French structures of the period. Military institutions, personnel, and technology were the focus of modernizing reforms from early in the nineteenth century in MENA. As was true in Europe, medical progress was invariably tied to the military.

3. It will be demanded that all Ottoman subjects having completed their twentieth year, regardless of whether they possess property or fortune, shall have the right to vote. Those who have lost their civil rights will naturally be deprived of this right.

4. It will be demanded that the right freely to constitute political groups be inserted in a precise fashion in the constitutional charter, in order that article 1 of the Constitution of 1293 AH be respected.

7. The Turkish tongue will remain the official state language. Official correspondence and discussion will take place in Turkish.

9. Every citizen will enjoy complete liberty and equality, regardless of nationality or religion, and be submitted to the same obligations. All Ottomans, being equal before the law as regards rights and duties relative to the State, are eligible for government posts, according to their individual capacity and their education. Non-Muslims will be equally liable to the military law.

10. The free exercise of the religious privileges which have been accorded to different nationalities will remain intact. . . .

14. Provided that the property rights of landholders are not infringed upon (for such rights must be respected and must remain intact, according to law), it will be proposed that peasants be permitted to acquire land, and they will be accorded means to borrow money at a moderate rate.

16. Education will be free. Every Ottoman citizen, within the limits of the prescriptions of the Constitution, may operate a private school in accordance with the special laws.

17. All schools will operate under the surveillance of the state. In order to obtain for Ottoman citizens an education of a homogenous and uniform character, the official schools will be open, their instruction will be free, and all nationalities will be admitted.

Instruction in Turkish will be obligatory in public schools. In official schools, public instruction will be free. Secondary and higher education will be given in the public and official schools indicated above; it will use the Turkish tongue. Schools of commerce, agriculture, and industry will be opened with the goal of developing the resources of the country.

18. Steps shall also be taken for the formation of roads and railways and canals to increase the facilities of communication and increase the sources of the wealth of the country. Everything that can impede commerce or agriculture shall be abolished.

Mutual Incomprehension?: Women, Education, and Public Behavior

In 1901 a girls' school with four grades was established [in Tehran] and then other schools under the direction of Iranian women were founded. But these schools did not have the same curriculum and were not under the guidance of the Ministry of Education. It was customary that Persian and French were taught. Some ladies might remember that at that time, some of these schools had yearly exams. I was invited to attend as an examiner. I well remember a five-year-old girl, whose parents had requested for her to learn simultaneously the Persian and French alphabet, consequently mix up the pronunciation.

—Journalist and educator, Sidiqah Dawlatabadi, account from 1901

In the mid-nineteenth century, young women of well-to-do families could be hindered from gaining an education by family members who feared that schooling outside the home might dishonor the family's reputation. However, women were at times encouraged by their fathers to acquire a modern education through private tutors, whereas their mothers resisted the idea of advanced studies for daughters since it could decrease their chances for a good marriage. `A'isha Taymur (1840–1902) became one of Egypt's most highly regarded litterateurs at a time when women's presence in literature or science was almost unknown. As Taymur relates, she belonged to a family of historians and playwrights; she herself wrote poetry in Arabic, Persian, and Turkish. Her father, of Kurdish origin [as was Qasim Amin—see p. 85] and connected to the Egyptian court, arranged for her education that included Quranic studies and Islamic law. But she could not escape all customs and was married at the age of fourteen. She experienced tragedy, as her husband died at a relatively young age as did her daughter, whose loss she memorialized in poetry. In this memoir, she recounts her eagerness to gain an education, her mother's opposition, and her father's solution.

When my mind was ready to develop. . . . , my mother, the goddess of compassion and virtue, and the treasure of knowledge and experience, brought the tools of weaving and embroidery and exerted herself in teaching me. She explained things clearly and cleverly but I was not receptive. I was not willing to improve in the feminine occupations. I used to flee from her like a prey escaping the net.

[At the same time] I used to look forward to attending the gatherings of prominent writers without any awkwardness. I found the sound of the pen on paper to be the most beautiful, and I became convinced that membership in that profession was the most abundant blessing. To satisfy my longing I would collect any sheets of paper and small pens. Then I would go someplace . . . and imitate the writers as they scribbled. Hearing that sound was very enjoyable. When my mother would find me out, she would scold me and threaten me. This only increased my rejection of embroidery and did not improve my skills. . . . My mother—may God rest her in the heavenly gardens—was hurt by my actions. She would reprimand, threaten, warn, and promise to punish. She also appealed to me with friendly promises of jewelry and pretty costumes.

[Finally] my father reasoned with her, quoting the Turkish poet who said: 'The heart is not led, through force, to the desired path. So do not torment another soul if you can spare it.' He also cautioned her: . . . 'If our daughter is inclined to the pen and paper, do not obstruct her desire.'

'Let us share our daughters. You take 'Afat and give me 'Asmat [another of 'A'isha's names] If I make a writer out of 'Asmat, then this will bring me mercy after my death'. My father then said: 'Come with me 'Asmat. Starting tomorrow, I will bring you two instructors who will teach you Turkish, Persian, *fiqh* [Islamic jurisprudence] and Arabic grammar. Do well in your studies and follow what I instruct you to do, and beware of making me ashamed before your mother.'"

This portrait of a group of middle-school girls in the mid-1880s is taken from the huge collection of photo albums that Sultan Abdul Hamid II ordered put together so as to visually demonstrate the modernization of the Ottoman Empire. Fifty-one large-format albums containing nearly two thousand photographs resulted from the project covering the period from 1880 to 1893. Prominent in this collection are students, educational institutions, modern government buildings, military staff and facilities, and hospitals.

The Egyptian popular press criticized Egyptians who appeared to ape Western ways, especially women. Women's dress and public behavior were considered important markers of traditional culture with its emphasis on modesty as opposed to "modern" public behavior. A poem from 1895 captures the mood of the more conservative Egyptians at a time when an open call for women's education had not yet been made.

> The lady is walking with the veil
> Though her eyes wander everywhere
> And on the road she walks playfully
> She really knows all the ins and outs
> The woman is walking in the quarter
> Continuously teasing and calling out to men
> These are the times but oh, what a great loss!

. . . The name of Qasim Amin (1865–1908) is firmly linked with the movement for women's emancipation in Egypt in the opening years of the twentieth century. After completing his study of law in France in 1885,

Amin returned to Egypt where he served as a judge and participated in the founding of the Egyptian University [1908—now Cairo University]. Amin's first book, *The Liberation of Women*, published in 1899, called for greater freedom for Egyptian women, justified on the basis of Islamic principles, while at the same time he defended the status of Egyptian women against European criticism. His book aroused a furor, attacked by Muslim clerics and moralists who opposed granting rights to women. Angered at this criticism, Amin published *The New Woman* in 1900, from which this selection is taken. Here he reversed course and justified women's education as necessary for progress as the Western example demonstrated. In doing so he attacked traditional practices, ignored Islamic sources permitting women's education, and evoked freedom as the cornerstone for human progress. Amin now sought to integrate Darwinian ideas of selective advancement of the species with the idea of progress for all societies. Implicitly at least, women's liberation would place Egypt on the path to modernity, but achieving that freedom required challenging traditional practices and institutions as well as those opposed to change.

"Women's Freedom"

"Freedom allows the human species to progress, and is the ladder to happiness. It is considered one of the most precious human rights by those nations who understand the secrets of success. 'Freedom' here means a person's independence of thought, will, and action, as long as this does not exceed legal limits and maintains the moral standards of society. Nobody need submit to the will of others, except in insanity and childhood. . . .

This is the freedom—with such broad parameters—that should be the basis for the education of our women. Some people are amazed at my request for women's freedom and question whether women are in bondage. If they understood the meaning of freedom they would share my opinion. I do not wish to say that a woman today is bought and sold in the market. . . . [but] common sense defines anyone who is not in control of his own thought, will, and actions as a slave.

I do not think an objective reader will disagree when I say that a woman in the eyes of a Muslim is an incomplete human being, or that a Muslim man thinks he has the right to dominate her or treat her accordingly; this is well attested. . . . It is improper for a woman to sit with men or eat with them. On numerous occasions I have seen a man sitting at a table eating while his wife stands by chasing away flies and his daughter carries the water pitcher . . . especially in the rural areas. . . .

However, women's enslavement may take different forms among other classes or in the cities. The man who forbids his wife to leave the house for any reasons except when he wishes does not respect her freedom. Here the woman is a slave, in fact a prisoner. . . . [and] although the number [of such cases] has decreased we are all aware that a woman can rarely choose where she will go or what she will do.

If Muslims adopt the opinions of their ignorant jurisprudents, who to them seem knowledgeable, they will think it their duty to imprison their women and forbid them to go out except to visit their relatives at the two religious feasts, or even think it preferable that a woman not leave her house under any circumstances. Indeed they have found pride in confining the woman to her quarters until she is carried to her grave!

Giving a man the right to imprison his wife certainly denies the woman her freedom that is her inalienable and natural right. A woman whose father handed her like an animal to a husband she did not know—because she was prevented from making her own critical appraisal of him—cannot be considered free. . . . [but] in reality a slave. . . . Fathers, regardless of class, marry off their daughters this way. . . . [Whereas] a man, though he too may be unfamiliar with his fiancée, is in a different situation, for he can rid himself of the consequences of his ignorance by divorcing the woman anytime he wishes, or he can simultaneously marry a second, third, or fourth wife. A woman who suffers from an unpleasant match is unable to rid herself of her husband. Marrying a man to a woman she does not know and depriving her of her right to terminate that relationship (while allowing the man the freedom to keep or dismiss his wife whenever he wishes) is true slavery. . . .

The woman who must conceal her limbs and the external features of her body—thus hindering her from walking, riding or breathing, and disabling her from looking or talking without difficulty—is a slave because her enclosure in a piece of fabric . . . meant to hide her appearance, and the confinement of her natural human form from the gaze of every man except those of her lord and master, is a form of slavery. . . .

What is the relationship between a woman's freedom and the uncovering of her face and her interaction with men? . . . The veil, originally intended for wives only, was finally extended to daughters, sisters and then all women because every women either is a wife, was a wife, or will become a wife. Veiling is the symbol of ancient ownership and is one of the vestiges of the barbaric behavior that characterized human life for generations. It existed before it was realized that as person should not be owned simply because she as a female—just as people with black skin should not be slaves for the white man. . . . The first step for women's liberation is to tear off the veil and totally wipe out its influence. . . .

Bahithat al-Badiya was the pseudonym ["Seeker in the Desert"] of Malik Hifni Nasif (1886–1918). Born into an educated, literary family, she graduated from the first teacher training school for women in Egypt. An active writer, she published essays on women and lectured at the Egyptian University. The Umma Party was a reformist Egyptian political party that embraced the writings of Qasim Amin with regard to women. But, as Bahithat al-Badiya indicates in this 1909 lecture at the Umma Party Club, women's hopes for full education and the right to choose their husbands had to be tempered by caution to avoid public backlash. Here, she walks a fine line between advocating equal rights for women, for which men are not yet prepared in her view, and remaining aware of criticism of women who showed too much independence in public and appeared immodest. Her comments mirror those found previously regarding a woman walking in the street, but as a nationalist her call for a boycott on imported products and for ousting foreigners is nearly identical to that of Hasan al-Banna, founder of the Muslim Brotherhood.

Ladies, . . . I applaud your kindness in accepting the invitation to this talk where I seek reform. . . . Complaints about both men and women are rife. Which side is right? Complaints and grumblings are not reform. . . . An Arab proverb says there is no smoke without a fire. . . . There is some truth in our claims and those of men. . . . Men blame the discord on our poor upbringing and haphazard education while we claim it is due to men's arrogance and pride. . . .

Men say when we become educated we shall push them out of work and abandon the role for which God has created us. But isn't it rather men who have pushed women out of work? Before, women used to spin and to weave cloth for clothes for themselves and their children, but men invented machines for spinning and weaving and put women out of work. In the past women sewed clothes for themselves, but men invented the sewing machine. . . . The men took up the profession of tailoring and began making clothes for our men and children. Before, women winnowed the wheat and ground flour on grinding stones for the bread they . . . [made] with their own hands. . . . Then men established bakeries employing men. They gave us rest but at the same time pushed us out of work. . . .

. . . I do not mean to denigrate these useful inventions which do a lot of our work. . . . But, I simply wanted to show that men are

Obviously a staged studio portrait, this image of an elite Ottoman woman was taken by Ottoman Armenian subjects, the Abdullah brothers who organized a celebrated photographic business in Istanbul from 1858 to 1900 and were appointed official photographers to the sultan in 1863. Bahithat al-Badiyya might have approved of the woman's outer garment if drawn tightly when in public, but might have criticized the type of veil worn by the woman in this photograph.

the ones who started to push us out of work and that if we were to edge them out today we would only be doing what they have already done to us.

The question of monopolizing the workplace comes down to individual freedom. One man wishes to become a doctor, another a merchant. Is it right to tell the doctor he must quit his profession and become a merchant or vice versa? No. Each has the freedom to do as he wishes. Since male inventors have taken away a lot of our work, should we waste our time in idleness or seek other work to occupy us? Of course, we should do the latter. Work at home does not occupy more than half the day. We must pursue an education in order to occupy the other half of the day, but that is what men wish to prevent us from doing under the pretext of taking their jobs away. Obviously I am not urging women to neglect their homes and children to go out and become lawyers or judges or railway engineers. But, if any of us wish to work in such professions our personal freedom should not be infringed. It might be argued that pregnancy causes women to leave work but there are unmarried women, others who are barren or who have lost their husbands or are widowed or divorced or those whose husbands need their help in supporting the family. It is not right that they should be forced into lowly jobs. These women might like to become teachers or doctors with the same academic qualifications. . . . if pregnancy impedes work inside the house, it also impedes work outside the house. . . . how many able-bodied men become sick from time to time and have had to stop work?

Men say to us categorically 'You women have been created for the house and we have been created to be breadwinners'. Is this a God-given dictate? How are we to know since no holy book has spelled it out? . . .

Specialised work for each sex is a matter of convention. It is not mandatory. . . . If men say to us that we have been created weak, we say to them, 'No, it is you who made us weak through the path you made us follow'. . . . women [in the past] have excelled in learning and the arts and politics. Some have exceeded men in courage and valour, such as Hawla bint al-Azwar al-Kindi who impressed Umar Ibn Khattab [the second Caliph] with her bravery and skill in fighting when she went to Syria to free her brother held captive by the Byzantines. Joan of Arc who led the French army after its defeat by the English encouraged the French to continue fighting. . . . While there is no fear now of our competing with men because we are still in the first stage of education and our oriental habits do not allow us to pursue much study, men can rest assured in their jobs. As long as they can see seats in the schools of law, engineering, medicine and at the university unoccupied by us, men can relax because what they fear is distant. . . . [But] Nothing irritates me more than when men claim they do not wish us to work because they wish to spare us the burden. We do not want condescension, we want respect. They should replace the first with the second. . . .

Men criticise the way we dress in the streets. They have a point because we have exceeded the bounds of custom and propriety. We claim we are veiling but we are neither properly covered nor unveiled. I do not advocate a return to the veils of our grandmothers because it can rightly be called being buried alive, not *hijab*, correct covering. The [urban] woman used to spend her whole life within the walls of her house not going out in the street except when she was carried to her grave. I do not, on the other hand, advocate unveiling, like Europeans, and mixing with men because they are harmful to us.

Nowadays, the lower half of our attire is a skirt that does not conform to the standards of our modesty (*hijab*) while the upper half [is] like age, the more it advances the more it is shortened. Our former garment was one piece. When a woman wrapped herself in it, her figure was totally hidden. The wrap shrunk little by little but it was still wide enough to conceal the whole body. Then we artfully began to shrink the waist and lower the neck and finally two sleeves were added and the garment clung to our back and was worn only with a corset. We tied back our headgear so that more than half the head including the ears were visible and the flowers and ribbons ornamenting the hair could be seen. Finally the face veil became more transparent than an infant's heart. . . . I believe the best practice for outdoors is to cover the head with a scarf and the body with a dress of the kind women call a *cache poussière*, a dust coat, to cover the body right down to the heels, and with sleeves long enough to reach the wrist. This is being done now in Istanbul I am told. . . .

If we had been raised from childhood to go unveiled and if our men were ready for it, I would approve of unveiling for those who want it. But the nation is not ready for it now. . . .

Veiling should not prevent us from breathing fresh air or going out to buy what we need if no one can buy it for us. It must not prevent us from gaining an education, nor cause our health to deteriorate. . . . But we should be prudent and not take promenades alone. And we should avoid gossip. We should not saunter, moving our heads right and left. . . . The imprisonment in the home of the Egyptian woman of the past is detrimental while the current freedom of the Europeans is excessive. I cannot find a better model [than] today's Turkish woman. She falls between the two extremes and does not violate what Islam prescribes.

I have heard that some of our high officials are teaching their girls European dancing and acting. I consider both despicable—a detestable crossing of boundaries and a blind imitation of Europeans. Customs should not be abandoned except when they are harmful. . . . What good is there . . . in women and men holding each others waists dancing or daughters appearing on stage before audiences acting with bare bosoms? This is contrary to Islam and a moral threat we must fight as much as we can. . . .

On the subject of customs and veiling, I would like to remind you of something that causes us great unhappiness—the question of engagement and marriage. Most sensible people in Egypt believe it is necessary for fiancés to meet and speak with each other before their marriage. It is wise and the Prophet, peace be upon him and his followers, did not do otherwise. It is a practice in all nations, including Egypt, except among city people. . . . In my view the two people should see each other and speak to each other after their engagement and before signing the marriage contract [as opposed to more extended contact prior to engagement]. . . . We have all seen family happiness destroyed because of this old betrothal practice.

By not allowing men to see their prospective wives following their engagement, we cause Egyptian men to seek European women in marriage. They marry European servants and working class women thinking they would be happy with them rather than daughters of pashas and beys hidden away in a 'box of chance'. If we do not solve this problem we shall become subject to occupation by women of the West. We shall suffer double occupation, one by men and the other by women. The second will be worse than the first because the first occurred against our will but we will have invited the second by our own actions. . . . Most Egyptian men who have married European women suffer from the foreign habits and extravagance of their wives. The European woman thinks she is of a superior race to the Egyptian and bosses her husband around after marriage. . . .

If we pursue everything western we shall destroy our own civilisation and a nation that destroys its civilisation grows weak and vanishes. Our youth [who go to Europe to study] claim that they bring European women home because they find them more sophisticated than Egyptian women. By the same token they should bring European students and workers to Egypt because they are superior to our own. The reasoning is the same. . . . I am the first to admire the activities of the western woman and her courage and I am the first to respect those who deserve respect but respect for others should not make us overlook the good of the nation. . . . In many of our ways we follow the views of men. Let them show us what they want. We are ready to follow their views on condition that their views do not do injustice to us nor trespass on our rights.

Our beliefs and actions have been a great cause of the lesser respect men accord us. How can a sensible man respect a woman who believes in magic, superstition and the blessings of the dead . . . [and how] can he respect a woman who speaks only about the clothes of her neighbor and the jewelry of her friend and the furniture of the bride? This is added to the notion imprinted in a man's mind that a woman is weaker and less intelligent than he is. If we fail to do something about this, it means we think our condition is satisfactory. . . . if it is not, how can we better it in the eyes of men? . . . We should get a sound education, not merely the trappings of a foreign language and the rudiments of music. Our education should also include home management, healthcare and childcare. If we eliminate immodest behaviour on the street and prove to our husbands through good behaviour and fulfillment of duties that we are human beings with feelings, no less human than they are, and we do not allow them under any condition to hurt our feelings or fail to respect us, if we do all this, how can a just man despise us? As for the unjust man, it would have been better for us not to accept marriage to him.

We shall advance when we give up idleness. The work of most of us at home is lounging on cushions all day or going out to visit other women. . . . Being given over to idleness or luxury has given us weak constitutions and pale complexions. . . . Now I shall turn to the path we should follow. If I had the right to legislate, I would decree;

1. Teaching girls the Quran and the correct Sunna.
2. Primary and secondary education for girls and compulsory school education for all.
3. Instruction for girls on the theory and practice of home economics, health, first aid, and child care.
4. Setting a quota for females in medicine and education so they can serve the women of Egypt.

5. Allowing women to study any other advanced subjects they wish without restrictions.

6. Upbringing for girls from infancy stressing patience, honesty, work and other virtues.

7. Adhering to the *Sharia* concerning betrothal and marriage, and not permitting any woman and man to marry without first meeting each other in the presence of the father or male relative of the bride.

8. Adapting the veil and outdoor dress of the Turkish women of Istanbul.

9. Maintaining the best interests of the country and dispensing with foreign goods and people as much as possible.

10. Make it incumbent on our brothers, the men of Egypt, to implement this programme.

For many Egyptians, modernization and exposure to Western practices brought alienation from Egyptian culture as shown in a skit by the journalist and playwright 'Abdullah al-Nadim (1845–1896) that first appeared in 1881 and was reprinted in 1907. Here a young Egyptian, Za'it, returns to Egypt from France and is greeted by his parents, Egyptian peasants: the father is Ma'it, the mother Ma'ika. On seeing Za'it, his father embraces and kisses him, resulting in mutual incomprehension, as Za'it considers himself to be "modern," having abandoned his family's traditional ways.

Za'it: "Oh God, you Muslims still have this very ugly habit of hugging and kissing.

Ma'it: But, son, how are we supposed to greet each other?

Za'it: You say *bonne arrivée* and shake hands once and that's it.

Ma'it: But son, I've never denied I am a *fallah* [peasant].

Za'it: Fallah or not, you Egyptians are like farm animals.

Ma'it: Thank you, Za'it, you are so kind. Come on, let's go. [they go home where Ma'ika has prepared a meal of baked meat and onions.] When Za'it sees the pot, he yells

Za'it. Why did you put so much of that . . . that . . . *comment ça s'appele?* [what is it called?]

Ma'ika: That . . . that what, Za'it?

Za'it: That thing . . . called?

Ma'ika: Called what, pepper?

Za'it: *Non, non*, the thing you plant.

Ma'ika: Garlic. I swear son, there is no garlic in it!

Za'it: No I mean the thing that brings you to tears, they call it *des oignons* [onions].

By the 1870s, Beirut had emerged as a major Mediterranean city for commerce and trade; thus, this branch of the Ottoman Bank was built there. Established in 1856 in Istanbul's Galata business district, the Ottoman Bank at first operated as a joint venture involving British and French banking interests as well as the Ottoman government.

There were 72 of us, we went to Beirut where we remained for eight days, living outdoors. . . . Finally, one night the Beirut agent came and said 'let's go.' They directed us through a small canyon and we continued walking until we got to the sea. There were three Turkish officers there whom they bribed. Then they put us in an open boat and took us to Cyprus which was under British rule. And they got us tickets for a French ship.

—Michel Haddy, Lebanese emigrant to the United States, interview, 1962

Ma'ika: I swear, son! I put no *des oignons* in there. This is just meat with *basal* [onions].

Za'it: *C'est ça! Basal! Basal!*

Ma'ika: What's happened to you, Za'it? You forgot *basal?* You always used to eat it.

Emigration: The Search for Livelihood Abroad

Emigration from Ottoman lands to the New World began in the late nineteenth century, mainly from the overpopulated Mount Lebanon to North and South America. By the last decades of the nineteenth century, Ottoman officials both in the region and stationed in European ports became alarmed at the loss of their laboring populations, as this 1889 letter from Yusuf Bey, Ottoman consul, Barcelona, to Istanbul demonstrates. Mostly peasants, they left their homeland on ships from Beirut that docked in European ports, where they then boarded ships going on the trans-Atlantic voyage. The letter suggests that many initially had money only for the first part of their journey.

A crowd of men, women and children dressed in rags, wandering about in the streets of Marseille, Havre, and Barcelona and other French and Spanish cities and begging for mercy and alms. When questioned why they had to leave their homes in such large numbers, they invent ridiculous stories about the massacre of their wives and children . . . all to increase the compassion and thus the alms they can elicit. The better-informed people ignore such outrageous calumnies, but the simple-minded folk are deceived, and a great harm is being done to our [Ottoman] national image.

Letter from Nuam Pasha, governor of Mount Lebanon, to the Ottoman Minister of the Interior, 1895, explaining reasons for Lebanese migration. Labor migration proved a powerful source of change for family, society, and the state. This was particularly true when many emigrants later returned home to Lebanon or other parts of the Ottoman Empire with capital amassed in the New World as well as new ideas and ways of organizing daily life.

Most of Mount Lebanon is rocky and uncultivable land. Mulberry trees constitute its principle plantation, and silk production the major source of income for the Lebanese in general. The continuous decline of silk prices over the last years, however, multiplied the difficulties which Lebanese encounter in maintaining their sustenance. The stringent conditions in Mount Lebanon contrast sharply with the opportunities of making a much better living abroad. . . . Under the circumstances the Lebanese become eager to try their fortunes overseas. . . .

Colonel Hakki Bey, Captain of the Imperial Ironclad Frigate *Mahmudiye*, stands at attention on deck in this late-nineteenth-century portrait. Ironclad ships were first introduced into the Ottoman imperial navy during the late 1860s and early 1870s and formed the core of the Ottoman fleet, most of which was constructed by British, French, and Italian yards as part of the sultan's modernization efforts.

CHAPTER 3

World War I and Its Aftermath, c. 1914–1923

The British officer and administrator General Edmund Henry Allenby [1861–1936] captured Jerusalem from the Ottoman army on December 9, 1917. Allenby chose to enter Jerusalem, on foot through the Jaffa Gate because of the city's status as a religious center, in contrast to Kaiser Wilhelm's entry on horseback, suggesting the entrance of a conqueror, in 1898. British troops line the streets.

In northern Africa by 1900, only the Kingdom of Morocco and the Ottoman province of Tripolitania (modern-day Libya) remained more or less independent of European rule, although European competition for Morocco was intense between Spain, France, and Germany, while Italy clearly had imperial designs on Tripoli province. Between 1899 and 1912, French armies progressively occupied parts of Morocco, using Algeria as a base. In 1912, the French and Spanish protectorates were declared, with the lion's share of Moroccan territory going to France. Nevertheless, it took France several decades to quell the numerous Moroccan revolts sparked by military occupation that had scarcely been suppressed when the Moroccan nationalist movement emerged in the post-World War I era. Italy invaded Libya in 1911.

World War I marked a fateful turning point in Middle Eastern and North African history. The war pitted two coalitions or alliances of states and empires against each other. The Triple Alliance was composed of Germany, the Austria-Hungarian Empire, and the Ottoman Empire. Opposing that coalition was the Triple Entente, which counted Great Britain, France, and Russia, although Russia withdrew from the war following the 1917 Bolshevik Revolution; Italy joined the alliance in 1915. After four years of brutal warfare, Great Britain and France emerged victorious in 1918 following the entry of the United States into the war on their side in 1917.

One of the ironies of colonialism was that native peoples were either forced into the imperial armies of the French, British, Italian, and other empires or volunteered with the expectation that their service

The French weekly *Le Miroir* in April 1915 depicted the sufferings of wounded North African colonial soldiers, fighting under France's flag, on the European front as they were evacuated from the battlefield.

would hasten their country's independence. Moroccan, Algerian, and Tunisian soldiers all served under the French flag in Europe in large numbers. Over 173,000 Algerians served in the French army during the "Great War." France sent tens of thousands of these soldiers to fight in the trenches in Europe. Britain did the same with its Indian troops, although most fought in the Middle East and East Africa. The North African units were segregated from French soldiers and often housed and fed in an inferior manner compared to European combatants. In addition, the war forced West African French colonial subjects by the hundreds of thousands, notably Senegalese, into the killing fields of Europe. The casualties for African soldiers were high because they became ill more easily, and did not receive the same quality food rations or medical assistance as white, European soldiers.

Many West Africans and North Africans served bravely under France's flag, as did Indian troops fighting for Britain, believing that military service would be rewarded with greater self-government for their countries after the hostilities ended. But their imperial masters refused to expand their political rights, leading to intensified nationalist, anticolonial movements against Britain as well as France that included Egypt as well as India. Thousands of Egyptians had been forcibly employed in labor battalions and sent to serve in Gallipoli and in Palestine without proper clothing or food; many died. In short, although the major combatants were European powers, those who fought included many imperial subjects, as well as many of British origin from lands such as Australia, New Zealand, and Canada.

The war brought the collapse of three imperial dynasties, the Russian Romanovs, the Austro-Hungarian Hapsburgs, and the Ottoman Turks whose lineage traced to the end of the thirteenth century but whose empire began with the fall of Constantinople in 1453. The overthrow of the Romanov Dynasty ended Tsarist rule stretching back to the fifteenth century and led to the creation of the communist Soviet Union; Poland once more emerged as an independent state after beating back Soviet efforts to retake Warsaw. The defeat of the Austro-Hungarian empire signaled the end of the Hapsburg Dynasty, which had ruled Austria from 1278–1918 and Hungary from 1699–1918. In its place emerged newly independent states such as Austria, Hungary, Czechoslovakia, and Yugoslavia.

The dismantling of the Ottoman Empire led eventually to the new, independent state of Turkey by 1923, and the transfer of the capital to Ankara in central Anatolia. However, the destiny of the diverse peoples residing in Greater Syria and Mesopotamia—lands that were predominantly Arab in terms of language or ethnicity, but that encompassed many different religions, races, and ethnic groups—was subjugation to new political masters. Great Britain and France determined during the war, principally through secret agreements, to take over Greater Syria, including Palestine, and Mesopotamia (the future Iraq), which had been under Ottoman rule since the sixteenth century. With utter disregard for the collective desires and future well-being of the region's inhabitants, France and Great Britain imposed a political system known as "Mandates" that represented a thinly disguised form of colonial rule.

Under the terms of the mandates, overseen by the newly created League of Nations, Britain and France were theoretically responsible for preparing these regions and their inhabitants for eventual political independence, although at some unspecified future date. Yet the reality was otherwise, as both France and Great Britain, whenever possible, blocked changes in the system that might have produced fully independent nation-states. In the case of Palestine, Britain promised future independence to Zionism, a Jewish national movement, although Jews were only 10 percent of Palestine's population at the time. At stake, especially for the new country of Iraq, was control over the region's resources—mainly oil fields—as well as strategic concerns. As a result, Anglo-French postwar imperialism carved out the present-day states of Iraq, Syria, Lebanon, Israel, formerly Palestine, and the future Kingdom of Jordan, which the British separated from the Palestine mandate. Many of the current conflicts in the Middle East today can be traced directly to World War I and its aftermath.

Although most of the fighting occurred in Europe, major campaigns took place in the Middle East with severe social and economic consequences. Civilians in combat zones of Turkey, Syria, Palestine, and Mesopotamia suffered enormous hardships during the war. Hundreds of thousands of the inhabitants of Syria, Lebanon, and northern Palestine died of famine from 1915–1918. People starved—or were allowed to starve—to death for lack of food. In a move calculated to inflict suffering

This 1917 poster for an exposition of Moroccan art depicts a wounded Moroccan soldier who had fought in Europe observing a Moroccan artisan painting a traditional ceramic bowl. The poster advertised a campaign to collect money for the war effort through a public exhibit held in Paris.

on civilian populations, an Anglo-French blockade along the Mediterranean coast impeded shipments of food to those in most dire need. The reasoning was that as Ottoman subjects, these peoples—mainly women, children, and the old or infirm—would rebel against the Ottoman government. To these woes were added others—locust swarms that destroyed what harvests existed, local wartime hoarding of food supplies, and the requisitioning of animals and food crops by Ottoman troops. Finally there was the Ottoman displacement and killing of hundreds of thousands of Armenians, actions whose causes are still debated today.

On the other hand, wartime conditions induced the Ottoman government to encourage women in Istanbul to assume an active, public part in the war effort as relief workers, organizers, nurses, and so forth. As was also true in Europe or the United States, these expanded wartime roles for women led to wider social and political reforms for Turkish women in the new republic that emerged after the war.

When World War I first broke out in August 1914, the Ottoman government had prudently assumed a position of neutrality, but by October it had joined with the coalition of Central Powers. As the Ottoman government entered the war on the side of Germany, the Shaykh al-Islam, the highest-ranking Muslim authority in the empire, issued a religious edict (*fetva*, Arabic: *fatwa*) in the name of Sultan Mehmed V (r. 1909–1918) calling all Muslims to rise up against those countries now at war with Turkey, namely, Britain, France, and Russia. The Ottomans hoped that Muslims under British or French colonial rule in North Africa, Egypt, and India would rebel against their overlords. Britain especially feared that Indian Muslims serving in the British army would refuse to fight against the Ottomans. This encouraged the British to approach the Sharif Hussein of Mecca (1854–1931) for an alliance against the Turks in 1914–1915. In this proclamation on November 23, 1914, the Ottoman Sultan Mehmed V alludes to the fetva as he urged Muslims to aid the Ottoman as well as German and Austro-Hungarian cause. His explanation of the outbreak of the war was inaccurate. Ottoman ships, some under German command, opened fire on Russian vessels, not vice-versa as suggested here.

"To my army! To my navy! — Sultan Mehmed V

Immediately after the war between the Great Powers began, I called you to arms in order to be able in case of trouble to protect the existence of empire and country from any assault on the part of our enemies, who are only awaiting the chance to attack us suddenly and unexpectedly as they have always done.

While we were thus in a state of armed neutrality, a part of the Russian fleet, which was going to lay mines at the entrance of the straits of the Black Sea, suddenly opened fire against a squadron of our own fleet at the time engaged in manoeuvres. While we were expecting reparation from Russia for this unjustified attack, contrary to international law, the empire just named, as well as its allies, recalled their ambassadors and severed diplomatic relations with our country. The fleets of England and France have bombarded the straits of the Dardanelles, and the British fleet has shelled the harbour of Akabah on the Red Sea.

In the face of such successive proofs of wanton hostility we have been forced to abandon the peaceful attitude for which we always strove, and now in common with our allies, Germany and Austria, we turn to arms in order to safeguard our lawful interests.

The Russian Empire during the last three hundred years has caused our country to suffer many losses in territory, and when we finally arose to that sentiment of awakening and regeneration which would increase our national welfare and our power, the Russian Empire made every effort to destroy our attempts, either with war or with numerous machinations and intrigues. Russia, England, and France never for a moment ceased harbouring ill-will against our Caliphate, to which millions of Mussulmans, suffering under the tyranny of foreign dominations, are religiously and whole-heartedly devoted, and it was always these powers that started every misfortune that came upon us.

Therefore, in this mighty struggle which now we are undertaking, we once for all will put an end to the attacks made from one side against the Caliphate, and from the other against the existence of our country. The wounds inflicted, with the help of the Almighty, by my fleet in the Black Sea, and by my army in the Dardanelles, in Akabah, and on the Caucasian frontiers against our enemies, have strengthened in us the conviction that our sacred struggle for a right cause will triumph. The fact, moreover, that today the countries and armies of our enemies are being crushed under the heels of our allies is a good sign, making our conviction as regards final success still stronger.

My heroes! My soldiers!

In this sacred war and struggle, which we began against the enemies who have undermined our religion and our holy fatherland, never for a single moment cease from strenuous effort and from self-abnegation. Throw yourselves against the enemy as lions, bearing in mind that the very existence of our empire, and of 300,000,000 Moslems whom I have summoned by sacred Fetva to a supreme struggle, depend on your victory. The hearty wishes and prayers of 300,000,000 innocent and tortured faithful, whose faces are turned in ecstasy and devotion to the Lord of the universe in the mosques and the shrine of the Kaabah, [in Mecca] are with you.

My children! My soldiers!

. . . Right and loyalty are on our side, and hatred and tyranny on the side of our enemies, and therefore there is no doubt that the Divine help and assistance of the just God and the moral support of our glorious Prophet will be on our side to encourage us. I feel convinced that from this struggle we shall emerge as an empire that has made good the losses of the past and is once more glorious and powerful. . . . Let those of you who are to die a martyr's death be messengers of victory to those who have gone before us, and let the victory be sacred and the sword be sharp of those of you who are to remain in life.

Mehmed-Reshad

Wartime Conditions

In addition to horrendous conditions in the fronts in Anatolia and the Caucasus, western Syria, Mt. Lebanon, and Palestine suffered severe famine and disease during the war caused by several factors. Britain and France maintained a blockade of the coastline to prevent supplies from being sent to Turkish troops. This meant that Ottoman forces often commandeered what local food was available, which was barely enough to sustain the soldiers. Ahmet Emin, a Turkish journalist close to military officers such as Mustafa Kemal, the future leader of independent Turkey, was invited to write an account of the Turkish experience in World War I by the Carnegie Endowment in New York.

The [Ottoman] army, which was expected to show the highest degree of endurance, was badly clothed and badly fed. There were instances where soldiers, equipped for a hot climate, were suddenly sent to the Caucasus front in winter time. As only a one-third ration could be issued, the death rate due to exposure, hunger and resulting disease was great.

On the Syrian front soldiers had often not only to live on half rations, but they were given the same flour soup for months and months and at last became incapable of touching a spoonful of it. Various food supplied . . . bought for the army were consumed be-

Liman von Sanders (1853–1929) commanded German troops on the Ottoman Front in the Caucasus. This 1916 report is from that campaign.
"Great losses are caused by lack of subsistence and lack of warm clothing [in winter conditions]. Many Turkish soldiers are dressed in thin summer garments, have no overcoats or boots. Their feet are mostly wrapped in rags from which the toes protrude. No wonder that under such conditions whole detachments were found in caves dead from hunger and cold after blizzards and other heavy weather."

hind the front and never reached the fighting units. On the eve of the third battle of Gaza . . . The Turkish soldiers . . . had not enough bread to maintain their strength. They received almost no meat, no butter, no sugar, no vegetables, no fruit. . . . they were wretchedly clothed. They had no boots at all, or what they had were so bad that they meant injury to the foot. . . . and men so placed could not but see that their German comrades on the same front were well fed and enjoyed every sort of comfort and amusement. With the exception of the Dardanelles campaign, such conditions were the ordinary thing. . . . Owing to the blockade, medical supplies and instruments were lacking. During the latter period of the war, serious surgical operations had to be undertaken without anesthetics.

Only the wealthy could afford food, which was scarce owing in part to grain hoarding by rich merchants in eastern Syria. With the Arab revolt against the Ottomans, led by Emir Feisal (1883–1933) from 1916 on, grain traders preferred selling to those forces since they were paid in gold supplied by the British High Command in Cairo. The Turkish female writer, activist, and nationalist Halide Edib Adivar (1884–1964) recalls her experiences working with the Islamic version of the Red Cross, the Red Crescent, when she was sent by the Ottoman government on a mission to Syria.

I was getting glimpses of the many-sided lives and peoples of Syria. There were the rich Lebanon and Beirut Christian nobility, an Arab imitation of the Parisian world; the dresses, the manners, the general bearing were of French importation. Strange to say, they still had something of their own which they tried hard to hide; there were the Moslem and Druze nobility, who fiercely, proudly kept their own way and personality. There was a great deal of profiteering and war wealth, all made on wheat. Among the Syrian masses, famine in its cruelest form was fast approaching. In the rich streets of Beirut, men in rags and with famished faces, solitary waifs and strays of both sexes, wandered; lonely children, with wavering, stick-like legs. Faces wrinkled like centenarians, eyes sunken with bitter and unconscious irony, hair thinned or entirely gone, moved along. There is an endless vista of road in my mind's eye where these nameless little figures move on and on. There is a vision of rich marble steps before stately mansions, where on a skeleton baby arm one of those miserable little heads rests in unutterable abandon and longing to die. The first time I heard the cry it echoed and echoed through my brain and heart. . . . I was driving home through the streets of Beirut . . . when I heard it: '*Dju'an*' [I'm hungry [i.e. starving] . . . I have heard that '*Dju'an*' so often since. . . .

The schools finally got up an exhibition of Syrian artists, most of whom I had come to know. . . . There was a small group of statuary by an amateur which was instinct with the utmost significance of Syria's suffering. . . . The group represented an Arab mother feeding a baby at her emaciated breasts, with two small children, one lying dead at her feet and the other agonizing, clutching her torn skirts, while the woman, with her fallen unkempt hair and dying eyes, was the very emblem of the starving women of Syria.

In Syria, Palestine, and Lebanon, civilian and military casualties exceeded rates in Europe. Out of a pre-1914 population of about 3.5 million inhabitants, as many as 18 percent perished during the war, or one out of six people. Desperate for manpower to field armies, the Ottomans forcibly conscripted men from the region between the ages of 17 and 55. With the men absent from towns and villages, no protection, no work, and often barely enough food, some young women sought spouses among the British troops or solicited as this British soldier's 1917 memoir shows. The grandmother of one of the families providing hospitality to the author of this memoir, H. P. Bonser, had previously worked as a family servant in New York and had returned to Lebanon speaking American English. She was part of those waves of mainly Christian Lebanese emigration from the region from the 1890s and had obviously returned from the United States to rejoin her family.

My first experience of war was at the Second Battle of Gaza [1917] when we were in reserve. It was a nightmare of interminable marching, thirst, and tiredness. . . . September of this year found us on the borders of Palestine. . . . We trekked northwards, rigging up signal offices wherever we stopped, until we settled down in the Wady Surar as a transmitting office to the divisions. It was a mud and misery winter. Supply lorries were stuck fast in the mud, and supplies often scarce. Our Christmas Day ration was two biscuits, a tin of bully to four [men], and a tin of jam to seventeen men. We were sleeping in wet clothes, and even sleep was scarce, as pressure of work in the signal office necessitated us working all through every alternate night. . . . By Christmas we were in Sidon [now in Lebanon] maintaining lines of communication. Hugh and I had many a day's ramble in the hills around Sidon, often striking villages where British troops had not been seen before. At one such they prepared a wonderful feast at which Hugh and I were guests of honour. The "grandma" of another had been in domestic service in New York, and greeted us in strident American. After entertaining us to figs preserved in aniseed, she produced two attractive Syrian girls. "These are my nieces," she explained. "They are good gals."

"You're married," she added, to me. Then turning to Hugh, she shot out: "You're not. I want my nieces to marry Englishmen. Which one will you have?" These were Christian villages, and I think the hand of the Turk had been heavy. There came orders to proceed to Beirut. Hugh and I, doing rations and orderly room work, got a comfortable room as combined office and quarters. We'd hardly settled in when a knock came at the door and two young women who spoke pleasant English made the proposition that they share room and rations with us. We declined and they apologized. Afterwards they often called to see if there was any mending they could do for us— "Won't Mamma be pleased!" was their usual exclamation if we gave them a tin of bully or jam for darning our socks. They never referred to their original proposal again, though once, when I asked the elder girl why they chose that livelihood, she answered, "It was this or starve, Mr. Harri." A chaste friendliness with a prostitute seems a contradiction, yet I felt a tribute in their tears when we came away. We were out of touch with our ordinary conventions, and I think fellows hammered out standards for themselves.

Journalism, Truth, and War Reporting

British war correspondent Ellis Ashmead-Bartlett (1881–1931) filed this report to his newspaper depicting operations in the Gallipoli Peninsula where Anglo-French forces engaged the Turks for most of 1915, were defeated, and ultimately forced to withdraw. This published report on the ultimately unsuccessful Battle of Sari Bair exudes a sense of exhilaration despite the fact that the Allied attacks failed. Compare this account to Ashmead Bartlett's private letter to the British prime minister that follows.

The great battle, the greatest fought on the Gallipoli Peninsula, closed on the evening of August 10th. . . . I have visited the ground over which the Anzac [Australian/New Zealand] corps advanced in its desperate efforts, extending over four consecutive days, to reach the crest of Sari Bair, commanding the ridge overlooking the Dardanelles. The New Zealand infantry, the Gurkhas, and some other battalions almost reached the objective, but were unable, through no fault of their own, to hold their position. . . . The Turks . . . counter-attacked in great force, and the gallant men [in the British army] . . . were driven from the crest to the lower spurs beneath. It was a bitter disappointment . . . but there was no alternative.

The Anzac corps fought like lions and accomplished a feat of arms in climbing these heights almost without a parallel. All through, however, they were handicapped by the failure of the corps to make good its positions on the Anafarta hills, further north, and thus check the enemy's shell fire.

When all the details of these complicated arrangements are collected and sifted, they will form one of the most fascinating pages of the history of the whole war. . . . if one point stands out . . . it is the marvelous hardihood, tenacity, and reckless courage shown by the Australians and New Zealanders. . . . In this extraordinary struggle . . . both sides fought with utter disregard of life. The wounded and dead choked the trenches almost to the top, but the survivors carried on the fight over heaps of bodies . . . The capture of Lone Pine, the most desperate hand-to-hand fight that has taken place on the peninsula . . . was but a diversion . . . to the main movement northward, which began the same evening under cover of darkness. For the final assault on Sari Bair. . . . The advance on the morning of the 9th was preceded by a heavy bombardment by the naval and land guns. The advance of No. 3 column was delayed by the broken nature of the ground and the enemy's resistance.

. . . Meantime throughout the day and night the New Zealanders succeeded in maintaining their hold on Sari Bair, although the men were thoroughly exhausted. During the night of the 9th the exhausted New Zealanders were relieved by two other regiments. At dawn the Tenth Regiment of the Turks, which had been strongly reinforced, made a desperate assault on our lines. . . . They hurled themselves, quite regardless of their lives, on the two regiments which, after desperate resistance, were driven from their position by artillery fire and sheer weight of numbers further down the slopes of Sari Bair. Following up their success, the Turks charged right over the crest and endeavoured to gain the great gully south of Rhododendron Ridge, evidently with the intention of forcing their way between our lines and the Anzac position. But . . . This great charge . . . was plainly visible to our warships and all our batteries on land . . . and they were swept away by hundreds in a terrific storm of high explosive shrapnel, and common shells from the ships' guns and our howitzers and field pieces. As the shells from the ships exploded, huge chunks of soil were thrown into the air, amid which you saw human bodies hurled aloft and then chucked to earth or thrown bodily into deep ravines. . . . Hardly a Turk got back to the hill. . . . In a few minutes the entire division had been broken up and the survivors scattered everywhere. If they succeeded in driving us from the crest of Sari Bair, the Turks paid a terrible price for their success. Thus closed, amid these bloodstained hills, the most ferocious and sustained "soldiers' battle" since Inkerman [i.e., the Anglo-French defeat of Russian forces, Crimean War, November 1854].

In a private letter to British Prime Minister Herbert Asquith (1852–1928), Ashmead-Bartlett wrote a highly negative account of the very same battle he had praised in his newspaper report, reserving his harshest criticism for the Allied leadership. Aware that the contents of his letter could never pass military censorship, Ashmead-Bartlett had arranged for a fellow journalist, Keith Murdoch (1885–1952), [father of media executive Rupert Murdoch], to take it to England for personal delivery to the prime minister. Murdoch was intercepted at Marseilles and the letter taken from him, leading Murdoch to write his own letter based on Ashmead-Bartlett's. The criticism of the high command, especially Commander-in-Chief Sir Ian Hamilton (1853–1957), may have been a factor in Hamilton's removal from command and in the eventual evacuation of the Dardanelles. The contradictions between Ashmead-Bartlett's published newspaper article and private letter remind us of the well-founded saying that "the first casualty of war is the truth." The Gallipoli campaign was eventually abandoned at the close of 1915.

September 8th 1915

Dear Mr Asquith

I hope you will excuse the liberty I am taking in writing to you but I have the chance of sending this letter through by hand and I consider it absolutely necessary that you should know the true state of affairs out here. Our last great effort to achieve some definite success against the Turks was [a] . . . most ghastly and costly fiasco. . . . All efforts now to make out that it only just failed owing to the failure of the 9th Corps to seize the Anafarta Hills bear no relation to the real truth. The operations did for a time make headway in an absolutely impossible country more than any general had a right to expect owing to the superlative gallantry of the Colonial Troops and the self-sacrificing manner in which they threw away their lives against positions which should never have been attacked. . . . The main attack with the best troops was delivered against the side of the Turkish position which is a series of impossible mountains and valleys covered with dense scrub. The Staff seem to have carefully searched for the most difficult points and then threw away thousands of lives in trying to take them by frontal attacks. . . . The failure of the 9th Corps was due not so much to the employment of new and untried troops as to bad staff work. The generals had but a vague idea of the nature of the ground in their front and no adequate steps were taken to keep the troops supplied with water. In consequence many of these unfortunate volunteers went three days in very hot weather on one bottle of water and were yet expected to advance carrying heavy loads and to storm strong positions.

The Turks having been given ample time to bring up strong reinforcements to Anafarta, where they entrenched themselves in up to their necks, were again assaulted in a direct frontal attack on August 21st. The movement never had the slightest chance of succeeding and led to another bloody fiasco. . . . As the result of all this fighting our casualties since August 6th now total nearly fifty thousand killed, wounded, and missing. The army is in fact in a deplorable condition. Its morale as a fighting force has suffered greatly and the officers and men are thoroughly dispirited. The muddles and mismanagement beat anything that has ever occurred in our Military History. The fundamental evil at the present moment is the absolute lack of confidence in all ranks in the Headquarters staff. The confidence of the army will never be restored until a really strong man is placed at its head. It would amaze you to hear the talk that goes on amongst the Junior commanders of Divisions and Brigades. Except for the fact that the traditions of discipline still hold the force together you would imagine that the units were in an open state of mutiny against Headquarters.

The Commander in Chief and his Staff are openly spoken of, and in fact only mentioned at all, with derision. One hates to write of such things but in the interests of the country at the present crisis I feel they ought to be made known to you. . . . At the present time the army is incapable of a further offensive. The splendid Colonial Corps has been almost wiped out . . . and the new formations have lost their bravest and best officers and men. Neither do I think, even with enormous reinforcements, that any fresh offensive from our present positions has the smallest chance of success. . . . We do not hold a single commanding position on the Peninsula and . . . we are everywhere commanded by the enemy's guns. . . . Our troops will have to face the greatest hardships from cold wet trenches and constant artillery fire. I believe that at the present time the sick rate for the army is roughly 1000 per day. . . .

I have only dealt with our own troubles and difficulties. The enemy of course has his. But to maintain as I saw stated in an official report that his losses in the recent fighting were far heavier than ours is a childish falsehood which deceives no one out here. He was acting almost the whole time on the defensive and probably lost about one third of our grand total. You may think I am too pessimistic but my views are shared by the large majority of the army. The confidence of the troops can only be restored by an immediate change in the supreme command. . . . The cost of this campaign in the east must be out of all proportion to the results we are likely to obtain now, in time to have a decisive effect on the general theatre of war. Our great asset against the Germans was always considered to be our superior financial strength. In Gallipoli we are dissipating a large portion of our fortune and have not yet gained a single acre of ground of any strategical value. . . . I am of course breaking the censorship regulations by sending this letter through but I have not the slightest hesitation in doing so as I feel it is absolutely essential for you to know the truth. I have been requested over and over again by officers of all ranks to go home and personally disclose the truth but it is difficult for me to leave until the beginning of October.

Hoping you will therefore excuse the liberty I have taken.

Believe me

Yours very truly

E. Ashmead-Bartlett
The Rt. Hon. H. H. Asquith
10 Downing Street

The Armenian Question

Long a pawn in Ottoman-Russian relations, Armenians had suffered previous Turkish attacks and casualties, in part out of Turkish fears that Armenians backed a Russian takeover of eastern Turkey. Some Armenians had joined the Russian forces that had invaded eastern Turkey in late 1914, leading to charges that Armenians in general were disloyal to the Ottomans. These were the "provocations" to which Dr. Martin Niepage [1886–1953], then an instructor at a German technical school in Aleppo] refers to in his "The Horrors of Aleppo," a report he sent to his superiors in Istanbul in 1916. Beginning in mid-1915, Ottoman troops helped by local Kurds began attacking the Armenian population residing in areas close to the Russian frontier. Thousands were killed near their homes, hundreds of thousands more died from starvation in their forced flight out of the region. Debate still rages as to how many Armenians actually died. Some estimates reach a million, and the matter has become a sensitive issue in Turkey whose government consistently denies that

the killings and evacuations were part of official policy at the time. As Niepage's report suggests, those who reached Syria were not guaranteed survival, as Ottoman administrators there restricted the assistance that could be given to them.

When I returned to Aleppo in September, 1915, from a three months' holiday at Beirut, I heard with horror that a new phase of Armenian massacres had begun which were far more terrible than the earlier massacres under Abdul-Hamid, and which aimed at exterminating, root and branch, the intelligent, industrious, and progressive Armenian nation, and at transferring its property to Turkish hands.

Such monstrous news left me at first incredulous. I was told that, in various quarters of Aleppo, there were lying masses of half-starved people, the survivors of so-called "deportation convoys." In order, I was told, to cover the extermination of the Armenian nation with a political cloak, military reasons were being put forward, which were said to make it necessary to drive the Armenians out of their native seats, which had been theirs for 2,500 years, and to deport them to the Arabian deserts. I was also told that individual Armenians had lent themselves to acts of espionage.

After I had . . . made inquiries on all sides, I came to the conclusion that all these accusations against the Armenians were, in fact, based on trifling provocations, which were taken as an excuse for slaughtering 10,000 innocents for one guilty person, for the most savage outrages against women and children, and for a campaign of starvation against the exiles which was intended to exterminate the whole nation. To test . . . my information, I visited all the places in the city where there were Armenians left behind by the convoys. In dilapidated caravansaries (*khans*) I found quantities of dead, many corpses being half-decomposed, and others, still living, among them, who were soon to breathe their last. In other yards I found quantities of sick and starving people whom no one was looking after. In the neighbourhood of the German Technical School, at which I am employed as a higher grade teacher, there were four such khans, with seven or eight hundred exiles dying of starvation. . . . I [then] thought it my duty to compose the following report [on behalf of teachers in the German Technical School at Aleppo]:

"We feel it our duty to draw attention to the fact that our educational work will forfeit its moral basis and the esteem of the natives, if the German Government is not in a position to put a stop to the brutality with which the wives and children of slaughtered Armenians are being treated here.

Out of convoys which, when they left their homes on the Armenian plateau, numbered from two to three thousand men, women and children, only two or three hundred survivors arrive here in the south. The men are slaughtered on the way; the women and girls, with the exception of the old, the ugly and those who are still children, have been abused by Turkish soldiers and officers and then carried away to Turkish and Kurdish villages, where they have to accept Islam.

They try to destroy the remnant of the convoys by hunger and thirst. Even when they are fording rivers, they do not allow those dying of thirst to drink. All the nourishment they receive is a daily ration of a little meal sprinkled over their hands, which they lick off greedily, and its only effect is to protract their starvation. . . .

And what becomes of these poor people who have been driven in thousands through Aleppo and the neighbourhood into the deserts, reduced almost entirely, by this time, to women and children? They are driven on and on from one place to another. The thousands shrink to hundreds and the hundreds to tiny remnants, and even these remnants are driven on till the last is dead. Then at last they have reached the goal of their wandering, the 'New Homes assigned to the Armenians,' as the newspapers phrase it. . . .

These Armenian orphans whose families had been driven out of Anatolia became wards of the Committee for Near East Relief in Palestine during 1915–1916. The refugee children are learning a trade—carpentry—in courtyard of a chapel in Nazareth so that they could earn some income.

LEST THEY PERISH

CAMPAIGN for $30,000,000

AMERICAN COMMITTEE
FOR RELIEF IN THE NEAR EAST
ARMENIA - GREECE - SYRIA - PERSIA
ONE MADISON AVE., NEW YORK.   CLEVELAND H. DODGE, TREASURER

With the outbreak of war in the Middle East and Europe, the American Committee for Relief in the Near East sought to collect money to aid civilian populations devastated either by hostilities or by disastrous economic conditions in Greater Syria, Armenia, Greece, and Persia. The iconic image in this 1917 poster for the Lest They Perish campaign shows a village woman, standing amidst the ruins of warfare, with her baby strapped to her back.

What we saw with our own eyes here in Aleppo was really only the last scene in the great tragedy of the extermination of the Armenians. It was only a minute fraction of the horrible drama that was being played out simultaneously in all the other provinces of Turkey. Many more appalling things were reported by the engineers of the Baghdad Railway, when they came back from their work on the section under construction, or by German travellers who met the convoys of exiles on their journeys. Many of these gentlemen had seen such appalling sights that they could eat nothing for days. . . .

The object of the deportations is the extermination of the whole Armenian nation. . . . A Swiss engineer was to have been brought before a court-martial because he had distributed bread in Anatolia to the starving Armenian women and children in a convoy of exiles. The Government has not hesitated even to deport Armenian pupils and teachers from the German schools at Adana and Aleppo, and Armenian children from the German orphanages, without regard to all the efforts of the Consuls and the heads of the institutions involved. The Government also rejected the American Government's offer to take the exiles to America on American ships and at America's expense. . . .

It is utterly erroneous to think that the Turkish Government will refrain of its own accord even from the destruction of the women and children, unless the strongest pressure is exercised by the German Government. Only just before I left Aleppo, in May, 1916, the crowds of exiles encamped at Ras-el-din on the Baghdad

Railway, estimated at 20,000 women and children, were slaughtered to the last one."

Promises, Promises: Britain, France, and the Arab Movement

Great Britain's loss of prestige during the disastrous Gallipoli campaign furthered British interest in an alliance with the Emir of Mecca, Sharif Hussein Ibn Ali (1854–1931). The office of Emir of Mecca was a prestigious position in the Islamic world because the holder acted as guardian of the Holy Places in Mecca, the birthplace of the Prophet Muhammad and of Islam, and Medina, the sites of the annual pilgrimage. Appointed Emir by Sultan Abdul Hamid II in 1908, Sharif Hussein was eager to secure the hereditary rule of his family in Mecca and Medina, independent of Ottoman control, and had contacted British officials in Egypt before the war seeking their backing.

Following British overtures, Sharif Hussein approached the British High Commissioner in Egypt, Sir Henry McMahon (1862–1949) in a series of letters known as the Hussein-McMahon Correspondence. In them he inquired about Britain's willingness to recognize an independent Arab kingdom in exchange for Hussein's proclamation of an Arab revolt against his Ottoman overlords. Hussein's territorial demands, drawn up by Syrian nationalists in Damascus, included Palestine, Syria, and Iraq. The Sharif Hussein's first note to Sir Henry McMahon illustrates Hussein's key demands regarding territory.

Mecca, Ramadan 2, 1333. [July 14, 1915.]

Whereas the entire Arab nation without exception is determined to assert its right to live, gain its freedom and administer its own affairs in name and in fact;

And whereas the Arabs believe it to be in Great Britain's interest to lend them assistance and support in the fulfillment of their steadfast and legitimate aims to the exclusion of all other aims;

And whereas it is similarly to the advantage of the Arabs, in view of their geographical position and their economic interests, and in view of the well-known attitude of the Government of Great Britain, to prefer British assistance to any other;

For these reasons, the Arab nation has decided to approach the Government of Great Britain with a request for the approval, through one of their representatives if they think fit, of the following basic provisions: . . .

1. Great Britain recognises the independence of the Arab countries which are bounded: on the north, by the line Mersin-Adana

In 1868, an Ottoman society parallel to the Red Cross had been formed, which registered with the Red Cross. After the disastrous 1876–1878 Russian-Ottoman War, the society became fully operational, using a "red crescent" as its emblem. This image, probably from Ottoman Jerusalem, shows a clinic run by the Turkish Red Crescent and its physicians, including a female nurse seated on the left.

to parallel 37° N. and thence along the line Birejik-Urfa-Mardin-Midiat-Jazirat (ibn 'Umar)—Amadia to the Persian frontier; on the east, by the Persian frontier down to the Persian Gulf; on the south, by the Indian Ocean (with the exclusion of Aden whose status will remain as at present); on the west, by the Red Sea and the Mediterranean Sea back to Mersin.

2. Great Britain will agree to the proclamation of an Arab Caliphate for Islam.

3. The Sharifian Arab Government undertakes, other things being equal, to grant Great Britain preference in all economic enterprises in the Arab countries. . . .

5. Great Britain agrees to the abolition of Capitulations in the Arab countries, and undertakes to assist the Sharifian Government in summoning an international congress to decree their abolition. . . .

McMahon's careful replies, especially in his October 24, 1915, letter, appeared to meet Hussein's requests except as specified. But McMahon's reference to "the interests of her ally France" meant that Britain left open the possibility of denying Arab independence in Syria; Palestine was never mentioned specifically in the exchanges but was included within the boundaries outlined in Hussein's first letter. Based on British promises of an independent Arab state with vaguely defined borders, Hussein proclaimed a revolt against the Ottoman Empire on June 10, 1916, and issued his own call to jihad. Hussein's tribal forces, commanded by his son, Feisal, fought in concert with British operations during the drive that led to the capture of Damascus in October 1918. As Feisal strove to set up an Arab government in Damascus, contradictions appeared between earlier British pledges to Sharif Hussein, buttressed by later pledges promising Arab independence, and subsequent agreements the British government had made to the French in 1916 [Sykes-Picot Agreement] and to the Zionists in 1917 [Balfour Declaration].

Cairo, August 30, 1915.

We have the honour to tender the gratitude due to you for the sentiments of sincere friendship for England which you display. . . . In earnest of this, we hereby confirm to you the declaration of Lord Kitchener as communicated to you through ʻAli Efendi, in which was manifested our desire for the independence of the Arab countries and their inhabitants, and our readiness to approve an Arab caliphate upon its proclamation.

We now declare once more that the Government of Great Britain would welcome the reversion of the caliphate to a true Arab born of the blessed stock of the Prophet [as was Sharif Hussein].

As for the question of frontiers and boundaries, negotiations would appear to be premature and a waste of time on details at this stage, with the War in progress and the Turks in effective occupation of the greater part of those regions. All the more so as a party of Arabs inhabiting those very regions have, to our amazement and sorrow, overlooked and neglected this valuable and incomparable opportunity; and, instead of coming to our aid, have lent their assistance to the Germans and the Turks; to that new despoiler, the German, and to that tyrannical oppressor, the Turk.

Here is Sharif Hussein's reply to McMahon.

Mecca, September 9, 1915

. . . . your statements in regard to the question of frontiers and boundaries—namely that to discuss them at this stage were unprofitable and could only result in a waste of time since those regions are still occupied by their sovereign governments . . . reflect . . . reluctance or something akin to reluctance on your part.

The fact is that the proposed boundaries and frontiers represent not the suggestions of one individual but . . . the demands of our people who believe that these frontiers form the minimum necessary to the establishment of the new order for which they are striving. This they are determined to obtain; and they have decided to discuss the matter . . . with that Power in whom they place their greatest confidence and reliance, . . . the pivot of justice, Great Britains. . . .

In a letter to British Foreign Secretary Sir Edward Grey (1862–1933), dated October 26, 1915, Sir Henry McMahon refers to his promises to Sharif Hussein in his October 24th letter as being couched in terms enabling Britain to award the same lands to France after the war.

The composition of a reply [to Sharif Hussein] which would be acceptable to the Arab Party and which at the same time would leave as free a hand as possible to HMG [His Majesty's Government] has been a difficult task.... While recognizing the towns of Damascus, Homs, Hama and Aleppo as being within the circle of Arab countries, I have endeavoured to provide for possible French pretensions to those places by a general modification to the effect that HMG can only give assurances in regard to those territories "in which she can act without detriment to the interests of her ally, France"....

McMahon then replied to Sharif Hussein.

Cairo, October 24, 1915

.... Having realized from your last note that you considered the question [of frontiers and boundaries] important, vital and urgent, I hastened to communicate to the Government of Great Britain the purport of your note. It gives me the greatest pleasure to convey to you, on their behalf, the following declarations....

The districts of Mersin and Alexandretta, and portions of Syria lying to the west of the districts of Damascus, Homs, Hama and Aleppo cannot be said to be purely Arab, and must on that account be excepted from the proposed delimitation....

As for the regions lying within the proposed frontiers, in which Great Britain is free to act without detriment to the interests of her ally France, I am authorised to give you the following pledges on behalf of Great Britain....

1. That, subject to the modifications stated above, Great Britain is prepared to recognize and uphold the independence of the Arabs in all the regions lying within the frontiers proposed by the Sharif of Mecca....

2. That, when circumstances permit, Great Britain will help the Arabs with her advice and will assist them in the establishment of governments to suit those diverse regions;

5. That, as regards the two vilayets of Baghdad and of Basra, the Arabs recognise that the fact of Great Britain's established position and interests there will call for special administrative arrangements to protect these regions from foreign aggression, to promote the welfare of their inhabitants, and to safeguard our mutual economic interests....

British-French negotiations to divide up the Arab lands promised to Sharif Hussein began in December 1915, before the Hussein-McMahon correspondence had ended. Ultimately, the Sykes-Picot Agreement, concluded in London on May 16, 1916, included Russia with respect to Ottoman territory (only those clauses dealing with Britain and France are provided here). Clause 1 refers to supposedly independent Arab states, A and B, that would be under the supervision of either France or Britain, as opposed to the Blue and Red areas, Clause 2, where Britain and France would have absolute authority. Palestine was to be internationalized, but Britain gained control over the port cities of Haifa and Acre to link them by railway to Baghdad to run oil pipelines from Iraq through French-dominated Syria to these cities where oil refineries were to be built (Clauses 4, 5, and 7). Per Clause 12, Britain and France would control the importation of arms into the supposedly independent Arab areas, A and B. Neither the Sharif Hussein nor

his supporters were informed of this agreement, which contradicted the promises for Syrian independence that McMahon had made in his letter of October 24, 1915, to Hussein.

Text of the Agreement Concluded in London on May 16, 1916

A.

1. France and Great Britain are prepared to recognise and uphold an independent Arab State or a Confederation of Arab States in the areas shown as (A) and (B) on the annexed map, under the suzerainty of an Arab Chief. France in area (A) and Great Britain in area (B) shall have a right of priority in enterprises and local loans. France in area (A) and Great Britain in area (B) shall alone supply foreign advisors or officials on the request of the Arab State or the Confederation of Arab States.

2. France in the Blue area and Great Britain in the Red Area shall be at liberty to establish such direct or indirect administration or control as they may desire or as they may deem fit to establish after agreement with the Arab State or Confederation of Arab States.

3. In the Brown area [Palestine] there shall be established an international administration of which the form will be decided upon after consultation with Russia, and after subsequent agreement with the other Allies and the representatives of the Sharif of Mecca.

4. There shall be accorded to Great Britain

(a) The ports of Haifa and Acre [in Palestine]

(b) Guarantee of a specific supply of water from the Tigris and the Euphrates in area (A) for area (B). . . .

7. Great Britain shall have the right to build, administer and be the sole owner of the railway connecting Haifa with area (B) [Iraq]. She shall have, in addition, the right in perpetuity and at all times of carrying troops on that line. It is understood by both Governments that this railway is intended to facilitate communication between Baghdad and Haifa, ...

12. It is understood, moreover, that measures for controlling the importation of arms into the Arab territory will be considered by the two Governments.

Promises to Keep: Britain, Palestine, and the Zionist Movement

The Zionist intent was to create a Jewish national home in all of Palestine, leading to a Jewish state. British cabinet debates led to the Balfour Declaration, a letter of November 2, 1917, from British Foreign Secretary Arthur James Balfour (1848–1930), to Lord Lionel Walter Rothschild (1868–1937), a leader of the British Jewish community, for transmission to the Zionist Federation. The declaration modified initial Zionist demands by suggesting only part of Palestine might become the Jewish national home, but it restricted the Arab (non-Jewish) population to having civil and religious rights, reserving political rights for Jews once they gained a majority in Palestine. Although Balfour interpreted the document to signify an eventual Jewish state, many British politicians and diplomats were uncertain as to the outcome. The British decision to promise a Jewish state was made partially out of sympathy for past Jewish persecution in Europe but also for wartime propaganda reasons and imperial concerns. The Zionists promised that once in Palestine, they would ally themselves with British interests on the east side of the Suez Canal against any future French threat from Syria.

Foreign Office, November 2nd, 1917

Dear Lord Rothschild,

I have much pleasure in conveying to you, on behalf of His Majesty's Government, the following declaration of sympathy with Jewish Zionist aspirations which has been submitted to, and approved by, the Cabinet.

His Majesty's Government view with favour the establishment in Palestine of a national home for the Jewish people, and will use their best endeavours to facilitate the achievement of this object, it being clearly understood that nothing shall be done which may prejudice the civil and religious rights of existing non-Jewish communities in Palestine, or the rights and political status enjoyed by Jews in any other country.

I should be grateful if you would bring this declaration to the knowledge of the Zionist Federation.

Yours sincerely

Arthur James Balfour

Initial Zionist Draft to British Foreign Office, July 1917

1. His Majesty's Government accepts the principle that Palestine should be reconstituted as the national home of the Jewish people.
2. His Majesty's Government will use their best endeavours to secure the achievement of this object and will discuss the necessary methods and means with the Zionist Organisation.

Postwar Settlements: The Great Powers and the Middle East

In this January 1918 speech to Congress, President Woodrow Wilson (1856–1924) outlined United States' war aims. Known as the "Fourteen Points," Wilson believed that they could form the basis for a just, lasting peace. Article XIV became the basis for the Covenant of the League of Nations. Alarmed by his criticism of colonialism (Article V), Prime Ministers David Lloyd George (Great Britain—1863–1945) and Georges Clemenceau (France)—1841–1929) sought to change Wilson's position at the Paris Peace Conference held after the war. France and Great Britain promoted the idea of "mandates," meaning that the territories taken as spoils of war from the losers, the Germans and the Ottomans, came with the obligation to prepare the inhabitants for future self-government. This would meet Wilson's wish, Article V, that the wishes of the inhabitants of regions be equal to those of the power controlling the country.

Gentlemen of the Congress . . .

It will be our wish and purpose that the processes of peace . . . shall be absolutely open and that they shall . . . permit henceforth no secret understandings of any kind. The day of conquest and aggrandizement is gone by; so is also the day of secret covenants entered into in the interest of particular governments. . . .

What we demand in this war, therefore, is nothing peculiar to ourselves. It is that the world be made fit and safe to live in; and particularly that it be made safe for every peace-loving nation which, like our own, wishes to live its own life, determine its own institutions, be assured of justice and fair dealing by the other peoples of the world as against force and selfish aggression. All the peoples of the world are in effect partners in this interest, and for our own part we see very clearly that unless justice be done to others it will not be done to us. The program of the world's peace, therefore, is our program; and that program, the only possible program, as we see it, is this:

"The Big Four, 1919." In January 1919, diplomatic representatives from dozens of nations, as well as from nationalist groups aspiring to nationhood, gathered in Paris to decide the future and fate of peoples in Europe and MENA as well as in former colonial possessions in Africa, Asia, and the Pacific. Paris functioned as a sort of center of world government. This image shows the leaders of the four "Great Powers." From right to left, President Woodrow Wilson of the United States, Prime Minister Georges Clemenceau of France, Italian Prime Minister Vittorio Orlando, and Prime Minister David Lloyd George of Great Britain. Wilson was the first American President to visit Europe while in office, and his "Fourteen Points," advocating self-determination, had won the hearts and minds of many people across the globe, especially in former Ottoman lands.

I. Open covenants of peace, openly arrived at, after which there shall be no private international understandings of any kind. . . .

V. A free, open-minded, and absolutely impartial adjustment of all colonial claims, based upon a strict observance of the principle that in determining all such questions of sovereignty the interests of the populations concerned must have equal weight with the equitable claims of the government whose title is to be determined. . . .

XII. The Turkish portions of the present Ottoman Empire should be assured a secure sovereignty, but the other nationalities which are now under Turkish rule should be assured an undoubted security of life and an absolutely unmolested opportunity of an autonomous development, and the Dardanelles should be permanently opened as a free passage to the ships and commerce of all nations under international guarantees. . . .

XIV. A general association of nations must be formed under specific covenants for the purpose of affording mutual guarantees of political independence and territorial integrity to great and small states alike. . . .

An evident principle runs through the whole program I have outlined. It is the principle of justice to all peoples and nationalities, and their right to live on equal terms of liberty and safety with one another, whether they be strong or weak.

Unless this principle be made its foundation, no part of the structure of international justice can stand. The people of the United States could act upon no other principle; and to the vindication of this principle they are ready to devote their lives, their honor, and everything that they possess. . . .

Although not ratified until January 1920, the Covenant of the League of Nations was written as part of the Versailles Peace Treaty in June 1919 and its text was publicized. Article 22 explained the idea of mandates, divided into three classes, of which the Arab lands of the Ottoman Empire were Class A, considered nearly ready for independence. The reference to "the wishes of the communities" in Clause 4 applied only to this mandate category, but it would be omitted from the Palestine Mandate. Although President Wilson signed the Covenant in June 1919, the United States Senate never ratified it, and the United States did not join the League of Nations because of Congressional opposition.

Preamble to Covenant:

In order to promote international co-operation and to achieve international peace and security by the acceptance of obligations not to resort to war, by the prescription of open, just and honourable relations between nations, by the firm establishment of the understandings of international law as the actual rule of conduct among Governments, and, by the maintenance of justice and a scrupulous respect for all treaty obligations in the dealings of organised peoples with one another.

Article 22

1. To those colonies and territories which as a consequence of the late war have ceased to be under the sovereignty of the States which formerly governed them and which are inhabited by peoples not yet able to stand by themselves under the strenuous conditions of the modern world, there should be applied the principle that the well-being and development of such peoples form a sacred trust of civilisation and that securities for the performance of this trust should be embodied in this Covenant.

2. The best method of giving practical effect to this principle is that the tutelage of such peoples should be entrusted to advanced nations who by reason of their resources, their experience or their geographical position can best undertake this responsibility, and who are willing to accept it, and that this tutelage should be exercised by them as Mandatories on behalf of the League.

3. The character of the mandate must differ according to the stage of the development of the people, the geographical situation of the territory, its economic conditions, and other similar circumstances.

4. Certain communities formerly belonging to the Turkish Empire have reached a stage of development where their existence as independent nations can be provisionally recognized subject to the rendering of administrative advice and assistance by a Mandatory until such time as they are able to stand alone. The wishes of these communities must be a principal consideration in the selection of the Mandatory.

5. Other peoples, especially those of Central Africa, are at such a stage that the Mandatory must be responsible for the administration of the territory under conditions which will guarantee freedom of conscience and religion, subject only to the maintenance of public order and morals, the prohibition of abuses such as the slave trade, the arms traffic, and the liquor traffic, and the prevention of the establishment of fortifications or military and naval bases and of military training of

the natives for other than police purposes and the defence of territory, and will also secure equal opportunities for the trade and commerce of other Members of the League.

6. There are territories, such as South-West Africa and certain of the South Pacific Islands which, owing to the sparseness of their population, or their small size, or their remoteness from the centres of civilisation, or their geographical contiguity to the territory of the Mandatory, and other circumstances, can be best administered under the laws of the Mandatory as integral portions of its territory, subject to the safeguards above mentioned in the interests of the indigenous population. . . .

8. The degree of authority, control, or administration to be exercised by the Mandatory shall, if not previously agreed upon by the Members of the League, be explicitly defined in each case by the Council.

9. A permanent Commission shall be constituted to receive and examine the annual reports of the Mandatories and to advise the Council on all matters relating to the observance of the mandates. . . .

I. Original Members of the League of Nations— Signatories of the Treaty of Peace:

United States of America, Belgium, Bolivia, Brazil, British Empire, Canada, Australia, South Africa, New Zealand, India, China, Cuba, Ecuador, France, Greece, Guatemala, Haiti, Hedjaz, Honduras, Italy, Japan, Liberia, Nicaragua, Panama, Peru, Poland, Portugal, Roumania, Serb-Croat-Slovene State, Siam, Czecho-Slovakia, Uruguay.

Protests and Rebellion

As a direct response to the League of Nations Covenant, on July 2, 1919, the General Syrian Congress issued its Resolutions of Damascus, at a time when Britain occupied Syria, in an attempt to undermine its commitment made to France under the Sykes-Picot Agreement of 1916. Emir Feisal, son of the Sharif Hussein of Mecca, headed the Damascus government. The resolutions' rejection of France as a mandatory mirrored Sharif Hussein's objection to any French role in the region as stated in the Hussein-McMahon correspondence. In the end, Great Britain abandoned Feisal in September 1919, leaving him to negotiate with French officials seeking to create a protectorate over Syria with Feisal ruling in name only. French forces invaded Syria from Lebanon in July 1920, ousting Feisal. Britain later orchestrated Feisal's installation as King of Iraq. The boundaries defined here included Palestine.

We, the undersigned, members of the General Syrian Congress assembled in Damascus on the 2nd of July 1919 and composed of delegates from the three zones, namely the southern, eastern and western, and furnished with credentials duly authorising us to represent the Moslem, Christian and Jewish inhabitants of our respective districts, have resolved to submit the following as defining the aspirations of the people who have chosen us to place them before the American Section of the Inter-Allied Commission. With the exception of the fifth clause, which was passed by a large majority, the Resolutions which follow were all adopted unanimously:

1. We desire full and absolute political independence for Syria within the following boundaries: on the north, the Taurus Range; on the south, a line running from Rafah [Gaza] to al-Jauf and following the Syria-Hejaz border below ''Aqaba; on the east, the boundary formed by the Euphrates and Khabur rivers and a line stretching from some distance east of Abu-Kamal to some distance east of al-Jauf; on the west, the Mediterranean Sea.

2. We desire the Government of Syria to be a constitutional monarchy based on principles of democratic and broadly decentralised rule which shall safeguard the rights of minorities, and we wish that the Amir Faisal who has striven so nobly for our liberation and enjoys our full confidence and trust be our King.

3. In view of the fact that the Arab inhabitants of Syria are not less fitted or gifted than were certain other nations (such as the Bulgarians, Serbs, Greeks and Rumanians) when granted independence, we protest against Article XXII of the Covenant of the League of Nations which relegates us to the standing of insufficiently developed races requiring the tutelage of a mandatory power.

4. . . . We rely on President Wilson's declarations that his object in entering the War was to put an end to acquisitive designs for imperialistic purposes. In our desire that our country should not be made a field for colonisation, and in the belief that the American nation is devoid of colonial ambitions and has no political designs on our country, we resolve to seek assistance in the technical and economic fields from the United States of America on the understanding that the duration of such assistance shall not exceed twenty years.

In a July 1919 interview with the head of the American Zionist movement, U.S. Supreme Court Justice Louis Brandeis (1856–1941), Arthur Balfour noted that Clause 4 of Article 22 of the League of Nations Covenant [Doc. 3.12] would not be enforced for all the Arab regions that became mandates, notably Palestine.

Palestine presented a unique situation. We are dealing not with the wishes of an existing community but are consciously seeking to re-constitute a new community and definitely building for a numerical majority in the future. . . .

· wished for a democraticly envisioned/organized const. monarchy w/ Faisal

→ " we don't need your intervention; our race is not subordinate to yours "

This Palestinian Arab protest in the spring of 1920 in Jerusalem was in response to publication of the Balfour Declaration, and heightened European Zionist immigration into Palestine with some of the immigrants calling for an immediate Jewish state. The banner in the far upper left contains the word for Palestine [Filastin].

5. In the event of the United States finding herself unable to accede to our request for assistance, we would seek it from Great Britain, provided always that it will not be allowed to impair the unity and absolute independence of our country and that its duration shall not exceed the period mentioned in the preceding clause.

6. We do not recognise to the French Government any right to any part of Syria, and we reject all proposals that France should give us assistance or exercise authority in any portion of the country.

7. We reject the claims of the Zionists for the establishment of a Jewish commonwealth in that part of southern Syria which is known as Palestine, and we are opposed to Jewish immigration into any part of the country. We do not acknowledge that they have a title, and we regard their claims as a grave menace to our national, political and economic life. Our Jewish fellow-citizens shall continue to enjoy the rights and to bear the responsibilities which are ours in common. . . .

   The lofty principles proclaimed by President Wilson encourage us to believe that the determining consideration in the settlement of our own future will be the real desires of our people; and that we may look to President Wilson and the liberal American nation, who are known for their sincere and generous sympathy with the aspirations of weak nations, for help in the fulfillment of our hopes.

We also fully believe that the Peace Conference will recognise that we would not have risen against Turkish rule under which we enjoyed civic and political privileges, as well as rights of representation, had it not been that the Turks denied us our right to a national existence. We believe that the Peace Conference will meet our desires in full, if only to ensure that our political privileges may not be less, after the sacrifices of life which we have made in the cause of our freedom, than they were before the War. . . .

The British writer and diplomat Gertrude Bell (1856–1926) traveled widely in the Middle East before World War I, usually alone, although she was frequently accompanied by local guides. During the war, she worked for British intelligence and was often based in Cairo. She went to Iraq with British officials after the war and died in Baghdad in 1926. In her diary, Bell writes from Cairo in 1919 just after the British had abandoned Feisal in Damascus, leaving him to deal with the French occupation of Syria. Egyptian nationalists led by Saad Zaghlul (1859–1927) were demanding an end to the British occupation of their country. The Milner Commission was then in Egypt to investigate the causes of Egyptian riots against British rule and demands for independence. According to Bell, General Gilbert Clayton (1875–1929) admitted the logic of the Egyptian argument for greater self-rule while seeking to preserve British primacy in military matters and issues dealing with imperial lines of communications.

Monday Sep 29. [September 29, 1919]. Cairo. Temp. something over 80°. General Clayton came to lunch. He says that . . . it seems likely that the boycott [of the Milner Commission] will take place; the Egyptians refuse to have anything to do with it on the ground that they have sent their representatives to Paris and entrusted them with their views, which they will give to no others. General Clayton interviewed the Egyptian delegation before it left. The case they made was a very strong one. They said we had come here with the declared intention of remaining only till we had restored tranquility to the country. These declarations had been renewed repeatedly, but at longer and longer intervals, which as time went on it became clear that far from educating the natives of the country to govern themselves, we employed an ever growing number of Englishmen in the smaller administrative posts.

At the same time they would admit that we had been of great benefit to the country. At the outbreak of war the old link with Turkey was broken without any consultation with Egyptian feeling.

In an August 11, 1919, memo to Lord George Curzon (1859–1925) of the British Cabinet, British Foreign Secretary Arthur Balfour noted that none of the European leaders' promises and agreements with their MENA counterparts squared with any other and all violated the Covenant of the League of Nations drawn up after the war.

In short, so far as Palestine is concerned, there is no statement of fact which is not admittedly wrong and no declaration of policy which, at least in the letter, they [the Powers] have not always intended to violate.

Nevertheless, Egyptians, satisfied that the Allies were fighting for the smaller nationalities, had raised no protest. In our first proclamation we declared that we would take all the burden of the war upon ourselves, but Egypt found herself obliged to provision our armies and provide labour corps both inside and outside the country. The Egyptian government had spontaneously contributed £4000000 to war expenses. The trade of the country had suffered and prices had risen. Then came the enunciation of principles favourable to Egyptian independence, Wilson's 14 points, warmly adhered to by Lloyd George, and much talk of self determination. Acting on the principles to which we had given utterance, the Egyptians had asked to be allowed to send a deputation to London to expose their views. The request was refused on the ground that H.M.G. had not time to listen to the deputation, though it was supported by the High Commissioner. When it was persisted in, the deputies were imprisoned. It would be impossible to maintain that they were not representative of the country. Saad Zaghlul was Vice President of the [Council] Legislative Assembly which is chosen by an elected body, several others were members of the [Council] Assembly, and all had held high official posts of one kind or other.

Clayton said that while it was possible to pick holes in details of the argument, substantially it held good. In his view our object should now be to guard a. Imperial necessities in Egypt, b. international interests for which we had made ourselves responsible, and let all the rest go. We must maintain control of the Suez Canal, the Nile water (leaving the details of irrigation in native hands with a general British supervision)[,] the army and the police. He would leave the Egyptian ministers without British advisers, but give the High Commissioner a British adviser in each department with a general supervision over the department but without executive powers. No doubt the Egyptians would make grave mistakes and tie the departments into serious knots; but they have the right, as they claim, to a fair trial and to be given the opportunity of showing whether they cannot learn from their own mistakes. Concessions on these lines would, he thinks, win the majority of the country to our side; immediate prejudice apart, they do not wish for any outside assistance except from us and do not believe that they can stand without ours. If however we refuse to take very bold liberal measures we shall create in Egypt an Oriental Ireland. As far as his knowledge goes, he would advise us in Mesopotamia to begin as we intend to go on, so as to avoid the position which has arisen in Egypt. However poor our material, he would create independent Arab ministries with departmental advisers to the High Commissioner. The ministers could form a Council with an Arab President without portfolio who would partly be occupied by social duties and who might easily be developed into a permanent head of the state. Meantime the sovereignty of the state would be vested in the Council. As for justice, the capitulations are at present in suspense here. He does not wish for their renewal and hopes that some other means may be found to protect foreign rights. The revision of the Code has been interrupted by the war and is still far from completion. It is a very long and delicate business.

Egyptian Protests

In March 1919, the British sent the Egyptian nationalist leader, Saad Zaghlul into exile on the island of Malta. British officials had refused Egypt the right to send a delegation to the Paris Peace conference, as Britain intended at that time to maintain the protectorate it had established in 1914. News of Zaghlul's exile sparked a major revolt in the cities and the countryside. Mass demonstrations occurred, displaying an unprecedented unity among Muslims and Christians; Azhar ulema spoke in Coptic churches and Coptic bishops in mosques. Equally significant was the banding together of Cairene women, led by Hoda Shaarawi (1879–1947), a noted feminist and married to an ally of Zaghlul's. Hoda Shaarawi was Muslim; Regina Khayyat, who stopped her at one point to protect her, was a Coptic Christian. As Shaarawi recorded in her diary

We women held our first demonstration on 16 March to protest the repressive acts and intimidation practised by the British authority. In compliance with the orders of the authority we [had] announced our plans to demonstrate in advance but were refused permission. We . . . [later] read in *al-Muqattam* that the demonstration had received official sanction. We got on the telephone . . . , telling as many women as possible that we would proceed according to schedule the following morning. Had we been able to contact more than a limited number of women, virtually all the women of Cairo would have taken part in the demonstration.

On the morning of 16 March I sent placards to the house of the wife of Ahmad Bey Abu Usbaa, bearing slogans in Arabic and French painted in white on a background of black—the colour of mourning. Some of the slogans read 'Long Live the Supporters of Justice and Freedom', others said 'down with Oppressors and Tyrants', and 'Down with Occupation'.

We assembled . . . in Garden City Park where we left our carriages. [and] . . . set out in columns toward the legation of the United States and intended to proceed from there to the legations of Italy and France. However, when we reached Qasr al-Aini Square, I observed that the young women in front were deviating from the original plan and had begun to head in the direction of *Bait al-Umma* (The House of the Nation), as Saad Zaghlul's house was called. . . . According to our first plan we were to have ended our demonstration there. . . . No sooner were we approaching Zaghlul's house than British troops surrounded us. They blocked the street with machine guns, forcing us to stop along with the students who formed columns on both sides of us.

I was determined the demonstration should resume. When I advanced a British soldier stepped toward me pointing his gun, but I made my way past him. As one of the woman tried to pull me back, I shouted in a loud voice, "Let me die so Egypt shall have an Edith Cavell [an English nurse executed by the Germans during World War I who became an instant martyr]. Continuing [toward] the soldiers, I called on the women to follow. A pair of arms grabbed me and the voice of Regina Khayyat rang in my ears. 'This is madness. Do you want to risk the lives of the students? It will happen if the British raise a hand against you'. At the thought of our unarmed sons doing battle against the weaponry of the British troops, . . . I came to my senses and stopped still. We stood still for three hours while the sun blazed down on us. . . . We stood up to the heat and suffered no harm. The British also brought out Egyptian soldiers armed with sticks.

Shaarawi's account is juxtaposed with the condescending report, included in his memoirs, of the same demonstration by Sir Thomas Russell Pasha (1879–1954), the British commandant of the Cairo police.

At a given signal I closed the cordon and the ladies found their way opposed by a formidable line of Egyptian conscript police who had been previously warned not to use violence but to stand still . . . considerable license was given them by their officers to practise their ready peasant wit on the smart ladies who confronted them.

According to Hoda Shaarawi, when the soldiers taunted the women,

The women rebuked the soldiers. Some were moved to the point of tears. Eventually Russell Pasha arrived: "You have conducted your demonstration in defiance of orders . . . you are requested to return home. . . ." Permission had not been granted and the news it had was false.

Russell Pasha wrote his father about the incident, describing the demonstration in a sarcastic tone.

My next problem was a demonstration by the native ladies of Cairo. This rather frightened me as if it came to pass it was bound to collect a big crowd and my orders were to stop it. Stopping a procession means force and any force you use on women puts you in the wrong. Well, they assembled in motor cars etc., got out and started to walk in a procession. . . . I let them get a little way and then blocked them in with police supported by troops and there the poor dears had to remain for an hour and a half in the hot sun with nothing to sit on except the curb stone.

In mid-April 1919, Zaghlul was released from Malta and allowed to go to France to seek, unsuccessfully, Allied recognition of Egyptian independence. At this point, organized demonstrations turned into mass celebrations that became violent, triggered in part by the behavior of British troops and European residents of Cairo. Russell notes in this letter to his father on April 9, 1919, how European troops and residents sparked violence by shooting at Egyptian demonstrators.

For two days the city has been given over to frenzied demonstrations of joy. I thought there was just the chance of getting through without trouble, but yesterday evening things were precipitated by some British and Australian soldiers getting loose and starting a fight with some Egyptian Army soldiers. Two of my Mounted Troop men got killed by stray bullets . . . and there were two bad scrapes in the night caused by infuriated Australians getting loose and eight or ten Egyptians getting killed. Yesterday was bad but today is far worse. The roughs of the town are out. Tearing down telephone wires, barricading streets and pillaging. . . . [Russell wrote on April 13th] . . . We have gone through some very ticklish days. The rioting . . . [of] last Wednesday was got in hand by the troops after a number of people had been killed and wounded. Much of the trouble started by low-class Europeans losing their heads and firing at the demonstrators from their houses, with the result that the mob attacked and set fire to the houses, killing the inhabitants. Some ghastly murders were perpetrated on individual British and Indian soldiers. . . .

Egyptian songs and slogans often mocked British actions and policies, while demanding full independence. Reginald Wingate (1861–1953) was High Commissioner in Egypt in 1918 and early 1919. This song accurately recalls British use of Egyptian laborers to help move supplies across the Sinai and into Palestine/Lebanon, many of whom were forcibly conscripted. Thousands died, many freezing to death in the winter climate as they

W oe on us, Wingate who has carried off our corn [wheat], carried off cotton, carried off camels, carried off children, leaving only our lives: For love of Allah, now leave us alone."

—An Egyptian protest

had only the clothes they wore when taken into service in Egypt. In the middle of the Egyptian Revolt of 1919, a British Foreign Office Report dated April 1 stated that "this is the song which the little boys in the streets of Cairo and the ladies in the harems have been singing lately."

Laborers and soldiers were forced to travel, leaving their land.
They headed to Mount Lebanon and to the battlefields and
    the trenches!
And now they [the British] blame us? [for revolting]
Behold the calamities you have caused! Had it not been for
    our laborers, you
(And your rifles) would have been helpless in the desert sand!
Oh, you who are in authority, why didn't you go all alone to
    the Dardanelles?
Oh Maxwell [British commander in Egypt 1915] now you
    feel the hardships, so why don't you drink it up?
The Egyptian is resilient; and now he is willing and able and
    can do anything.
His achievements are worthy of praise, and he will do his all
    to gain a constitution.
We are the sons of Pharaohs, which no one can dispute.
When necessary, we can fight with clubs and sticks and even
    head-butts.
Long live Egypt! Long live Egypt!. Best of all nations; mother
    of the brave;
And this has been for all times.
A new life, oh glorious Egypt! We have gained our eternal
    purpose. There is no disputing that.
So leave us alone! . . .
Oh Wilson [U.S. President Woodrow], we have gathered
    together and to whom shall we address ourselves?
For we have no real newspapers—only those lunatics in the
    Muqattam.[pro-British] . . .
We want it to be known—total independence is our goal!
If only 'they' leave our nation! We would surpass Japan in
    civilization!
Return to your country. Pick up your belongings! What
    audacity and rudeness.
You are true calamity—do you have to stick to us like glue?

Until November 1917, Britain and Russia shared control over Iran [referred to here as Persia] according to the 1907 Anglo-Russian accord. Following the Bolshevik revolt of November 1917, the new Soviet gov-

ernment withdrew its forces. This gave Britain a free hand after the war to attempt to secure a treaty with the Shah that would guarantee its primary role in Iranian affairs, evading parliamentary approval. The Iranian parliament eventually reviewed the treaty and refused to ratify it, but the turmoil surrounding its announcement contributed to the reassertion of parliamentary rights and the ultimate overthrow of the Qajar dynasty in 1925. The documents following provide the treaty and American diplomatic evaluation of the Iranian public's views of its significance.

741.91/81: Telegram

The Minister in Persia (Caldwell) to the Secretary of State

TEHERAN, August 13, 1919, 7 p.m.

[Received August 17, 11:30 a.m.]

162. Strictly confidential. Public sentiment running against the present Cabinet on account of recent British treaty which many Persians consider to be in effect a mandate for Great Britain over Persia, thus circumventing League of Nations. The treaty was secretly, and surreptitiously, prepared and suddenly announced. Public, including other Legations, greatly surprised and attribute to Cabinet lack of good intention and to Great Britain bad faith. Full text . . . follows by cable. See my 160, August 11, 6 p.m.

CALDWELL

741.91/22: Telegram

The Minister in Persia (Caldwell) to the Secretary of State

TEHERAN, August 16, 1919, 7 p.m.

[Received August 21, 7:57 p.m.]

163. The following is the full text of the agreement between Great Britain and Persian Government: Persian patriots claim that this treaty amounts to a protectorate over Persia by Great Britain but the Persians are prevented from public expression of opinion or giving vent to feelings in any manner by the existing martial law and controlled press, as well as the fact that British Army now occupy Persia. While by the provision of the Persian Constitution, treaties are not effective until ratified by Persian Mejliss, nevertheless, it is understood that steps have been taken to immediately put into effect the provisions of this agreement. Moreover the current elections throughout the provinces are entirely controlled by the present

Cabinet, members of which have been chosen as representatives of provinces wherein they have never been.

CALDWELL

741.91/23: Telegram

The Ambassador in Great Britain (Davis) to the Secretary of State

LONDON, August 18, 1919, 7 p.m.

[Received August 19, 2:22 a.m.]

Agreement between Great Britain and Persia, Signed at Teheran,

August 9, 1919

No. 1

AGREEMENT BETWEEN THE GOVERNMENTS OF GREAT BRITAIN AND PERSIA

PREAMBLE: In virtue of the close ties of friendship which have existed between the two Governments in the past, and in the conviction that it is in the essential and mutual interests of both in future that these ties should be cemented, and that the progress and prosperity of Persia should be promoted to the utmost, it is hereby agreed between the Persian Government on the one hand, and His Britannic Majesty's Minister, acting on behalf of his Government, on the other, as follows:

1. The British Government reiterate, in the most categorical manner, the undertakings which they have repeatedly given in the past to respect absolutely the independence and integrity of Persia.

2. The British Government will supply, at the cost of the Persian Government, the services of whatever expert advisers may, after consultation between the two Governments, be considered necessary for the several departments of the Persian Administration. These advisers shall be engaged on contracts and endowed with adequate powers, the nature of which shall be the matter of agreement between the Persian Government and the advisers.

3. The British Government will supply, at the cost of the Persian Government, such officers and such munitions and equipment of modern type as may be adjudged necessary by a joint commission of military experts, British and Persian, which shall assemble forthwith

for the purpose of estimating the needs of Persia in respect of the formation of a uniform force which the Persian Government proposes to create for the establishment and preservation of order in the country and on its frontiers.

4. For the purpose of financing the reforms indicated in clauses 2 and 3 of this agreement, the British Government offer to provide or arrange a substantial loan for the Persian Government, for which adequate security shall be sought by the two Governments in consultation in the revenues of the customs or other sources of income at the disposal of the Persian Government. Pending the completion of negotiations for such a loan the British Government will supply on account of it such funds as may be necessary for initiating the said reforms.

5. The British Government fully recognising the urgent need which exists for the improvement of communications in Persia, with a view both to the extension of trade and the prevention of famine, are prepared to co-operate with the Persian Government for the encouragement of Anglo-Persian enterprise in this direction, both by means of railway construction and other forms of transport; subject always to the examination of the problems by experts and to agreement between the two Governments as to the particular projects which may be most necessary, practicable, and profitable.

6. The two Governments agree to the appointment forthwith of a joint Committee of experts for the examination and revision of the existing Customs Tariff with a view to its reconstruction on a basis calculated to accord with the legitimate interests of the country and to promote its prosperity.

Signed at Tehran, August 9, 1919.

Tribes in Iraq [former Mesopotamia] rebelled in June 1920 against British policies designed to centralize control over them. T. E. Lawrence (1888–1935), who had worked with British intelligence in Cairo and served with Feisal's army in the Arab Revolt, wrote an article for *The Sunday Times*, in August 1920, to object to British military tactics, including airplanes, to suppress the revolt. He argued that they were creating more opposition rather than less and that a small cabal of officials were directing policy and ignoring directives from London. Ultimately, the legacy of the revolt, and the installation of Feisal as king enabled Feisal to negotiate a type of mandate far more lenient than that found elsewhere. Unlike the other Arab mandates [Syria, Lebanon, Palestine], Iraq would gain formal independence in 1932 and enter

"On the Aerodrome at Amman, TransJordan, April, 1921." Pictured here are some of the architects of the postwar order for Palestine. In the center wearing the white pith helmet is Herbert Louis Samuel (1870–1963), the first British High Commissioner for Palestine under the Mandate. On his right is T. E. Lawrence (1888–1935), who served as military advisor during the Arab Revolt of 1916–1918 against the Ottomans. Emir Abdullah (1882–1951), son of the Sharif Hussein of Mecca and soon-to-be named king of the artificially created client state of Transjordan, stands to Samuel's left.

the League of Nations, albeit with arrangements for British military installations to remain. *The Sunday Times* states that it requested his article to illustrate issues presumably not being openly discussed by the government.

Ex.-Lieut.-Col. T. E. Lawrence, *The Sunday Times*, 22 August 1920

[Mr. Lawrence, whose organization and direction of the Hedjaz against the Turks was one of the outstanding romances of the war, has written this article at our request in order that the public may be fully informed of our Mesopotamian commitments.]

"The people of England have been led in Mesopotamia into a trap from which it will be hard to escape with dignity and honour. They have been tricked into it by a steady withholding of information. The Baghdad communiques are belated, insincere, incomplete. Things have been far worse than we have been told, our administration more bloody and inefficient than the public knows. It is a disgrace to our imperial record, and may soon be too inflamed for any ordinary cure. We are to-day not far from a disaster.

The sins of commission are those of the British civil authorities in Mesopotamia (especially of three 'colonels') who were given a free hand by London. They are controlled from no Department of State, but from the empty space which divides the Foreign Office from the India Office. They availed themselves of the necessary discretion of war-time to carry over their dangerous independence into times of peace. They contest every suggestion of real self-government sent them from home. A recent proclamation about autonomy circulated with unction from Baghdad was drafted and published out there in a hurry, to forestall a more liberal statement in preparation in London, 'Self-determination papers' favourable to England were extorted in Mesopotamia in 1919 by official pressure, by aeroplane demonstrations, by deportations to India. . . .

We said we went to Mesopotamia to defeat Turkey. We said we stayed to deliver the Arabs from the oppression of the Turkish

Government, and to make available for the world its resources of corn [wheat] and oil. We spent nearly a million men and nearly a thousand million of money to these ends. This year we are spending ninety-two thousand men and fifty millions of money on the same objects.

Our government is worse than the old Turkish system. They kept fourteen thousand local conscripts embodied, and killed a yearly average of two hundred Arabs in maintaining peace. We keep ninety thousand men, with aeroplanes, armoured cars, gunboats, and armoured trains. We have killed about ten thousand Arabs in this rising this summer. We cannot hope to maintain such an average: it is a poor country, sparsely peopled; but [former Sultan] Abd el Hamid would applaud his masters, if he saw us working. We are told the object of the rising was political, we are not told what the local people want. It may be what the Cabinet has promised them. . . . Cromer controlled Egypt's six million people with five thousand British troops; Colonel [Arnold] Wilson fails to control Mesopotamia's three million people with ninety thousand troops.

We have not reached the limit of our military commitments. Four weeks ago the staff in Mesopotamia drew up a memorandum asking for four more divisions. I believe it was forwarded to the War Office, which has now sent three brigades from India. If the North-West Frontier cannot be further denuded, where is the balance to come from? Meanwhile, our unfortunate troops, Indian and British, under hard conditions of climate and supply, are policing an immense area, paying dearly every day in lives for the willfully wrong policy of the civil administration in Baghdad. . . .

The Government in Baghdad have been hanging Arabs in that town for political offences, which they call rebellion. The Arabs are not at war with us. Are these illegal executions to provoke the Arabs to reprisals on the three hundred British prisoners they hold? And, if so, is it that their punishment may be more severe, or is it to persuade our other troops to fight to the last?

We say we are in Mesopotamia to develop it for the benefit of the world. All experts say that the labour supply is the ruling factor in its development. How far will the killing of ten thousand villagers and townspeople this summer hinder the production of wheat, cotton, and oil? How long will we permit millions of pounds, thousands of Imperial troops, and tens of thousands of Arabs to be sacrificed on behalf of colonial administration which can benefit nobody but its administrators?

Portrayals

Women, Work, Education, War, and Peace, c. 1800–Present

This image is part of the Library of Congress photo albums in the Abdul Hamid II Collection which documents the Ottoman Empire during the reign of one of its last sultans. The 1,819 photographs date from about 1880 to 1893 and emphasize the modernization of the Ottoman Empire, particularly in the realm of schooling, educational facilities, and students. The two girls portrayed here attended a modern secondary school in Istanbul named after a notable, Molla Gürani Rüşdiyesi. Many of the schools for girls in the Ottoman Empire were patterned after French educational institutions, although British and American schooling also provided inspiration. Judging by their dress, these two unnamed girls were from the elite or bourgeoisie.

This picture essay surveys representations and portrayals of women from diverse sources—painting, photography, and posters. It addresses four principal themes: women in the artist's eye and camera's lens, schooling and education, work, and women in war and in peace. In part, the essay draws inspiration from the contemporary period in which misleading images of, and uncritical assertions about, women in MENA are rife in the media, greatly affecting collective attitudes and policy making. In addition, Islam and Muslims have been demonized by the West for centuries; the events of 9/11 and the "War on Terror" have in many respects fed into, and off of, those earlier negative representations. Thus, it is especially challenging to dismantle prejudices and stereotypes, nurtured largely by commonly held, but frequently unexamined, beliefs about the region's women. Emphasizing diversity within the large framework of encounters with modernity offers an antidote to the widespread notion that women have "always and everywhere been oppressed." The various kinds of images following illustrate the complexities inherent in depicting women's lives from 1800 until the present. Since World War I constituted a sea change for MENA, the essay is strategically located after chapter 3 to simultaneously gaze in several directions—to the past as well as forward in time.

What emerges is that there was (and is) no monolithic Turkish, Arab, or Persian "woman"—to name only three major ethnolinguistic groups—nor did an undifferentiated Muslim, Jewish, or Christian woman exist. Wide-ranging elements determined women's legal, social, political, and cultural roles in each society or community and historical era. The nature of the state, class formation, family organization, local laws, and interpretations of religious traditions, educational practices, and resource structures all shaped women's status, lives, and life opportunities. Finally, women have always been fundamental, not marginal, to the origins, beliefs, and practices of world religious traditions because religion is inseparable from patriarchy and patriarchal systems of domination.

I. Women in the Artist's Eye and Camera's Lens

From the early nineteenth century, women in MENA were extensively painted, portrayed, photographed, written about, and imagined, mainly by European (and later North American) artists, literati, and photographers who were largely male. Orientalist painters, for example, Eugène Delacroix, and novelists, such as the French writer Pierre Loti, were not innocent bystanders in these depictions; nor were they unbiased or objective in visual or textual representations of women from other cultures and societies. Moreover, artistic and literary production were directly implicated in Western justifications for empire building in MENA and globally. Indeed, image making and dissemination served as handmaiden to imperialism. Across Africa and Asia, European armies employed the camera's lens to

The Women of Algiers (In Their Apartment), 1834.

This oil on canvas painting by Eugène Delacroix has long been infamous for its explicit sexual connotations. Although the artist never, as far as we know, gained entry to a harem or Muslim household, nevertheless the image purports to document Algerian concubines. The hookah, a water pipe used to smoke tobacco, hashish, or opium, became an iconic prop in many European paintings and photographs of MENA's women. Note the languid, fey poses of the women as an African servant or slave attends to their needs. The painting later inspired Pablo Picasso to execute a series of drawings during the 1950s. It is currently located in the Louvre, Paris, France.

chronicle and celebrate military exploits, first in French Algeria and British India during the 1850s. Nevertheless, the rapid progress of photography never eclipsed other forms of visual artistic production, documentation, or commemoration; portraiture and photos, image and icon fed into one another. Nor were all portrayals of MENA's women by foreign artists necessarily distorted or demeaning.

While many of the nineteenth-century depictions were fashioned by Europeans or North Americans, some individuals from the region took up camera, pen, and brush to represent themselves or memorialize their dynasties. In Persia/Iran, Shah Nasir al-Din (r. 1848–1896) became enamored of the camera long before his state trips to Europe beginning in 1873. He employed Francis Carlhian, a French photographer, to organize a royal photo studio in the Golestan palace in Tehran. Breaking with religious and social moral conventions, the Shah even had the royal women and children of his harem photographed. Commissioned by Nasir al-Din Shah to document royal ceremonies, scenes, and structures, the Armenian-Georgian Antoin Sevruguin (1830–1933) became prominent in Iran, taking thousands of on-site photos of peoples

Scenes of daily life in the Ottoman capital, Constantinople.

Appointed imperial architect to Sultan Selim III, the German artist Antoine Ignace Melling spent eighteen years in the Ottoman Empire where he observed, painted, and participated in court life between roughly 1786 and 1803. His daily experiences confer authenticity on his images. Melling's *Voyage pittoresque de Constantinople et des rives du Bosphore* was illustrated with engravings such as this one published in Paris in 1819 depicting a daily market. Notice the two women in the middle bottom of the picture who appear to be bargaining with a fruit seller.

Druze Woman of the Mount Lebanon, c. 1889.

Done by the French photographer, Tancrède R. Dumas, in a local studio, this image of a woman in the typical tall Druze female headdress was probably sold in numerous prints in Europe where demand was high for images of exotic foreign women, a demand fueled in part by the world's fairs discussed in chapter 1.

and places between 1870 and 1930. Sevruguin also established a highly successful studio in nineteenth-century Tehran where photos were modeled on French photography known as "scenes and types." Closely tied to the emerging scientific fields of ethnography and ethnology, these were portraits of ethnic, racial, or religious groups deemed "typical." Their intended audiences were Europeans unfamiliar with, but intrigued by, MENA's cultures, regional costumes, and traditional handicrafts; portrayals of female dress were in high demand. Due to photography's growing popularity, most urban areas in MENA by the late nineteenth century boasted studios where cherished moments in family life cycles—births, weddings, and school events—were recorded. It is critical to remember that many images were staged and arranged by European or European-trained photographers who employed the culturally and aesthetically determined visual canons of their times. Until recently in the Middle East and North Africa, clothing served as critical markers for social class and religious identity particularly in public spaces. As is true of all images, these can be "read" and interpreted in a multitude of ways because they served scientific, political, polemical, and propagandistic purposes, depending on the objectives of those producing them. Moreover, viewers perceived and received images differently. Nothing shaped the camera's probing eye more than imperialism.

After its 1830 invasion of Algeria, the French army set about visually depicting, and thus classifying, people, places, and things to rule more effectively, a pattern detected in modern colonial regimes worldwide. In addition to cannons and rifles, the French expedition included a cohort of skilled artists and draftsmen, as had Napoleon's 1798 expedition to Egypt. Since photography had not yet been invented, military artists portrayed Algerians of all social classes and ethnic, racial, or religious backgrounds. The women of Algiers—rich, poor, Jewish, and Muslim—were a favorite topic. With the rapid spread of photography, colonial officials and settlers manipulated images of the "Algerian woman," inevitably portrayed as exotic or even erotic, in thousands of picture postcards printed in France or in Algeria. Portraits done in studios were frequently contrived so as to give the sensation of a sly, illicit glance into the intimacy of the family and household. In any case, Algerian women were increasingly open to public gaze, once again for the ends of empire. Colonial officials used the allegedly degraded status of Muslim women to argue against conferring political rights on the Algerians.

By the late nineteenth century, contrived photographic images of the "Arab," "Jewish," or "Middle Eastern" woman were widely available as well as posters, engravings, and other media. Many were fashioned in studios with the same stage "props"—water pipes, oriental carpets, lavish "traditional" costumes, and allegedly "native" women and men. Often, however, the people posing were not from MENA but Europeans dressed up as "Orientals." Visually representing women in strange ways served to distance Middle Eastern societies from modern, enlightened, Western societies, and thus to justify colonial rule. Once again, images and representations have always served state or imperial aims and agendas.

In 1932, a Turkish woman won an international beauty competition, the Miss Universe contest held in Spa, Belgium, after having been elected earlier that same year "the most beautiful Turkish

Algerian types, Moorish Woman, c. 1860–1890.

Although numerous other photos more offensive than this exist in the canon of French colonial images of Algerian women, this suggests sexual availability—that the woman is a prostitute—as well as indolence. Other posed, sexually suggestive, often racist, photo postcards featured men and women who were supposedly "native" in a demeaning manner, but often it is difficult to know the identity of the sitters.

Egypt or a Daughter of the Nile, 1887.

After the mid-nineteenth century, North Americans were increasingly enthralled by Orientalist depictions of MENA and its peoples in art and literature. The popularity of world fairs, the growth in American Protestant missions to the region, and organized tourist tours to the Middle East, particularly to Egypt, produced a kind of "Egypto-mania" in North America. This theater poster is one example among many of the keen interest in things Egyptian. The American actress, Effie Ellsler (c.1855–1942) starred in a number of theatrical productions at Macauley's Theatre in Louisville, Kentucky, between 1878 and 1901.

woman" in a national pageant. The winner Keriman Halis Ece symbolized womanhood and modernity as defined by the Turkish republic in the period. Born in 1913 in Istanbul, Keriman Halis was a model and pianist with a relatively advanced education. A few decades earlier, most reputable Ottoman Muslim women would not have appeared in public dressed in this fashion and might have donned a face veil. Now the state and nationalist press promoted

The Turkish Beauty Queen, 1932, Bayan Keriman.
The daughter of a merchant in Istanbul, Keriman's uncle was a well-known opera composer and her aunt a musician. Turkish beauty pageants were first held in 1929 and promoted by the leading newspaper *Cumhuriyet* (*Republic*). In July 1932, she was crowned Miss Universe, less than a decade after the founding of the Republic, and thus represented the new state of Turkey to the world.

Turkey's participation in this novel social event with support from the president, Mustafa Kemal, or Ataturk. In 2002, a Turkish woman, Azra Akin, was crowned in London as "Miss World." Nevertheless, questions arise about women's commodification and commercialization as well as the uses made of them by political elites and states.

II. Education and Schools

In the course of the nineteenth century, schooling outside the home came to be associated with modernity itself among certain social sectors. In nineteenth-century Egypt, the ruler, Muhammad Ali Pasha, organized the School for Midwives in 1832 whose goal was to train young women not only in obstetrics but also in modern medicine. Later in the century, formal photos of educational institutions for girls and boys as well as students in class were taken in cities ranging from Istanbul and Cairo to Tehran where rulers used photography to document the pace of reforms and modernization. Indeed, the Abdul Hamid II collection, over 1,800 photographs in fifty-one albums assembled between 1880 and 1893, is a perfect example of this. However, MENA's elite families had educated women and girls at home with private tutors, long before the emergence of modern schooling. And cities, towns, and villages boasted religious schools for children of ordinary status, although girls were not permitted to attend beyond a certain age to protect their virtue and family honor. Households and kin members provided home-based learning in the domestic arts, but female (and male) illiteracy was very high relative to Western Europe or North America. Many state-organized educational institutions in MENA were patterned on France, although Catholic and Protestant missionaries from Europe and North America introduced a variety of schools and curricula from the nineteenth century on. Missionary and secular schooling became central to the practice of empire, particularly in French and British colonies. However, girls' education proved a contentious issue in many colonies because European officials and taxpayers did not want to fund instruction for native children. Instead handicraft schools were frequently substituted for a truly modern education, although these institutions did provide income to girls and their families. In precolonial Tunisia, one of the ruling princes of the Husaynid Dynasty, Ahmad Bey (r. 1837–1855), gave permission to a French Catholic congregation of female missionaries to establish girls' schools in Tunis in 1840 that were both academic and vocational; these institutions later inspired other experiments in education in Tunisia.

As schools became increasingly seen as crucibles for citizens and modernity in MENA, movements for educational reforms arose;

Arab school of embroidery, Algiers, 1899.

This photograph from French Algeria depicts embroidery and lace-making classes overseen and organized by a French woman, Eugènie Luce. Luce went to Algeria in 1832 where she founded one of the first academic schools for Muslim girls in 1845. Due to French colonial opposition to instructing native girls, she later organized handicraft schools often located inside family residences.

at first these tended to be the purview of middle-class, urban men and women involved in nationalist movements. During anticolonial protests, school girls and boys demonstrated in the streets for rights and freedom. For example, in 1925 in Lebanon, then under French rule, a group of one hundred Lebanese girl scouts in uniform, between the ages of twelve and sixteen, paraded through the streets of Beirut to publicize the fact that the colonial regime had closed down their school. The Iranian woman, Bibi Khanum Astarabadi (c.1858–1921), was a writer, educator, and women's rights activist whose educational path blended the older tradition of instruction with modern education. Her mother, Khadijah Khanum, had served as a tutor in the royal household of one of Nasir-al-Din Shah's wives. Astarabadi was educated at home by her mother and became a teacher herself, establishing one of the first modern schools for girls in her Tehran residence in 1906. She and her two daughters penned numerous articles calling for women's rights within the family, particularly in the domain of marriage, and for girls' education. In Iran in 1934, the University of Tehran, previously a male-only institution, admitted women students as part of Reza Shah's sweeping universal education program. In Turkey, the University of Istanbul was reorganized in 1933 and the country's academies, colleges, and universities were made open to women.

Ataturk visits Istanbul University.

In giving women access to higher learning, the Turkish Republic built on Ottoman schooling policies. As early as 1915, the predecessor to the modern University of Istanbul boasted a separate section for girl students. This undated photo of Mustafa Kemal at Istanbul University most likely was taken in the mid-1930s.

III. Women at Work

Until well into the twentieth century, many communities in MENA were overwhelmingly rural; the vast majority lived in villages earning their livelihood from farming and animal husbandry, but they were not as well documented in photographs or other media as MENA's urban dwellers. Many girls and women of ordinary means in the countryside did not enjoy full access to formal modern schooling until after independence from colonial rule in the mid-twentieth century. In addition, large pastoral-nomadic communities in eastern Turkey, Iran, North Africa, the Arabian Peninsula, and elsewhere moved between mountains and plains or among desert oases. In southwestern Persia/Iran, the tribal Bakhtiari confederation laboriously trekked through the high passes of the Zagros Mountains to summer pasturage, involving fifty thousand people—men, women, and children—and countless animals. Women played a fundamental role in the pastoral-nomadic economy. The Pahlavi Dynasty (1925–1979), successor to the Qajars, set up tribal schools, but the intent was often state surveillance of the tribesmen.

Rural women, whether sedentary or transhumant, produced a multitude of commodities—tents, clothing, bed linens, mats, rugs, sacks for the storage or transport of grains, cooking utensils, and so forth; many of them were sold or bartered in markets. Raw materials came from diverse sources—wool from flocks, grasses for weaving mats, and clay for pottery. Women and girls labored hard in fields, farms, or in family workshops until the advent of industrialization, which affected different regions, peoples, and economies in varying degrees. In short, women's work was crucial, and the clan and village could not survive without it. After 1850, European merchants in the region began organizing local village families into workshops that produced raw materials for sale in foreign markets, a form of international "putting out." During the 1860s and 1870s, young women in Mount Lebanon and Syria were recruited into French-owned silk factories, which grew into long-term export enterprises. In cities or towns, women of modest means served feminine society as heal-

Girls weaving a large carpet, Iran, 1870s–1930s.

Carpet production was a crucial part of village and pastoral nomadic economies, particularly with the rise of European and then global demand for Middle Eastern carpets. The wool used often came from flocks raised in villages or by tribesmen.

ers, midwives (*qabla*), and beauticians, such as the *hannana* who specialized in applying henna to brides, dancers, and singers. Women musicians performed at weddings both in cities and the countryside, although the profession was frequently not highly regarded because female public performance was morally suspect. MENA's cities (and often towns) boasted numerous bathhouses that offered employment to female attendants. Numerous women and girls worked in home-based carpet, lace, and embroidery production, as servants, and sold produce in local markets.

IV. Women in War and Peace

States have always enlisted women into warfare in diverse ways; in the modern era, gendered images and representations became central to wartime propaganda. During World War I, visually dramatic posters depicting women and children as suffering victims garnered popular support and donations for the international Red Cross, the Islamic Red Crescent, and other aid

Girl selling bread in the bazaars, Baghdad, 1932.

Children had to work as well, often peddling products made in the home for sale. This rare photo from Baghdad shows one of the popular markets in the Iraqi capital; in addition to the little girl in the foreground, another girl can be seen in the background with a basket of wares on her head for sale.

societies. In the twentieth century, women were encouraged to serve as nurses and medical staff as well as assume men's work in heavy industry and agriculture, jobs normally unavailable to them in peacetime. Nevertheless, female warriors—women as soldiers bearing arms—was highly controversial until very recently. Here Fatima the Moroccan combatant, billed as an example of "women who fight," sits confidently on a horse. We have no additional information on Fatima or how she arrived at the French front. Did she disguise herself as a man, which historically was one way for women to follow men-folk into battle? Or was she in France before the war's outbreak and volunteered when Moroccan units, perhaps

Fatima the soldier, 1915, France.

This photo from the French newspaper, *Le Miroir*, is entitled "Fatima the Moroccan: Women Who Fight as True Soldiers" and reads "Fatima the Moroccan woman, whose portrait we reproduce here, followed into battle from the beginning of the war our [North African] units and fought courageously like a man." The paper also notes that it "would pay any price for photographic documents relating to the war and presenting a particular interest to the public.

including family members, arrived to fight against Germany? And how was her image used? Was this photo meant to encourage Moroccan soldiers to struggle for a cause that was not theirs? Or was this image aimed at European audiences to advertize the loyalty of colonized troops in a world war of Europe's making? The questions posed by Fatima's image can be raised regarding the others in this essay. In addition, it signals a rupture with the countless colonial photographs of the idle, sensuous, "Eastern" woman either clothed in oriental finery, or unclothed, and posed reclining in a studio photograph in accordance with the dictates of male fantasies.

As discussed in chapter 3, civilians in European colonies were exhorted to collect money, food, and supplies to aid the war effort through posters mobilizing support for fund-raising campaigns. During the First World War, millions

In order that they may return, Algiers, 1918.

This 1918 French poster from World War I depicts a native Algerian soldier in uniform who has been conscripted into the colonial army bidding farewell to his wife and child, who are dressed in traditional costumes, as he prepares to go to Europe to fight with an "Algerian Company." The image's intent is clear: "To subscribe to (war bonds) means victory and will hasten his homecoming" [LC].

of people became refugees or died due to the hostilities, famines, and epidemics. But the armistice in 1918 ushered in neither peace nor stability for many. Hundreds of thousands were forcibly uprooted and resettled in ethnic population exchanges between Turkey and Greece decreed by international treaties concluded by the major European victors.

As nationalist movements for independence from European rule erupted after World War I in MENA, women became pivotal as "mothers of the nation," organizers, street protesters, political agents, and combatants, particularly in murderous colonial conflicts, such as the Algerian war for independence, waged from 1954 to 1962. When the war of liberation broke out in 1954, women joined the FLN (National Liberation Front) or served in support capacities as nurses, spies, clandestine arms dealers, and so forth. Urban women who participated in the nationalist struggle were often young, middle-class graduates of French *lycées*, for example, Djamila Boupacha, shown here. They were particularly critical during the Battle of Algiers, which took place in 1957 and was later immortalized by Italian film maker, Gillo Pontecorvo, in his 1965 film, *La bataille d'Alger* (*The Battle of Algiers*). A number of these young women were captured by the French police or army, imprisoned, and subjected to horrible torture. After 1962, the independent Algerian government registered nearly 11,000 women as war veterans, but this figure greatly undervalued the actual number who actively contributed to the war effort.

After World War I, new national and international women's organizations emerged that included female participants and activists from MENA. In 1936, the International Feminist Congress was held in Istanbul with the backing of the Turkish republic; the Turkish Women's Union played a leading role in its deliberations. In Iran, the Women's National Rights Association was created in Tehran in 1923.

Djamila Boupacha, 1962.

This photo features Djamila Boupacha as she addressed a 1962 meeting of the National Liberation Front in the capital city. Many former female fighters or activists joined the newly formed Algerian government to militate for women's rights and socio-legal reforms, but their hopes for true change were dashed [LC].

These organizations' activities were documented by photography and have increased our fund of images. Women's international associations eventually resulted in transnational peace and human rights organizations so important in today's world. Women as peacemakers have been active in the ongoing Palestinian-Israeli conflict over the status of the occupied territories, the West Bank, and Gaza. The Coalition of Women for Peace in Palestine and Israel, which includes Israelis and Palestinians, has steadfastly organized pro-peace demonstrations for years. In addition, female artists, literati, and filmmakers have made enormous contributions to social reform and women's advancement.

Two internationally known political and social activists from MENA are Shirin Ebadi and Dr. Nawal el Saadawi. Born in Iran in 1947, Ebadi was awarded the Nobel Peace Prize in 2003 [Doc. 7.16] for her advocacy of freedom of speech and human rights, especially for women and children. Egypt's best known writer, novelist, and social critic, Nawal el Saadawi was born in 1931 and earned a medical degree in 1951 at Cairo University. For decades, she too has been a

Nawal el Saadawi.

Dr. Nawal el Saadawi was imprisoned in 1981 by the Egyptian president, Anwar Sadat, because of her political and social views on civil liberty and women's rights. In addition to publishing many books and articles, she served as a member of the United Nations Women's Programme in Africa and the Middle East and has been awarded a number of international prizes. This image shows Dr. Saadawi at a 2011 demonstration for the Global Women's Strike.

tireless advocate for human and women's rights, particularly health and reproductive rights, in the Arab world and internationally. However, Saadawi's work as a feminist has attracted severe condemnation from Muslim clerics as well as secular political leaders in her own country and elsewhere.

The "Arab Spring," whose popular uprisings demanding freedom began in December 2010 in Tunisia and spread to Egypt, Libya, Syria, Yemen, Bahrain, and elsewhere in MENA, have featured women in frontline positions as protestors, fighters, organizers, medical personnel, and media commentators. Nevertheless, women's multiple acts of courage in the face of often brutal state and military repression have not always been rewarded. Indeed, the photo of a young Egyptian woman in *hijab* being dragged half-naked by riot police through the streets of Cairo near Tahrir Square on December 17, 2011, remains the iconic image of the Arab Spring, one seen around the world [see chapter 7]. The shocking incident caused hundreds of thousands of women in MENA and across the globe to engage in collective protests and earned Egypt's military a public rebuke from Secretary of State, Hillary Clinton.

Egypt: Woman dragged half-naked through the street, 2011.

As riot police pulled off the unnamed woman's clothing to reveal her undergarments, the world watched. She became the symbol of the Egyptian people's revolution and fight against military rule of then-president Husni Mubarek.

CHAPTER 5

From the Great War to World War II, c. 1923–1950

"Mustafa Kemal's Speech at Mersin, March 17, 1923." This photo was taken two years before his speech found on p. 157. Here we see Mustafa Kemal in military uniform, not his later civilian dress where he wore a broad-brimmed hat. But the headwear of the men listening to him in 1925 resembled that seen in this 1923 photo.

The post-World War I era witnessed five major developments that were intertwined. First, political readjustments saw a fully independent Turkish republic emerge in 1923 from the ashes of the Ottoman Empire while the dismantling of the Ottoman state enabled France and Britain to take over the remaining Arab lands of the empire as mandates. As for Iran, the Qajar dynasty, in power from 1795, was abolished by the upstart Pahlavi dynasty, which lasted until the Islamic Revolution of 1979. Second, a wide variety of struggles for national independence came to maturity in those regions under European imperial rule. Third, debates and even clashes in many societies of North Africa and the Middle East emerged between local advocates of Western-style secular reforms inspired by European institutions, social norms, and practices and more "traditionalist" communities or groups. The latter included religious or social conservatives whether Muslim, Jewish, or Christian who defended long-accepted values and who regarded the wholesale adoption of European law and customs as an assault on religion and society.

Fourth, the further development of modern civil society and its multiple manifestations—political clubs, trade unions, sports associations, musical societies, and so forth—can be detected from Morocco to Iran. For example, in the city of Algiers under French colonial rule since

153

1830, new forms of associational life, an index of civil society, flourished during the 1920s and 1930s. And in the British-controlled oil fields of southwestern Iran, where Iranian workers' labor was exploited by the Anglo-Persian Oil Company, a workers' movement came into existence after 1941. Finally, from 1918 on, the European and North American competition to control, extract, and monopolize North African and Middle Eastern resources—principally, but not exclusively, oil—intensified during the interwar period.

Whereas Turkey and Iran were self-governing, nationalist movements in other regions demanded liberation from foreign control, but these efforts were not fully realized in most cases until the 1950s in the aftermath of World War II. The exception was Iraq, which became nominally independent in 1932 and entered the League of Nations, but was forced to tolerate the presence of British military installations. British rule in Palestine strove to facilitate the creation of a Jewish state. This triggered Palestinian resistance in the 1930s leading to the Palestinian Arab revolt (1936–1939).

As World War II loomed in Europe, many movements for independence were suppressed and martial law imposed by the imperial powers—France, Great Britain, Italy in Libya and Spain in northern Morocco. In 1939, fearing Arab uprisings against its Palestine policies, Britain issued a White Paper [an official government policy statement] that, if fully implemented, would have reversed its backing for a Jewish state. Turkey, Iran, and Egypt experienced turmoil caused by struggles between political elites calling for secular states and their opponents who viewed secularism as a challenge to the centrality of Islam. In contrast, the Kingdom of Saudi Arabia, officially recognized in 1932, saw the emergence of a state founded on conservative Sunni Muslim principles. The ruling Ibn Saud family allied itself with the rigid tenets of the Wahhabi Muslim reform movement, founded in the eighteenth century to purify Islam of accretions unknown at the time of the Prophet Muhammad.

By far, the most successful example of modern state building during the period was the republic of Turkey. There a national military hero, Mustafa Kemal (1881–1938), consolidated power and embarked on a major social and political revolution to secularize the nation. In doing so, Kemal, building on reforms implemented by the Ottomans before and during World War I, refashioned Turkish state and society, especially among its urban inhabitants. Islam remained a source of identity in outlying rural areas and would reappear as a political factor after World War II. He abolished the Caliphate and religious courts in 1924 and in 1928 replaced the (modified) Arabic script for the Turkish language with the Latin script. His goal was not to abolish religion entirely

[handwritten margin notes: · age of imperialism · British is doing what the US is now trying to (invading countries, control political & economic motives through military interventions & financial positions)]

[handwritten note at bottom: westernizing the country (like Hussein's autobio.)]

but to remove it from direct involvement in the exercise of government and public life. In addition, Turkey's first president strongly advocated the emancipation of women by banning polygamy, encouraging women to abandon the veil, and granting women the right to vote in 1930 and to run for office in national elections in 1934, not long after American women won suffrage in 1920. He also decreed that all Turks should have a family name, emulating the West, and he was awarded the name of Ataturk (Father of the Turks) by the parliament in 1934. No other Middle Eastern nation went as far as did Turkey.

The first Pahlavi ruler, Reza Shah (1878–1944), imitated Mustafa Kemal's state-building program in Iran by attempting to secularize the government and courts. He met with only partial success, though not simply because of Shia clergy opposition. A major factor was his own small circle of support. He was not a nationalist hero as was Mustafa Kemal, owing to the latter's military exploits during World War I and his leadership in defeating a Greek invasion of Anatolia in 1920–22. In Egypt, Western-oriented and educated intellectuals and nationalists were divided. Many called in the 1920s for more democratic and secular political institutions but also tolerated British control of major aspects of Egyptian life; others, more nationalistic, called for Egypt's immediate independence as did Muslim opponents of secular change, which they linked to Western corruption and negative aspects of British imperial occupation. In interwar Egypt, the most effective of these groups was the Muslim Brotherhood, founded in 1928, which in 2012 won unrestricted Egyptian elections and has spread throughout the Islamic world. New literary voices and genres emerged in the region as did new cultural and communication forms, especially the radio and the cinema.

The most visible and controversial sign of secularization for many was the drive to emancipate women through legal, social, and cultural changes. Some women, mainly urban and educated, in Turkey, Iran, and Egypt, abandoned the veil and adopted forms of European dress in public but, more important, advocated expanded girls' education as well as revisions of legal codes prejudicial to women's status. These same women, for example, the Egyptian Hoda Shaarawi, participated in international feminist congresses held with greater frequency after WWI; indeed, the Turkish republic hosted the 1936 International Feminist Congress in Istanbul. For the builders of new states, women were cast in the role of "mothers of the nation," which meant that they had to be educated and enjoy certain rights to advance national interests. But to those religiously or socially conservative groups, such radical transformations in women's status threatened the family, community morality, and social values.

"Egyptian Feminists Meet with American Counterparts in Cairo, 1925." Hoda Shaarawi (also mentioned in chapter 3) stands second from left with an Egyptian colleague and two American members of the international woman's movement who visited Cairo. Shaarawi attended women's conferences in Europe and led efforts to encourage the greater engagement of Egyptian women in public life.

Another arena of intense ferment in the interwar period was the question of labor, particularly in modern industry. Mass workers' movements and labor organizations arose, often influenced by socialist ideologies imported from Europe; the best example is Iran's oil industry. In North Africa and in Palestine, European and Arab workers at first banded together in the same labor unions but later became antagonists owing to the growing appeal of nationalist movements for independence.

World War II spared Turkey, whose leaders wisely declared neutrality; but Iran was occupied by British, American and Soviet troops to guarantee supplies to the Soviets via the Persian Gulf. All of northern Africa was engulfed by the war, with major campaigns fought in Egypt, Libya, and Tunisia before German and Italian forces surrendered in late 1943. The end of the war brought full awareness of the Holocaust, the deliberate killing of six million European Jews approved by Adolf Hitler (1889–1945) who had assumed power in Germany in 1933; this news created international backing for a Jewish state in Palestine. Israel then declared its independence in May 1948 in much of what had been Palestine, in the aftermath of a United Nations partition plan passed in November 1947, accepted by the Zionist leadership and rejected by Palestinians. The resultant conflicts saw the flight and the forced mass exile of hundreds of thousands of Palestinians, who became refugees during the first of several Arab-Israeli wars. Syria and Lebanon gained independence from France in 1946, but North Africa suffered colonial conflict, and in the case of Algeria, a long, bloody struggle for independence culminating in the 1962 birth of the Algerian republic.

Since historical events in the Middle East and North Africa diverged so greatly during the period under consideration here, this chapter follows different strands of political, social, economic, and cultural developments, beginning with Turkey and Iran and ending with Palestine and Israel.

Reforms and Their Motivations: Turkey and Iran

After World War I, Istanbul was occupied by British and French forces, and Greece, with British encouragement, invaded Anatolia. The Turks defeated the Greeks and gained international recognition of their independence in the 1923 Treaty of Lausanne. The leader of Turkish resistance was Mustafa Kemal , who established himself as the new head of the Turkish state with his own agenda to fully modernize and secularize Turkey, breaking all ties to Islam and the Ottoman past. Kemal's at times authoritarian approach as a ruler and as a reformer alienated many including supporters of reform. . . .

In a speech during a regional tour in August 1925, he openly mocked persons who wore the traditional headgear, the fez. He wore the Western broad-brimmed hat, which was European and hence civilized, but it also prevented Muslims from praying in public by bowing their heads to the ground.

I see a man in the crowd in front of me [pointing at him]. He has a fez on his head, a green turban [wound around] the fez, a smock on his back, and on top of that a jacket like the one I'm wearing. . . . Now what kind of an outfit is that!? Would a civilized man put on this preposterous garb and go out to hold himself up to universal ridicule? Gentlemen, the Turkish people who founded the Turkish republic are civilized . . . in history and reality. . . . [But] the truly civilized people of Turkey must prove that they are civilized and advanced people also in their outward aspect. . . . A civilized international dress is . . . boots or shoes on our feet, trousers on our legs, shirt and tie, jacket and waistcoat, and of course to complete these, a cover with a brim on our heads. I want to make this clear. This head-covering is called 'a hat.'

Educated women in the large cities had already begun abandoning the veil, but it remained part of Turkish life in rural areas. Along with this campaign, he pushed for female education at all levels and equal rights for women in divorce proceedings.

In some places I have seen women who put a piece of cloth or a towel or something like that over their heads to hide their faces, and who turn their backs or huddle themselves on the ground when a man passes by. What are the meaning and sense of this behavior? Gentlemen, can the mothers and daughters of a civilized nation adopt this strange manner, this barbarous posture? It is a spectacle that makes the nation an object of ridicule. . . ."

• modernize/westernize nation by endorsing west. fashion

adopted family name

↓

Mustafa Kemal (Ataturk)

↑

Arab origin

In a 1926 speech, Kemal called for transforming the Ottoman script to Latin characters, to be read left to right, not right to left. This brought a complete break with Islamic as well as Ottoman literary and literate traditions.

My friends. . . . We must free ourselves from these incomprehensible signs that for centuries have held our minds in an iron vice. You must learn the new Turkish letters quickly. . . . Regard it as a patriotic and national duty . . . and when you perform that duty, bear in mind that for a nation to consist of 10 to 20 percent of literates and 80 to 90 percent of illiterates is shameful. . . . The fault is not ours; it is of those who failed to understand the character of the Turk and bound his mind in chains. . . . Our nation will show with its script and its mind that its place is in the civilized world.

This 1934 *New York Times* article notes that family names were seldom used in Middle Eastern society. Six months later, a law decreed that all Turks should adopt family names and register those names with the government. Mustafa Kemal adopted the name of "Ataturk," meaning "father of the Turks," to associate himself with the modern Turkish nation that he founded, and he dropped the name Mustafa, considered of Arab origin. His prime minister, Ismet Pasha, became Ismet Inönü (1884–1973), the latter name taken from a river where he had won a battle against the Greeks in 1922; the name and title "Pasha," a traditional Ottoman office, were dropped to symbolize a break with the past.

ISTANBUL, Jan. 3—Foreigners visiting Turkey are surprised when registering with the police and at hotels at the request to give, in addition to their own names, those of their fathers. The reason is that family names practically disappeared in Turkey, particularly in the towns, and the Turk is known by one name only. The total number of such names in Turkey being very limited, some means of distinguishing had to be found, and for a long time now reference to the father's name has provided the distinction for official purposes. Thus Mehmet Ahmet is Mehmet son of Ahmet. So many Mehmets are sons of Ahmets, however, that further means of identification were found necessary, and where many Mehmets abound they are distinguished by reference to physical peculiarities or callings. The Shushman (fat) Mehmet is not confused with Altin Dish (gold-toothed) Mehmet or with Bakchivan (gardener) Mehmet.

Sabiha Gökçen (1913–2001): Turkey's first female Aviator

Sabiha Gökçen [Gueukschehn] was legally adopted by Ataturk as an eleven-year-old girl living in poverty; he sponsored her education and oversaw her career. As this obituary notes, she symbolized for many Turks the accomplishments women achieved owing to Ataturk's reforms. Her fame was such that Istanbul's newest international airport is named after her.

Ankara-Turkish Daily News, March 23, 2001

Turkey's first female aviator Sabiha Gökçen passed away Wednesday night in Ankara's GATA military hospital aged 88. Born in Bursa in 1913, Sabiha Gökçen was unofficially adopted by Atatürk in 1925. She entered the Turkish Aviation Authority (THK) Turk Kusu School of Civilian Aviation in 1935 where she first learned how to pilot gliders.

She completed her glider training along with seven male students in Russia. Sabiha joined the THK School of Military Aviation in 1936 and became a military pilot before being posted to the Eskisehir First Aircraft Regiment, where she flew bombers. Sabiha Gökçen took part in military exercises in the Aegean and Thrace in 1937 as well as the Dersim operation that same year. The following year she toured the Balkans with her plane as a guest of the Balkan countries before being appointed Senior Instructor at the THK Turk Kusu School of Aviation in 1938. She served in this position until 1955.

In an interview last year, Sabiha Gökçen recalled her memories of Atatürk and could not hold back her tears. She noted there had been an increase in defamatory attacks on the memory of the man who founded the Turkish Republic. Flags at the Sabiha Gökçen International Airport in Pendik [Istanbul] were flying at half mast in a display of respect.

"Sabiha Gökçen, c. 1936." Sabiha Gökçen, here pictured in front of a Turkish aircraft. She was one of eight children Mustafa Kemal adopted, mostly young women whose education he personally sponsored.

Halide Edib Adivar (1884–1964) was a Turkish novelist, political leader, activist, and champion of democracy. A volunteer with the Turkish Red Crescent during World War I, she served as a soldier in the Turkish army during the post-World War I independence struggle. Born to an elite family in Istanbul, she was the first Turkish Muslim woman to graduate from the American College for Girls in Istanbul. She backed Mustafa Kemal when he took power, but then broke with him over his opposition to two-party democracy and to any criticism of him in the press. She and her husband went into exile in Europe and the United States in 1924, returning only after Kemal's death in 1938.

In 1929, the *Yale Review* published her measured critique of Kemal's reforms along with appreciation for the earlier political achievements of the Young Turks just prior to, and during, World War I.

What is of supreme interest is the change of a democratic state . . . without even an altering of the form or the closing of the National Assembly. . . . But the continuation under the dictatorial regime of

1925–1929 in Turkey of reforms—some of them begun long ago—
... are more interesting and profitable to consider than the terroristic
methods by which they are supposed to have been made possible. ...
The first and most spectacular of these was the so-called 'hat law'
passed in 1925. It was also the most futile and superficial. ... [B]ut
it was the only one [in original] which accomplished a change over-
night. ... To tell a Turk to put on a headdress and "get civilized' or
be hanged or imprisoned is absurd to say the least. ... The interesting fact ... is that of all the changes of the last four years, it attracted
the most attention in the western world. ... [while] the many fundamental changes taking place in Turkey have been either unnoticed,
criticized, or treated as unimportant ... in Western papers. ... The
first substantial result of the hat law was that it enriched European hat
factories at the expense of the already impoverished Turk. ...

The adoption of the Swiss code in place of Islamic family law
in 1926 was ... of a much more serious nature. ... The prevalent
journalist stuff published in the West about Turkish women declaring that they had been freed from harems in the thousands, that their
veils were lifted, and that they were first allowed to enter public life
as a result of this law, is both absurd and untrue. All Turkish men of
the progressive type ... especially from 1908 on, have ... helped to
give [Turkish women] rights and opportunities. ... From the moment Turkish women entered the economic field there has been no
discrimination whatever of the kind which European feminists complain of. Women in Turkey have always received the same salaries or
wages as men, and the fact of their being married or unmarried has
never hampered them in their search for work. ... In 1916 the University of Istanbul opened its doors to [women]. ... Naturally the
Great War gave these movements a practical turn. The governmental
departments as well as financial houses and trades had to employ a
great number of women ... [who] were forced to go to work in order
to support their families. ... The large amount of public work which
women were thus obliged to do led to a natural social freedom and
did away entirely with their partial seclusion in the majority of cities.

... The change of the Turkish alphabet from the Arabic to the
Latin characters is as important as the adoption of the Swiss family
law in its future significance.

**Reza Shah overthrew the Qajar ruler and established his own Pahlavi
dynasty in 1925. Relatively uneducated compared to Turkey's Mustafa
Kemal, Reza Shah also lacked Kemal's reputation as a war hero and
thus did not have widespread popular support for his regime. Reza**

"Reza Shah Visits Mustafa Kemal." This photo
was taken during the visit Reza Shah, on the
right, made to Turkey in 1934 to bolster his
political standing back home in Iran. In contrast
to Mustafa Kemal, Reza Shah rashly ordered the
veil's abolition, which triggered social resistance
among women and men.

Shah attempted to impose a state-sanctioned "women's awakening" project from 1936, which had only modest success compared to Turkey. Unlike Kemal, Reza Shah permitted polygamy to continue, in part, as a close adviser noted, because Reza Shah had more than one wife.

Of course in this business one must not forget the role of some of Reza Shah's advisers. For the removal of the veil, Teymourtache was very influential . . . and another was my father. During the time my father was in court, he would often speak about this issue with Reza Shah. Once, even now I don't know who else was there, [but] there were two or three people who were talking about the necessity of removing the veil and these things. The Shah said: 'Well, if this is a change that is really necessary . . . , very well let it come. It should not be an obstacle to the progress of the country. But I think I will divorce my two wives at that time.' But, later he did not do this because he went to Turkey and changed his outlook. And when Reza Shah came back, he decided to remove the veil in Iran [but retained polygamy].

Living in Two Worlds

Born in Beirut, Lebanon, in 1925 during the French Mandate created after World War I, Etel Adnan's (1925–) story illustrates the manner in which individual lives crossed religious and ethnic boundaries. The child of a Muslim/Christian marriage, with family in Damascus as well as Beirut, she attended a French school taught by Roman Catholic nuns in Beirut. Many Christian Lebanese, Maronite Catholics especially, identified with France, and private schools in Lebanon were predominantly French, dating to before World War I. A retired university professor of literature living in California, Adnan recalled her Lebanese upbringing in this 1986 address delivered to the Association of Middle Eastern Women's Studies meeting in Boston.

My mother was a Greek from Smyrna [Izmir in Turkey], and my father was a Syrian from Damascus who belonged to a family where the men served in the army of the Ottoman Empire. He was the commander of Smyrna during the First World War and although he was already married and the father of a boy and two girls, he married my mother who was about twenty years younger than he was. His first family had remained in Damascus. At the end of the war, he came to settle in Beirut [where] . . . I was born in 1925.

Lebanon was newly created as a state by the French. The French turned Syria and Lebanon into mandates under their rule. They expanded the already existing French schools in the country and favoured the establishment of new ones. They created in Lebanon,

Syria, 1928

The French do not seem able to distinguish between a mandate and a colony. The British, in Palestine, Irak and Transjordan, act as if they really expect some day to get out . . . even if, way down in their hearts, they do not intend that their wards shall be completely independent when they grow up, that, like Ireland, Egypt and other places . . . they must forever remain loyal to the empire . . . , Whereas the French act as if they intend to stay in Syria forever. They treat the Syrians . . . very much as they treat the Senegalese.

—Harry A. Franck

"Damascus, c. 1928." This photo captures one of the main city squares of Damascus, then ruled by France. We see a 19th-century Ottoman administrative building to the right, local shops on the left, with modern apartment buildings in the background.

and imposed on it, a system of education totally conforming to their schools in France, an education which had nothing to do with the history and geography of the children involved.

So at age five I started speaking French and then, only French, as Arabic was a forbidden language in these French schools . . . [which] were run by members of the French Catholic Church. . . . Arabic was forbidden [but] the Lebanese children spoke it at home. My mother not knowing Arabic [she knew Turkish and Greek] French took over as the language at home: we spoke less and less Turkish and Greek and more and more French. . . . The French nuns . . . behaved like colonialists and like missionaries: they had the dual purpose of extolling the virtues of French civilisation and the infallibility of the Church in matters of religion. . . . So I grew up thinking the world was French. And that everything that mattered, that was 'in books' or had authority (the nuns) did not concern our environment. This is what is called alienation. . . .

I was the only 'only' child at school, the only one among the children considered 'natives' by the ever-present nuns. . . . I was also the only child of mixed background: my father was a Muslim and my mother a Christian. Such a mixed marriage was an anomaly. . . . my mother was scorned by some for having married a Muslim. She was pitied by others.: 'Such a beautiful woman like you married to a Turk' some women neighbours would say. For most people my father, although an Arab, was a Turk because of his service in the Ottoman Empire. To marry a Muslim Turk was somehow worse than having married an Arab, at least in the eyes of the Maronite Christians who were more and more in positions of power in the new Lebanon. . . .

My father and I used to go very regularly to Damascus, where my aunt Fahima lived with her husband and two sons. My father loved Damascus, the city of his own childhood, with tenderness. He was different when he was there: relaxed, mysterious, romantic. And I was happy there, in a house where Arabic and Turkish were spoken, never French. It was another world, with Muslim feasts involving dinners on huge copper trays put on rugs, and trays of sweets brought in from the market by boys carrying them on their heads.

Damascus was the East, with its splendour, its specific qualities, its hushed conversations, its sense of history and grandeur. There I was a child of city Arabs mixed with Turkish blood and culture, of Arabs who were wondering if the Ottoman Empire was really any worse than the new colonisation. In Beirut it was puzzlement and everyday life, in Damascus it was magic and recreation. In Beirut I was a little Christian. In Damascus I was at the door of the Islamic world.

Thus I got used to standing between situations, to being a bit marginal and still a native, to getting acquainted with notions of truth which were relative and changed like the hours of the day and the passing of the seasons.

I ended up not being religious, seeing in the discourse held by the nuns some vague trap, some temptation I was refusing, some challenge to the world of my father, a father who always appeared weaker than my mother but always dignified. In my adolescence I viewed him as a tragic figure. . . .

My parents each having been uprooted many times, we had at home my father's Quran, my mother's book of Gospels in Greek, a Turkish-German dictionary from my father's War College days in Istanbul, and a few novels in Greek about Cleopatra, Egyptian saints of the desert and love stories . . . books my mother at some time in her life read aloud to her niece who came to live with us for a while . . .

Egypt: European Influences and the Definition of Culture

"Shepheard's Hotel, Cairo, c. 1920–25." Originally built in 1841, it became the hotel of choice for wealthy tourists by the end of the 19th century, its veranda an eagerly sought-after site for European social interactions. For many Egyptians the hotel symbolized British power and control. Egyptian rioters burned it to the ground in January 1952 as part of nationalist demonstrations against continued British control of a 200-square-mile sector of the Suez Canal Zone, a prelude to the Egyptian revolution of July 1952; several guests were killed.

In 1936 Great Britain signed a treaty with the Egyptian government granting more freedom to Egyptians generally. Egypt was permitted to station embassies abroad, and a military academy for officers was created, opening the way for native Egyptian officers in the Egyptian army. The capitulations were abolished in 1937, removing foreigners from immunity from Egyptian law. But Britain remained the dominant power in Egypt, and British influence permeated Egyptian life with the currency pegged to the British pound. As this 1937 tourist guide shows, Imperial Airways linked Egypt to Australia and to New Zealand as well as to British-controlled Palestine, India, and East Africa. These lines served European imperial interests, as did the Dutch KLM links to the Dutch East Indies. Moreover, foreign tourism was a major source of revenue and Egypt was promoted as a desirable vacation spot for tourists worldwide, including Japan, as the list of shipping lines indicates.

To the traveler contemplating a holiday in Egypt, there is one question that might very well be put: 'Which Egypt is that you wish to visit?' . . . Is it the land of sunshine, the Egypt of golden days and starry nights? The land where pearly sunrises usher in days of radiant warmth, where flaming sunsets give way to a sky of midnight blue? The favoured country where the convalescent regains strength, the tired worker finds rest and relaxation, where all may store up health and energy which will counteract the cold and damp of Northern winters? Is it the Egypt of ancient lore, the oldest country in the world? . . . Is it perhaps the magic of the East which attracts you? The Egypt where legends still linger of brave Arab warriors, of gallant Crusading knights? The city of Cairo . . . where a thousand minarets stand out in silhouette against the clear Eastern sky?

Or, it may be, you delight in contrast and wish to see, in its age-old setting, the new-born Egypt of today. Here, for you to behold, is a nation advancing by leaps and bounds in the path of modern progress. Here are cities with wide modern streets, tall modern buildings, electric trains, broadcasting stations, and all the adjuncts of twentieth-century civilisation. And yet, often within a stone's throw of all that is new, the same cities still possess the old covered bazaars, the winding lanes, the overhanging windows of mediaeval times. Perhaps your bent is sport and you feel the call of a land where outdoor games are practically exempt from worry about weather conditions. Bathing, boating, fishing, shooting, golf and tennis are only a few of Egypt's sporting attractions. . . .

Coordination between the Egyptian Government, steamship, railway and air lines and, last but not least, the many hotels and pensions in Egypt, has made the country easily accessible even to the traveler of moderate means. . . . The Egyptian monetary system is a simple one . . . and the Egyptian pound is pegged to sterling. . . . Foreign money may be changed at any bank or travel agency. Facilities for every kind of sport abound in Egypt. Temporary membership of the many sporting clubs is available to visitors. . . .

. . . Sea and air traffic between Europe and America, India, Far East, and Australia must necessarily make a call at Egyptian ports or aerodromes, and the shipping and air transport companies which undertake the Far East and Australian services are consequently available to passengers to Egypt. In addition . . . steamship lines from Europe to Egypt [and] direct lines from the United States to Egypt are also available.

[Among the many shipping companies are]: Aberdeen and Commonwealth Line, England to Port Said, stopping at Malta, . . . proceeding to Colombo [Ceylon, now Sri Lanka] and Australia; American Export Lines; British-India Steam Navigation Company, . . . Dollar Steamship Line; . . . Nederland Royal Mail Line; Nippon Yusen Kaisha; . . . Royal Roumanian State Line. . . .

IMPERIAL AIRWAYS operates five services a week between England and Egypt. Times takes 36 hours. The following are the new stopping places on the route: Southampton, Marseilles, Rome, Brindisi, Athens, Alexandria, Cairo. . . . Other services to and from South Africa, East Africa, Australia, Malaya, India, Iran and Palestine are also operated by Imperial Airways. . . . THE ROYAL DUTCH AIRLINES (K.L.M.) operate three regular services a week between Amsterdam, Leipzig, Budapest, Athens, Rhodes and Alexandria. . . . the service continues to the Dutch East Indies [today, Indonesia] whence the return journey is made thrice weekly.

Blind from early childhood, Taha Hussein (1889–1973), was educated first at the Muslim al-Azhar University in Cairo and later earned his doctorate at the Sorbonne in Paris. He served as Minister of Education and as president of the Egyptian University. The greatest scholar/litterateur of his generation, he wrote *The Future of Culture in Egypt* soon after the Anglo-Egyptian Treaty of 1936, motivated also by major cultural and political debates then current in Egypt, in particular the growing role of Islam and Islamic groups in Egyptian life. By 1928 a major new force had appeared with the founding of the Muslim Brotherhood to challenge the perceived pervasiveness of Western cultural and secular values in Egypt. At the same time, some of Taha's former allies in calling for secular culture and an identification with the Pharaonic civilization of ancient Egypt had begun to present Islam as the basis for Egyptian culture , motivated by what Taha refers to sarcastically as the spiritual nature of "the East" as opposed to the "materialistic West." Alarmed, Taha insisted on the importance of Egypt's ties with Europe and Western civilization, but denied that Egypt should slavishly imitate Western culture.

. . . . The subject to be treated . . . is the future of culture in Egypt, now that our country has regained her freedom through the revival of the constitution and her honor through the realization of independence. . . . Like every other patriotic, educated Egyptian who is zealous for his country's good reputation, I want our new life to harmonize with our ancient glory. . . . I do not like illusions. . . . I therefore believe that the new Egypt will not come into being except from the ancient eternal [Pharaonic] Egypt. I believe further that the new Egypt will have to be built on the great old one, and that the future of culture in Egypt will be an extension, a superior version of, the humble, exhausted feeble present. . . . At the outset we must ask this fundamental question: Is Egypt of the East or of the West? Naturally I mean East or West in the cultural, not the geographical sense. It seems to me that there are two distinctly different and bitterly antagonistic cultures on the earth. Both have existed from time immemorial, the one in Europe, the other in the Far East. . . . Is the Egyptian mind Eastern or Western in its imagination, perception, comprehension and judgment? . . . Which is easier for the Egyptian mind: to understand a Chinese or Japanese, or to understand an Englishman or a Frenchman? . . . The contacts between ancient Egypt and the lands of the East scarcely went beyond Palestine, Syria and Mesopotamia, that is the East that falls in the Mediterranean basin. . . . Historians tell us that the kings of Egypt extended their sway over them. Ancient Egypt was a major power politically and economically not only in comparison with her neighbors but with the countries that cradled the European civilization with which we are examining our kinship.

It would be a waste of time . . . to detail the ties binding Egypt to the ancient Greco-Aegean civilization. . . . [true] an Eastern nation, Persia, successfully invaded our country at the end of the sixth century, B.C. but we resisted fiercely until the Alexandrian era, having recourse at one time to Greek volunteers. . . . The meaning of all this is very clear: the Egyptian mind had no serious contact with the Far Eastern mind; nor did it live harmoniously with the Persian mind. The Egyptian mind has had regular, peaceful and mutually beneficial relations only with the Near East and Greece . . . influenced from earliest times by the Mediterranean Sea and the peoples living around it. . . .

[When] Islam arose . . . Egypt was receptive and hastened . . . to adopt it as her religion and to make the Arabic of Islam her language. Did that obliterate her original mentality? Did it make her an Eastern nation in the present meaning of the term? Not at all! Europe did not become Eastern nor did the nature of the European mind change because Christianity, which originated in the East, flooded Europe and absorbed the other religions. If European philosophers . . . deem Christianity to be an element of the European mind, they must explain what distinguishes Christianity from Islam; for both were born in the geographical East, both issued from one noble source and were inspired by the one God in whom Easterners and Westerners alike believe. . . . The essence and source of Islam are the essence and source of Christianity. The connection of Islam with Greek philosophy is identical to that of Christianity. . . .

In order to become equal partners in civilization with the Europeans, we must literally and forthrightly do everything they do; we must share with them the present civilization, with all its pleasant and unpleasant sides, and not content ourselves with words or mere gestures. . . . [On the other hand] I am pleading for a selective approach to European culture, not wholesale and indiscriminate borrowing. Europe is Christian. I do not call for the adoption of Christianity, but for the adoption of the motive-forces of European civilization. Without them, Egypt cannot live, let alone progress and govern herself. . . .

[Some] objectors to Western civilization . . . assert that it is ultra-materialistic and a source of misery both to Europe and the rest of the world. [Or] they insist that Europe is tired of her own civilization as evidenced by the . . . writers, scholars and philosophers who are turning away from it and seeking nourishment in the spirituality of the East. . . .

Certainly there is a good deal of materialism in European civilization, [but] it is absurd to deny that it possesses spiritual content. The brilliant successes of modern science and the inventions that have changed the face of the earth spring from imaginative and creative minds. . . . Moreover what is this spiritual East? It is assuredly not our Near East which, as . . . noted, is the cradle of the mind I have been lauding. . . . The spiritual east by which some Europeans are fascinated is clearly . . . the Far East. . . . Do we want to embrace the religion, philosophy and motive forces of the Chinese just when they are rapidly Westernizing themselves? This talk of a spiritual East is sheer nonsense. . . . The younger generation must be protected from such false knowledge, and the best, if not the only, method is to provide them with a sound education. . . .

In his 1947 novel, *Midaq Alley*, Neguib Mahfouz (1911–2006) portrayed the daily rhythms of neighborhood life in Cairo as seemingly indifferent to the impact of outside events, despite the blackouts, air raids, and

"King Farouk of Egypt, c. 1937." Farouk (1920–1965) succeeded to the throne in 1936, following the death of his father, Fuad. Only sixteen at the time of succession, he was initially seen by many Egyptians as a possible savior of Egyptian dignity who would resolve the many issues of political rivalries and corruption, but he himself became immersed in these rivalries, exacerbated by the close oversight imposed by the British ambassador, Sir Miles Lampson (1880–1964). Rumors about his personal life furthered his reputation as a playboy, unconcerned with Egyptian affairs, well before he was sent into exile after the officers' coup of July 1952; he died in Italy.

the greatly increased foreign military presence during World War II. But those inhabitants of Midaq Alley who attempted to abandon the quarter found themselves corrupted or disappointed in their contacts with the British, suggesting that its isolation preserved its integrity. Naguib Mahfouz won the Nobel Prize for Literature in 1988.

Many things combine to show that Midaq Alley is one of the gems of times gone by and that it once shone forth like a flashing star in the history of Cairo. Which Cairo do I mean? That of the Fatimids, the Mamlukes or the Sultans, [former rulers of Egypt]? Only God and the archaeologists know the answer to that, but . . . , the alley is certainly an ancient relic and a precious one. How could it be otherwise with its stone-paved surface leading directly to the historic Sanadiqiya Street. And then there is its coffeeshop known as "Kirsha's." Its walls decorated with multicolored arabesques, now crumbling, give off strong odors from the medicines of olden times, smells which have now become the spices and folk-cures of today and tomorrow. . . . Although Midaq Alley lives in almost complete isolation from all surrounding activity, it clamors with a distinctive and personal life of its own. Fundamentally and basically, its roots connect with life as a whole and yet, at the same time, it retains a number of the secrets of a world now past.

The sun began to set and Midaq Alley was veiled in the brown hues of the glow. . . . The noises of daytime life had quieted now and those of the evening began to be heard, a whisper here and a whisper there: "Good evening, everyone." "Come on in; it's time for the evening get-together." . . . Two shops, however, Uncle Kamil's, the sweets seller to the right of the alley entrance and the barber's shop on the left, remain open until shortly after sunset. It is Uncle Kamil's habit, even his right, to place a chair on the threshold of his shop and drop off to sleep with a fly-whisk resting in his lap. . . . He is a hulk of a man, his cloak revealing legs like tree trunks and his behind large and rounded like the dome of a mosque, its central portion resting on the chair and the remainder spilling over the sides. He has a belly like a barrel, great projecting breasts, and he seems scarcely to have any neck at all. . . . People are always telling him he will die suddenly because of the masses of fat pressing round his heart. He always agrees with them. But how will death harm him when his life is merely a prolonged sleep?" . . .

"The many times I've told you," shouted Hussain. . . . "Shake off this miserable life, close up your shop, leave this filthy alley behind. Rest your eyes from looking at Uncle Kamil's carcass. Work for the British army. It's a gold mine that will never be exhausted. . . . The war isn't a disaster. . . . It's a blessing. God sent it to us to rescue us from our poverty and misery. Those air-raids are throwing gold down on us. . . . The war will last at least another twenty years." . . .

One morning Midaq Alley awoke to a tumult of . . . noise and confusion. Men were setting up a pavilion in a vacant lot. . . . The sight distressed Uncle Kamil who thought they were constructing a funeral pavilion. In his high shrill voice he wailed "We all belong to God and to Him we shall return; Oh Almighty, Oh Omniscient One, Oh Master." He [asked] a youth passing in the street . . . who had died. "The pavilion isn't for a corpse, it's for an election campaign," answered the boy with a laugh. . . .

Hamida, a young woman desired by two men in Midaq Alley but eager to escape its confines, was seduced by an Egyptian pimp who trained women to learn English and appeal to English and American soldiers. Abbas, a former barber in the alley who had hoped to marry Hamida, discovered she was a prostitute. He entered a bar to find her surrounded by English troops. He hurled a cup, hitting her in the face, and the soldiers retaliated.

Hussein, . . . said hoarsely, 'Father, Abbas has been killed, the British murdered him. [When] he saw her in the midst of the soldiers . . . he went wild. . . . The soldiers got mad and . . . beat him 'til he fell down senseless. . . . Was she killed?' asked Kirsha [Hussein's father]. 'I don't think so,' answered Hussein. 'Too bad, he lost his life in vain.' Kirsha then quoted 'We are all God's creatures and to him we must return'. . . . This crisis too, like all the others, finally subsided and the alley returned to its usual state of indifference and forgetfulness. It continued, as was its custom, to weep in the morning when there was material for tears, and resound with laughter in the evening. . . .

Born into a family of religious notables, Hasan al-Banna (1906–1949), from an early age was preoccupied with questions of moral laxity and abandonment of religious values. He attended a teachers' training college in Cairo from 1923 to 1927 where he was dismayed by the wholesale adoption of European customs by the Egyptian ruling classes. To him, this behavior, especially the advocacy of more freedom for women and the adoption of European dresses, symbolized decadence and the loss of national as well as religious identity and culture. In short, al-Banna linked the British occupation of his country to cultural as well as political imperialism.

His beliefs were strengthened during his years as a teacher in Ismailiyah, on the Suez Canal, where the British Army, despite the 1936 treaty, retained control of a two-hundred-square-mile zone, a constant reminder of Egypt's impotence and shame. It was in Ismailiyah, in 1928, that he founded the *Ikhwan al-Muslimun*, the Muslim Brotherhood. For al-Banna, Islam, by offering social as well as moral guidance, provided the only possible resistance to foreign domination. In "Yesterday and To-day," al-Banna presents the early Islamic community, or *umma*, as the ideal to be restored and offers a treatise on how the Muslim Brotherhood might prevail in reforming and liberating modern Islamic societies.

In the Name of God, the Merciful, the Compassionate! . . .

The Europeans worked assiduously to enable the tide of [their] materialistic life, with its corrupting traits and its murderous germs, to overwhelm all the Islamic lands toward which their hands were outstretched. . . . They deluded the Muslim leaders by granting them loans and entering into financial dealings with them. . . . and thus they were able to obtain the right to infiltrate the economy and to flood the countries with their capital, their banks, and their companies; to take over the workings of the economic machinery . . . and to monopolize, to the exclusion of the inhabitants, enormous profits and immense wealth. After that, they were able to alter the basic principles of government, justice, and education, and to imbue political, juridical, and cultural systems with their own peculiar character in even the most powerful Islamic countries. They imported their half-naked women into these regions, together with their liquors, their theaters, their dance halls, their amusements, their stories, their newspapers, their novels, their whims, their silly games, and their vices. Here, they countenanced crimes they did not tolerate in their own countries, and decked out this frivolous, strident world, reeking with sin and redolent with vice, to the eyes of deluded, unsophisticated Muslims of wealth and prestige, and to those of rank and authority. This being insufficient for them, they founded schools and scientific and cultural institutes in the very heart of the Islamic domain, which cast doubt and heresy into the souls of its sons and taught them how to demean themselves, disparage their religion and their fatherland, divest themselves of their traditions and beliefs, and to regard as sacred anything Western, in the belief that only that which had a European source could serve as a model to be emulated in this life. These schools took in the sons of the upper class alone, and became a preserve restricted to them. . . . This drastic, well-organized social campaign had a tremendous success, . . . and some Islamic countries went overboard in their admiration for this European civilization and in their dissatisfaction with their own Islamic character, to the point that Turkey declared itself a non-Islamic state and imitated the Europeans with the utmost rigor in everything they did. . . . In Egypt the manifestations of this mimicry increased and became so serious that one of her intellectual leaders [Taha Hussein] could say openly that the only path to progress was to adopt this civilization with all it contained of good and evil, sweet and bitter, the appealing and the hateful, the praiseworthy and the reprehensible. . . .

Our General Aims: What do we want, Brethren? Do we want to hoard up wealth, which is an evanescent shadow? Or do we want an abundance of fame, which is a transient accident? Or do we want dominion over the earth. . . . Rather always bear in mind that you have two fundamental goals:

(1) That the Islamic fatherland be freed from all foreign domination, for this is a natural right belonging to every human being, which only the unjust oppressor or the conquering exploiter will deny.

(2) That a free Islamic state may arise in this free fatherland, acting according to the precepts of Islam, applying its social regulations, proclaiming its sound principles, and broadcasting its sage mission to all mankind. . . .

We want to realize these two goals in the Nile Valley and the Arab domain, and in every land which God has made fortunate through the Islamic creed: a religion, a nationality, and a creed uniting all Muslims.

Our Special Aims: Following these two aims, we have some special aims without . . . which our society cannot become completely Islamic. Brethren, . . . more than sixty per cent of the Egyptians live at a subhuman level; . . . they get enough to eat only through the most arduous toil, . . . there are more than 320 foreign companies in Egypt, monopolizing all public utilities and all important facilities in every part of the country; that the wheels of commerce, industry, and all economic institutions are in the hands of profiteering foreigners. . . .

Recall also that . . . Egypt is still backward; with no more than one-fifth of the population possessing any education, and of these more than 100,000 have never gone farther than the elementary school level. Recall that crime has doubled in Egypt, and that it is increasing at an alarming rate to the point that the prisons are putting out more graduates than schools. . . . Among your aims are to work for the reform of education; to war against poverty, ignorance, disease, and crime; and to create an exemplary society which will deserve to be associated with the Islamic Sacred Law.

Going to the Movies

The cinema expanded in the Middle East and North Africa after World War I. It aroused condemnation by Muslim moralists, such as Hasan al-Banna, and by Christian clergy who feared its corrupting influence, particularly on youth. Groups in Europe and the United States at the time also viewed the cinema as a negative social influence. Pierre Cachia (1921–] was born in Egypt of a Maltese father and a Russian mother. His father's family had long been established in Egypt and because they were Maltese, were British subjects. When Pierre was a boy, his family lived in a part of Egypt known as the Fayyum where his father was employed with a bank. His account of going to the movies illustrates the mixture of nationalities in Egyptian society.

The main entertainment we shared with adults was the cinema. There was only one 'picture palace' in the town, and it offered a change of program twice a week, so twice a week all who could afford it were herded in, no matter what was being shown. The owner was a dapper little man with a waxed moustache, whose love of histrionics gave rise to the rumor that he was a disbarred lawyer. As the building was the only one that could accommodate an occasional visit from a theatrical company, it had a small stage in front of the screen, and on this he would stride back and forth every evening to tell the audience what the next attraction was to be. He got his biggest round of applause when the trap that could accommodate a prompter's box was left open and he slipped into it. Of course he could impose his taste on the public and his taste rather oddly embraced Greta Garbo and Lon Chaney, the father. Thanks to him I saw the first film to experiment with sound. It was *the Phantom of the Opera*, which was not a 'talkie', but embodied one scene in which Lon Cheney's mad laughter was heard. There I also saw Abel Gance's *Napoleon*, later hailed as a masterpiece. I saw it again half a century later in New York. . . .

Except for the cinema, families made their own entertainment and frequently visited one another. One such family was headed by a Muslim called Zaki, married to a Frenchwoman. They had two daughters. The elder, Madeleine, was Vivienne's [Cachia's sister] closest friend. She was entirely French in appearance and culture. The very fact that she bore a European name was extremely unusual for a girl who was at least nominally a Muslim. . . . On the contrary,

Western Cinema in the Middle East

The introduction of American as well as European films into the Middle East challenged traditional centers of authority. In Beirut during the 1920s, the spiritual head of the Maronite Catholic Church, the Patriarch Anoine Arida, demanded that French colonial officials close down cinema houses. In the prelate's view, "It is France that perverts our people and introduces immorality to them."

her younger sister, Leila, was unmistakably Egyptian in every respect. Some thirty-five years after we had gone our separate ways, Madeleine saw a book of mine in a bookshop in Alexandria and wrote to me in Scotland, so on my next visit to Egypt I looked her up. The difference between the two sisters had had accentuated consequences. The law would not have allowed either one of them to marry a non-Muslim, and Madeleine had chosen not to marry at all, whereas Leila, widowed after bearing six children, was the hub of a noisy, chaotic, and happy household!"

One of Tunisia's best known writers, Albert Memmi (1920–), born into a Tunisian Jewish family of humble origins, went on to achieve a university education as well as international literary fame. In this memoir, Memmi recalls his childhood under French colonial rule and the interactions of the different European communities from working class populations that resided and worked in Tunis during the interwar period. Mostly Catholic, they were prejudiced against Jews.

I went to the movies on Saturdays. More than anything else, it was the way we spent our leisure time that showed up the difference between ourselves and our [wealthier] schoolmates; we used to go to the Kursaal [movie house in Tunis] which they considered a dive, having never set dainty foot there. Certainly they were not altogether wrong. In order to get in for the three o'clock show, we had to queue up at one, be jostled and elbowed and attacked by kids of our own age, older boys, and even adults, until the box office opened. Often the queue grew too long and dissolved into sudden confusion; by the time things had straightened out, we had lost our places. Once the tickets were torn out of my hand before I could identify the thief; Bissor in his rage couldn't refrain from railing at me while I burst into tears. So we went to complain to the manager and he allowed us into the theater despite his mistrust. . . .

[Once] I got to the Kursaal long before the box office opened, but there was already a big crowd. To my delight, a policeman was there lording it over the whole square. The Sicilian laborers who composed our aristocracy, with slicked-down hair and bright ties; the ragged bootblacks who were its lowest class and had to gather the price of a ticket by collecting cigarette butts; the fritter vendors in their greasy fezzes; the Maltese cabbies with their cap visors coquettishly broken; the porters with professional ropes thrown over their shoulders; all these people, so brutal and dishonest in past weeks, were now miraculously orderly, almost polite, waiting under the eyes of the of the Mohammadan policeman, an enormous fellow with a pock-marked face and a pointed black mustache. I felt happy being where I was: the façade of the Kursaal built to look like a dragon's head, spat out its flames; there were colored posters glued to the monster's cheeks, and the crowd itself was disturbing but full of living joy; all this contributed to give me each time the same glow of happiness. On this particular day there was also the promise of security. The posters on the dragon's cheeks announced two Tom Mix films and one Rin-Tin-Tin. We were used to this but we never tired of exulting in the triumphs of our wonderful cowboy. We joined him in his pursuit of the stagecoach that contained the gold and the exquisite blond heroine and was being driven away by bandits . . . for a few minutes we all forgot our individual fears and hatreds and became a single unit in the noisy expression of our emotions.

North African Experiences with France and the United States

Tawhida Ben Sheikh (1909–2010) was the first North African Muslim woman to earn a medical degree from the Faculty of Medicine in Paris, in 1936, while Tunisia was still under colonial rule. After she was awarded her medical diploma in France, Madame Ben Sheikh returned to Tunis, where she opened a women's reproductive health clinic, often providing free medical services for poor women. She was active in the nationalist movement until independence from France was won in 1956. In this 1992 interview with Dr. Ben Sheikh, she describes how she got to medical school.

"I come from a well-known Tunisian family. I never knew my father: we were four children, three girls and a boy. The son was born after my father's death. I was thus raised by my mother who was a most extraordinary woman. She was educated in Arabic and did not speak French. She was a devout Muslim and very open minded. Despite the fact that she was alone, widowed young, she managed to see to it that all of us had secondary school educations. My sisters and I were the first Tunisian girls to complete secondary school. That's the way she was, my mother, she wanted us to go as far as we wanted in school. I was the first girl to pass the baccalauréat degree in Tunisia, in 1928. But, of course then came the question, what was I going to do with it?

It was about then that I met a Russian woman, the wife of a well-known French doctor, Dr Burnet. He was the Deputy Director of the Pasteur Institute here in Tunis. His wife was a wonderful woman; she knew one of my professors at secondary school, who was interested in what I would do next. I wanted to do social work, help others; I thought I could work in one of the institutes or charities or the Pasteur Institute, So this woman suggested that I talk with her husband. Dr Etienne Burnet was a literary man, a philosopher who had studied Greek and Latin. He was also a famous medical researcher. I still remember going to see him. It was a summer day, in June or July. They lived on a hill in the Belvedere neighbourhood of Tunis. I went alone. It was 1929. I remember it so well. As soon as I arrived he asked, 'Now my little one, what is it you would like to do?' 'I would like to do something, perhaps study medicine,' I replied, 'but there is no medical school here in Tunis—so perhaps Algiers?' He looked at me; he hesitated, then said. 'My little one. If you want to accomplish something, to study medicine, you must enter by the big door. You must go to Paris.' I almost laughed. 'You are dreaming, sir.' 'I can help you.' he said. 'I know many people in Paris and can arrange for you to go there.' So I went home and told my mother, sisters and brother. My brother had received his baccalauréat at the same time as I, but my mother hadn't yet thought about sending him off to pursue university studies. I watched my mother's reaction to my story. She didn't reject it outright so I began to think that perhaps there was hope.

My mother had never left Tunisia, but she was very broad-minded and very courageous. Everyone—her mother, brothers, sisters—all of them said she shouldn't let me go. In the meantime Dr Burnet started writing to his friends in Paris to try to find a family in which I could live while I studied. Finally he found an opening in a brand new centre for women students, a centre founded by an American woman, a Mrs Anderson. It had one hundred student rooms and was called the Foyer International des Etudiantes. They telegraphed Dr Burnet saying there was an opening and, without even consulting me, he reserved a room for me. He was about to leave for Geneva to take up a new position there but, luckily, his wife was staying on a few weeks and would join him later. It meant that I could travel to France with her just before the university classes commenced in October. People in our strict family began to say that my mother had gone crazy. I had one uncle whom I thought I could count on because he had studied in France. He joined the other, saying, 'Your mother is crazy: she is sending you off to a city of perdition.'

I began to prepare my departure. On the day I was to leave, one of my mother's brothers was to send his car to take me to the port and the boat for France. A family meeting was called with my uncle Tahar Ben Amar and the husband of an aunt who was our legal guardian, and an Islamic cleric. This was necessary, of course. Here was this young girl, an orphan, who wanted to go off to France to study on her own. As I was waiting for the car, I saw another one arriving. In it was the cleric, my two uncles and a cousin who was just a bit older than I. As he brushed passed me he whispered in my ear. 'You know, everybody knows, you aren't to be allowed to leave.'

My aunt told my mother to cover herself and run to receive these men. My mother replied, 'Have them go upstairs, these aren't the first men or the last men that I will see.' So there we were, on the first floor in a sitting-room with our male guests, while the other women, my aunts, grandmother and sisters were all out of sight downstairs. Discussion, arguments, discussion—and in the meantime the car had arrived to take me to the port. I managed to tell the driver not to leave without me, no matter who told him to go away. And the discussions continued, slowly, slowly. 'How can a young girl who has never even been out of the city of Tunis'— I knew a bit of the city but not really even that much—'be permitted to go so far away?' Mother answered simply that many people travelled, for pleasure or for health treatment, and that it wasn't such a big thing. She added: 'My daughter wants to learn, to study and you know that in Islam it is an obligation for both men and women to learn and improve themselves.' The cleric became silent. Finally one of my uncles said, 'Well, then she can leave next week because a young girl should only travel with her father, a maternal uncle or a brother.' Again my mother replied. 'She is leaving with a woman of whom I am as confident as my own self.' At this point I put on my coat and ran downstairs to the car because I knew we were about to miss the boat. In fact, the boat sailed a few minutes late that day because of me."

Ahmed ben Messali Hadj was born in Algeria in 1898 and died in France in 1974. He was from a working class family and sought employment in the factories in France. In Paris, he came into contact with Marxist ideology as well as with trade unionism. In 1927, he was elected as leader of an Algerian workers' association based in Paris. A dedicated nationalist, he founded a number of political parties demanding Algerian independence from France. In 1937 he was arrested, put on trial for political agitation, and imprisoned. Here, in 1933, he demanded immediate Algerian independence as well as restoration of the lands seized by European settlers in Algeria from the peasants. He couched his appeal in Islamic as well as Marxist terms, pointing out that the landlord classes included European colonists as well as native "feudalists," wealthy Algerians who sided with

The Tunisian labor activist, M'hamed Ali, calling for a Tunisian labor federation in 1924 declared that,

The creation of a Tunisian federation does not mean that we shall not be united with the workers of the world as a whole. France, Germany, and England have national federations. Why are we denied similar rights? The only reason for their [the European Left's] attitude is that they would like to consider us as part of France. Is not imperialism a denial of equality? Why such accusations from Socialists and Communists? Are they also deceiving us?

the French and expanded their landed wealth at the expense of Algerian farmers. In contrast, Bourguiba's critique of French policy was more moderate. He appealed to France to grant more rights, modifying his criticisms with praise of French culture. Messali Hadj's demands were inspired in part by the French celebration in 1930 of the centenary of their occupation of Algeria in 1830. That anniversary and French celebration also sparked Algerian nationalist protests.

First Part

Immediate abolition of the odious Code de l'Indigénat and all measures of exception;

Amnesty for all those who are imprisoned, under special surveillance or exiled for infractions to the Indigénat or for political crimes;

1. Absolute freedom to travel to France and overseas;

2. Freedom of the press, association, gathering, political and union rights;

3. Replacement of the Financial Delegations elected through a restricted suffrage by an Algerian Parliament elected through universal suffrage;

4. Suppression of mixed communes and military territories. Replacement of these organisms by municipal assemblies elected through universal suffrage; . . .

9. Granting of agricultural credit to small fellahs, and a more rational organization of irrigation. Development of means of communication. Non-reimbursable assistance to the victims of periodic famines.

Second Part

1. The total independence of Algeria;

2. Total withdrawal of occupation troops;

3. Constitution of a national army.

Revolutionary national government:

1. A constitutional assembly elected through universal suffrage;

2. Universal suffrage at all levels and the eligibility of Algerians for all assemblies;

3. The Arabic language shall be considered an official language;

4. The hand over to the Algerian state of the banks, mines, railroads, ports and public services taken by the conquerors;

5. The confiscation of great properties taken by feudalists allied to the conquerors, the colonists and financial societies, and the return of confiscated land to the peasants. Respect for middle-sized and small property. The return to the Algerian state of Algerian lands and forests taken by the French state;

6. Free and mandatory instruction at all levels in Arabic;

7. Recognition by the Algerian state of the right to unions, coalitions and strikes; the elaboration of social laws.

8. Immediate assistance to fellahs by the granting to agriculture of interest-free credits for the purchase of machinery, seed, and fertilizer; the organization of immigration and the improvement of means of communication, etc

France occupied Tunisia in 1881. By the turn of the century, members of a new intelligentsia with a modern education and outlook founded the Young Tunisian movement. In 1920, the Tunisian Liberal Constitutional (Destour) Party was formed demanding expanded political and civil rights, but the French colonial regime rejected their appeals and disbanded the party by force. In the 1930s, a new generation of nationalists arose under the leadership of Habib Bourguiba (1903–2000) that appealed to the Tunisian masses to support demands for greater liberties under French rule. Bourguiba, the first president of independent Tunisia from 1956 until 1987, was educated in Tunis and later studied law in Paris where he developed an appreciation of France and its culture and even married a French woman. In his 1936 note to Pierre Vienot, the Undersecretary for French Foreign Affairs, Bourguiba expressed his hope that the new government in Paris would grant Tunisians expanded rights. After World War II, he and other nationalists demanded full independence, achieved in 1956.

It is indisputable that since the establishment of the protectorate [1881] and especially since the Great War, French policy in Tunisia has been dictated by the hostility of the Tunisian people toward France (which had imposed the new regime by force). . . . This [French] policy has taken an even more accelerated pace especially since the Great War—despite all the voluntary sacrifices that the Tunisians have made in favor of France—uniquely, please believe us, because of the appearance on the day after the armistice

"France Celebrates 100 Years of Ruling Algeria, 1830–1930." This French poster was designed to show Algerian prosperity under a century of French rule. It depicts Algerians catering to the tourist trade and goods arriving at the port of Algiers. France's celebration of its rule came at a time when Algerians were demanding independence from France.

of the liberal Tunisian constitutional [Destour] party that claimed by means of a written constitution the establishment of a less despotic, more liberal regime, more in touch with the stage of evolution at which the people have arrived and perfectly compatible with the principle of the protectorate. This normal phenomenon, which might have been foreseen in a people deeply influenced by a contact of 40 years with the genius of France, unleashed . . . an extremely violent reaction that strongly impressed the several residents-general who have succeeded one another in Tunis since that time. From there [came] these accusations of xenophobia, fanaticism, and of wishing to "throw the French into the sea" against the leaders of our party, so as to compromise our movement. . . . From there [came] this policy of systematic denationalization of the country that manifestly violated the treaties and that was destined to break the framework of the Tunisian nation. . . .

From there [came] this policy of unremitting settlement . . . and official colonization, destined by the vow of its promoters to counterbalance the numerical preponderance of the indigenous element judged unsure or hostile to France. From there [came] this obsession progressively to dissolve Tunisian sovereignty by . . . [turning] the protectorate into a convenient screen behind which . . . the pure and simple annexation of the country will be accomplished. From there [came] this system of political, economic, and fiscal inequalities and privileges, destined to keep the Tunisian perpetually in a state of inferiority beside the Frenchman and even the foreigner, . . . From there finally [came] this repressive system of the utmost perfection, which, I repeat, especially since the war and by use of an excessive legislation of common law, claimed to condemn an entire nation to silence under a regime of awful terror.

Such, in broad terms, is the general policy that has been practiced until now in the name of France by a narrow and irresponsible bureaucracy, a policy that must keep Tunisia "indissolubly linked to France." It is not an exaggeration to state today that this policy has completely failed, . . . But what must be underlined immediately is that . . . neither the Tunisian people, nor its chiefs—exiled into the desert—despaired of France, which they never confused with certain of those whose mission nevertheless was to represent it. It can be affirmed today that their hopes have not been disappointed. . . . From conversations that I have had with leaders responsible for French policy in Tunisia, I have been persuaded that France has decided to abandon the follies of the past, . . . and to attempt loyally with them to apply the formula for government that, in effective and progressive association with the administration of public affairs, can only reknit the bonds that unite them with the protecting power. . . . From now on, vigorous measures are necessary to encourage this evolution. . . .

(1) Cessation of official colonization . . .

(2) . . . the remodeling of the statute on the civil service so as to unify salaries on a fair basis . . . without any distinction between nationalities. . . . France must take full or limited responsibility for the expenses of . . . the policy of settlement which it thought necessary to practice for purely political reasons in favor of French immigration and which Tunisia is materially incapable of continuing to support. . . .

(5) Finally, in the political domain, the great reform that the Tunisian people have always demanded, that . . . will reconcile the Tunisian people with the protectorate and lead it toward emancipation within the orbit of France, namely, the replacement of the present despotic regime . . . by a constitutional and democratic regime that permits the people to share in the power and to take an active part in lawmaking and in voting on the budget. The institution of universal suffrage and the extension of the powers in this direction may be the bait for a deeper reform in the direction of the democratization of the regime. But all these reforms cannot be carried out until the Tunisian administration has been cleansed of all reactionary elements still imbued with the spirit of conquest and racial prejudice. . . .

Palestine from World War I to 1948

The mandates for Mesopotamia, to be known as Iraq, Syria, Lebanon, and Palestine, were assigned by the Supreme Court of the League of Nations to Britain and France at its San Remo meeting in April 1920. Britain and France then wrote the mandate drafts [see p. 182] for their assigned regions that were then officially approved by the Council of the League of Nations in July 1922. Their principles, however, had been imposed from April 1920. French forces invaded Lebanon and occupied Syria in July 1920, forcing Feisal to flee; he would later become King of Iraq under British auspices. In the Mandate for Palestine [July 24, 1922], the League of Nations recognized the "historical connection of the Jewish people with Palestine" and the "grounds for reconstituting their national home

Behold, we the American holy warriors have arrived. . . . We have come to set you free.

—American propaganda script broadcast to Berber tribes in Algeria on November 8, 1942

"Crowds Welcome Tunis's' Liberation, May 1943." Tunisia became a major battleground in 1943 as German troops moved in from the south, pushed eastward by Britain's Eighth Army following the battle at El Alamein, Egypt, in October 1942. They then clashed with American troops seeking to entrap them. German forces finally surrendered after escaping northward to the Cap Bon region, the northeastern most point of Tunisia. Here crowds of primarily European residents of French-controlled Tunis welcome Allied forces. Tunisian/Algerian encounters with American troops were often at odds with American propaganda: "We became ruthless with the Arabs," a First Division soldier wrote. "If we found them where they were not to be, they were open game, much as rabbits in the States during hunting season. . . ." "[another soldier] I saw men from another outfit shoot Arabs just to watch them jump and fall. . . . I could hear them yell and laugh each time and there was nothing I could do about it. . . . I saw them do it, like you're shooting gophers. I could hear them: 'Wow, I got another one.' Those guys were murderers."

in that country." This meant that the Balfour Declaration was included in the mandate, an act that violated Article 22 of the League of Nations Covenant on which the mandate was based. That clause stated that the mandatory had the obligation to prepare the inhabitants of the country, that is, the Palestinians, who were 90 percent of the population, for future self-government. Article 25 of the mandate accepted the British separation of land east of the Jordan River from Palestine to become Transjordan, later the Hashemite Kingdom of Jordan. It would be ruled by Emir Abdullah (1882–1951), a son of the Sharif Hussein of Mecca.

The World Zionist Organization established its office in London after World War I with Chaim Weizmann as its head. As Weizmann indicates, Zionists had constant access to and debated with British officials on how the responsibilities of the mandate should be defined.

By the autumn of 1921.... Curzon [Lord George]; (1859–1925) had taken over from Balfour at the Foreign Office and was in charge of the actual drafting of the mandate. On our side we had the valuable assistance of Mr. Ben V. Cohen.... one of the ablest draftsmen in America and he and Curzon's secretary—young Eric Forbes-Adam (1888–1925), highly intelligent, efficient and most sympathetic—fought the battle of the Mandate for many months. Draft after draft was proposed, discussed and rejected.... The most serious difficulty arose in connection with a paragraph in the Preamble—the phrase which now reads: 'Recognizing the historical connection of the Jews with Palestine.' Zionists wanted it to read 'Recognizing the historic rights of the Jews to Palestine.' But Curzon would have none of it, ... As a compromise Balfour suggested 'historical connection' and 'historical connection' it was.

The Council of the League of Nations:

"Whereas the Principal Allied Powers have agreed, for the purpose of giving effect to the provisions of Article 22 of the Covenant of the League of Nations, to entrust to a Mandatory selected by the said Powers the administration of the territory of Palestine, which formerly belonged to the Turkish Empire, within such boundaries as may be fixed by them; and

Whereas the Principal Allied Powers have also agreed that the Mandatory should be responsible for putting into effect the declaration originally made on November 2nd, 1917, by the Government of His Britannic Majesty, and adopted by the said Powers, in favour of the establishment in Palestine of a national home for the Jewish people, it being clearly understood that nothing should be done which might prejudice the civil and religious rights of existing non-Jewish communities in Palestine, or the rights and political status enjoyed by Jews in any other country ; and

Whereas recognition has thereby been given to the historical connection of the Jewish people with Palestine and to the grounds for reconstituting their national home in that country; and

Whereas the Principal Allied Powers have selected His Britannic Majesty as the Mandatory for Palestine; and ...

Confirming the said mandate, defines its terms as follows:

Article 1. The Mandatory shall have full powers of legislation and of administration, save as they may be limited by the terms of this mandate.

Article 2. The Mandatory shall be responsible for placing the country under such political, administrative and economic conditions as will secure the establishment of the Jewish national home, as laid down in the preamble, and the development of self-governing institutions, and also for safeguarding the civil and religious rights of all the inhabitants of Palestine, irrespective of race and religion. . . .

Article 4. An appropriate Jewish agency shall be recognised as a public body for the purpose of advising and co-operating with the Administration of Palestine in such economic, social and other matters as may affect the establishment of the Jewish national home and the interests of the Jewish population in Palestine, and, subject always to the control of the Administration, to assist and take part in the development of the country.

The Zionist organisation, so long as its organisation and constitution are in the opinion of the Mandatory appropriate, shall be recognised as such agency. . . .

Article 6. The Administration of Palestine, while ensuring that the rights and position of other sections of the population are not prejudiced, shall facilitate Jewish immigration under suitable conditions and shall encourage . . . close settlement by Jews, on the land. . . .

Article 11. . . . The Administration may arrange with the Jewish agency mentioned in Article 4 to construct or operate, upon fair and equitable terms, any public works, services and utilities, and to develop any of the natural resources of the country, in so far as these matters are not directly undertaken by the Administration. . . .

Article 13. All responsibility in connection with the Holy Places and religious buildings or sites in Palestine, including that of preserving existing rights and of securing free access to the Holy Places, religious buildings and sites and the free exercise of worship, while ensuring the requirements of public order and decorum, is assumed by the Mandatory,

Article 15. . . . No discrimination of any kind shall be made between the inhabitants of Palestine on the ground of race, religion or language. No person shall be excluded from Palestine on the sole ground of his religious belief. The right of each community to maintain its own schools for the education of its own members in its own language, while conforming to such educational requirements of a

"Lord Balfour Visits Zionist Settlements, 1925." Arthur Balfour, as an ardent Gentile Zionist and issuer of the 1917 Balfour Declaration, was invited to Palestine in 1925 to participate in the laying of the foundation stone of the Hebrew University of Jerusalem. Here he, in light suit, is welcomed at one of the Zionist agricultural settlements during his visit.

general nature as the Administration may impose, shall not be denied or impaired. . . .

Article 22. English, Arabic and Hebrew shall be the official languages of Palestine. Any statement or inscription in Arabic on stamps or money in Palestine shall be repeated in Hebrew, and any statement or inscription in Hebrew shall be repeated in Arabic.

Article 25. In the territories lying between the Jordan and the eastern boundary of Palestine as ultimately determined, the Mandatory shall be entitled, with the consent of the Council of the League of Nations, to postpone or withhold application of such provisions of this mandate as he may consider inapplicable to the existing local conditions, and to make such provision for the administration of the territories as he may consider suitable to those conditions. . . . Done at London the twenty-fourth day of July, one thousand nine hundred and twenty-two.

Issued by the Colonial Secretary, Winston Churchill (1874–1966), a month before the official declaration of the mandate, this British White Paper of June 1922 on European Jewish immigration to Palestine sought to allay Palestinian Arab fears and calm social unrest. Jewish immigration since the end of the war had led to clashes between Arabs and Jews, as some immigrants called for transferring Palestinian Arabs to other Arab lands. Although the statement seemed to modify assumptions that a Jewish state in all of Palestine was intended, that remained Zionist policy. The Palestinian response to the White Paper follows.

"The Secretary of State for the Colonies has given renewed consideration to the existing political situation in Palestine, with a very earnest desire to arrive at a settlement of the outstanding questions which have given rise to uncertainty and unrest among certain sections of the population. . . .

The tension which has prevailed from time to time in Palestine is mainly due to apprehensions . . . entertained both by sections of the Arab and by sections of the Jewish population. These apprehensions, so far as the Arabs are concerned are partly based upon exaggerated interpretations of the meaning of the [Balfour] Declaration. . . . Unauthorized statements have been made to the effect that the purpose in view is to create a wholly Jewish Palestine. Phrases have been used such as that Palestine is to become "as Jewish as England is English." His Majesty's Government regard any such expectation as impracticable and have no such aim in view. Nor have they at any time contemplated, as appears to be feared by the Arab delegation, the disappearance or the subordination of the Arabic

population, language, or culture in Palestine. They would draw attention to the fact that the terms of the Declaration referred to do not contemplate that Palestine as a whole should be converted into a Jewish National Home, but that such a Home should be founded 'in Palestine.' In this connection it has been observed with satisfaction that at a meeting of the Zionist Congress, the supreme governing body of the Zionist Organization, held at Carlsbad in September, 1921, a resolution was passed expressing as the official statement of Zionist aims "the determination of the Jewish people to live with the Arab people on terms of unity and mutual respect, and together with them to make the common home into a flourishing community, the upbuilding of which may assure to each of its peoples an undisturbed national development."

It is also necessary to point out that the Zionist Commission in Palestine, now termed the Palestine Zionist Executive, has not desired to possess, and does not possess, any share in the general administration of the country. Nor does the special position assigned to the Zionist Organization in Article IV of the Draft Mandate for Palestine imply any such functions. That special position relates to

"Palestinian Leaders Protest British Policy, 1930." Palestinian leaders of various backgrounds met, as shown here, to prepare to present petitions to a visiting British delegation after major riots erupted in 1929. In the front row, second left, is Hajj Amin el-Husseini (1897–1974), mufti of Jerusalem and leader of the Palestine Arab Party. To his left is Musa Kazim el-Husseini (1850–1934), former mayor of Jerusalem and cousin of Hajj Amin. To his left is Raghib al-Nashashibi (1881–1951), who succeeded to the mayoralty in 1920, the primary Arab Muslim rival of Hajj Amin. To his left (far right, front row) is Alfred Roch, a Palestinian of Greek Catholic faith, and a member of Hajj Amin's Palestine party.

the measures to be taken in Palestine affecting the Jewish population, and contemplates that the organization may assist in the general development of the country, but does not entitle it to share in any degree in its government. . . . So far as the Jewish population of Palestine are concerned it appears that some among them are apprehensive that His Majesty's Government may depart from the policy embodied in the Declaration of 1917 . . . that Declaration . . . is not susceptible of change.

During the last two or three generations the Jews have recreated in Palestine a community . . . [with] its own political organs; . . . Its business is conducted in Hebrew as a vernacular language, and a Hebrew Press serves its needs. It has its distinctive intellectual life and displays considerable economic activity. This community . . . has in fact "national" characteristics. When it is asked what is meant by the development of the Jewish National Home in Palestine, it may be answered that it is not the imposition of a Jewish nationality upon the inhabitants of Palestine as a whole, but the further development of the existing Jewish community, with the assistance of Jews in other parts of the world, in order that it may become a centre in which the Jewish people as a whole may take, on grounds of religion and race, an interest and a pride. But in order that this community should have the best prospect of free development and provide a full opportunity for the Jewish people to display its capacities, it is essential that it should know that it is in Palestine as of right and not on the sufferance. That is the reason why it is necessary that the existence of a Jewish National Home in Palestine should be internationally guaranteed, and that it should be formally recognized to rest upon ancient historic connection. . . . For the fulfillment of this policy it is necessary that the Jewish community in Palestine should be able to increase its numbers by immigration. . . . It is essential to ensure that the immigrants should not be a burden upon the people of Palestine as a whole, and that they should not deprive any section of the present population of their employment. . . .

The Palestinian Arab Response to the Churchill White Paper

. . . (4). The Memorandum goes on to discuss the existing Jewish Community in Palestine which it says possesses 'national characteristics' because it has 'its own political organs, an elected assembly . . .

etc.' We would here remark that all those outward signs of a 'national' existence are also possessed by other communities in Palestine, and if these are to be considered as a reason why the Jews outside Palestine should be allowed into Palestine 'as of right and not on sufferance', it is the more reason why the Arabs should be confirmed in their national home as against all intruders and immigration placed in their control. . . .

The White Paper of 1939 reversed the commitment Great Britain had made to European Zionists in the 1917 Balfour Declaration by declaring that Britain had never intended to go against the wishes of the majority Arab population of Palestine when issuing the declaration. The White Paper severely restricted Jewish land purchases and immigration at a time when Jews were fleeing Nazi racial laws and seeking access to Palestine. It stemmed from a major Palestinian Arab revolt of 1936 to early 1939 over fears resulting from greatly increased Zionist immigration following Hitler's rise to power in 1933. Yet Britain issued this 1939 White Paper appearing to promise an Arab majority state within ten years, just after crushing the Arab Revolt. The reason was the looming war in Europe and fears that Arabs in other areas controlled by Britain [Egypt and Iraq] might rebel against Britain because of concern at the fate of Palestinians. The Zionist leadership, recognizing that they could not oppose Britain when it was fighting Nazi Germany, vowed to "fight the war as if there was no white paper, and then fight the white paper as if there was no war." Once the German threat receded from the Middle East at the end of 1942, Zionists began storing stolen weapons and planning for a revolt against the British at the end of the war.

The Mandate for Palestine . . . embodies the Balfour Declaration. . . . Previous commissions of Enquiry have drawn attention to the ambiguity of certain expressions in the Mandate, such as the expression 'a national home for the Jewish people', and they have found in this ambiguity . . . a fundamental cause of unrest and hostility between Arabs and Jews. His Majesty's Government are convinced that in the interests of the peace and well being of the whole people of Palestine a clear definition of policy and objectives is essential. . . . Their views

"The Peel Commission in Jerusalem, 1936–1937." Following Arab strikes against greatly increased Jewish immigration triggered by Hitler's rise to power in Germany in 1933, London appointed Sir William Peel (1867–1937) to head a commission to recommend future policy. Here we see members of the commission in front of the Dome of the Rock. The Commission's report, issued in 1937, sharply criticized British policy goals for assuming Arab acceptance of a Zionist state in Palestine, but went on to recommend partition of Palestine into two states. The Zionist portion amounted to 25% of the area, but included the wealthiest, citrus crop region where half the population was Arab; it would have to be moved into the Arab sector and landowners compensated for their losses. The proposed Palestinian state, while much larger, would include Transjordan, and the ruler of the new Palestinian state would be Transjordan's Emir Abdullah, not a Palestinian. Zionists hesitantly accepted the plan while requesting more land. Palestinians rejected it, resulting in major outbursts of violence known as the Arab Revolt that lasted into early 1939.

and proposals are set forth below under three heads, Section I, "The Constitution," Section II, "Immigration," and Section III, "Land."

Section I. "The Constitution" . . . His Majesty's Government believe that the framers of the Mandate in which the Balfour Declaration was embodied could not have intended that Palestine should be converted into a Jewish State against the will of the Arab population of the country. . . . His Majesty's Government therefore now declare unequivocally that it is not part of their policy that Palestine should become a Jewish State. They would indeed regard it as contrary to their obligations to the Arabs under the Mandate, as well as to the assurances which have been given to the Arab people in the past, that the Arab population of Palestine should be made the subjects of a Jewish State against their will.

[As for Jewish immigration] . . . , since . . . 1922 . . . more than 300,000 Jews have immigrated to Palestine, and that the population of the National Home has risen to some 450,000, or approaching a third of the entire population of the country. . . .

His Majesty's Government are charged as the Mandatory authority "to secure the development of self governing institutions" in Palestine. . . . [and] The objective of His Majesty's Government is the establishment within 10 years of an independent Palestine State in such treaty relations with the United Kingdom as will provide satisfactorily for the commercial and strategic requirements of both countries in the future. The proposal for the establishment of the independent State would involve consultation with the Council of the League of Nations with a view to the termination of the Mandate.

The independent State should be one in which Arabs and Jews share government in such a way as to ensure that the essential interests of each community are safeguarded. . . . During the transitional period [of ten years]. . . . Both sections of the population will have an opportunity to participate in the machinery of government, and the process will be carried on whether or not they both avail themselves of it. . . .

Section II. Immigration.

. . . [I]n the Command Paper [Churchill White Paper] of [July]1922 [Doc. 5.17A] it was laid down that for the fulfilment of the policy of establishing a Jewish National Home:

" . . . It is essential to ensure that the immigrants should not be a burden upon the people of Palestine as a whole, and that they should not deprive any section of the present population of their employment."

. . . Although it is not difficult to contend that the large number of Jewish immigrants who have been admitted so far have been absorbed economically, the fear of the Arabs that this influx will continue indefinitely until the Jewish population is in a position to dominate them has produced consequences which are extremely grave for Jews and Arabs alike and for the peace and prosperity of Palestine. The lamentable disturbances of the past three years are only the latest and most sustained manifestation of this intense Arab apprehension. The methods employed by Arab terrorists against fellow Arabs and Jews alike must receive unqualified condemnation. But it cannot be denied that fear of indefinite Jewish immigration is widespread amongst the Arab population and that . . . [if] immigration is continued up to the economic absorptive capacity of the country, regardless of all other considerations, a fatal enmity between the two peoples will be perpetuated, and the situation in Palestine may become a permanent source of friction amongst all peoples in the Near and Middle East. . . .

. . . [But] to abruptly stop further immigration would be unjust to the Jewish National Home. . . . above all, His Majesty's Government are conscious of the present unhappy plight of large numbers of Jews who seek refuge from certain European countries, and they believe that Palestine can and should make a further contribution to the solution of this pressing world problem. . . . by adopting the following proposals . . . :

Jewish immigration during the next five years will be at a rate which . . . will bring the Jewish population up to approximately one third of the total population of the country. . . . this would allow of the admission, as from the beginning of April this year, of some 75,000 immigrants over the next five years. . . .

After the period of five years, no further Jewish immigration will be permitted unless the Arabs of Palestine are prepared to acquiesce in it.

His Majesty's Government are determined to check illegal immigration, and further preventive measures are being adopted. . . .

Section III. Land.

. . . The Reports of several expert Commissions have indicated that, owing to the natural growth of the Arab population and the steady sale in recent years of Arab land to Jews, there is now in certain areas no room for further transfers of Arab land, whilst in some other areas such transfers of land must be restricted if Arab cultivators are to maintain their existing standard of life and a considerable landless Arab population is not soon to be created. In these circumstances, the High Commissioner will be given general powers to prohibit and regulate transfers of land. These powers will date from the publication of this statement of policy and the High Commissioner will retain them throughout the transitional period. . . .

The end of World War II revealed the extent of the Holocaust. Over half a million Jewish refugees from the concentration camps survived and were placed in internment camps until arrangements for their destinations could be made. Most refugees hoped to go to the United States but were persuaded by Zionist representatives from Palestine to say that they longed to go to Palestine to focus world attention on the need for a Jewish state and negate the 1939 British White Paper. The British, hoped to retain control of Palestine with American support, while U.S. President Harry S Truman, to British dismay, insisted on linking Holocaust survivors to Palestine. In addition to his own sympathies, this position held political benefits for Truman; there was a by-election in November 1946 and Truman was advised that backing the introduction of 100,000 Jews to Palestine would be politically advantageous to the Democratic Party. A month before the election, President Truman issued the following White House statement supporting the transfer of 100,000 Jews to Palestine. In February 1947, weakened by the war and dependent on American financial aid, Great Britain decided to withdraw from Palestine by October 1948 at the latest and handed the issue over to the United Nations.

"I have learned with deep regret that the meetings of the Palestine Conference in London have been adjourned and are not to be resumed until December 16, 1946. In the light of this situation it is appropriate . . . to state my views on the situation as it now exists.

It will be recalled that, when Mr. Earl Harrison reported on September 29, 1945, concerning the condition of displaced persons in Europe, I immediately urged that steps be taken to relieve the situation of these persons to the extent at least of admitting 100,000 Jews into Palestine. In response to this suggestion the British Government invited the Government of the United States to cooperate in setting up a joint Anglo-American Committee of Inquiry. . . . The unanimous report of the Anglo-American Committee of Inquiry was made on April 20, 1946, and I was gratified to note that among the recommendations contained in the Report was an endorsement of my previous suggestion that 100,000 Jews be admitted into Palestine. The administration immediately concerned itself with devising ways and means for transporting the 100,000 and caring for them upon their arrival. . . . The British Government cooperated with this group but made it clear that in its view the Report must be considered as a whole and that the issue of the 100,000 could not be considered separately. . . .

I have, . . . repeatedly made known and have urged that steps be taken at the earliest possible moment to admit 100,000 Jewish refugees to Palestine. . . . Meanwhile, the Jewish Agency proposed a solution of the Palestine problem by means of the creation of a viable Jewish state in control of its own immigration and economic policies in an adequate area of Palestine instead of in the whole of Palestine.

It proposed furthermore the immediate issuance of certificates for 100,000 Jewish immigrants. This proposal received wide-spread attention in the United States, both in the press and in public forums. From the discussion which has ensued it is my belief that a solution along these lines would command the support of public opinion in the United States. . . . In the light of the situation which has now developed I wish to state my views as succinctly as possible:

1. . . . I believe and urge that substantial immigration into Palestine cannot await a solution to the Palestine problem and that it should begin at once. Preparations for this movement have already been made by this Government and it is ready to lend its immediate assistance.

In the light of the terrible ordeal which the Jewish people of Europe endured during the recent war and the crisis now existing, I cannot believe that a program of immediate action along the lines suggested above could not be worked out with the cooperation of all people concerned. The administration will continue to do everything it can to this end.

Israel's Declaration of Independence on May 14, 1948, resulted from the events that followed the UN General Assembly partition recommendation of 1947. Fighting erupted between Jewish and Palestinian forces. The Zionists triumphed by the end of April 1948, causing hundreds of thousands of Palestinians to flee. The British officially withdrew on May 14, 1948, with David Ben-Gurion (1886–1973), Israel's first prime minister and former head of the Jewish Agency, immediately declaring the independent state of Israel. Ben-Gurion refers to

"The Zionist Refugee Ship, Exodus, 1947." The closing months of World War II disclosed the extent of the Holocaust and led Zionists in Palestine and, outside Palestine, especially in the United States, to demand the settlement of Holocaust survivors and other Jewish refugees in Palestine. Britain hoped to retain Palestine in the face of Zionist terror attacks against their troops and civilian employees, and sought to block Zionist-sponsored refugee ships such as the Exodus, a former American cargo ship during the war, from reaching Palestine. The British commandeered the ship and brought it into port as shown here. But rather than sending the passengers to Cyprus, the normal policy, British officials forced it to return to Europe where, after various refusals to allow it to dock, it berthed in Germany where its passengers were again placed in barbed wire camps, albeit with adequate food. The fate of the Exodus and its passengers became a major propaganda victory for the Zionist leadership in Palestine, as it occurred during the visit of a British commission that would ultimately recommend partition to the newly formed United Nations, seeing no other way to resolve the Zionist-Palestinian impasse. That recommendation would be approved in November, meeting Zionist approval and Palestinian rejection.

Arab armies that had initiated attacks following the British withdrawal. Better armed and slightly outnumbering the Arab forces, Israeli troops defeated the Arabs and, in the process, ousted another three hundred and fifty thousand Palestinians. Armistice agreements were drawn up between Israel and surrounding Arab states during 1949, but technically a state of war still existed.

Eretz-Israel [The Land of Israel] was the birthplace of the Jewish people. Here their spiritual, religious and political identity was shaped. Here they first attained to statehood, created cultural values of national and universal significance and gave to the world the eternal Book of Books. After being forcibly exiled from their land, the people remained faithful to it throughout their Dispersion and never ceased to pray and hope for their return to it and for the restoration in it of their political freedom. . . .

In the year 5657 (1897), at the summons of the spiritual father of the Jewish State, Theodor Herzl, the First Zionist Congress convened and proclaimed the right of the Jewish people to national rebirth in its own country This right was recognized in the Balfour Declaration of the 2nd November, 1917, and re-affirmed in the Mandate of the League of Nations which, in particular, gave international sanction to the historic connection between the Jewish people and Eretz-Israel and to the right of the Jewish people to rebuild its National Home.

The catastrophe which recently befell the Jewish people—the massacre of millions of Jews in Europe—was another clear demonstration of the urgency of solving the problem of its homelessness by re-establishing in Eretz-Israel the Jewish State, which would open the gates of the homeland wide to every Jew and confer upon the Jewish people the status of a fully privileged member of the comity of nations. Survivors of the Nazi holocaust in Europe, as well as Jews from other parts of the world, continued to migrate to Eretz-Israel, undaunted by difficulties, restrictions and dangers, and never ceased to assert their right to a life of dignity, freedom and honest toil in their national homeland. In the Second World War, the Jewish community of this country contributed its full share to the struggle of the freedom—and peace-loving nations against the forces of Nazi wickedness and . . . gained the right to be reckoned among the peoples who founded the United Nations.

On the 29th November, 1947, the United Nations General Assembly passed a resolution calling for the establishment of a Jewish State in Eretz-Israel. . . . This recognition by the United Nations of the right of the Jewish people to establish their State is irrevocable. This right is the natural right of the Jewish people to be masters of their own fate, like all other nations, in their own sovereign State.

Accordingly, we, members of the People's Council, representatives of the Jewish community of Eretz-Israel, and of the Zionist movement, are here assembled on the day of the termination of the British mandate over Eretz-Israel and, by virtue of our natural and historic right and on the strength of the resolution of the United Nations General Assembly hereby declare the establishment of a Jewish state in Eretz-Israel, to be known as the state of Israel. . . .

The state of Israel will be open for Jewish immigration and for the Ingathering of the Exiles; it will foster the development of the country for the benefit of all its inhabitants; it will be based on freedom, justice and peace as envisaged by the prophets of Israel; it will ensure complete equality of social and political rights to all its inhabitants irrespective of religion, race or sex; it will guarantee freedom of religion, conscience, language, education and culture; it will safeguard the Holy Places of all religions; and it will be faithful to the principles of the Charter of the United Nations. . . .

We appeal to the United Nations to assist the Jewish people in the building-up of its State and to receive the State of Israel into the comity of nations. We appeal—in the very midst of the onslaught launched against us now for months—to the Arab inhabitants of the State of Israel to preserve peace and participate in the upbuilding of the State on the basis of full and equal citizenship and due representation in all its provisional and permanent institutions.

"Declaration of the State of Israel, May 14, 1948." Here David Ben Gurion (1886–1973), first prime minister of Israel, reads the Israeli declaration of independence beneath a photograph of Theodor Herzl, first president of the World Zionist Organization.

We extend our hand to all neighboring states and their peoples in an offer of peace and good neighborliness, and appeal to them to establish bonds of cooperation and mutual help with the sovereign Jewish people settled in its own land. The State of Israel is prepared to do its share in a common effort for the advancement of the entire Middle East.

We appeal to the Jewish people throughout the Diaspora to rally round the Jews of Eretz-Israel in the tasks of immigration and upbuilding and to stand by them in the great struggle for the realization of the age-old dream—the redemption of Israel.

Placing our trust in the Almighty, we affix our signatures to this proclamation at this session of the Provisional Council of the State, on the soil of the homeland, in the city of Tel Aviv, on this Sabbath eve, the 5th day of Iyar 5708 (14 May 1948).

Iraqi Jews in the 1930s and 1940s

Most Iraqi Jews migrated to Israel after its independence in 1948, but not all were eager to leave. The Jewish community had deep roots in Iraq dating to the pre-Christian era, and many Jews were well integrated in broader Iraqi society and culture. But there had been two days of attacks on Jews in 1941, known as the *Farhud* (Violent Dispossession) following a failed Iraqi nationalist attempt to oust the monarchy, with many Jews killed and injured. More pressures emerged following Israel's declaration of independence and organized Zionist efforts in Iraq to encourage emigration to Israel.

An educated Baghdadi Jew and student of English literature, Nissim Rejwan (1924–), was a journalist and a bookstore owner in Baghdad, and later a journalist and author in Israel and the United States. The *farhud* to which he refers in this memoir erupted after a pro-German Iraqi nationalist, Rashid Ali al-Gailani, led a short-lived revolt against Britain and the Iraqi monarchy in May 1941, hoping to liberate Iraq from British control with German help, which never came. In Karrada, as in other upscale Baghdad neighborhoods, Iraqi Jews and Muslims of various sects lived together. Rejwan's account disproves claims that Arabs generally backed Nazi Germany against Britain. Many, including a young Egyptian officer, Anwar al-Sadat, sought to use Germany to rid their countries of British occupation, but that did not mean he accepted Nazi racist ideology toward Jews.

.... Throughout the [civil] war [May 1941].... The populace in Iraq's major cities was in a state of euphoria which alternated between attacks of fear and xenophobia. There were some cases of minor molesting of Jews, whose every movement tended to be interpreted as some satanic pro-British device.... On May 31, after ... the [Hashemite] regent announced he would return to Baghdad ... the Jews started to relax [but were then attacked by Iraqi soldiers loyal to Gailani who had been allowed to return to Baghdad—British troops remained outside Baghdad]. Various versions have been told as to what actually happened that Sunday and the following day. According to official figures the riots and murders ... those two days claimed a total of 110 dead, among them 28 women, and 204 injured, and that the victims were from both sides, Jews and Muslims.

[As for] The number of homes and shops assaulted and broken into ... [Jewish community statistics indicate] 586 shops and stores alone, while the total value of goods, valuables and money looted as 271,402 Iraqi dinars. As to homes the community gave the figure as 911, with 3,395 families and 12,311 inhabitants.... Unlike the official version ... which mentioned no cases of rape, the community [estimated] three or four such cases.

The Jews of Baghdad were caught completely unaware.... Seeing that not only soldiery but some ... policemen [took] part ... the mobs in ... [some] destitute] areas—where Muslims and Jews lived in close proximity—became more systematic, and by early afternoon large trucks were seen moving furniture and other household goods....

These forages, often accompanied by physical violence resulting in deaths and injuries ... [provoked] no effective reaction on the part of the police. ... The *farhud* ... spread throughout the poor neighborhoods. ... It is interesting to note here that Karrada and some of the more fashionable suburbs of Baghdad where Jews constituted the majority of the inhabitants, witnessed the least trouble, some of them none at all. In many cases, armed Muslim neighbors stood guard and managed to chase away mobs intending to attack and loot....

Totally unaware of what was going on in other parts of the city, I left the house a little after 4:00 p.m. that same Sunday and took the bus to Bab al-Sharqi where the open-air cafes and snack bars were. As usual, my friends and I ... [discussed] the month's events for the nth time. Although a true patriot himself, my Muslim friend Salman was pleased with the outcome of Rashid Ali's rebellion since the British and their allies were fighting the Nazis and Fascists. Anti-British he certainly was, but like many moderate Iraqis with left-wing leanings, he was content with leaving his anti-imperialist sentiments in abeyance. ... It was only when we approached Suq el-Shorja ... that I began to feel something was definitely wrong. ... We duly saw our friend safely home, refusing to leave him until he was inside the house. Then Salman decided, and I did not object, that he should see me home as well. I will never forget the way I was let in.... Only after assuring the people inside it was me did they [agree] to open the door.... They ... [had] simply [given] me up for dead, killed by one of those murdering bands of agitated Muslims roaming the streets and alleyways. [As for our home] Without even being approached, the three older sons of our aging neighbor [Muslim] ... assured us we could rely on their protection....

The psychological consequences that the *farhud* had on the Jews of Iraq, and its effects on their morale, were far-reaching. The Jews of Baghdad, the most influential and well-established single element in the city, were shocked, terrorized and demoralized. ... It could well be said that the mass exodus of 1950–1951, when almost all the Jews of Iraq were hurriedly transferred to Israel, was the end result of a process that had started on those two fateful days of June. ... [Although] there were other factors and pressures—notably the situation created by Iraq's participation in the Palestine conflict in 1948 and the defeat the Arabs suffered at the hands of the new state of Israel. . . .

The oral histories presented here recount the experiences of two Iraqi women, one Jewish, the other Shii Muslim, who grew up in Iraq in the 1940s and recall the interactions of different communities.

Siham's Story—She Went to Israel in 1949

"When I grew up in the late 1930s and 1940s, I lived in a multi-cultural society. We had equal opportunities in school and with jobs. I never thought that being Jewish meant being different. My family was traditional Jewish. We were proud of being Iraqi and of being Jewish. We were living in Karrada, a mixed neighbourhood in Baghdad. I had three sisters and four brothers. Even in '48, when Israel was established, most Iraqi Jews refused to go. But when they [Iraqi officials] started to harass people and sack them from their jobs, they started to think about leaving. In 1949, they arrested my elder sister, my middle sister, and one of my brothers, because of their communist ideology and activism rather than because they were Jewish. Both of my sisters had studied, one medicine and the other civil engineering, but both ended up in prison. One of them was imprisoned for life, but she was released after the revolution in '58.

Zeynab's Story—a Shii Muslim, She Lives in Dearbigan, Michigan

"We were all friends. We celebrated holidays together. When we had the celebration in commemoration of Imam Husayn, they came with us. Even Jews and Christians joined us. We never thought about race, religion or anything else. Schools were open to everybody. In schools, we had Jewish, Christian, Sunni and Kurdish classmates. There were no bad feelings toward anyone. I myself came from a very conservative family. We wore abaya [in original] and long dresses. But when I look at some family pictures, some of my cousins had sleeveless shirts and short skirts. I tried to put pressure on my dad so we could do what my cousins were allowed to do. But the king's mother and sisters were covered like us. We never saw them. Religion was part of the country. Religion was reflecting the mosaic of our country. We had lots of celebrations on religious holidays and we would celebrate each other's holidays whether they were Muslim, Jewish, or Christian.

The UN General Assembly passed Resolution 194 concerning Palestinians right of return in December 1948. Primarily known for its clauses dealing with Palestinian refugees, the resolution also called for the creation of a Conciliation Commission for Palestine. This commission would seek to make Jerusalem an international zone as foreseen by the United Nations partition recommendation of November 1947. Israel rejected this idea as a violation of its sovereignty. As for the approximately 750,000 Palestinians then refugees in regions surrounding the new state of Israel [Gaza, Jordan, Syria, Lebanon], the resolution called for either the repatriation of refugees to Israel or resettlement outside the country with adequate compensation. Israel objected, stating that it had taken in hundreds of thousands of Jews from Arab lands and that this resettlement of Jews balanced the flight of Palestinian Arabs for which Israel admitted no responsibility. This burning question remained a primary issue in consideration of Arab-Israeli peace from that period until the present where the question of a Palestinian right of return is an item to be negotiated.

The General Assembly,

Having considered further the situation in Palestine. . . .

4. Requests the [Conciliation] Commission to begin its functions at once, with a view to the establishment of contact between the parties themselves and the commission at the earliest possible date. . . .

7. Resolves that the Holy Places—including Nazareth—religious buildings and sites in Palestine should be protected and free access to them assured in accordance with existing rights and historical practices; . . . that the United Nations Conciliation Commission in presenting to the . . . General Assembly its detailed proposal for a permanent international regime for the territory of Jerusalem, should concern recommendations concerning the Holy Places in that territory. . . .

8. Resolves that in view of its association with the three world religions, the Jerusalem area, including the present municipality of Jerusalem plus the surrounding villages

"Palestinian Refugees Fleeing Palestine, October–November 1948." The United Nations Partition recommendation, November 1947, led to outbreaks of violence between Zionist forces, divided into three separate groups and Palestinian irregulars aided by volunteers from other Arab states. Over 400,000 Palestinians either fled or were driven out by Zionist forces before independence. With the Arab state attack, which Israel successfully repelled and gained more territory, 350,000 more Palestinians were driven out of Palestine. This photo shows Palestinians walking north from Galilee, originally allotted to a Palestinian state, to Lebanon in October–November 1948.

and towns, the most Eastern of which should be Abu Dis, the most southern Bethlehem; the most western Ein Karem . . . should be accorded special and separate treatment from the rest of Palestine and should be placed under effective United Nations control; . . . .

11. Resolves that the refugees wishing to return to their homes and live at peace with their neighbors should be permitted to do so at the earliest practicable date, and that compensation should be paid for the property of those choosing not to return and for loss or damage to property which, under principles of international law or in equity, should be made good by the governments or authorities responsible;

Instructs the Conciliation Commission to facilitate the repatriation, resettlement and economic and social rehabilitation of the refugees and the payment of compensation and to maintain close relations with the Director of the United Nations Relief for Palestinian Refugees and, through him, with the appropriate organs and agencies of the United Nations.

America and Saudi Arabia— The Oil Connection

This U.S. Senate committee report of 1952 traces the development of Saudi Arabian oil and the American-backed company that developed it, Aramco, to the point where in 1950 it was producing just over half a million barrels a day; in 2011 it was producing nearly 9 million barrels a day. The fifty-fifty agreement of December 1950, although a landmark in the history of Middle Eastern oil concessions, was not the first; Venezuela had gained such an agreement in 1943. Aramco copied the Venezuela arrangement. It allowed for increased taxes paid to the host country to be deducted from taxes paid to the home country of the company, with special privileges for U.S. military needs.

The Arabian American Oil Co. has extensive oil operations in Saudi Arabia, and, except for the Bahrein Petroleum Co.' s operations on Bahrein Island, is the only company holding an important oil concession in the Middle East that is exclusively American-owned and operated. In recent years the Arabian American Oil Co. (hereafter called Aramco) has increased its operations to such a point that, in 1950, it accounted for 5.3 percent of world production and about 35 percent of all production in the Middle East. Although Aramco did not discover oil in Saudi Arabia until 1938, production increased from an average of 11,000 barrels per day in 1939 to 547,000 in

1950, which made it the second largest producer of oil in the Middle East, exceeded only by the operations of Anglo-Iranian in Iran. The rapid development by Aramco of the oil resources of Saudi Arabia can be traced directly to the ingenuity and persistence on the part of the participating American companies in the face of numerous obstacles. . . .

. . . After Standard Oil Co. of California discovered oil on Bahrein in 1932, interest immediately shifted to Saudi Arabia, where it was believed the same geological formations existed. . . . The concession granted to Standard Oil Co. of California on May 29, 1933, and assigned to California Arabian Standard Oil Co. a wholly owned subsidiary, on December 29, 1933, covered approximately 360,000 square miles, an area comparable in size to the States of Washington and Oregon. In addition, the company was given a preference right to acquire additional oil concessions in Saudi Arabia by meeting the terms of any other offers made to the Government. The concession agreement was to run for 66 years. As consideration for the concession, the company was to make an initial loan of 30,000 pounds, in gold or its equivalent plus an annual payment of 5,000 pounds payable in advance; and, if the agreement was not terminated in 18 months, the company was to make a second loan of 20,000 pounds. The loans were not repayable and were to be recovered by deductions from royalties. Upon discovery of oil in commercial quantities, the company was to advance the Government 50,000 pounds and a similar amount was to be paid 1 year later—both payments to be recoverable by deductions from royalties. On all oil produced, the company was to pay a royalty per ton of 4 shillings gold or its equivalent. If paid in dollars, adjustments for changes in the exchange rate between dollars and 4 shillings gold were to be made in accordance with a formula set forth in the agreement. . . .

The company was required to erect a refinery to supply the Government with sufficient gasoline and kerosene to meet ordinary requirements, and it was understood that ordinary requirements were not to include resale of products inside or outside the country. To meet these "ordinary requirements" the company, upon completion of the refinery, was to supply free to the Government 200,000 gallons of gasoline and 100,000 gallons of kerosene annually. . . .

. . . on October 16, 1938, oil was discovered in commercial quantities in the Dammam field. There then ensued a rush by various parties, particularly representatives of the Axis nations (Germany,

Italy, and Japan) to obtain a concession in Saudi Arabia. . . . But the California Arabian Standard Oil Co. was the successful bidder, and on May 31, 1939, a supplemental agreement was concluded between the company and the Saudi Arabian Government, which added approximately 80,000 square miles to the original concession area. This increased the total concession area held for the exclusive use of the company to about 440,000 square miles, equal to about one-sixth the area of the United States. The company agreed to pay the Saudi Arabian Government 140,000 English pounds in gold, or its equivalent, at the time the supplementary agreement became effective. In addition, the company was to pay an annual rental of 20,000 English pounds in gold, or its equivalent, until oil was discovered in the "additional area" in commercial quantities or until the company relinquished the area. However, if oil were discovered in the additional areas, the company was to pay 100,000 English pounds in gold, or its equivalent, and increase the quantity of free gasoline and kerosene supplied to the government. No change was made in the per ton royalty payments, but the terms of the concession were extended for 60 years, dating from 1939. . . .

. . . by the end of 1941 three important oil fields had been discovered . . . [and] sufficient exploration and development work . . . prove[d] beyond question the existence of vast oil reserves in the Aramco concession. . . . Thus the owners of Aramco, i.e., Standard of California and the Texas Co., were faced with the problem of finding an outlet for an extremely large quantity of oil.

In 1941, the owners of Aramco offered to sell petroleum products to the United States Government at reduced prices if . . . the United States Government would advance $6,000,000 annually for 5 years to the King of Saudi Arabia. Aramco would [then] contract with the King to produce the products ($6,000,000 worth annually) and deliver them to the United States Government. . . . In essence, it was a three-cornered arrangement; the advance payments would give financial relief to the King of Saudi Arabia, the United States Government would obtain petroleum products at special prices, and Aramco would have a market for its products as well as relief from the burden of making further advances to the King against future royalties. . . . Because of their strategic location, the Aramco and Bahrein operations benefitted from the war. A big refinery was constructed at Ras Tanura which turned out large quantities of Diesel and fuel oil for the Navy. . . . A new oil field was discovered in 1945, making a total of four fields in the Aramco concession. Also, because

Aramco was an important supplier of oil products to the military, it was able to assemble and maintain a technical organization. This combination of circumstances placed Aramco in a position to expand rapidly when the war ended. . . . Aramco emerged from the war as one of the important foreign oil holdings of the world with not only a tremendous potential to produce crude but a necessity of producing in substantial quantities to increase the total royalty payment to the King of Saudi Arabia. . . . On December 30, 1950, Aramco and the Saudi Arabian Government agreed to a revision of the 1939 concession agreement. The important change related to tax payments to be made by Aramco to the Government. During 1950, the Saudi Arabian Government issued two income tax decrees which, for the first time, imposed income taxes on petroleum producers. In effect, the income taxes which were imposed, together with royalties and other payments to the Government, amounted to 50 percent of Aramco's profits after allowing for income taxes paid to other countries. Aramco agreed to pay taxes up to but not exceeding 50 percent of its net profits, after income taxes to the United States were deducted. . . . In return for the additional payment, Aramco was permitted to pay taxes in any currency which it received and in the same proportions as received, and to obtain Saudi Arabian riyals (the local currency) at the prevailing rate of exchange rather than at a premium. . . .

CHAPTER 6

Struggles for Independence and New Forms of Political Community, c. 1950–1980

"Khomeini Throws Out the Shah." This poster from the revolution shows the Shah humbly departing bottom left as Khomeini takes charge.

Decolonization and the end of empire marked the post-World War II era (1950–1980). These twin processes were closely intertwined, often in cruel and paradoxical ways, but they should not be confused with one another. Around the globe, colonized peoples engaged in collective action that included both peaceful resistance and armed revolt; wars of national liberation were fought in MENA as well. But with the demise of colonial regimes, newly independent nations did not necessarily enjoy more freedom under indigenous nationalist leaders, nor could they claim full economic control or political sovereignty. In many respects, those nations remained subject to the hegemony of former colonial masters or international corporate capitalist interests. The same period witnessed the emergence of bitter American-Soviet rivalry, the "Cold War," which lasted until the collapse of the USSR in 1991. Each side sought to co-opt new nations into its orbit, which succeeded in many cases. However, former colonial states and peoples often manipulated superpower rivalry to their own advantage as recipients of military and economic aid.

The end of empires resulted in the overthrow of monarchies and political groups controlled by members of local landed elites who had previously been allied with European colonial rulers. In their place emerged new leaders, frequently military officers, who called for major social and economic reforms and for dismantling the old order, epitomized by the 1952 revolution in Egypt. There Gamal Abd al-Nasser (1918–1970) ousted King Farouk, rejected the "business as usual" of Egyptian parliamentary politics, and instituted critical transformations first in land ownership and later in the country's economic organization through nationalization, which ultimately proved disastrous. Nasser also seized the leadership of pan-Arab nationalist movements that demanded full independence from the West, including from anti-Soviet military alliances sponsored by the United States. In consequence, populist regimes headed by military officers in Egypt, Syria, and Iraq after 1958 confronted traditional powers, often the shaykhs or shahs of oil-producing states, such as Saudi Arabia and Iran, that maintained strong ties to the West, along with ruling elites of Jordan, the Persian Gulf, and Morocco.

Two major crises emerged in Iran and Algeria during the post-World War II era. In Iran, Prime Minister Muhammad Mossadegh (1882–1967) [literally transliterated Mussadiq] nationalized the British-controlled oil industry, which had constituted a "state within a state." This led to an Anglo-American boycott of Iranian oil that shut down Iranian oil facilities. The stalemate was resolved by a joint British-American sponsored coup that restored the young shah, Muhammad Reza (1918–1980), to the "peacock throne" in 1953. As American military aid poured into Iran, the shah became an increasingly dictatorial ruler until his regime was overthrown by the 1979 revolution that saw the Ayatollah Ruhollah Khomeini (1902–1989) ultimately assume power as head of government led by Shii clerics, the only theocracy in MENA.

***

For North Africa, France's loss of Vietnam in 1954–1955 made it all the more important, not only for its fading imperial prestige, to retain Algeria, which had been fully incorporated into the French state; major oil and natural gas deposits had been discovered in the mid-1950s. France granted Tunisia and Morocco independence in 1956 to suppress the Algerian nationalist movement. The struggle for Algeria lasted from 1954 to 1962 and cost over a million lives. It brought down the French Fourth Republic and, as the grueling war ground to a halt, caused the departure of nearly one million Europeans for France and elsewhere. Together with the massive departures of settlers from Tunisia and Morocco, this movement of former colonials represented the single largest trans-Mediterranean population transfers of the period after World War II.

The French military's systematic torture of Algerian civilians, including the rape of thousands of women during the war, brought the issue of human rights and torture to global consciousness. Finally, the "Algerian Question" became a major Cold War issue. In the postcolonial era, the Algerian regime assumed a leadership position in the Third World bloc and offered a refuge for revolutionary movements and leaders, including the American Black Panther radical, Eldridge Cleaver (1935–1998).

The political direction taken by the three former French colonies, Morocco, Algeria, and Tunisia, diverged sharply after 1962. In Tunisia, Habib Bourguiba (1903–2000) declared a republic, secularized the court system, pushed public education for all, and put in place one of the most progressive family codes in the region, which greatly favored women's rights. The Moroccan dynasty in power since the seventeenth century continued to rule the country, while independent Algeria installed a state-dominated socialist economy under the FLN (National Liberation Front). In Libya, freed from Italian imperial rule after World War II, the Idrisid monarchy was overthrown in 1969 by young colonels led by Muammar al-Qaddafi (1946–2011) who was ousted and killed in a popular uprising backed by NATO (North Atlantic Treaty Organization) military aid in the fall of 2011.

During the period, Arab states and Israel were locked in an ongoing conflict. Israel joined Britain and France in invading Egypt during the 1956 Suez Crisis that resulted after Nasser nationalized the Suez Canal in July, an important Egyptian asset controlled by foreign companies. Both the Soviet Union and the United States strongly opposed the invasion, the United States angered that countries linked to Western European imperialism could take actions benefiting Soviet propaganda. But the administration of President Dwight D. Eisenhower (1890–1969) still sought to overthrow Nasser to blunt his appeal to the Arab world.

Syrian-Israeli strife in the mid-1960s, coupled with Arab state rivalries, especially between Syria and Egypt, led to the June 1967 Arab-Israeli War whereby Israel occupied the Sinai Peninsula, West Bank, and Syria's Golan Heights. While Israel continues to occupy the West Bank and Golan Heights [which it annexed in 1981], it returned the Sinai to Egypt after long negotiations following the 1973 Arab-Israeli War that ultimately produced the 1979 Egyptian-Israeli peace treaty, the first such treaty signed by an Arab state with Israel.

[handwritten margin notes: Palestinian resistance leader]

[handwritten margin notes: • led by Arafat, PLO sponsored by Egypt (Nasser), against Israel (Britain & USA)]

The Great Disillusion

The end of decolonization should have brought with it freedom and prosperity. The colonized would give birth to the citizen, master of his political, economic, and cultural destiny. After decades of imposed ignorance, his country, now free, would affirm its sovereignty. Opulent or indigent, it would reap the rewards of its labor, of its soil and subsoil. Once its native genius was given free rein, the use of its recovered language would allow native culture to flourish. Unfortunately, in most case[s], the long anticipated period of freedom ... brought with it poverty and corruption, violence and sometimes chaos.... There has been a change of masters but, like new leeches, the new ruling classes are often greedier than the old.... When have the privileged ever given up their privileges except under the threat of losing them?

—Albert Memmi, *Decolonization and the Decolonized*

The 1967 Arab-Israeli War had important social, religious, and demographic implications for both Egypt and Israel. For Israel, the capture of the West Bank, considered part of the ancient lands of Samaria and Judea, led to calls for retaining the occupied Palestinian territories and ultimately to intensive expropriation of and settlement on Palestinian-owned land designed to ensure that they remained part of Israel in violation of the intent if not the letter of UN Resolution 242. Organized Palestinian resistance to Israel had begun before the 1967 War and contributed to its outbreak, especially the Syrian-sponsored raids into Israel of al-Fatah, among whose leaders was Yasser Arafat (1929–2004). Another group, the Palestine Liberation Organization (PLO), was formed in Cairo in 1964 under Egyptian sponsorship, in part a reaction to Syrian accusations that Nasser had no interest in the Palestinian cause. Following the 1967 war, the PLO absorbed Fatah, with Arafat appointed PLO head. The PLO then became the official vehicle for Palestinian resistance, although it was riven with factions sponsored by various Arab states. After 1970, the PLO leadership and many members relocated from Jordan to Lebanon following abortive efforts by radical PLO groups to overthrow Jordan's King Hussein (1935–1999).

For Egypt, the humiliating defeat in the 1967 War created widespread disillusionment with the secular Arab nationalist ideals espoused by President Nasser, but increasingly unfavorable social and economic conditions played a major role as well; relentless population growth, the lack of land for the peasantry, and the growing gap between rich and poor fed enormous resentment. Many turned to Islamic leaders and institutions, notably the Muslim Brothers who were permitted to operate publicly by Nasser's successor, Anwar al-Sadat (1918–1981), to counter his secular political opponents. Though Sadat's assassination in 1981 could be partially attributed to the 1979 peace treaty with Israel, a major impetus came from conservative Islamist movements who turned against Sadat and called for the establishment of an Islamic state and social order. In attempting to reform the Egyptian economy, Sadat had introduced a policy known as the infitah, or opening to private investment from the West. Such investment did occur, but the individuals who gained the contracts had close ties to Sadat, a process known as "crony capitalism." The resulting conspicuous displays of wealth and widened gaps with the mass of Egyptians angered many of the Muslims whose activities Sadat had tolerated. Radical Islamists inspired by the writings of Sayyid Qutb (1906–1966) broke with the Muslim Brothers and conspired to overthrow the regime.

In the midst of these developments, the 1950s and 1960s witnessed the beginnings of large-scale worker migrations to Europe and to the Arab oil-producing states short of labor. Egyptians and Palestinians *worked in Iraq and the Gulf States, Yemenis labored in Saudi Arabia, Turkish workers went to Germany in search of employment, and North Africans after 1962 poured into France and Western Europe. The remittances these workers sent back to their families at home boosted the latter's economic status while masking the deep-seated economic problems found in their societies. Finally, significant social, artistic, and literary experiments in education, women's rights, film, and literature also marked the period.*

Immigrations and Displacements

Two years after independence, Israel passed a law of return establishing official policy regarding immigration. Prior to this law, Israel had encouraged the influx of Jews without restrictions to welcome European survivors of the Holocaust but also to boost the population to settle vacant or seized Palestinian lands. In principle, all Jews were encouraged to immigrate, but in practice the rising costs of health care for immigrants, especially refugees, led to a decision to reserve the right of refusal based on the applicant's health as noted in Section 2, (b), (2). Palestinians then and now point to the idea of the right of return as expressed in Section 1 as contrasted with the refusal to allow a Palestinian right of return to their former homeland.

Right of Aliyah [immigration of Jews to Israel.]

1. Every Jew has the right to come to this country as an oleh [(pl. *olim*) a Jew who is immigrating to Israel.].

Oleh's visa   2. (a) Aliyah shall be by oleh's visa.

(b) An oleh's visa shall be granted to every Jew who has expressed his desire to settle in Israel, unless the Minister of Immigration is satisfied that the applicant

- (1) is engaged in an activity directed against the Jewish people; or
- (2) is likely to endanger public health or the security of the State.

Oleh's certificate   3. (a) A Jew who has come to Israel and subsequent to his arrival has expressed his desire to settle in Israel may, while still in Israel, receive an oleh's certificate.

(b) The restrictions specified in section 2 (b) shall apply also to the grant of an oleh's certificate, but a person shall not be regarded as

- What was the attitude that Israel had towards diasporan Jews in the post-world war world? What about Palestinians? How were they regarded?

endangering public health on account of an illness contracted after his arrival in Israel.

Residents and persons born in this country   4. Every Jew who has immigrated into this country before the coming into force of this Law, and every Jew who was born in this country, whether before or after the coming into force of this Law, shall be deemed to be a person who has come to this country as an oleh under this Law.

Implementation and regulations   5. The Minister of Immigration is charged with the implementation of this Law and may make regulations as to any matter relating to such implementation and also as to the grant of oleh's visas and oleh's certificates to minors up to the age of 18 years.

David Ben-Gurion

Prime Minister

With the creation of the Israeli state in 1948, the status of Arab Jews in many Arab countries became untenable. Most Egyptian Jews stayed until the 1956 Israeli-British-French attack on Egypt, preceded by discovery of an Israeli spy ring in Egypt in 1954 that included Egyptian Jews. In Iraq, the centuries-old Jewish presence gradually disintegrated. The 1941 riots (*farhud*) against them for suspected pro-British sympathies left a legacy of resentment intensified by Zionist actions in Palestine leading to Israel's creation in 1948. A covert Zionist campaign to encourage Iraqi Jews to leave for Israel existed, though not all Jews wanted to leave their homelands for Israel, as in the case of Siham, an Iraqi communist, who relates her experience following. Her mother forced her to leave after Iraqi secret police gave them a choice: either Siham would be deported, because of her communist activities, or go to prison. Life was difficult for many new immigrants during the early years of Israel's independence, but Jewish immigrants from Arab lands [*Sephardim (North African Jews) or Mizrahim* (Jews from the eastern Arab world)] were discriminated against due to the bias in favor of Jews of European descent (*Ashkenazi*).

They [Iraqi police] took me by force from home. I tried three times to run away from them. First they took me to Basra and then in a very terrible boat to Ahwas in Iran. It was winter . . . and very cold. They took us by bus from Ahwas to Tehran. There were other people with us. Some older people and some children died along the way. Israeli agents and the Iranians worked together. When I ran away from the camp in Tehran the Iranian police brought me back. I begged them to bring me back to Iraq but they sent me back to the camp. The same day an airplane took me to Israel. In the boat there were [had been] five or six people, but in the camp there were hundreds of people who wanted to go to Israel. The Zionist movement worked very hard and so many people believed they were going to paradise.

In Israel they put us in a camp and we lived in tents. They sprayed us with DDT when we arrived. I stayed for three months in a camp called Shaar Aliya near Haifa. I was actually in a very difficult situation until I met my brother who came later. Once he told me there is a very important person to see me. It was a communist who wanted to go to Russia. I went with him to the Communist Party in Israel and stayed in a youth camp established by the party. It was a very difficult life. After a year and a half my father came with my younger sister and brother. I left the communist camp to be with them, so we lived in a tent again. For about three years we lived in a tent. They asked us, "Do you know how to eat with a fork and knife?" Although our community was the most educated community of all refugees. One of our friends, who was a solicitor, had to take an exam before his degree was recognized [in Israel]. He went to Jerusalem and died of starvation.

Mahmoud Darwish (1941–2008) is considered to be the Palestinian national poet. This poem, *Identity Card*, written in 1964 when he still lived in Israel, captures the Palestinian feeling of homelessness and rage.

> Record!
> I am an Arab
> And my identity card is
>   number fifty thousand
> I have eight children
> And the ninth is coming after
>   a summer
> Will you be angry?
> Record!
> I am an Arab
> Employed with fellow workers at a quarry
> I have eight children
> I get them bread
> Garments and books
> from the rocks.
> I do not supplicate charity at your doors

Handwritten margin notes:
- DDT is an insecticide
- What was life like for Jewish Arabs & their emigration (or deportation) to Israel?

"Yasser Arafat and Georges Habash with Mahmoud Darwish Between Them, 1980." Darwish, the noted Palestinian poet, left Israel in 1970 and settled in Lebanon. Here he is flanked by bitter rivals, Arafat, a Sunni Muslim and head of Fatah and the PLO, and Habash, a Greek Orthodox Christian and head of the Popular Front for the Liberation of Palestine, both groups based in Lebanon during the 1970s (p. 228). The PFLP in particular was responsible for several terrorist attacks including plane hijackings during the 1970s.

Nor do I belittle myself at the footsteps of your chamber
So will you be angry?
Record!
I am an Arab
I have a name without a title
Patient in a country
Where people are enraged
My roots
Were entrenched before the birth of time
And before the opening of the eras
Before the pines, and the olive trees
And before the grass grew
My father . . . descends from the family of the plow
Not from a privileged class
And my grandfather . . . was a farmer
Neither well-bred, nor well-born!
Teaches me the pride of the sun
Before teaching me how to read
And my house is like a watchman's hut
Made of branches and cane
Are you satisfied with my status?
I have a name without a title!
Record!
I am an Arab
You have stolen the orchards of my ancestors
And the land which I cultivated
Along with my children
And you left nothing for us
Except for these rocks.
So will the State take them
As it has been said?!
Therefore!
Record on the top of the first page:
I do not hate people
Nor do I encroach
But if I become hungry
The usurper's flesh will be my food
Beware . . .
Beware . . .
Of my hunger
And my anger!

Nationalism and Cold War Tensions: Egypt, Lebanon, Iran

Egyptian army officers led by Colonel Gamal Abd al-Nasser overthrew the Egyptian government on July 23, 1952, and sent King Farouk into exile, ending the dynasty founded by Muhammad Ali in 1805. As Nasser and his colleagues were young officers unknown to the public, they appointed a general, Muhammad Neguib (1901–1984), as head of government. In spring 1954, Nasser ousted Neguib and took over the regime.

The officers publicly justified their 1952 coup on the basis of government corruption and submission to foreign control. In his book *Egypt's Liberation: The Philosophy of the Revolution*, published in English in 1955, Nasser argued that specific crises did not spark the revolution, but his references to certain events suggest otherwise. In the defective arms scandal, persons close to King Farouk bought surplus arms from World War II battlefields and sold them for huge profits to the Egyptian Defense Ministry. These weapons and ammunition were often useless, but Egyptian troops were forced to use them in the 1948 conflict with Israel. When news of the scandal became public, political leaders refused to hold a trial to curry favor with King Farouk in hope of being appointed to head the government. Here Nasser argues that the army should remain in power to lead a divided country, justifying military rule that has lasted in various guises to the present.

It is not true that the successful revolution of 1952 stemmed from what happened in the Palestinian War; nor is it true that it was due to the defective weapons which caused the death of our men and officers. . . . In my view . . . had the Army officers attempted the revolt [because of these events] . . . it could not have been called a revolution—mutiny would have been a more appropriate name. . . .

Is it not clear that . . . these seeds of revolution . . . were implanted in us before we were born and that they were a hope concealed in our subconscious, put there by the generation before us? [once the 1919 revolution failed to oust Britain from Egypt]

. . . But why the Army? Before July 23rd, I had imagined that the whole nation was ready and prepared, waiting for nothing but a vanguard to lead the charge . . . and . . . I had imagined that our role [the Army] was to be this commando vanguard . . . [a] role that would never take more than a few hours. . . . Then suddenly came reality after July 23rd. The vanguard . . . threw out Farouk and . . . then [waited] for the serried ranks to come up in their sacred advance toward the great objective . . . but how different is the reality from the dream . . . the masses that came were disunited and . . . the

Politicians don't know Orientals like we do, they don't know that the only way you deal with them is to kick them in their backsides.

—Brigadier M. F. Farquharson-Roberts (1897–1963), British Expeditionary Force, prior to the Suez attacks of October/November 1956 picture boded danger. . . . We needed order but we found nothing . . . but chaos. We needed unity but we found nothing . . . but dissension. We needed work but we found . . . only indolence and sloth.

We [Egyptian people] were not yet ready. So we [Young Officers] set about seeking the views of leaders of opinion and . . . of those who were experienced. . . . [But] every man we questioned had nothing to recommend except to kill someone else. Every idea we listened to was an attack on another idea. . . . I had met many eminent men . . . of every political tendency and color but when I would ask them about a problem in the hope he could find a solution, I would never hear anything but 'I'. Economic problems? . . . Political issues? He alone was expert. . . .

This whole situation and . . . my reflections thereon . . . brought me the answer to the question which had long bothered me, namely: 'Was it necessary for us, the Army, to do what we did on July 23rd [?] The answer is yes . . . we did not ourselves define the role given us to play; it was the history of the country that cast us in that role [saviors of the country]. I can now state that we are going through two revolutions, not one revolution. Every people on earth goes through two revolutions: a political revolution by which it wrests the right to govern itself from the hand of tyranny or from the army stationed on its soil against its will; and a social revolution, involving the conflict of classes, which settles down when justice is secured for the citizens of the united nation.

Peoples preceding us on the path of human progress have passed through two revolutions but they had not had to face both simultaneously. . . ; their revolutions were centuries apart in time. . . . , We are having both revolutions at the same time.

Shortly after the Suez Crisis, President Eisenhower announced in January 1957 the Eisenhower Doctrine, a policy that would authorize a Middle Eastern nation to request American military assistance if threatened directly or indirectly by "International Communism." Despite Washington's opposition to the Suez attacks, this declaration was aimed at Nasser's popularity after the crisis. The United States would

This June 1956 photo was taken at Port Said, the Mediterranean entrance to the Suez Canal, a month before Egyptian leader Gamal Abd al-Nasser nationalized the canal. Nasser's anti-imperialism and appeals for Arab unity made him a major figure in Arab politics, especially after the Suez crisis.

bolster pro-Western states [Iraq, Lebanon, and Jordan] previously receiving aid from either Britain or France, the latter now discredited by their participation in the Suez venture. Congress approved the doctrine in March.

The Middle East has abruptly reached a new and critical stage in its long and important history.... Just recently there have been hostilities involving Western European nations that once exercised much influence in the area. Also the relatively large attack by Israel ... has intensified the basic differences between that nation and its Arab neighbors. All this instability has been heightened and, at times, manipulated by International Communism.... The reason for Russia's interest in the Middle East is solely ... power politics. Considering her announced purpose of Communizing the world, it is easy to understand her hope of dominating the Middle East.... Thus, ... The free nations of the Middle East need, and for the most part want, added strength to assure their continued independence....

Under [these] circumstances . . . a greater responsibility now devolves upon the United States.... The action which I propose would have the following features. It would ... authorize the United States to assist any nation or group of nations in . . . the Middle East in the development of economic strength dedicated to the maintenance of national independence . . . [and] authorize the Executive to undertake . . . programs of military assistance . . . with any nation . . . which desires such aid. It would [also] authorize such assistance . . . to include the employment of the armed forces of the United States to secure and protect the territorial integrity and political independence of such nations, requesting such aid, against overt armed aggression from any nation controlled by International Communism.... The proposed legislation is primarily designed to deal with the possibility of Communist aggression, direct or indirect.... Such authority [military action] would not be exercised except at the desire of the nation attacked.

In 1957, the Lebanese President, Camille Chamoun (1900–1987), a Maronite Catholic, decided, apparently with U.S. backing, to pack the parliament in upcoming elections to gain support for a second consecutive presidential term in 1958, a violation of the Lebanese constitution. Simmering tensions erupted into civil war in June 1958 following the assassination of a Maronite journalist who had criticized Chamoun.

Chamoun asked the United States to invoke the Eisenhower Doctrine to preserve stability, arguing it was a Christian-Muslim confrontation, when in fact many Maronite Catholics and other Christians opposed

• Eisenhower doctrine ≈ if a Middle East nation is threatened by communism, US. will assist militarily

• Does the U.S. really care about ~~the~~ helping countries? • what other motives could they have. (think world powers & Cold War)

Throughout the [1957 parliamentary] elections, I traveled regularly to the presidential palace with a briefcase full of Lebanese pounds.

—A former CIA agent in Lebanon recounting U.S. funding of backers of Lebanese President Camille Chamoun him. But Eisenhower, viewing the matter in Cold War terms, relented in mid-July, 1958, and ordered Marines to land in Lebanon once the Iraqi revolution occurred, overthrowing the Hashemite Dynasty established there after World War I.

We [Eisenhower and his advisers] [shared a] deep-seated conviction that the Communists were principally responsible for the trouble and that President Chamoun was motivated only by a strong feeling of patriotism. . . . [The landing was a success because] the Communists came to be aware of our attitude . . . [and] the peoples of the Middle East, inscrutable as always to the West, have nevertheless remained outside the Communist orbit.

The U.S. Marine Corps Official Account of Intervention in Lebanon
        Although pledged to act only in behalf of nations threatened by Communist aggression, the United States undertook to interfere in Lebanon's internal affairs to support a pro-Western government that was endangered largely by a crisis of its own making.

The Anglo-Iranian Oil Company (AIOC) emerged after World War I out of the oil concessions negotiated by William D'Arcy in 1901. Britain retained control of the company following the war. AIOC's ongoing refusal to provide Iranian governments an accounting of profits became a nationalist cause, and popular political pressure built in Iran to renegotiate the oil contract after World War II. British refusal to do so led in 1951 to Iranian nationalization of the company and in retaliation, a British boycott of Iranian oil. These developments were directly tied to Soviet-Western tensions as the Cold War developed. The symbol of Iranian nationalism was Muhammad Mossadegh, who became prime minister in 1951. The Truman administration questioned the British boycott and sought to negotiate British-Iranian differences. Once Dwight D. Eisenhower took office, the United States, fearing that Moscow could exploit Iranian unrest, backed the British in overthrowing the democratically elected Mossadegh. In this 1952 speech, Mossadegh appealed for negotiations.

June 25, 1953: Anglo-American Coup in Iran

[J]ohn] Foster Dulles was finally finished on the telephone. Picking up the thick paper which had been placed in front of him, he looked casually at the group and said: 'So this is how we get rid of that madman, Mossadegh!'

[To] our great regret the diplomatic relations between the two states [Great Britain and Iran] have reached the present stage, [yet] the Government and people of Iran can easily demonstrate . . . that from the very beginning they have been desiring . . . to come to a settlement of the oil dispute. . . . While on the contrary the covetous Company, who was conscious of the fact it enjoyed full protection of the British Government . . . took resort in threats and . . . rumors . . . that the Government and people of Iran were not prepared to arrive at a settlement of the oil dispute. . . .

Taking . . . world developments . . . as regards the self-determination of nations, the Iranians could no longer tolerate the behavior of the former Company; and the best interests of the nation demanded . . . the nationalization of the oil industry. . . . In other words the Iranians availed themselves of the birthright of any free and independent nation. Many other countries and particularly the United Kingdom, have availed themselves of the right to nationalize their industries. . . . In order to settle the differences, the Iranian Government showed its readiness to pay compensation to the former Company in accordance with nationalization laws enacted in Great Britain. . . . [T]his proposal . . . was also rejected. . . .

These steps compelled the Government of Iran to sever diplomatic relations with the British Government and to leave the resumption of relations to such time as the British Government may care to revisit their policy, with regard to world developments and the awakening of the people of Iran and with due consideration for the principles of justice and equity.

George McGhee (1912–2005), a foreign service officer and former ambassador to Turkey, served in several American administrations. Here, he reflects on the differences in U.S. policy toward oil nationalization under the Truman and Eisenhower presidencies. As he notes, Iranians never forgot the United States' role in toppling Mossadegh, which, together with Washington's blind support for the shah, became a major factor in the Islamic revolution in 1979.

When I first joined the State Department in 1946, I was not exposed to covert operations. . . . I knew of a few relatively insignificant cases—I even participated in some—of giving innocuous aid to influential individuals and groups because we wanted to keep them "on our side." But I do not recall any actions aimed at overthrowing a government or assassinating a leader.

The situation changed abruptly during the Eisenhower administration, as a result of the (John) Foster-Allen Dulles combination [John Foster Dulles [1888–1959], Secretary of State, and his brother, Allen Dulles, [1893–1969], who was CIA Director]. . . . A plethora of daring covert actions all around the world date from that period, including one in Iran in 1953 which led to the overthrow of Prime Minister Mohammed Mossadegh and the return of the Shah. Kermit Roosevelt (1916–2000), the CIA officer who, with British intelligence, ran Operation Ajax, wrote a book about the incident . . . despite CIA efforts to block it. . . . This book, as well as a public award

Supporters of Iranian Prime Minister Mohammed Mossadegh demonstrate in Tehran prior to his overthrow in an Anglo-American sponsored coup.

Having backed the 1953 coup that restored the Mohamed Reza Shah to power, the United States met many of the Shah's demands for military aid but made little progress in encouraging the Iranian ruler to embark on democratic political and social reforms. Roy Wilkins headed the U.S. delegation to the International Conference on Human Rights, which met in Tehran in 1968. Here Wilkins is greeted at a royal reception for conference delegates by the Shah and his wife, Empress Farah.

to Roosevelt presented by President Eisenhower, confirmed for the Iranians that we had played the key role in overthrowing their constitutionally elected leader. Mossadegh had freed Iran from AIOC-British control without loss of blood and was considered a national hero. His overthrow led to anti-United States attitudes in Iran. We became the incarnate of evil, the Great Satan of the Khomeini era.

Algeria's War of Independence: Torture and Colonial Rule

The Algerian National Liberation Front (FLN) issued this manifesto on October 31, 1954, calling for the end of the colonial regime established in 1830. France rejected offers to negotiate and the Algerian revolt began. For eight years, until 1962, the French army brutally suppressed the uprising; the struggle resulted in the deaths of at least a million people, mostly Algerian civilians, and the destruction of much of the country's agriculture and infrastructure. A contributing factor to French determination to retain hold over Algeria was the discovery of major oil fields in the south of the country in 1957.

Proclamation of the Algerian National Front, Liberation Front, (FLN) November 1954

After decades of struggle, the National Movement has reached its final phase of fulfillment. At home, the people are united behind the watchwords of independence and action. Abroad, the atmosphere is favourable, especially with the diplomatic support of our Arab and Moslem brothers. Our National Movement, prostrated by years of immobility and routine, badly directed, was disintegrating little by little. Faced with this situation, a youthful group . . . judged that the moment had come to take the National Movement out of . . . [its] impasse . . . and to launch it into the true revolutionary struggle at the side of the Moroccan and Tunisian brothers. . . . Our movement gives to compatriots of every social position, to all the purely Algerian parties and movements, the possibility of joining in the liberation struggle.

GOAL: National independence through:

1. The restoration of the Algerian state, sovereign, democratic, and social, within the framework of the principles of Islam;

2. The preservation of fundamental freedoms, without distinction of race or religion.

INTERNAL Objectives:

1. Political house-cleaning through the destruction of the last vestiges of corruption and reformism

EXTERNAL Objectives:

1. The internationalization of the Algerian problem;
2. The pursuit of North African unity in its national Arabo-Islamic context;
3. The assertion, through United Nations channels, of our active sympathy toward all nations that may support our liberating action.

"A Former Algerian Revolutionary." As a college student, Zohra Drif had encountered discrimination at the University of Algiers because she was a Muslim; most students were of European background. She joined the Algerian National Liberation Front (FLN) as an undercover combatant accused of planting bombs in areas in the European quarter; she was imprisoned but survived the war and married one of the founders of the FLN. She became a lawyer and then vice-president of the upper house of the Algerian Parliament.

MEANS OF STRUGGLE: Struggle by every means until our goal is attained. Exertion at home and abroad through political and direct action, with a view to making the Algerian problem a reality for the entire world. The struggle will be long, but the outcome is certain. To limit the bloodshed, we propose an honourable platform for discussion with the French authorities:

1. The opening of negotiations with the authorized spokesmen of the Algerian people, on the basis of a recognition of Algerian sovereignty, one and indivisible.
2. The inception of an atmosphere of confidence brought about by freeing all those who are detained, by annulling all measures exception, and by ending all legal action against the combatant forces.
3. The recognition of Algerian nationhood by an official declaration abrogating all edicts, decrees, and laws by virtue of which Algeria was "French soil."

In return for which:

1. French cultural and economic interests will be respected, as well as persons and families.
2. All French citizens desiring to remain in Algeria will be allowed to opt for their original nationality, in which case they will be considered as foreigners, or for Algerian nationality, in which case they will be considered as Algerians, equal both as to rights and as to duties.

3. The ties between France and Algeria will be the object of agreement between the two Powers on the basis of equality and mutual respect.

Algerians: The F. L. N. is your front; its victory is your victory. For our part, strong in your support, we shall give the best of ourselves to the Fatherland.

French troops and police not only tortured Algerians but also French citizens in Algeria who backed Algerian independence. Those French who opposed government interrogation methods in Algeria compared them to those used by the Nazi Gestapo against French citizens during the German occupation. Some of the methods described following were used at the U.S. prison at Guantanamo after the attacks of September 11, 2001. Here, Henri Alleg, a French Communist living in Algiers, describes his experience when tortured by French troops in 1957.

Ja—, smiling all the time, dangled the clasps at the end of the electrodes before my eyes . . . [and] attached one of them to the lobe of my right ear and the other to a finger on the same side. Suddenly a

The bitter war for Algerian independence, 1954–1962, saw numerous attacks and retaliations by both sides that claimed hundreds of thousands of civilian lives. Here French paratroopers search Algerians, Arab and European, in July 1957.

flash of lightening exploded next to my ear and I felt my heart racing in my breast. I struggled screaming . . . while . . . Cha—repeated a single question. . . . 'Where have you been hiding?' . . . Still smiling above me, Ja—had attached the pincers to my penis. The shocks going through me were so strong that the straps holding me to the board came loose. . . . All around me, sitting on packing cases, Cha—and his friends emptied bottles of beer. Later electrodes were placed in my mouth: my jaws were soldered to the electrode by the current and it was impossible for me to unlock my teeth. [Then] they picked up the plank to which I was . . . attached and carried me into the kitchen [where] . . . my head was rested against the sink [and] . . . a rubber tube fixed to the metal tap was placed in my mouth . . . the rag [in my mouth] soaked rapidly, Water flowed everywhere. . . . I had the impression of drowning and a terrible agony, that of death itself, took possession of me. . . . In spite of myself, the fingers of my two hands shook uncontrollably. 'That's it, he's going to talk' said a voice. The water stopped running [and] . . . in the gloom I saw the . . . captain who, with a cigarette in his lips, was hitting my stomach with his fist to make me throw out the water. . . .

'Listen', said Cha— . . . ' Where can it get you—all this? If you won't say anything we'll take your wife. Do you think she'll stand it?' . . . In this nightmare I . . . knew they were capable of torturing Gilberte. . . . I learnt later on that they had even tortured Madame Touri [the wife of a well-known Radio Algiers actor] in front of her husband in order to make him talk. . . .

I have written these lines four months after having left the paras [paratroopers], in cell 72, of the civil prison of Algiers. . . . It is only a few days since the blood of three young Algerians has joined that of the Algerian Fernand and Yveton in the courtyard of the prison. In the immense cry of pain which sprang from the prisoners in all the cells at the moment when the executioner went to get the condemned . . . the soul of Algeria vibrated. . . . All the cells had been shuttered by the guards but we were able to hear one of the condemned cry out before he was gagged 'Tahia El Djezair! Vive l'Algerie', And with a single voice . . . the anthem of free Algeria rose from the women's section of the prison.

'Out of our struggle rise the voices of free men: They claim independence for our country. I give you everything I love, I give you my l[i]fe, O, my country . . . O my country.'

All this I have to say for those Frenchmen who will read me. . . . the Algerians do not confuse their torturers with the great people of France from whom they have learnt so much and whose friendship is so dear to them. But they must know what is done IN THEIR NAME.

C. L. Sulzberger (1912–1993), a noted foreign affairs columnist for the *New York Times*, **interviewed many world leaders and investigated numerous crises, here the Algerian revolution. French officials had acknowledged to Sulzberger that Algerian resistance had not been crushed even though torture had won the 1955–1957 battle for Algiers. In this diary entry, Sulzberger discusses the Algerian war with the Tunisian President, Habib Bourguiba, whose government supplied much-needed weapons and other supplies to the Algerian rebels. President Bourguiba bemoaned Western backing for colonial occupation.**

Tunis, March 5, 1959—.

Last night I dined with President Habib Bourguiba at his home in Monastir, about one hundred miles away [from Tunis]. . . . Bourguiba talked a lot, starting on Algeria which overshadows everything in this part of the world:

"Habib Bourguiba Calls for Tunisian Independence, January 1952." Head of the Neo-Destour nationalist party since the 1930s, Habib Bourguiba speaks at a rally in the coastal city of Bizerte, January 15, 1952. After brief clashes, France granted both Tunisia and Morocco independence in 1956 to focus its efforts on retaining Algeria.

'The situation is not ripe for settlement now. It will ripen; eventually it will have to ripen—but at what price? The French live totally apart from reality. They are fighting a full-scale war in Algeria with all their power just exactly as they did in Indochina, and the result will be just exactly the same. They imagine they will win the war. They say it is a question of honor and prestige. They say that by winning it, they will be able to diminish the impression made on the world and on their own people by their having to leave Indochina, Syria, Tunisia, and Morocco. They still seem to consider the liberation of these countries as due to the treason of the *système* of the French regime. They don't yet recognize that this liberation movement is a natural phenomenon. After all it happened to the British and the Dutch. It should be faced coolly and logically. The French think they are stronger and smarter than the British. How unclever they really are.'

Bourguiba thought that French insistence on pushing this uncompromising war . . . was pushing Morocco toward neutrality and Algeria toward communism. . . . Bourguiba complained that there is a ridiculous situation in the world today. Dictatorships, such as Russia's and China's, which deny human rights to their own people, appear before the world as the champions of liberation, while the countries where true freedom reigns oppose such colonial liberation.

Women, Education, and the Public Sphere

In this interview the Tunisian physician, Tawhida Ben Sheikh (1909–2010) recalls her experiences as a physician in Tunisia during the 1950s and 1960s, the period of Tunisia's struggle for independence from France, and Habib Bourguiba's policies toward women. She became interested in family planning.

. . . I was asked to go into politics [1960s] and always refused. When necessary, of course, one gets political. During the independence struggle, I was vice President [in original] of the Tunisian Red Crescent [Islamic Red Cross]. In 1952, the French army had stormed a village in Cap Bon, destroyed homes, killed and raped the inhabitants. I went there, wrote a report, and presented it to the French authorities. . . . I had also gone to New York [1961] to work in a family planning clinic there, to learn what was being done. As soon as contraceptives were allowed in Tunisia, in 1963, I started a family

How have North African States' (like Tunisia) progressed socially ∧ (look @ women's rights/roles).

planning service at Charles Nicole Hospital [in Tunis] where I was Head of the Gynaecological department [in original]. . . . Women learned about the contraceptive services by word of mouth very quickly. They were supposed to have the permission of their husbands of course. . . . There were some husbands who would have the loop removed if they were going on a trip and leaving the wife alone. . . . That practice still exists today [1990].

President Bourguiba had well prepared us in family planning. He was a leader in women's rights. He had abolished polygamy, had created a legal basis for women's rights in Tunisian law which . . . gave women the right to ask for a divorce. He was very advanced for his time, not only in North Africa, but across the Arab world and Africa.

France declared Morocco a Protectorate in 1912 and reinforced the patriarchy of the reigning dynasty, the Alawis, and of the leaders of the great tribes to assure that Morocco remained "traditional," untouched by modernity. The colonial administration transformed cities, built roads, and introduced rudimentary health care, but severely circumscribed modern education, especially for girls. Faced with Moroccan demands for independence after World War II, repressive measures backfired. In 1953, the colonial regime exiled the ruler, Sultan Mohammed V (1909–1961), who had ruled in tandem with the French occupation since 1927; his exile transformed him into a nationalist symbol and political leader and ignited a guerrilla war against the French military. As was true in Algeria and Tunisia, Moroccan women proved key to the struggle, since they could move about more freely than Moroccan men due to the colonial assumption that colonized Muslim women, veiled or not, were apolitical. In 1956, the French, embroiled in a deadly war in Algeria, decided to grant independence to both Morocco and Tunisia.

Independence, however, was bittersweet for certain social classes, particularly women of ordinary means. Illiteracy among women and girls was much higher in Morocco than in Tunisia or Egypt. In 1955, only six girls had attained secondary school diplomas. Five decades later, the situation has dramatically changed, as shown in the case of Leila Abouzeid (1950–), a well-known Moroccan writer. In *Return to Childhood*, a narrative of her family's struggles during the nationalist fight for independence, she reveals the contradictions and ambiguities that people—particularly women—encountered on a daily basis. Her mother, illiterate, courageously brought food to Abouzeid's father after he was incarcerated in colonial prisons for his militant opposition to the French Protectorate. But Abouzeid's mother, while offering biting insights into the politics of oppression, did not, unlike her husband, want her daughters to attend modern schools.

Then my mother told us, 'The Nasara [Christians or French] have put your father in prison. Not because he did anything bad, but because he is a nationalist. 'Nationalist' means someone who wants the Nasara to get out of our country, and that's honorable.' But her moaning disturbed me much more than the news. Still, her distress made it difficult not to think of prison as something bad. In El Ksiba, where we lived after leaving Rabat, certain [Moroccan] inmates of the local prison were assigned to us by the French administration to do errands in the village. Those prisoners had been arrested for minor infractions of the law; most had injured somebody or stolen something. One had been arrested because he did not salute the French *contrôleur général* when he passed him on the street. One day, while still serving his sentence, he [the Moroccan prisoner] was taking the dough for our bread to the village bakery when he met the same Frenchman, riding his horse. He put the breadboard on the ground and saluted him with both hands. The Frenchman asked, "Two salutes, why?" "One is for you and the one is for the horse," answered the inmate. Every time my mother heard that story she would say, "The poor man must have told himself, 'If he could put me in jail because I did not salute him, he might increase my punishment if I don't salute his horse.'" Then she would add, in a sad tone, "It is the law of the powerful. The law of the jungle. . . . "

The summer was over. We were getting ready to enter school and my mother's old aunt Zineb came to her and said, "Is it true that you intend to enroll the girls at school?" "Yes." "Are you crazy? Who's going to buy them notebooks and pens?" "The nationalists, aunt. They are taking care of us. They send us money every month." "Send them to learn a craft and forget about school." "I would do that if it were only up to me, but their father says every time I visit him, 'Take them to school,' and I've never gotten a letter from him in which he does not emphasize it." "He spent his time having affairs with other women and spending money, then he went off to prison and now he decides to say school! What will a girl study, for heaven's sake and what for? A girl's destiny is marriage, pregnancy and breast-feeding, isn't it? One would think that they are going to learn that language you need to deal with djinns!" "But my dear aunt, the Sultan Sidi Mohammed Ben Youssef [Muhammad V] himself has ordered the nationalists to send their girls to school. And every time I visit Si Hmed in prison he insists that I take them to school. I can't disobey him." "Your husband's crazy and you're crazier than he is. You should be the one to decide. The proverb says, 'Show your friend the way, but if he refuses to see it, go your own way and leave him.'" We did go to school, as my father had insisted. But before we began, there was always laundry day and bath day. The laundry and the bath came every week, but in those days before we started school, my mother made special occasions out of these weekly rituals.

The Jordanian Constitution of 1952 guaranteed women's right to work as does Article 2 of the 1966 Labor Law still in force. Thus, Jordanian laws enshrine two basic principles of citizenship—the right to work and equality before the law—that have encountered opposition. The persistence of customary laws governing women's activities and patriarchal institutions, structures, and attitudes have frequently conspired to render laws and constitutions a dead letter. In places like Jordan, conservative religious figures condemned the sexual mixing of the modern workplace because serious moral problems might arise; some Muslim clerics maintained that Islamic law forbade women from working outside the home. In this edict, the Jordanian religious scholar, Marwan Ibrahim al-Kaysi (1950–), represents one position in the decades-long debate that has pitted advocates of women's right to work against those seeking to prohibit that right.

W ork is the right of all citizens. Jobs are based on capability. All Jordanians are equal before the law. There will be no discrimination between [Jordanians] regarding rights and duties based on race, language or religion.

—Article 6 of the 1952 Jordanian Constitution

"1. The husband has the right to stop his wife from leaving the home after having paid her advanced dowry. However, this right like any other right should not be misused by the man.

2. A Muslim woman should not go out too much, leaving her home must be for an important reason.

3. A Muslim woman should prefer to bear children and raise them, and watch out for her family's needs rather than work outside the home. However, there is nothing against her going out to work if there is a need as when there is no one to support her, but on condition that her work be according to conditions laid down by Islam, i.e. that this work be allowable by the *shari'a*, that said, work does not take her away from her husband or children and that it not be in a situation where she would work with men."

Arab-Israeli Conflicts: The 1967 War and the Lebanese Civil War

Israel still occupies both the West Bank and the Golan Heights as a result of the 1967 Arab-Israeli War; it annexed the Golan Heights to Israel in 1981. The Sinai Peninsula, also taken in the war, was returned to Egypt following the Egyptian-Israeli peace treaty of 1979. As efforts progressed

during summer 1967 to draft a declaration to address the new situation created by Israel's victories, Israel's attitude toward retention of some of the newly conquered territories changed. It unilaterally annexed the old city of East Jerusalem on June 27 and would insist on retaining some land for security purposes in any peace agreement with Arab states.

UN Security Council Resolution 242 (SCR242) remains the basis for settlement of issues pertaining to the 1967 War. Lord Caradon (Hugh Foot, 1907–1990), British Ambassador to the United Nations, is credited with the final draft. He was deliberately ambiguous in its wording, explaining to the delegates that, "All delegations might have their own views and interpretations and understandings, but only the resolution would be binding." Although the resolution appears to condemn retention of territories acquired by war in its preamble, Article 1, Section (i) was worded to allow Israel to retain land it claimed essential for "secure and recognized boundaries," Section (ii). Caradon did this by removing the word "the" just before "territories" so that Israel could claim it did not have to withdraw from *all* the territories. The extent of lands Israel could retain remained deliberately undefined, although the United States interpreted it to mean minor border rectifications.

542. United Nations Security Council Resolution 242

New York, November 22, 1967.

The Security Council,

Expressing its continuing concern with the grave situation in the Middle East,

Emphasizing the inadmissibility of the acquisition of territory by war and the need to work for a just and lasting peace in which every State in the area can live in security,

Emphasizing further that all Member States in their acceptance of the Charter of the United Nations have undertaken a commitment to act in accordance with Article 2 of the Charter,

1. Affirms that the fulfillment of Charter principles requires the establishment of a just and lasting peace in the Middle East which should include the application of both the following principles:

i.   Withdrawal of Israeli armed forces from territories occupied in the recent conflict;

ii. Termination of all claims or states of belligerency and respect for and acknowledgment of the sovereignty, territorial integrity and political independence of every State in the area and their right to live in peace within secure and recognized boundaries free from threats or acts of force;

Prior to the 1967 War that erupted on June 5, President Lyndon Johnson had declared on May 23 that the United States was committed to the territorial integrity of all states in the Middle East. In the aftermath of the war and Israel's victories, Johnson found himself under increasing pressure to allow Israel to retain some land it had occupied. Johnson and his aides acknowledged the problem, leading him to side with the Israeli position that led to the passing of UN Security Council Resolution 242.

To the leaders of all the nations of the Near East, I wish to say what three American Presidents have said before me—that the United States is firmly committed to the support of the political independence and territorial integrity of all the nations of the area. The United States strongly opposes aggression by anyone in the area, in any form, overt or clandestine. . . . [T]he record of the actions of the United States over the past twenty years, within and outside the United Nations, is abundantly clear on this point.

2. Affirms further the necessity

(a) For guaranteeing freedom of navigation through international waterways in the area;

(b) For achieving a just settlement of the refugee problem;

(c) For guaranteeing the territorial inviolability and political independence of every State in the area, through measures including the establishment of demilitarized zones;

3. Requests the Secretary-General to designate a Special Representative to proceed to the Middle East to establish and maintain contacts with the States concerned in order to promote agreement and assist efforts to achieve a peaceful and accepted settlement in accordance with the provisions in this resolution;

4. Requests the Secretary-General to report to the Security Council on the progress of the efforts of the Special Representative as soon as possible.

In spring 1967, before the Arab-Israeli War, Naomi Shermer (1930–2004) composed "Jerusalem the Gold," first performed at Israeli Independence Day ceremonies in mid-May. The song laments Israel's lack of control over the Old City of East Jerusalem with its holy places, especially the Temple Mount. Then the war broke out and East Jerusalem was captured, leading the composer to add two new triumphal stanzas beginning with "we have returned to the cisterns. . . ." The song contains a Zionist theme that parts of ancient Israel not controlled by the Israeli state and uninhabited by Israelis are empty even though inhabited by Palestinians. The Temple Mount, a focal point for Islam as well as Jews, houses the al-Aqsa mosque and the Dome of the Rock, a Muslim shrine. Israel later annexed West Bank land to create a new 'East Jerusalem' that extended north to Ramallah and south to Bethlehem, leading Israel to insist that this new East Jerusalem, not the Old City, was forever Israeli and not subject to negotiation.

> The mountain air is clear as wine
>> And the scent of pines
> Is carried on the breeze of twilight
>> With the sound of bells
> —And in the slumber of tree and stone
>> Captured in her dream
>> The city that sits solitary
>> And in its midst is a wall
> —Jerusalem of gold, and of bronze, and of light
>> Behold, I am a violin for all your songs
> —How the cisterns have dried

Johnson: "How do we get out of this predicament?"

McNamara: "We're in a heck of a jam on territorial integrity."

—Dialogue on June 13 between President Lyndon Johnson and Secretary of Defense Robert McNamara on the territorial integrity pledge

The market place is empty

And no one frequents the Temple Mount

    In the Old City

—And in the caves in the mountain

    Winds are howling

And no one descends to the Dead Sea

    By way of Jericho

—Jerusalem of gold, and of bronze and of light

    Behold I am a violin for all your songs.

—But as I come to sing to you today,

And to adorn crowns to you [sing your praise]

I am the smallest of the youngest of your children [the least

    worthy of doing so]

And of the last poet [of all the poets born]

—For your name scorches the lips

Like the kiss of a seraph

If I forget thee Jerusalem

    Which is all gold

—Jerusalem of gold, and of bronze, and of light

    Behold I am a violin for all your songs

These two verses were added after the 1967 War.

—We have returned to the cisterns

    To the market and to the marketplace

A ram's horn [shofar] calls out on the Temple Mount in the

    Old City

—And in the caves in the mountain

    Thousands of suns shine

We will once again descend to the Dead Sea

    By way of Jericho!

—Jerusalem of gold, and of bronze, and of light

    Behold I am a violin for all your songs

The Lebanese Civil War that erupted in 1975 was far more deadly and long-lived than that of 1958. Many local militias emerged, the most important being Maronite Catholic and later Shii groups, notably Hizbollah, created following Israel's invasion of Lebanon in 1982. Outside states intervened with Israel backing the Maronites, especially the Phalange of Bashir Gemayyel (1947–1982), since the PLO used Lebanon as a base for attacks on Israel. The Israeli-Maronite alliance led to Israel's invasion of Lebanon in 1982, where Israeli troops oversaw Maronite entry into the Palestinian refugee camps of Sabra and Shatila where hundreds of Palestinians were massacred. As the civil war continued,

"Maronite Phalange Give the Group's Salute to Leader Bashir Gemayel, Lebanese Civil War, Mid-1970s." The fragile Lebanese political system disintegrated in the early 1970s owing to internal rivalries and the influx of Palestinian militias as the Palestine Liberation Organization (PLO) established its headquarters outside Beirut after being ousted from Jordan. A civil war erupted that saw leftist Palestinian and Lebanese forces pitted against primarily Maronite Catholic groups. Initially influenced by European fascism in the 1930s, Bashir Gemayel's Phalange became the dominant Maronite militia in the mid-1970s, wiping out rival Maronite clan heads. Phalange personnel, seen in this poster, were trained by the Israeli military and ultimately allied with it during Israel's invasion of Lebanon in June 1982.

thousands died on all sides and local gangs fought for dominance of Beirut neighborhoods. This poem exemplifies the feelings of one poet in the mid-1970s.

> A bomb falls in the garden
> a man falls inside
> a child screams
> Darkness blinds me
> silence deafens me
> time stops
> My wild heart
> bleeds
> aches
> beats
> and does not die.

Qaddafi's *Green Book*: Path to the Future?

Muammar al-Qaddafi (literally *al-Qadhdhafi*) (1946–2011) led a coup in 1969 staged by young colonels that deposed the regime of Libya's King Idris (1889–1983). Whereas Idris belonged to the Senussi, a great tribal confederation, Qaddafi came from humble origins, rising to power via the military as had the then rulers of Egypt, Syria, and Iraq. He quickly established his control of the country, imposing a military regime that profited from Libya's large oil reserves. Presenting himself as a radical

Arab nationalist leader, he ended the American use of a major air base for NATO training purposes and intervened in Arab politics at will, but he retained close ties to European consumers of Libyan oil.

At the time he published the *Green Book* (1975), with its slogans calling for mass democracy, Qaddafi had already established an oppressive police state with a government-controlled press that tolerated no dissent. He later, in 1977, proclaimed Libya to be a *jamahiriyya* or people's republic, a term that matched the populist rhetoric of the *Green Book* but masked the reality of a dictatorship with wealth centered in his family and allies; the popular conferences to which he refers were overseen by members of the regime. The book became required reading in Libyan schools, similar to the book of Chairman Mao's sayings in Communist China. Qaddafi's reasoning was often inconsistent and simplistic, but his criticism of parliamentary democracy as a tool of special interests has recently been echoed in popular protests elsewhere. His remarks on women, despite his claims that they are equal to men, are reminiscent of conservative Muslim arguments in the nineteenth century that women should be confined to specific roles in society.

The Instrument of Government

. . . THE GREEN BOOK presents the ultimate solution to the problem of the proper instrument of government. . . . All political systems in the world today are a product of the struggle for power between alternative instruments of government. This struggle may be peaceful or armed, as is evidenced among classes, sects, tribes, parties or individuals. The outcome is always the victory of a particular governing structure . . . and the defeat of the people; the defeat of genuine democracy.

Political struggle that results in the victory of a candidate with, for example, 51 per cent of the votes leads to a dictatorial governing body in the guise of a false democracy, since 49 per cent of the electorate is ruled by an instrument of government they did not vote for, but which has been imposed upon them. Such is dictatorship. . . . [Which] is established under the cover of false

"Beirut: The Green Line, 1982." Numerous militias vied for control of Beirut during this period, Shi'a and Palestinian as well as Maronite. All were well-armed and left sections of the city, as shown here, in shambles. The "Green Line" divided the city into two quarters and served as a sort of DMZ.

democracy . . . the political systems prevailing in the world today . . . are dictatorial systems . . . that . . . falsify genuine democracy.

Parliaments

. . . Parliamentary systems are a false solution to the problem of democracy. . . . [because] True democracy exists only through the direct participation of the people, and not through the activity of their representatives. . . . The masses are completely isolated from the representative and he, in turn, is totally removed from them. . . . The prevailing traditional democracy endows the member of parliament with a sacredness and immunity which are denied to the rest of the people. Parliaments, therefore, have become a means of plundering and usurping the authority of the people. It has thus become the right of the people to struggle, through popular revolution, to destroy such instruments . . . which stifle the will of the people . . . [parliamentary] representation is a fraud, . . . based on propaganda to win votes, it is a demagogic system in the real sense of the word. Votes can be bought and falsified. Poor people are unable to compete in the election campaigns, and the result is that only the rich get elected. . . . The most tyrannical dictatorships the world has known have existed under the aegis of parliaments.

The Party

The [political] party . . . is the modern instrument of dictatorial government. . . . the modern equivalent of the tribal or sectarian system. A society governed by one party is similar to one which is governed by one tribe or one sect. . . . Just as tribal and sectarian rule is politically unacceptable and inappropriate, likewise the rule under a party system. . . .

THE GREEN BOOK presents the ultimate solution to the problem of the instrument of government, and indicates for the masses the path upon which they can advance from the age of dictatorship to that of genuine democracy. This new theory is based on the authority of the people, without representation or deputation. It achieves direct democracy in an orderly and effective form. It is superior to the older attempts at direct democracy which were impractical because they lacked popular organizations at base levels.

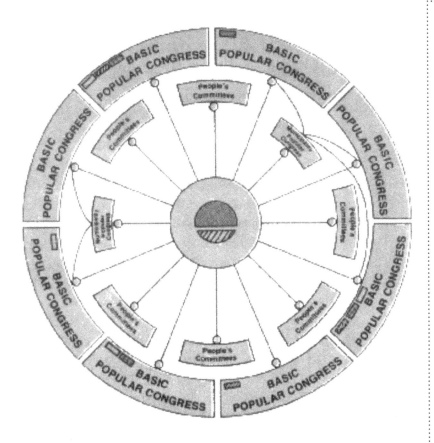

Popular Conferences and People's Committees

.... True democracy.... [the] Authority of the people has but one face which can only be realized through Popular Conferences and People's Committees....

First, the people are divided into Basic Popular Conferences. Each Basic Popular Conference chooses its secretariat.... Subsequently, the masses of the Basic Popular Conferences select administrative People's Committees to replace government administration. All public institutions are run by People's Committees which will be accountable to the Basic Popular Conferences which dictate the policy and supervise its execution. Thus, both the administration and the supervision become the people's and the outdated definition of democracy—democracy is the supervision of the government by the people—becomes obsolete. It will be replaced by the true definition: Democracy is the supervision of the people by the people....

Subjects dealt with by the Popular Conferences and People's Committees will eventually take their final shape in the General People's

Congress, which brings together the Secretariats of the Popular Conferences and People's Committees. Resolutions of the General People's Congress, which meets annually or periodically, are passed on to the Popular Conferences and People's Committees, which undertake the execution of those resolutions through the responsible committees, which are, in turn, accountable to the Basic Popular Conferences.

The General People's Congress is not a gathering of persons or members such as those of parliaments but, rather, a gathering of the Popular Conferences and People's Committees. Thus, the problem of the instrument of government is naturally solved, and all dictatorial instruments disappear. The people become the instrument of government, and the dilemma of democracy in the world is conclusively solved. . . .

Who Supervises the Conduct of Society?

The question arises: who has the right to supervise society, and to point out deviations that may occur from the laws of society? Democratically, no one group can claim this right on behalf of society. Therefore, society alone supervises itself . . . through the government of these people through People's Committees and the General People's Congress—the national congress—where Secretariats of the Popular Conferences and the People's Committees convene. In accordance with this theory, the people become the instrument of government and, in turn, become their own supervisors. . . .

The Press

An individual has the right to express himself or herself even if he or she behaves irrationally to demonstrate his or her insanity. Corporate bodies too have the right to express their corporate identity. . . . Since society consists of private individuals and corporate bodies, the expression, for example, by an individual of his or her insanity does not mean that the other members of society are insane. . . . The press is a means of expression for society: it is not a means of expression for private individuals or corporate bodies. Therefore, logically and democratically, it should not belong to either one of them. . . . The democratic press is that which is issued by a People's Committee, comprising all the groups of society. Only in this case, and not otherwise, will the press or any other information medium be democratic, expressing the viewpoints of the whole society, and representing all its groups. . . .

Women

It is an undisputed fact that both men and women are human beings. It follows as a self-evident fact that woman and man are equal as human beings. Discrimination between man and woman is a flagrant act of oppression without any justification. . . . But why are there man and woman? . . . the fact that a natural difference exists between man and woman is proved by the created existence of man and woman. This means . . . that there is a role for each one of them, matching the difference between them, . . . [i.e.,] woman is a female and man is a male. . . . Men and women must perform, not abandon, the role for which they are created. . . . The woman who rejects marriage, pregnancy or motherhood etc. because of work abandons her natural role. . . . Consequently there must be a world revolution which puts an end to all materialist conditions hindering woman from performing her natural role in life and driving her to carry out man's duties in order to be equal in rights. Driving woman to do man's work is unjust aggression against the femininity with which she is naturally provided for a natural purpose essential to life. . . . In general woman is gentle and man is tough by virtue of their inbred natures. . . . There is no difference in human rights between man and woman, the child and the adult. But there is no absolute equality between them as regards their duties.

Libyan leader Muammar Qaddafi (left) at an Arab summit meeting in 1977, two years after he published the *Green Book*. To his left are Algerian president Houarie Boumedienne and Syrian president Hafez al-Assad.

Sayyid Qutb: Jahiliyyah and Islamic Liberation

The rise of radical Islamist thinking and movements is often traced to the humiliations and defeat of the 1967 war as well as deteriorating social and economic conditions in many Middle Eastern societies and increasingly autocratic political regimes. Sayyid Qutb's (1906–1966)

ideas inspired Egyptian Islamists in the mid-1970s and subsequently influenced al-Qaida ("the base"), especially since several Egyptians linked to Anwar al-Sadat's 1981 assassination later went to Afghanistan to fight the Soviets. Key among them was Ayman al-Zawahiri [1951–] who served from the later 1980s as Osama Bin Laden's (1957–2011) chief adviser and succeeded him as the head of al-Qaida.

Born in upper Egypt to a devout family, Qutb took a university degree in modern literature and in 1948 received a government fellowship to study in the United States. Dark skinned and religiously conservative, he experienced American racism of the era and was appalled by the freedom of male–female relations at the colleges where he studied. He joined the Muslim Brotherhood on his return to Egypt and wrote an influential book, *Social Justice in Islam* (1951), a critique of Egyptian society with its extremes of wealth and poverty before the 1952 revolution. Qutb argued that while Islam permitted private capital and individual wealth, it also called for the more fortunate to aid their poorer brethren to create a stable community. Qutb and other Muslim Brothers were imprisoned on charges of sedition in 1954. Except for a brief respite in 1965, Qutb spent his remaining years in prison and was hung in 1966.

Whereas Hasan al-Banna had sought the restoration of Islam and the *shari'a* in the Islamic world, Qutb called for Islamic expansion to rule the entire world as the only means to achieve justice. He called for a vanguard of committed Muslims to initially overthrow all existing Islamic governments because they were corrupt and lived in ignorance, *jahiliyya* (ignorance of God's revelation), the term applied to Arabia before the revelation to the Prophet Muhammad.

The whole world is steeped in **Jahiliyyah**. This **Jahiliyyah** is based on rebellion against God's sovereignty on earth. . . . The result of this rebellion against the authority of God is the oppression of His creatures. Thus the humiliation of the common man under the communist system and the exploitation of individuals and nations due to greed for wealth and imperialism under the capitalist systems are but a corollary of rebellion against God's authority and the denial of the dignity of man given to him by God.

In this respect, Islam's way of life is unique. . . . Only in the Islamic way of life do all men become free from the servitude of some men to others and devote themselves to the worship of God alone. . . .

The beauty of this new system cannot be appreciated unless it take a concrete form. . . . In order to bring this about we need to initiate the movement of Islamic revival in some Muslim country. Only such a revivalist movement will eventually attain to the status of world leadership whether the distance is near or far.

How is it possible to start the task of reviving Islam?

It is necessary that there should be a vanguard which sets out with this determination and then keeps walking on the path, marching through the vast ocean of **Jahiliyyah** which has encompassed the entire world. . . . Our whole [Muslim] environment . . . is **Jahiliyyah,** even to the extent that what we consider to be Islamic culture, Islamic sources, Islamic philosophy and Islamic thought are also **Jahiliyyah.**

. . . [T]herefore . . . we should remove ourselves from all the influences of the **Jahiliyyah** . . . and return to that pure source [the Quran] . . . which is free of any mixing or pollution. . . . Our aim is first to change ourselves so that we may later change society.

The establishment of the dominion of God on earth . . . the taking away of sovereignty from the usurper and the bringing about of the authority of the divine **Shari'ah** and the abolition of man-made laws cannot be achieved only through preaching. . . . Since the objective of the message of Islam is a decisive declaration of man's freedom, not merely on the philosophical plane but also in the actual conditions of life, it must employ **Jihad** [holy war].

America and Iran: The Shah and the Islamic Revolution

In 1964, the Iranian Parliament (*majlis*) approved a law granting legal immunity to Americans and their dependents who were in Iran on U.S. government contracts. This law, the result of a U.S. government request, included civilians as well as diplomats and military personnel. Ayatollah Ruhollah Khomeini (1902–1989), then in exile for attacking the Shah's reforms and the latter's brutal repression of seminary student demonstrations, taped a sermon where he condemned this act as a return to Iran's submission to capitulations in the nineteenth century, a theme that resonated with many young Iranians, secular as well as religious. Khomeini's references to Israel were based in part on Iran's sale of oil to Israel; Israel maintained an unofficial embassy in Teheran.

Do you—the nation of Iran—know . . . that the majlis, pressured by the government, has quietly signed a treaty with America enslaving Iran, colonizing Iran. . . . Iran is now under American control. American advisers, military and non-military, together with their families, can with impunity disregard our institutions, our laws, and our judicial courts. . . . [They] have immunity from our laws. . . .

In an age when one colonized country after another is throwing off the shackles of imperialism, the Iranian government is reducing

I [suggested] that [Muhammad Reza Shah] do more to gauge public opinion. . . . 'But I already know what the people think,' he replied, 'I'm fed report after report from goodness knows how many sources.' I pointed out that such reports were calculated merely to set his mind at rest; to tell him only what he wants to hear. This went down very badly."

—From the diary of Asadollah Alam, chief counselor to the Shah, June 1970

Asadollah Alam [1919–1978], from a prominent Iranian family, served as chief counselor to the Shah for over thirty years. In this diary entry, he describes conditions in Tehran.

Friday, 26 December 1969:

"[After] two trucks . . . collided on the road to Farahabad, bringing traffic to a complete standstill. I waited and meanwhile got a glimpse of the life that goes on in that squalid district of [south] Teheran. The street running off the highway was filthy, not an ounce of asphalt since there's [little] risk of an inspection by [the shah] . . . A few men, women wearing the veil, on their way home from the communal bathhouse . . . a gaggle of children, the girls all veiled. The upper classes would not be up so early in the morning, nor would the girls wear veils. They converged, haggling, on a merchant selling hot beetroot. . . . It was both droll and desperately depressing; a scene from a top-heavy society. The Shah struggles day and night, confident that within a decade we will have surpassed much of the developed world; change can never come quickly enough for him. Yet no manner of wishful thinking can alter life in these streets."

Iran into the most backward country in the world. . . . I proclaim this disgraceful vote to be against the Holy Koran, against Islam, against the Muslim community, and thus to be null and void. . . . Everyone should realize that Iran's and the Muslim World's problems are all derived from America. In the past Britain oppressed us, exploited our natural resources, occupied our land, and interfered in our internal affairs. Now it is America that tramples over Islam and the Holy Koran, arms Israel against the Arabs . . . and wants the ulama to be incarcerated in prison—for it knows that the ulama are the real opponents of imperialism. . . .

"Massive Demonstrations in Support of Ayatollah Khomeini and Calling for Ouster of the Shah of Iran, February 1979." The collapse of the Shah's regime early in 1979 took the United States by surprise. Not only devout Shi'ites but also many secular Iranians participated in the demonstrations sparked by decades of draconian press censorship and widespread torture in Iran's prisons of political dissidents. Subsequently many Iranians who had opposed the creation of a religious state found themselves suspect, and Khomeini presented the country as the leader of a Shi'ite revolution that would represent and politically influence Islam generally.

Iran's ruling circle is busy creating chaos when it should be directing attention on the dismal economic situation, . . . providing the needy with bread, water and housing . . . the bazaar is no longer in Iranian and Muslim hands . . . all this because the Iranian economy is now in the clutches of America and Israel.

Yearnings for Love and Home ✡

[handwritten margin note: Islamism in this period]

Between 1950 and the 1970s, the spread of media—radio, television, film, the recording industry, and cassette players—exerted an immense impact in the region, since various kinds of communication were enhanced. The political implications of unrestrained, but concentrated, urban growth, combined with expanded media and communications, and were enormous. Indeed, Khomeini's speeches, banned in Iran until 1979, were disseminated underground by cassette recordings. In Egypt, TV, the most powerful medium for entertainment, propaganda, and education, made its appearance in 1960, furthering the singing career of Umm Kulthum (1898–1975), the most famous of all Arab vocalists, the "Star of the East." Her biography encapsulates the period from World War I until after the 1973 War between Egypt and Israel, but more widely the histories of North Africa and the Middle East in the transition from European imperialism to nation-state status and full participation in global modernity. In 1965, Umm Kulthum popularized the Arabic song translated here, *Inta Umri* ("You are my life").

> Your eyes took me back to my days that are gone
> They taught me to regret the past and its wounds.
> Whatever I saw before my eyes saw you was a wasted life.
> How could they consider that part of my life?
> With your light, the dawn of my life started
> How much of my life before you was lost
> It is a wasted past, my love.
> My heart never saw happiness before you
> My heart never saw anything in life other than the taste of
>   pain and suffering . . .
> I reconciled with days because of you
> I forgave the time because of you
> With you I forgot my pains
> And I forgot with you my misery.
> Your eyes took me back to my days that are gone
> They taught me to regret the past and its wounds.
> Whatever I saw before my eyes saw you was a wasted life.
> How could they consider that part of my life?
> You are my life that starts its dawn with your light.

Born in 1898 in a village, Umm Kulthum was a much celebrated Egyptian singer, songwriter, and actress. This 1968 concert was one of her last. In the decades since her 1975 death, she is still widely regarded as the greatest female singer in the Arab world.

The end of empire and their newfound political independence did not yield the expected fruits for many social classes in MENA. High underemployment or unemployment in rural economies from Morocco to Turkey drove first single male workers, and then entire families, to Europe where labor was in demand after the war. But the workers often lived in terrible conditions and moreover were not welcome as Africans, Arabs, Muslims, and outsiders. Moreover, the absence of fathers from households back home in Morocco frequently created many family tensions.

Haddou sat on the bed, thumbing through his passport. It was full of entry and exit stamps from his many trips between his family in Morocco and his job in Düsseldorf, Germany. As the pages flipped he stopped again to look at the visa he had received from the German government just that afternoon. He had to smile, for this newest visa guaranteed him a court hearing before any deportation measures could be taken against him. It made him feel relaxed. He did not need fear every time the boss yelled at him or every time the border guards interrogated him. He had had very few close calls over the years, but you could never be too careful. He thought of that time when while riding his bicycle to work the cops stopped him, claiming he had run a red light. They said to him, 'Hey, where do you think you are, Turkey? Here in Germany we obey the law. Do that again and you'll be riding that bike back in Istanbul'. Haddou was upset that they assumed he was a Turk. It further irritated him that they assumed he disobeyed the law when in fact he bent over backwards to keep his nose clean. With the new visa he would not have to jump every time a police car passed him. . . .

As far back as Haddou could remember he had worked. . . . [His] first job was a ticket taker on the local bus route between Kariat Arkman, a small town near his *char,* or lineage settlement, and Villa Nador, the Spanish provincial capital of the whole region. He got the job during the great drought of 1944–45, when he was only seven years old. Prior to that he had worked on the family farm, watching the goats or helping with the planting and harvesting. The drought proved to be so bad, however, that his father was forced to sell the goats—and that was after the goats had eaten what little of the barley actually sprouted that year. . . .

When in his late teens, Haddou finally landed a good paying job working in Kariat Arkman in an automobile upholstery shop. Since the business was owned by a Spaniard and all the customers were Spaniards, when the Spanish population in the region began to decline after independence, so, unfortunately, did the business. Before it closed, however, Haddou managed to save enough money to get married. That same year he and a friend from the shop decided to emigrate to Europe to look for work. . . .

Haddou has started as an unskilled construction worker on a job in the outskirts of Paris. He lived in a shack on the site to save money. Many other North Africans lived there also. They guarded the site at night in exchange for their room. That is how Haddou met the big bosses. Every Saturday evening after work was finished, the architect, contractor, and their cronies returned to the job site. Haddou would open the gate to let them in, after which they would enter his guard hut and pull out the cards and liquor and proceed to play poker until early in the morning. Haddou's job was to wash their cars and then wait outside and stand guard in case of trouble. Since he was a Muslim, they reasoned, he did not want to go out on the town or to play or drink with them. He could thus be trusted to stay nearby, sober and alert. He could also be trusted to guard their liquor stash during the week. They did not have to worry about his taking an extra nip behind their backs. They did not see the need to pay him extra for his special duties either. . . .

I earn a little by selling watercress and parsley but because I am here in the vicinity I learn when there is meat, chicken, eggs, or other items in the *gam'iyya* [government food cooperative] and I can always leave my basket either for my children or a friend here and run to the queue . . . If I was working in the factory, since I am illiterate, I would earn only ten pounds or so more, but I would have to buy more clothes since I could not go in my *gallabiyya* [traditional dress]. I would have to pay bus fare and then when I came home I would have to purchase food at the free-market price, wasting as much as fifteen to twenty pounds monthly.

—Umm Sabah, Cairo resident

CHAPTER 7

Unknown Destinies c. 1980–Present

It is difficult to adequately cover the diversity of forces at work in MENA during the past three decades, especially in light of the "Arab Spring" that exploded in Tunisia in December 2010 and saw the swift overthrow of the rulers of Tunisia and Egypt. But the consequences of these popular protests remain uncertain with respect to what types of governments will replace them and what repercussions these events will have elsewhere. Similar demonstrations in Bahrain were crushed by the royal family with Saudi assistance. Muammar al-Qaddafi (1942–2011) was killed in October 2011 after his Libyan regime had been overthrown with the assistance of NATO, and Syria's al-Bashar Assad (1965–) continued to struggle as of spring 2013 to quell a broadening wave of armed militias demanding his overthrow.

These events only add to the process of what the Egyptian Nobel Prize winning writer, Naguib Mahfouz (1911–2006), called a "whirling hem of change" to suggest that large social and political transformations are difficult to chart, much less to understand, for those living when they occur. The region has experienced an enormous range of developments since 1980, the period that followed the 1979 Iranian revolution. Its success had encouraged Islamic militancy that challenged state authority, especially in Algeria and Egypt where high unemployment, elite corruption, a huge demographic youth bulge, and the unequal distribution of social wealth had created immense tensions. Added to these internal crises were two wars during the 1980s whose consequences led to further strife extending into the twenty-first century. In 1980, Iraq's Saddam Hussein (1937–2006) initiated a war against Iran, a long drawn-out

German and Turkish flags fly next to each other as fans prepare for the 2008 European soccer championship between Germany and Turkey. Two of the Turkish players were born in, and lived in, Germany.

241

affair that lasted until 1988. The Soviet Union invaded Afghanistan late in 1979. This sparked Islamic resistance backed by the United States and Saudi Arabia that finally succeeded in driving out the Soviet invaders in warfare that wreaked havoc on Afghan society with serious repercussions throughout the region, including the creation of al-Qaida.

Both conflicts had unforeseen results. Iraq's need for debt relief after 1988 created tensions with Kuwait over oil and revenues that ultimately led to Iraq's invasion of Kuwait in August 1990. Iraq's action sparked the first Gulf War during which a U.S.-dominated coalition drove Iraqi troops out of Kuwait in February–March 1991 and forced Iraq's submission to devastating international economic sanctions. The Afghanistan conflict and Soviet defeat contributed to the collapse of the Soviet Union in 1991, ending the Cold War, but these events ushered in more conflicts and a power vacuum in Afghanistan ultimately filled by the Islamists known as the Taliban. During the 1990s, al-Qaida, based in Afghanistan, sponsored attacks on American military and political targets in the Middle East and Africa that culminated in the air assaults on the U.S. on September 11, 2001. These events triggered the U.S. invasion first of Afghanistan but then of Iraq in 2003, resulting in Saddam' Hussein's overthrow, trial, and death. American combat forces withdrew from Iraq at the end of 2011, as the Iraqi government refused to grant them legal immunity based on actions including torture of prisoners at prisons such as Abu Ghraib. U.S. troops were scheduled to withdraw from Afghanistan by the end of 2014. There is no assurance that political stability will have been achieved in either country.

In the midst of these developments, there erupted what has been called "The Arab Spring" in December 2010 when a street vendor's death in Tunisia led to a spontaneous outburst of popular demonstrations demanding more political and economic rights that forced out the authoritarian president Zine el-Abedin Ben Ali (1936–), whose regime had ruled since 1988. Events in Tunisia inspired similar, more sustained demonstrations in Egypt that caused the downfall of the Husni Mubarak (1928–) government, in power since 1981. Popularized in part by the latest technologies in social networking, including Twitter, mobile phones, and Web sites such as Facebook and YouTube, major demands for more political rights emerged elsewhere with uncertain consequences. Whereas the United States had applauded developments in Egypt and Tunisia, it remained silent as events in Bahrain unfolded; the U.S. Fifth Fleet is based in Bahrain. Likewise, in Iran where a major protest movement, the Greens, challenged the results of 2009 elections, many activists and young people, among them numerous students, were imprisoned, with the Iranian government using access to Web technologies to identify leaders of protests. Even in cases where greater constitu-

tional rights for citizens have been promised, as in Egypt and Tunisia, outcomes are unclear. Free elections in Tunisia in October 2011 saw the Muslim Nahda (Renaissance) Party gain 90 (forty-one percent) out of 217 seats in Parliament. Nahda's leaders have promised to preserve women's rights, but are challenged by Saudi-backed Salafists who called for restoration of Islamic law. In Libya, the anti-Qaddafi forces remain divided and the interim leader, Mustafa Abedel-Jalil, announced in late 2011 that he supported the restoration of polygamy; he left office in August 2012. There is no effective central government in Libya. Finally, in Syria the Assad regime continued its ferocious and bloody oppression of its own citizens demanding freedom and social justice, but the opposition forces are divided as to the society they hope to create.

During the 1980s, Palestinians, chafing under Israeli occupation in Gaza and the West Bank, erupted in a rebellion called the intifada *[literally a "shaking off"] at the end of 1987. With this rebellion appeared a new militant Islamic group in Gaza called Hamas whose growth had initially been encouraged by Israel to counter Palestinian nationalism centered on the PLO; Hamas would win Palestinian elections in January 2006. The intifada and related developments ultimately led to the 1993 Oslo agreement whereby Israel and the PLO agreed to seek a solution to the conflict. After the second Oslo agreement of 1995, these efforts collapsed when a militant Israeli who backed settlement expansion assassinated Israeli Prime Minister Yitzhak Rabin (1922–1995) in November. With the Likud Party led by Benjamin Netanyahu (1949–) elected to power after Rabin's death, the peace process stalled, due principally to Israeli settlement expansion in the West Bank. The failure of the Camp David peace talks of 2000, opposed by both the Palestinian Hamas and the Likud and other rightist Israeli parties, led to a second intifada, where violence on both sides, including terrorist attacks inside Israel, was not contained for several years*

But along with wars and internal turmoil, countries in the region witnessed peaceful change, social innovation, uneven economic growth, and cultural achievements in literature, film, and music. Both Algeria and Morocco established multiparty systems prior to the Arab Spring. Advocates for women's rights gained greater support in Egypt as well as in Morocco where the language of human rights is currently being used to advance feminist causes; the first league for human rights was established in Tunisia (1977). Equally crucial are popular perceptions of social unity or divisiveness, of social justice or injustice, and of respect for, or violation of, human rights. Local chapters of international human rights organizations have sprung up in some countries, often focusing on women's and children's rights. A good example is the Iranian lawyer and activist, Shirin Ebadi (1947–), (see p. 278) who was awarded the

Nobel Peace Prize in 2003 for her work in human rights, but who was later barred from legal practice by her government.

A long-standing problem is population growth, whose rapidity outstrips economic expansion. In many Middle East countries, at least fifty, if not more, percent of the population is under the age of eighteen. This vast reservoir of unemployed, and often undereducated, citizens created political and social problems that contributed to the uprisings in Tunisia and Egypt where students played a prominent role. Pressures on existing resources, together with the ravages of colonialism and colonial wars, led to massive worker migration to Western Europe, especially from North Africa, creating strains in European societies as well. Moreover, millions of expatriate Egyptians and Palestinians sought work in the Gulf States. Among the countries that publicly support family planning and other social programs are Turkey, currently ruled by an Islamist party, and Iran, although Tunisia has officially promoted women's reproductive rights since the 1970s. Thus, Islamist-party rule does not mean that state elites oppose efforts to curb population growth. Another apparent paradox is the fact that the Iranian cinema took off after 1979 and Iranian film producers, such as Abbas Kiarostami (1940–), produced films that won international recognition.

The dilemmas of uneven modernization that affected the Middle East in the nineteenth century, and debates over Western-inspired secular ideas regarded as in opposition to Islamic values, have reappeared in different forms and intensified during the last thirty years. In the most avowedly secularist Middle Eastern state, Turkey, an Islamist party first won elections in 1995, and the Justice and Development Party has governed since 2002. This democratic transition, following decades of often brutal military intervention to retain Ataturk's secular legacy, may foreshadow future compromises in other areas of MENA. Another important element is Turkey's desire for admission into the European Union. While globalization has enriched some social sectors in certain countries, further incorporation into the world economy has created profound social distress and discontents that are reminiscent of the economic imperialism of the nineteenth century.

Urban Transformations and Ethnic Interactions: Turkey and Germany

Both the Cairo of Naguib Mahfouz and the Istanbul of the celebrated contemporary writer and fellow Nobel Prize for Literature winner, Orhan Pamuk (1952–), have grown into gigantic cities that are home to millions of people. Much of their growth resulted from population movements from villages to the city. This four-part article, published in the German news magazine *Der Spiegel* online in 2007, illustrates the vibrant nature of Istanbul, absorbing extremely diverse inhabitants, balancing the traditional and the modern, and trying to accommodate the influx of impoverished peasantry from the countryside.

Istanbul's more affluent citizens live directly on the shore or pay a $1,000 premium for an apartment with a view of the Bosporus [a strait twenty miles long but at its narrowest point only two thousand feet wide]. [Kagan] Gürsel lives with his wife Merve, an interior designer and former show jumper, in one of Istanbul's most beautiful buildings: an old wooden Ottoman palace on the water in the Asian part of the city. . . . Built in 1860, the Gürsel's villa was once the home of a princess from Egypt, an Ottoman province at the time. The new elite is rediscovering old Istanbul's beauty and its historic legacy. . . . Pamuk talks of a "frenzy to turn Istanbul into a pale, poor second class imitation of a Western city. . . ." The Marmara hotel on Taksim Square, which Gürsel, as his father's heir, runs, is one of those much-maligned buildings from the 1970s. But the popular and well-managed property is one of the top addresses in the area. . . . From the Marmara, it's only a short walk to the restaurants and bars of Beyoglu . . . [which] boasts rooftop bars with an excellent view of the Istanbul skyline, palaces and magnificent mosques between the Sea of Marmara and the Golden Horn. . . . Every few hours the call of the muezzin cuts through the sound of the techno music, an aural reminder of Istanbul's position as the gateway between East and West.

Part 2: The Exploding City

The city . . . has exploded, overrun by a surge of poor immigrants from Anatolia in eastern Turkey and the Black Sea region. Migrant workers have built makeshift houses known as "gecekondus," illegal but tolerated, on Istanbul's fringes and interspersed throughout the city. . . . The city has granted amnesty to many gecekondus and has

"Naguib Mahfouz." Winner of the Nobel Prize for Literature in 1988, Naguib Mahfouz breakfasted daily at this table at the Aly Baba Café that fronted on Midan al-Tahrir (Liberation Square) in Cairo before going to work. He would greet and converse with other patrons in the café as well as with people in neighboring streets, which provided the writer with rich oral data for his stories.

If the city speaks of defeat, destruction, deprivation, melancholy and poverty, the Bosporus sings of life, pleasure and happiness.

—Nobel Prize-winning novelist, Orhan Pamuk

even upgraded some of them. . . . These crowded slums, bleak satellite cities, don't fit into the picture of a shimmering Istanbul, which has previously served as the capital of three different empires. . . . Istanbul is probably the most Western city in the Islamic world. But those who take the trouble to go to the Fatih neighborhood to pay a visit to the tomb of the conqueror Mehmed II, who brought down Byzantium in 1453 . . . will also discover the city's deeply Islamic side. Here the women wear black, full-length veils, and many men are bearded and wear religious caps and collarless shirts. One small section consisting of a few streets is populated almost entirely by members of a 14th-century Islamic order and has no televisions or alcohol.

But it is not just the tension between religion and the secular republic, between miniskirts and minarets, which characterizes Istanbul. The visible social inequality that plagues Turkey is more readily apparent. Wealth is ostentatiously displayed in the form of expensive cars, yachts and elite clubs like the Reina, which is designed to resemble the deck of a cruise ship. . . . [Still] there are possibilities for the poor to become upwardly mobile. Istanbul . . . [is] a place where Anatolian cotton porters and scrap dealers can become millionaires, like Haci Ömer Sabanci, whose family-owned holding company is now Turkey's second-largest corporation, or media mogul Aydin Dogan, one of Forbes' 500 richest people in the world. . . .

Part 3: 'You Can Make Something of Yourself Here'

Former residents of Istanbul who return to the city are amazed at how quickly it has changed. . . . Defne Koryürek started up an upmarket butcher's shop when she returned from New York. Defne . . . 38, and her husband spent five years in New York, where they ran a small restaurant. . . . Koryürek found surprising similarities between the Big Apple and Istanbul. "Both cities are dynamic and full of energy," she says. "You can make something of yourself here. It's up to you whether you want to be part of the whole, and whether you are willing to learn." Koryürek . . . studied history

"Dubai, 1990–2003." Whereas Istanbul's expansion reflects developments affecting a city that has existed for nearly 2,000 years, these two photos, one from 1990, the other from 2003, illustrate the extraordinary explosion of a former small Arab principality on the Persian Gulf into a major international urban center owing to oil revenues.

and cinematography, and worked as a TV producer until she discovered her love of cooking. When she returned to Istanbul, she brought back recipes for pancakes, quiches and Eggs Benedict from New York. She now runs "Dükkan," an exclusive butcher's shop specializing in dry-aged beef. Juicy, dark cuts of beef dry in a climate-controlled glass cabinet.... As Koryürek fills sausage skins with meat, the door of the shop opens and a hotel chef walks in. He bends over the meat counter and selects the best pieces. Dükkan has become a supplier to Istanbul's five-star restaurants, including the Hilton, the Four Seasons, the Ciragan Palace Kempinski and Les Ottomans, a luxury hotel on the banks of the Bosporus that is bringing the flair of the Ottoman era back to life.... Koryürek and her partner Emre Mermer, 38, an economist and the son of a cattle farmer, don't even have an official permit for their exclusive shop, which lies in the middle of Küçük Armutlu, a poor gecekondu settlement adjacent to the highway. They chose the spot because the rent was affordable. When they tried to register the company, officials at the city planning office told them the buildings weren't registered—and so it was impossible to register a business there. Nevertheless, the authorities tolerate Dükkan, and business is booming. That's just the way it goes in Istanbul....

The post-World War II era witnessed the unprecedented movement of labor from the Middle East to Europe and elsewhere. As this 2004 report from the Council of Europe's Parliamentary Assembly indicates, from the 1960s on, large numbers of Turkish migrants sought employment in Germany, which suffered from a shortage of unskilled and semiskilled workers for industrial growth. Jobs in Germany relieved pressures on labor markets within Turkey, and worker remittances sent back home to Turkish villages assured families of a decent living. The presence of several generations of Turkish workers, who were often poorly assimilated to their host societies, exerted a major impact on both the immigrants and on Europe as well.

1.... The first wave of Turkish emigration began in the early 1960s in response to the needs of the West German economy. Suffering from a labour shortage, West Germany signed a bilateral agreement with Turkey in October 1961 on the short-term emigration of Turkish workers. As the German term "Gastarbeiter" (guest worker) indicates, the Turkish migrants intended staying in Germany for only a short period before returning to their country of origin. However, it was clear by 1967 that the immigration that had been expected to be

For a man to make a major decision (for instance, to go to a foreign country), it must first be conceivable, then possible, and only lastly necessary.

—French anthropologist Germaine Tillion, 1958

temporary had become more long-term. In addition to West Germany, other European countries signed bilateral agreements with Turkey (Belgium, Netherlands, Austria, France, Sweden and Switzerland) and, with time, Turkish immigrant workers have become an integral part of society in many European countries.

2. According to Turkish Labour Ministry sources, 3,038,215 Turkish citizens were living in EU countries at the end of 1999, including one million of working age who were in employment or seeking employment. In terms of geographical distribution, there were over 730,000 in Germany, 76,000 in France, 57,000 in Austria, 51,000 in the Netherlands and 44,000 in the United Kingdom.

3. The Assembly wishes to look into the situation of the Turkish migrant workers living in Council of Europe member states because of their large numbers and the length of time they have spent in Europe. The issue is important, as it has economic, social and cultural implications. There is a need to clarify certain fundamental aspects of the migrants' legal status: firstly, the question of the integration of these migrant workers in their host society and that of their possible reintegration in their country of origin if they return home, particularly with regard to access to social rights (transfer of pensions, health insurance) and, secondly, the lack of arrangements enabling them to obtain employment in a country other than their host country.

4. The situation of the Turkish migrant workers in the European Union (EU) is based on an association agreement signed by the EU and Turkey in 1963, which lays down their rights in terms of employment, social protection and freedom of movement. If an even more consistent policy was properly implemented at Council of Europe level, it would enable them to enjoy treatment of a kind comparable with that of national workers....

8. The Assembly therefore calls on the Committee of Ministers:

i. to ask its relevant bodies to study the situation of Turkish migrant workers in Europe as regards their social integration, pension rights and more general social rights, as well as their possible entitlement to freedom of movement in terms of employment;

ii. to urge those member countries which have not already done so to sign and ratify the European Convention on the Legal Status of Migrant Workers and the European Convention on Social Security;

iii. to urge member countries to make sure that pension rights are transferable regardless of the country of destination of Turkish migrant workers and to provide adequate information on their entitlement to social housing, social protection, pensions and health services.

Netherlands, SOC

The impact of foreign migration to Europe was well-illustrated during the European soccer championship of 2008. It featured teams such as Germany and Turkey with players who were born and raised in the country of the opposing team. This was particularly true of the Turkish team, but for German fans their loyalties were also mixed, some choosing to root for the Turks. Published before the match, this *New York Times* article reports on the preparation of Berlin's police force in anticipation of violent sports fans. Germany defeated Turkey, and no fighting ensued.

Berlin, June 25, 2008:

When the German team takes the field Wednesday night against Turkey in Basel, Switzerland, in the semifinals of the European Championship, it will also face two German natives on the Turkish side. The versatile midfielder Hamit Altintop hails from the West German city of Gelsenkirchen and defender Hakan Balta is a Berliner. . . . [There are an] estimated 2.7 million people either of Turkish citizenship or heritage living in Germany, the country's largest minority . . . many Germans have cheered on the Turks and vice versa. Each Turkish victory in the tournament has brought enthusiastic fans draped in the country's red flag onto the streets, where they set off firecrackers and shot bottle rockets into the night sky, with parties often lasting until morning. German fans have packed pubs and beer gardens for their team's run to the semifinal.

Now the country is practically humming with anticipation for the match, with . . . an edge of nervousness that a friendly sporting rivalry could spill over into something more serious in the streets. Police officials say they are prepared, especially in Berlin where some 500,000 people are expected at the public viewing area at the Brandenburg Gate. . . . Mixed allegiances are hardly new to international soccer. . . . "Of course my heart lies first with the German team," said Rainer Krause, 63, a Berlin native who bought a red Turkish flag as well as a German one at a store in the heavily Turkish Neukölln neighborhood, where he works., "But over the decades the loyalties have grown together, there are such strong feelings of connection." Altintop, who plays for the German club champion, Bayern Munich, agrees. In an interview this week with Spiegel Online, he declared, "I owe much, actually everything, to Germany." But when asked whether he considered himself German at heart, Altintop, the Turkish team's mainstay, reinforced the sense of dual loyalty, saying: "No. Maybe I'm both." ... Some Germans have gone so far as to switch allegiances from their home team to Turkey, a sentimental favorite of the tournament if not quite a Cinderella, considering its run to the semifinals in the 2002 World Cup. "It's only fair," said Rosie Lambrecht, who was out shopping for a Turkey T-shirt on Tuesday morning and who roots with her Turkish friends and neighbors in Neukölln. "They've never won the tournament."

"I think it will go great, whichever team wins," said Murat Yalcin, 33, who works at a cafe in Neukölln back in Berlin. He was wearing a Turkey T-shirt, but said that if Germany wins, he would root for it in the final. "When you live here, when you were raised here, why root for anyone else?"

Islam, Women, Clothing, and Identity in France and MENA

One of the most popular singers and composers in Europe today is a Tunisian woman, Amina Annabi (1962–), whose music—and life—fuses traditional Arab, Middle Eastern, and West African musical genres with Western music, particularly blues, jazz, reggae, rap, and rock and roll. Amina's life is intertwined with the postcolonial reality of millions of North Africans who reside permanently in European nations; many were born there and are from second- or third-generation migrant families. She was born in Carthage, a suburb of Tunis, the product of a "mixed marriage"—her father is French, her mother Tunisian. Amina's mother came from a family that boasted gifted female musicians and composers, including her grandmother. Tunisia has hosted international summer musical festivals for decades in Carthage and Tabarka, which brought in vocalists, like James Brown, Tina Turner, Joan Baez, Algerian and Senegalese musicians, and performers from around the world.

In 1975 Amina went to Paris with her mother where she pursued music at France's leading world music station, Radio Nova. In 1991 she was named the "Best Female Singer of the Year" in France and represented France at the 1991 Eurovision Song Contest held in Rome, where she received a second place. Again in 1994, she was invited to participate in a multiartist album entitled "Paris," which celebrated the French capital. Born in Tunisia, Amina has represented France and French culture in international competitions—by combining the musical traditions of former French colonies with those of Europe or the West. While she has managed through art and performance to break out of the postcolonial

cultural and political ghetto experienced by so many African migrants residing in Europe, these songs suggest obstacles she faced.

1. "The Bad Seed":

> Me, I am like a bad seed that grows soundlessly without hatred
> You can walk on top of me at times but life will always overcome
> You do not rule the sky nor the earth nor the angels above my
>   bed.

2. "My Music Has Been Shattered":

> My music has been shattered, Monsieur
> I can no longer awaken, Monsieur
> My music has been shattered, Monsieur
> I can no longer awaken, Monsieur
> Yes, I have again sold my thoughts
> For a very small handful
> Of electricity, of electricity, of electricity
> For a little bit of progress
> Wear yourself out, wear yourself out, ah
> I must wake up
> Wear yourself out, wear yourself out
> I must wake up.

3. "Away from Doors that Slam":

> Away from doors that slam
> Away from doors that slam
> Away from screams, away from slaps
> From evil, from words, from evil
> From demonic words . . .
> I will not lower my eyes
> I will raise them to the sky
> And if even rumor has it that
> One day you will die because of it
> And if I were to die
> And if you were to die
> It is only a rumor.

The issue of clothing and its religious symbolism is not limited to the
Middle East. With a large Muslim minority, primarily from North Africa, French authorities reacted strongly against women students who
wore what were viewed as "Islamic" head scarves to public school.
This violated the French doctrine of *laïcité* or secularism, defined in

France's system of education as imposing the separation of church and state in the classroom. The ban, decreed in March 2004, reflected a controversy going back to 1989. Some observers saw the decision as, paradoxically, violating religious freedom, as this article from Human Rights Watch shows.

"The Great Mosque of Paris." The French government authorized the building of the mosque after World War I to acknowledge the sacrifices made by Muslim soldiers from French colonies; more than 100,000 died fighting on the Western front for France against Germany. During World War II, Paris mosque authorities provided shelter and fake Muslim birth certificates for Jewish children to save them from being sent to the extermination camps.

The proposed French law banning Islamic headscarves and other visible religious symbols [of all religions] in state schools would violate the rights to freedom of religion and expression, Human Rights Watch said today. The law . . . forbids "signs and dress that conspicuously show the religious affiliation of students". . . . "[It] is an unwarranted infringement on the right to religious practice," said Kenneth Roth, executive director of Human Rights Watch. "For many Muslims, wearing a headscarf is not only about religious expression, it is about religious obligation."

International human rights law obliges state authorities to avoid coercion in matters of religious freedom, and this obligation must be taken into account when devising school dress codes. The proposed prohibition on headscarves in France, as with laws in some Muslim countries that force girls to wear headscarves in schools, violates this principle. Under international law, states can only limit religious practices when there is a compelling public safety reason, when the manifestation of religious beliefs would impinge on the rights of others, or when it serves a legitimate educational function (such as prohibiting practices that preclude student-teacher interaction). Muslim headscarves, Sikh turbans, Jewish skullcaps and large Christian crosses—which are among the visible religious symbols that would be prohibited—do not pose a threat to public health, order or morals; they have no effect on the fundamental rights and freedoms of other students; and they do not undermine a school's educational function. . . .

[Furthermore], protecting the right of all students to religious freedom does not undermine secularism in schools. On the contrary, it demonstrates respect for religious diversity, a position fully consistent with maintaining the strict separation of public institutions from any particular religious message.... The impact of a ban on visible religious symbols, even though phrased in neutral terms, will fall disproportionately on Muslim girls, and thus violate antidiscrimination provisions of international human rights law as well as the right to equal educational opportunity. Indeed, the promotion of understanding and tolerance for such differences in values is a key aspect of enforcement of the right to education. In practice, the law will leave some Muslim families no choice but to remove girls from the state educational system.

Some in France have used the headscarf issue as a pretext for voicing anti-immigrant and anti-Muslim sentiments. Some arguments appear to be based on the premise that all Muslims want to oppress women, or that women and girls who choose to veil do not understand women's rights. Public debate has also touched on many other significant social issues: religious fundamentalism and political uses of religious symbols; oppression of girls and women; levels of immigration; discrimination and lack of economic opportunity for immigrant communities; pluralism and national integration.

"The proposed law has raised important issues about religious freedom and the role of the state in France," said Roth. "The resolution of this issue will have important implications throughout Europe and beyond. But simply banning headscarves and other expressions of religious belief from the schools is not the answer."

France allows French Catholic schools to permit the wearing of headscarves banned in state schools, even while providing state funding to those schools that qualify academically, as this 2008 article from the *New York Times* reports. In the Netherlands, Dutch officials have banned the wearing of headscarves in Dutch Catholic schools.

Marseille

The bright cafeteria of Saint Mauront Catholic school is conspicuously quiet: It is Ramadan and 80 percent of the students are Muslim. When the lunch bell rings, girls and boys stream out past the crucifixes and the large wooden cross in the corridor, heading for Muslim midday prayer. "There is respect for our religion here," said Nadia Oualane, 14, her hair covered by a black headscarf. "In the public school," she added, gesturing at nearby buildings, "I would not be allowed to wear a veil." Oualane, of Algerian descent, wants to be the first in her family to go to a university.

France has only four Muslim schools. So the 8,847 Roman Catholic schools have become a refuge for Muslims seeking what an overburdened, secularist public sector often lacks: spirituality, an environment in which good manners count alongside mathematics and higher academic standards. There are no national statistics, but Muslim and Catholic educators estimate that Muslim students now form more than 10 percent of the two million students in Catholic schools. In ethnically mixed neighborhoods in Marseille and the industrial north, the share can be more than half.

The quiet migration to fee-paying Catholic schools highlights how hard it has become for state schools, long France's tool for integration, to keep their promise of equal opportunity—irrespective of color, creed or zip code. Traditionally, the republican school, born of the French Revolution, was the breeding ground for citizens. The shift from these schools is another indication of the challenge facing the strict form of secularism known as "laïcité." After centuries of religious wars and squabbles between the nascent republic and a meddlesome clergy, a 1905 law granted religious freedom in predominantly Roman Catholic France but also withdrew financial support and formal recognition from all faiths. Religious education and symbols were banned from public schools.

As France has become home to five million Muslims, Western Europe's largest such community, new fault lines have emerged. In 2004, a ban on the headscarf in state schools prompted an outcry and a debate about loosening interpretations of the 1905 law. "Laïcité has become the state's religion and the republican school is its temple," said Imam Soheib Bencheikh, a former grand mufti in Marseille and founder of its Higher Institute of Islamic Studies. Bencheikh's oldest daughter attends Catholic school. "It's ironic, but today the Catholic church is more tolerant of, and knowledgeable about, Islam than the French state," he said.

For some, economics argue for Catholic schools, which tend to be smaller than public ones and much cheaper than private schools in other countries. In return for teaching the national curriculum and being open to students of all faiths, the government pays teachers' salaries and a subsidy per student. Annual cost for parents averages €1,400, or about $2,000, for junior high and €1,800 for high school, according to the Catholic teaching authority. . . . Religious instruction, such as Catholic catechism, is strictly voluntary. Catholic schools are free to allow girls to wear a headscarf. Many impose the state ban, but several, like Saint Mauront, tolerate a discreet version.

Tucked under an overpass in the city's northern housing projects, the school embodies the tectonic shifts in French society over the last century. Founded in 1905 in a former soap factory, the school initially served mainly French Catholic students, said the headmaster, Jean Chamoux. Before World War II, Italian and some Portuguese immigrants arrived; since the 1960s, Africans from former French colonies. Today there is barely a white face among the 117 students. About one in five girls covers her hair. Chamoux, a slow-moving, jovial man, has been here 20 years and seems to know each pupil by name. In his crammed office, under a crucifix, he extolled the virtues of Catholic schools. "We practice religious freedom, the public schools don't," he said. "We teach the national curriculum. Religious activities are entirely optional. If I banned the headscarf, half the girls wouldn't go to school at all," he added. "I prefer to have them here, talk to them and tell them that they have a choice. Many actually take it off after a while. My goal is that by the time they graduate they have made a conscious choice, one way or the other."

Defenders of secularism retort that such leniency could encourage other special requests and anti-western values, such as oppression of women. "The headscarf is a sexist sign and discrimination between the sexes has no place in the republican school," Education Minister Xavier Darcos said in a telephone interview. "That is the fundamental reason why we are against it." Chamoux suspects that some pupils—"a small minority," he said—wear the scarf because of pressure from family. He acknowledged that parents routinely demand exemptions from swimming lessons for daughters, who, when denied, present a medical certificate and miss class anyway. Recently he put his foot down when students asked to remove the crucifix in a classroom they wanted for communal prayers during Ramadan. The biology teacher has been challenged on Darwin's theory of evolution and history class can get heated when the crusades or the Israeli-Palestinian conflict is discussed. After the Sept. 11 attacks in 2001, Chamoux recalled, some Muslim students shocked staff with their glee.

The school deals swiftly with offensive comments, Chamoux said, but also tries to respect Islam. It takes Muslim holidays into account for parent-teacher meetings. For two years now, it has offered

"Selection of Headscarves, Whitechapel Road, London, May 2010." There is a large market for fashionable headscarves worn as a sign of Muslim identity in Europe, North America, and worldwide.

optional Arabic, in part to steer students away from Koran classes in neighborhood mosques believed to preach radical Islam. Seventeen students volunteered to stay after class for the month of Lent to prepare a slideshow on the 14 stations of the cross for the Easter sermon in church. Only four were Christian, said Nathalie Geckeler, who led the project. Ten of the 13 Muslim students attended the sermon.

Ask parents why they chose Catholic school, and the answer is swift: "We share the same God," said Zohra Hanane, who struggles to meet the €249 annual fee for her daughter Sabrina to attend Saint Mauront. But faith is not the only argument. Hanane, a single mother who is unemployed, said she did not want her children with "the wrong crowd" in the projects. Many local children attend the public school with six times as many students. "It's expensive and sometimes it's hard, but I want my children to have a better life," said Hanane. "Today this seems to be their best shot."

Across town, in the gleaming compound housing the Sainte Trinité high school in the wealthy neighborhood of Mazargues, the rules and conditions are different, but the arguments similar. Muslim girls do not wear headscarves. But Imene Sahraoui, 17, a practicing Muslim and the daughter of an Algerian diplomat-turned-businessman, is here above all to get top grades and head for business school, preferably abroad. "Public schools just don't prepare you in the same way," she said. . . . Catholic schools remain popular among Muslims even in cities where Muslim schools have sprung up: Paris, Lyon and Lille. Muslim schools have been hampered in part by the relative poverty of the Muslim community, which commands less real estate than the Catholic church. And only one Muslim school, the Averroës high school on one floor of the Lille mosque, has qualified for state subsidies. The three others charge significantly higher fees to survive.

Also, as M'hamed Ed-Dyouri, headmaster of a new Muslim school just outside Paris, noted: "We have to prove ourselves first." For now, he plans to enroll his son in a Catholic school.

The battle over head scarves has arisen in Turkey where, since 1950, there has been a gradual shift from the dominance of Ataturk's legacy toward greater toleration for the role of religion in politics, a shift interrupted by three military interventions to safeguard secular democracy. The Turkish parliament, controlled by members of the Islamist Justice and Development Party, voted in 2008 to permit women to wear headscarves in some public places. This vote inspired celebrations among those sympathetic to the Islamist parties and platforms and sparked outrage among those

loyal to Ataturk's secularist reforms, which forbade, as in France, the wearing of religious clothing in public schools and in government offices.

Istanbul, Feb. 9

Turkey's parliament voted Saturday to end a more than 80-year-old ban on women wearing head scarves at universities, acknowledging the rising influence of conservative Islam in the most determinedly secular republic of the Muslim world. Tens of thousands of secular Turks marched in the capital, Ankara, against lifting the ban. Many brandished portraits of Mustafa Kemal Ataturk, who founded modern Turkey in 1923 with the goal of making it a Westernized, secular republic. "Turkey is secular and will remain secular," the protesters chanted, swinging poles bearing the red flag of the Turkish republic. "This is catastrophic," Aylin Tok, a woman with uncovered hair, said in a busy shopping district in Istanbul, Turkey's commercial center. "We are in a minority now," she said, referring to Turkish women who do not cover their hair.

Ataturk, still revered even by many conservative Muslims, outlawed the wearing of Islamic attire at universities and in public offices. The ban stood until Saturday's vote by lawmakers. The governing Justice and Development Party, which is religiously conservative but has won wide support through pragmatic economic policies, holds a majority in parliament. It easily won passage of lifting the ban in a 411 to 103 vote. Crucially, Turkey's military made no immediate objection to the result . . . as the guardians of Ataturk's secular vision for their country, in the past generals have overthrown Islamic-oriented elected governments they saw as straying from his secular goal. Last year, generals forced an early national election simply by posting a statement on a military Web site expressing their concern about the rise of the Justice and Development Party. But voters rebuked the generals, making clear in the resulting elections last year that they were increasingly comfortable with conservative Islam and pleased with the party's economic policies.

The government news agency stressed that the style of head scarf legalized on Saturday was not necessarily Islamic. Justice and Development Party officials have promised to interpret the measure as allowing only head scarves that are tied under the chin, a style seen as traditionally Turkish rather than Islamic. The party says it will not allow women to wear more rigidly Islamic attire—veils that cover all of the hair and neck or the face, or cloaks that cover the body—in public offices. The wife of Turkish President Abdullah

Gul (1950–), also a member of the Justice and Development Party, had sued to be allowed to wear a head scarf in public institutions.

... "Everyone must respect the national will as it is manifested in parliament," Prime Minister Recep Tayyip Erdogan (1954–) told reporters in Munich, where he was attending a security conference. Opposition parties promised lawsuits to block the measure. In many ways, the vote was an acknowledgment that Turkey has become a more religiously conservative society. As economic prosperity increases the ranks of the middle class, observant Muslims are outnumbering the Western-looking elite. Polls consistently show that about 60 percent of people in Turkey favor allowing women to wear traditional head scarves in public.

"We're happy about the law, but we're not happy that they only accept one version on the head scarf," said Burcu Cakimanoglu, 22, who said she had to take off her scarf every time she went to her job at a university cafeteria. "Every style of head scarf must be accepted," she said. "God willing, this process will continue." Analysts said religious parties could easily draw millions into the streets in support of head scarves, dwarfing protests by secular Turks against the scarves. ... "This is a matter of Turkish democracy, so it's quite hard for the military to create a reaction," said Tanju Tosun, a political analyst at Ege University in the city of Ismir. "While most Turks love Ataturk and follow his cultural way of modernization, we know that unfortunately there is a growing trend of Islamic movements in Turkey," Tosun said. "The military has no choice—it must accept this result."

In contrast to Turkey, where clothing can signify those who remain secular and those seeking to wear signs of Muslim allegiance, the question of dress is often different in more conservative states. In Saudi Arabia, professional women have to accept severe restrictions on their public dress, but the *abaya*, the enveloping cloak that conceals a women's body, enables a woman to move about more freely in public space without being identified. Many Egyptian women shifted to various forms of Islamic dress for similar reasons in the 1970s, since such apparel permitted them to gain employment and move in large crowds without fear of harassment or condemnation for wearing western clothes.

The institution of physical concealment in public, as manifested in veiling, is criticized even less than segregation. The *abaya* [black concealing garment] is not portrayed as a restriction on their freedom but rather as key to women's accessibility to the public field. But other reasons account for why women have not severely criticized the institution of concealment. Judging by my own experience with veiling in Saudi Arabia, I can attest to the power and control a woman feels in having the advantage of being the seer, not the seen. Both men and women recognize this advantage of the *abaya*, and it has led women writers to frequently assert its existence in their texts, either to indicate a setting (i.e., that events are taking place in Saudi Arabia) or to symbolize oppression in relation to its black color, rather than to complain about its restrictive function.

"Algerian Secondary School Students on a Break from Classes, 2008." Unlike Saudi Arabian women, this young Algerian woman student wears a modern version of the modest head covering along with jeans as she and her male counterparts listen to music in a casual setting unacceptable in many Muslim countries.

The gap between legislation and custom goes beyond the question of Islamic dress. The 2004 Moroccan Family Law [in Arabic, *mudawwanat al-usra*, which translates literally as "family code"], a centerpiece of Morocco's self-proclaimed program of liberalization and reform, remains hotly debated. It aims to address women's inequality before the law. The code covers critical family matters such as divorce, child support, and inheritance. But in a country where 40 percent of the labor force is employed in rural areas and whose cities are populated by large communities of migrants from villages, it is difficult to introduce changes in family structures and customs. In the countryside, family disputes traditionally were resolved by local figures, but with the newly created family courts located in the cities, peasants are legally forced to seek legal redress outside their communities. Many interpret the family legal reforms as tantamount to the imposition of foreign values that undermine the traditional Moroccan family. Thus, the 2004 Moroccan Family Law espouses greater rights for women but allows traditional male authority to prevail in given circumstances, subject to court approval.

February 3, 2004: To Implement Law n° 70.03 as the Family Code

Preamble: Since acceding to the throne of his noble ancestors, His Majesty King Mohamed VI (1963–), our Chief Commander of the Faithful, may God protect him, has made the promotion of human rights a priority which lies at the very heart of the modernist democratic social project of which His Majesty is a leader. Doing justice to women, protecting children's rights and preserving men's dignity are a fundamental part of this project, which adheres to Islam's tolerant ends and objectives, notably justice, equality,

"Moroccan World Record Holder." Perhaps the greatest middle-distance runner during the decade from 1995 to 2004 when he retired, Hicham El Guerrouj [in middle] broke the world records in the 1,500 meters, twice, 1997 and 1998, and the mile records in 1997 and 1999. In each case he lowered his own record by five seconds. After winning a silver medal in the 1,500 meters at the 2000 Olympics, he scored a double gold medal in the 1,500 and 5,000 meters at the 2004 Olympic games, the first runner to accomplish that since 1924.

solidarity, *ijtihad* (independent juridical reasoning) and receptiveness to the spirit of our modern era and the requirements of progress and development. . . .

In the same vein, and following the right path of his august grandfather and father, His Majesty King Mohamed VI, may God glorify him—in order to illustrate his commitment to the policies of local democracy and participation, respond to the legitimate expectations of the Moroccan people, and further emphasize the shared will that unites the entire nation with its leader on the path of comprehensive reform, swift progress, and the strengthening of the Kingdom's civilizational enlightenment—has insisted, may God protect him, on making the Moroccan family—based upon shared responsibility, affection, equality, equity, amicable social relations and proper upbringing of children—a substantial major component of the democratization process, given that the family constitutes the essential nucleus of society. . . . We . . . [have] adopted the following fundamental reforms:

One: Adopt a modern form of wording and remove degrading and debasing terms for women. Place the family under the joint responsibility of both spouses, given that 'women are men's sisters before the law' in keeping with the words of my ancestor the Chosen Prophet Sidna Mohammed, Peace Be Upon Him, as reported, 'Only an honourable person dignifies women, and only a villainous one degrades them.'

Two: Entitle the woman who has come of age to tutelage as a right, and she may exercise it according to her choice and interests, on the basis of an interpretation of a holy verse stipulating that a woman cannot be compelled to marry against her will: 'place not difficulties in the way of their marrying their husbands, if it is agreed between them in kindness.' A woman may of her own free will delegate tutelage to her father or a male relative.

Three: Equality between women and men with respect to the minimum age for marriage, which is now fixed at eighteen years for both, in accordance with certain provisions of the Malekite School, and authorize the judge to reduce this age only in justified cases, and further, equality between girls and boys under custody who may choose their custodian at the age of fifteen.

Four: Concerning polygamy, we took into consideration the commitment to the tolerant principles of Islam in establishing justice, which the Almighty requires for polygamy to take place, as it is plainly stated in the Holy Koran: He said '. . . and if you fear that you cannot do justice (to so many) then one (only).' And since the Almighty ruled out the possibility for men to do justice in this particular case, He said: 'You will not be able to deal equally between (your) wives, however much you wish (to do so),' and he thus made polygamy quasi impossible under Sharia (religious law). We further adhered to the distinguished wisdom of Islam in allowing men to legitimately take a second wife, but only under compelling circumstances and stringent restrictions, with the judge's authorisation, instead of illegitimate polygamy occurring if we prohibit it entirely. From thence, polygamy shall be allowed only in the following circumstances and according to the following legal conditions:

—The judge shall not authorize polygamy unless he has verified the husband's ability to guarantee equality with the first wife and her children in all areas of life, and there is an objective and exceptional motive that justifies polygamy.

—The woman has the right to stipulate a condition in the marriage contract by which her husband will refrain from taking another wife, as Omar Ibn Al-Khattab, may God be pleased with him, is quoted as saying: 'The intersection of rights is in the conditions.' In the absence of such a condition, the first wife is summoned to obtain her consent, and the second wife must also be notified and consent to the fact that the husband is already married to another woman. Moreover, the first wife has the right to petition for divorce for harm suffered. . . .

Six: Make divorce, defined as the dissolution of marriage, a prerogative that may be exercised as much by the husband as by the wife, in accordance with legal conditions established for each party and under judicial supervision to control and restrict the abusive arbitrary practices of the husband in exercising repudiation, and this according to the rules established on the basis of the Hadith by Prophet Mohammed, Peace Be Upon Him, 'The most hateful to God among all lawful things is divorce.' The new legislation also reinforces the mechanisms for reconciliation and mediation both through the family and the judge. If the husband has the right of repudiation, the wife may also avail herself of this right through tamleek (assignation). In all cases, before repudiation may be authorized, it must be ascertained that the repudiated woman has received all of her vested rights. A new procedure for repudiation has been established that requires judicial permission, and the repudiation can not be registered until all vested rights owed to the wife and children have been paid in full by the husband. Irregular pronouncements of repudiation by the husband shall not be considered valid.

Seven: Expand the woman's right to file for divorce when the husband does not fulfil any of the conditions stipulated in the marriage contract, or for harm caused to the wife such as lack of financial support, abandonment, violence, and other harm, . . .

Eight: Protect children's rights by inserting provisions of international conventions ratified by Morocco into the Moudawana. Children's interests with respect to custody are also guaranteed by awarding custody to the mother, then to the father, then to the maternal grandmother. Should this prove impossible, the judge will entrust custody to the most qualified relative. . . .

Nine: Protect the child's right to acknowledgement of paternity in the event the marriage has not been officially registered for reasons of force majeure, where the court examines the evidence presented to prove filiation, and establish a five year time limit for settling outstanding cases in this regard to put an end to the suffering endured by children in this situation. . . .

Israeli-Palestinian Negotiations and Protests

In letters preceding the Oslo agreement of 1993, the Palestinian leader, Yasser Arafat (1929–2004), recognized Israel's right to exist; and Israeli prime minister, Yitzhak Rabin (1922–1995), recognized the Palestine Liberation Organization (PLO) as the representative of the Palestinian people. These letters inaugurated the Declaration of Principles, spelling out a tentative program for Israel's partial withdrawal from the Gaza Strip, and from one town in the West Bank, both occupied in the 1967 War.

Neither in this, nor in the second Oslo agreement of October 1995, did Israel recognize a Palestinian right to a state; further Israeli concessions in the second Oslo accord resulted in Rabin's assassination by a fellow Israeli opposed to giving up land for peace. Efforts after 1995 to widen peace agreements foundered because of growing divisiveness within Israeli and Palestinian societies owing to mutual violations of the Oslo accords, notably extensive Israeli settlement expansion. This discord and mistrust contributed to the failure of the peace conference at Camp David in July 2000 and led to the outbreak of the second Palestinian intifada in September 2000. Here is Arafat's letter, followed by Rabin's.

September 9, 1993

Yitzhak Rabin, Prime Minister of Israel

Mr. Prime Minister,

The signing of the Declaration of Principles marks a new era in the history of the Middle East. In firm conviction thereof, I would like to confirm the following PLO commitments: The PLO recognizes the right of the State of Israel to exist in peace and security. The PLO accepts United Nations Security Council Resolutions 242 and 338. The PLO commits itself to the Middle East peace process, and to a peaceful resolution of the conflict between the two sides and declares that all outstanding issues relating to permanent status will be resolved through negotiations.

The PLO considers that the signing of the Declaration of Principles constitutes a historic event, inaugurating a new epoch of peaceful coexistence, free from violence and all other acts which endanger peace and stability. Accordingly, the PLO renounces the use of terrorism and other acts of violence and will assume responsibility over all PLO elements and personnel in order to assure their compliance, prevent violations and discipline violators.

In view of the promise of a new era and the signing of the Declaration of Principles and based on Palestinian acceptance of Security Council Resolutions 242 and 338, the PLO affirms that those articles of the Palestinian Covenant which deny Israel's right to exist, and the provisions of the Covenant which are inconsistent with the commitments of this letter are now inoperative and no longer valid. Consequently, the PLO undertakes to submit to the Palestinian National Council for formal approval the necessary changes in regard to the Palestinian Covenant.

Sincerely,

Yasser Arafat, Chairman

The Palestine Liberation Organization

Rabin replied.

"Israel-Palestine Accord." Israeli Prime Minister Yitzhak Rabin shakes hands with PLO chairman Yasser Arafat with President Bill Clinton (1946–) smiling approvingly at the first Oslo Accord in September 1993. Rabin's assassination by a fellow Israeli in November 1995 following a huge peace rally in Tel Aviv seriously undermined chances of ongoing progress toward resolving Israeli-Palestinian issues.

September 9, 1993

Yasser Arafat

Chairman

The Palestine Liberation Organization

Mr. Chairman,

In response to your letter of September 9, 1993, I wish to confirm to you that, in light of the PLO commitments included in your letter, the Government of Israel has decided to recognize the PLO as the representative of the Palestinian people and commence negotiations with the PLO within the Middle East peace process.

Yitzhak Rabin

Prime Minister of Israel

The Israeli Likud Party, formed in 1973, has governed Israel on several occasions. It is committed, as its original (1977) platform states, to Israel's control of all land from the Jordan River to the Mediterranean Sea forever. It also rejects the idea of a Palestinian state. Hamas, a Sunni Muslim party formed in 1987, is labeled a terrorist organization in the West. It won free Palestinian elections, backed by the United States, in January 2006. The Bush administration immediately rejected the election results because Hamas had won. Its platform insists on Palestinian control of the same land, from the Mediterranean to the Jordan River, as an Islamic state, rejecting the idea of a state of Israel. The two party platforms regarding territory are the mirror images of each other.

Likud Platform on Land, 1977.

The Right of the Jewish People to the Land of Israel [Eretz Israel]

a. The right of the Jewish people to the land of Israel is eternal and indisputable and is linked with the right to security and peace; therefore, Judea and Samaria [West Bank] will not be handed to any foreign administration; between the sea and Jordan there will only be Israeli sovereignty.

b. A plan which relinquishes parts of western Eretz Israel [West Bank—west of Jordan River—Kingdom of Jordan considered eastern Eretz Israel], unavoidably leads to the establishment of a 'Palestinian State', [quotes in original],

"Ariel Sharon (1928–) Visits the Temple Mount/ Haram Al-Sharif, September 28, 2000." Likud leader Sharon had opposed the Camp David 2000 talks because he wished to retain the rest of the West Bank occupied by Israel. He visited the site, shown here, seeking to undermine further peace negotiations. His visit, accompanied by 800–1,000 security police and journalists, helped to spark the second intifada, which would lead to thousands of casualties on all sides as Palestinian suicide bombers for the first time attacked within Israel's 1967 boundaries.

jeopardizes the security of the Jewish population, endangers the existence of the State of Israel, and frustrates any prospect of peace.

Settlement

Settlement, both urban and rural, in all parts of the land of Israel is the focal point of the Zionist effort to redeem the country, to maintain vital security areas, and serves as a reservoir of strength and inspiration for the renewal of the pioneering spirit. The Likud government will call the younger generation in Israel and in the dispersions (overseas) to settle and help every group and individual in the task of inhabiting and cultivating the wasteland, while taking care not to dispossess anyone.

In its 1988 platform, Hamas rejects the existence of Israel. Each platform promises to ensure the safety and property of those who are not Jewish or Muslim.

Introduction

. . . The Islamic Resistance Movement emerged to carry out its role, struggling for the sake of its Lord. The movement joined hands with those of all warriors [*mujahidin*—those engaged in jihad] who are striving to liberate Palestine . . .

Article Six. Peculiarity and Independence.

Three Perspectives on the second Palestinian Israeli Agreement (Oslo II), of September 1995

Israeli Prime Minister Yitzhak Rabin attacked Israeli settlers as a threat to Israel's security: "the Oslo II Accord is a mighty blow to the delusion of a Greater Israel."

Likud Party head, Benjamin Netanyahu [1949–], violently opposed this accord and its implications: "no Jew hitherto ever longed to give up slices of the homeland."

Rabin was assassinated at a peace rally in November 1995 by a settlement supporter, Yigal Amir. His brother Hagai, who was convicted of abetting the assassination, declared on his release from prison in 2012: "I am proud of what I did."

"Israeli Arabs Protest Ariel Sharon's Temple Mount Visit." This Israeli Arab protest, at the village of Umm Fahm, was sparked by Ariel Sharon's Temple Mount visit. It turned deadly as Israeli Arabs who burned tires and threw stones were shot by Israeli snipers; thirteen protestors were killed.

The Islamic Resistance Movement is a unique Palestinian movement. It owes its loyalty to Allah, derives from Islam its way of life and strives to raise the banner of Allah over every inch of Palestine. Under the shadow of Islam, it is possible for followers of all religions to coexist in safety and with security for their lives, property and rights. . . .

Article Eleven. The Islamic Resistance Movement believes that the land of Palestine is an Islamic Waqf [endowment—subject to Muslim control] to all Muslim generations until the Day of Resurrection. It is not right to give up it or any part of it,

Article 13. . . . Giving up any part of Palestine is tantamount to giving up part of the religion. . . .

Afghanistan and Iraq before September 11, 2001

The George W. Bush (1946–) administration justified the American invasion of Iraq as well as Afghanistan as a response to the al-Qaida terrorist attacks of September 11, 2001, despite lack of evidence of Iraqi links to that organization. The roots of these developments lie in Cold War rivalries between the United States and Soviet Union. Soviet troops first entered Afghanistan on Christmas Eve 1979 to bolster an Afghan communist regime under threat from Afghan resistance. During the 1980s, U.S. intelligence allied itself with Saudi Arabia and Pakistan's Interservices Intelligence [ISI] to fund Islamic resistance in a holy war [*jihad*] to oust the Soviets. The jihad attracted Muslim militants from the broader Muslim world, and led ultimately to the formation of al-Qaida, including Egyptians linked to the assassination of Anwar al-Sadat in 1981.

After the Soviet defeat and withdrawal, many militants turned their attention to the large numbers of American troops stationed in Saudi Arabia after the 1991 Gulf War, demanding their immediate withdrawal. Leading this movement was an Islamic group called al-Qaida (meaning *the base* or *the foundation*), formed during the Afghan resistance to the Soviets, which now called for holy war against the United States from its sanctuary in Afghanistan. Various attacks sponsored by elements of al-Qaida on U.S. military and civilian institutions overseas during the 1990s culminated in the coordinated assaults of September 11, 2001, on New York City and the Pentagon. This inspired the American invasion of Afghanistan where al-Qaida was based, and later of Iraq to oust Saddam Hussein, in March 2003.

Less well known is that the United States had decided to militarily aid Afghan anti-Communists earlier in 1979, while recognizing that that decision might encourage Soviet invasion. In 1998, Zbigniew Brzezinski

(1928–), National Security Adviser in the Jimmy Carter administration, acknowledged this fact in an interview with the French newspaper *Le Nouvel Observateur*. Viewing the issue in Cold War terms, Brzezinski saw the action as an opportunity to gain revenge for the U.S. defeat in Vietnam.

Question: The former director of the CIA, Robert Gates, stated in his memoirs, that American intelligence services began to aid the Mujahadeen in Afghanistan 6 months before the Soviet intervention. In this period you were the national security adviser to President Carter. You therefore played a role in this affair. Is that correct?

Brzezinski: Yes. According to the official version of history, CIA aid to the Mujahadeen began during 1980, that is to say, after the Soviet army invaded Afghanistan, 24 Dec 1979. But the reality, secretly guarded until now, is completely otherwise. Indeed, it was July 3, 1979, that President Carter signed the first directive for secret aid to the opponents of the pro-Soviet regime in Kabul. And that very day, I wrote a note to the president in which I explained to him that in my opinion this aid was going to induce a Soviet military intervention.

Q: Despite this risk, you were an advocate of this covert action. But perhaps you yourself desired this Soviet entry into war and looked to provoke it?

B: It isn't quite that. We didn't push the Russians to intervene, but we knowingly increased the probability that they would.

Q: When the Soviets justified their intervention by asserting that they intended to fight against a secret involvement of the United States in Afghanistan, people didn't believe them. However, there was a basis of truth. You don't regret anything today?

B: Regret what? That secret operation was an excellent idea. It had the effect of drawing the Russians into the Afghan trap and you want me to regret it? The day that the Soviets officially crossed the border, I wrote to President Carter. We now have the opportunity of giving to the USSR its Vietnam War. Indeed, for almost 10 years, Moscow had to carry on a war unsupportable by the government, a conflict that brought about the demoralization and finally the breakup of the Soviet empire.

Q: And neither do you regret having supported the Islamic fundamentalism, having given arms and advice to future terrorists?

B: What is most important to the history of the world? The Taliban or the collapse of the Soviet empire? Some stirred-up Moslems or the liberation of Central Europe and the end of the cold war?

The Clash of Civilizations

The West won the world not by the superiority of its ideas or values or religion (to which few members of other civilizations were converted) but rather by its superiority in applying organized violence. Westerners often forget this fact, non-Westerners never do.

Q: Some stirred-up Moslems? But it has been said and repeated Islamic fundamentalism represents a world menace today.

B: Nonsense! It is said that the West had a global policy in regard to Islam. That is stupid. There isn't a global Islam. Look at Islam in a rational manner and without demagoguery or emotion. It is the leading religion of the world with 1.5 billion followers. But what is there in common among Saudi Arabian fundamentalism, moderate Morocco, Pakistan militarism, Egyptian middle pro-Western or Central Asian secularism? Nothing more than what unites the Christian countries.

Iraq contains diverse ethnic and religious populations. In addition to Sunni and Shii Muslim Arabs, there are Kurds who are Sunnis but not Arab, and Christian communities of long standing who reside in the Kurdish and Arab sectors. Many educated Iraqis were communists. After World War II, Iraq was plagued by political instability that impeded social progress. The Ba'ath Party took power in 1963 in a coup, and then established a brutal military dictatorship lasting from 1968 to 2003. Saddam Hussein assumed office as president in July 1979 and the next year invaded Iran. The oral histories following are from Iraqis, many of whom were forced to flee the country during purges and now live in Europe or elsewhere.

Dalal P [living in London—former communist]

Yes, there had been violence during the revolution in '58 [end of Hashemite monarchy] and afterwards, but this unfortunately happens when a mob is angry. But the violence was limited in comparison to the atrocities committed by the Ba'this throughout their long rule. It was clear that the Ba'th did not have the popular support that we communists had. So they had to rely on force, on arresting people, on show trials, on killing thousands who did not agree with them.... Many of my friends were arrested and some even killed....

Nevertheless, major modernization efforts occurred under the Ba'ath, including greater opportunities for women in public life during the 1970s, especially middle-class women.

Fedwa K.

I was not a Ba'thi and hated the regime, but at the same time there was something constructive happening in the country. The education system improved tremendously. We got excellent health care.... By the end of the 1970s, all of Baghdad was modernized. Although the mayor was cruel and Baghdadis hated him, he managed to make Baghdad very clean. UNESCO gave us a prize for our achievement in education, especially women's education....

Saddam Hussein's decision to initiate war with Iran [1980–1988] brought hardship and increasing repression of groups that opposed the regime, especially the Kurds of northern Iraq who sought autonomy if not independence. Saddam had begun an Arabization program in the later 1970s to seek to remove Kurds from homes and weaken Kurdish identity. During the Iran-Iraq war, he ordered the poison gas campaign against Kurds, killing thousands. Still, the U.S. government of President Ronald Reagan (1911–2004) decided to back the Iraqis against Iran, fearing the spread of Islamist tendencies. But when Saddam Hussein invaded Kuwait in August 1990, President George H. W. Bush [(1924–) ordered a buildup of forces in Saudi Arabia and neighboring Arab Gulf states to oust the Iraqi forces from Kuwait. Air attacks began in January, the ground assault on February 23; Kuwait was liberated in four days and a cease-fire imposed as of February 28. As part of this effort, the United States had encouraged uprisings of Kurds in northern Iraq and Shiis in the south. Saddam crushed the latter, but the United States established a safe zone in the north for Kurds that has lasted to the present. This account by an Iraqi Kurdish woman called Veyan K. on the Arabization program aimed at Kurds recalls these events and their impact on her life.

We returned to our village close to Irbil after having spent some months in Iran as refugees.... everyone was so depressed. My mother kept wailing . . . because . . . Barzani [Kurdish political leader] had fled to the USA. For me it was really difficult as we switched from Kurdish to Arabic. I failed some of my exams my first year. . . . we all had been taught in Kurdish before. There were always Saddam's soldiers threatening everyone and making us feel insecure. The only positive thing during that period [w]as that we were less poor. The government built better roads, schools, and hospitals. More girls started to go to school and even to university. Our living standards improved, but we were still living in fear.

Kurds renewed their separatist actions against Iraq during the Iraq-Iran war, leading to a violent reaction. Saheena K. recalls her life in 1985 once Kurds resumed resistance.

Our house was destroyed three times [by Saddam's soldiers]. We fled to the mountains. We lived there for four years. These mountains were controlled by Kurdish *peshmerga* [militias] from Turkey. We had no schools, no radio, no television. We had to cook, clean, and wash all day. It was like old times. We washed clothes in the river. We had to move every single day to avoid being bombed. Moving became part of our lives for four years.

Agiza, eight years old in 1988, was tending family livestock near her village when she saw Iraqi planes dropping poison gas bombs, one landing close to her family's house.

"Iraqi Kurds Dead After Chemical Weapons Attack, 1988." This stark image shows how quickly humans and animals died following the chemical weapons attack at Halabja in March 1988 perpetrated by Saddam Hussein.

It made smoke, yellowish-white smoke. It had a bad smell, like DDT, the powder they kill insects with. It had a bitter taste. After I smelled the gas, my nose began to run and my eyes became blurry. . . . I saw my parents fall down with my brother after the attack, and they told me they were dead. I looked at their skin and it was black and they weren't moving. And I was scared and crying and I did not know what to do.

Hana A. is an architect now living in Jordan. She comments on the first Gulf War.

In 1991 we were there during the war, but we left at the end of the year. I almost had a nervous breakdown after what happened during the war. Our house was hit by a missile. I did not feel that any of the wars were justified So I did not want to be part of them. I did not want my sons to go into the army. I managed to convince my husband. So we came here to Amman. My husband is a surgeon and found a teaching position here at the university. Our eldest son was then 16, the younger one 14. They started school here. I started working. Then we applied for immigration to Canada. In 1996, I and the boys went to Toronto. The boys went to college. We rented an apartment for them. I was planning to stay with them and to continue my studies in interior design. But about a month after I arrived in Canada, my mother had a stroke. She was in Amman. My husband was also in Amman, because he was not allowed to work in Canada. They did not need doctors at the time. So I had to come back and leave the boys alone. I spent two years taking care of my mother before she passed away in 1998. By then we had Jordanian nationality. My husband was allowed to have his own clinic. Then we got more attached to Jordan. My own work here was getting better as well. The boys graduated. One is still in Canada, the other one is in Qatar. . . .

It is very difficult for an Iraqi to become a Jordanian citizen. We had a big *wasta* (connection). My husband's relatives used to be in the government under the [Iraqi] monarchy, so they had a good relationship with the late King Hussein (of Jordan, 1935–1999). [Iraq was ruled by a branch of the Hashemite clan to 1958, as is Jordan still] Other people have to leave every three months. . . .

Ibtesam A., a Shii woman living in Dearborn, Michigan, recalled the 1991 Gulf War and the crushing of the Shiite uprising that followed it.

We hardly had anything to eat or drink during the Gulf War. It was so scary, especially at night . . . because there was no electricity. We could hear the airplanes and bombs flying just over our heads. . . . But we are all hopeful and in good spirits. My mother thanked God that our prayers were finally heard and that we were going to get rid of this monster [Saddam Hussein] But then when the war was finished and our people started to fight Saddam's troops, the Americans betrayed us. They watched our men being slaughtered by Saddam's soldiers. They watched our houses being demolished. One of my cousins died and my older brother disappeared.

American artillery shells and bombs were often coated with depleted uranium for greater penetration of armor; the life of such depleted uranium is measured in billions of years. Dr. Hala was formerly in the Iraqi Ministry of Health. In the early 1990s she joined her husband in a family pharmacy and assisted a friend, a pediatrician, at a Baghdad hospital.

"Iraqi Shiites Rebel after Saddam's Defeat Spring 1991." Once Iraqi forces had been driven from Kuwait and southern Iraq, the George H. W. Bush administration agreed to a cease-fire, as it did not wish to accept the consequences of overthrowing Saddam Hussein. Nonetheless, the administration encouraged Iraqi Shiites in southern Iraq as well as Kurds in the north to rebel, hoping to cause Saddam's downfall. But with a cease-fire in place, American troops watched as Saddam's forces crushed the poorly organized Shiite uprising shown in this photo.

"Kurds Return to Northern Iraq." The U.S.-led coalition successfully established the Kurdish area as protected by a no-fly zone, and Kurdish refugees returned to Iraq in 1991–1992. The Kurdish region in the north became and still is a semiautonomous area known as Iraqi Kurdistan whose power is divided between the rival Barzani and Talabani clans.

Every time I went to the hospital, I saw children with birth defects. There were many children without limbs. And lots of children suffering from cancer. We had never seen so many young children with leukaemia before. It was heart-breaking, seeing their little emaciated bodies wither away. We did not have the right medicines for chemotherapy. It was very expensive so it was only distributed in special hospitals. Sometimes we brought it from Amman, but we could not afford much of that. Even educated people were living in poverty.

Al-Qaida, 9/11, and the American Response: Prisoners, Refugees, and Human Rights

As a result of the first Gulf War, when the United States positioned hundreds of thousands of troops in Saudi Arabia, Saudi Arabia found itself buffeted by pressures from diametrically opposed viewpoints. In 1998, the Saudi Osama Bin Laden (1957–2011), head of al-Qaida, issued what he considered a legal judgment, a *fatwa*, declaring that all Muslims had an individual duty to kill Americans wherever found. He based this argument on the continued American military presence (he called them crusaders) in Saudi Arabia and the Gulf states of the Arabian Peninsula following the first Gulf War of 1991. He depicted that presence as an act of aggression, especially against the Iraqi people, as sanctions continued to be imposed on them. He also argued that this ongoing military presence served Israeli interests as well. In his view, an American-led war against Islam required retaliation.

Bin Laden had no official qualification as a legal scholar to issue such a fatwa, nor did Muslims have a legal obligation to obey him. The vast majority of Muslims rejected his call, and Sunni Iraqi Muslims who had initially fought against the American occupation of Iraq after March 2003 later turned on al-Qaida factions that entered the country, because the latter killed fellow Sunni Muslims who did not adhere to their specific beliefs.

Fatwa of February 23, 1998

Shaykh Usamah Bin-Muhammad Bin-Ladin

Ayman al-Zawahiri (1951–), amir of the Jihad Group in Egypt

Abu-Yasir Rifa'i Ahmad Taha, Egyptian Islamic Group

Shaykh Mir Hamzah, secretary of the Jamiat-ul-Ulema-e-Pakistan

Fazlur Rahman, amir of the Jihad Movement in Bangladesh

Praise be to Allah, who revealed the Book, controls the clouds, defeats factionalism, and says in His Book: "But when the forbidden months are past, then fight and slay the pagans wherever ye find them, seize them, beleaguer them, and lie in wait for them in every stratagem (of war)"; and peace be upon our Prophet, Muhammad Bin-'Abdallah, who said: I have been sent with the sword between my hands to ensure that no one but Allah is worshipped, Allah who put my livelihood under the shadow of my spear and who inflicts humiliation and scorn on those who disobey my orders.

The Arabian Peninsula has never—since Allah made it flat, created its desert, and encircled it with seas—been stormed by any forces like the crusader armies spreading in it like locusts, eating its riches and wiping out its plantations. All this is happening at a time in which nations are attacking Muslims like people fighting over a plate of food. In the light of the grave situation and the lack of support, we and you are obliged to discuss current events, and we should all agree on how to settle the matter. No one argues today about three facts that are known to everyone; we will list them, in order to remind everyone: First, for over seven years the United States has been occupying the lands of Islam in the holiest of places, the Arabian Peninsula, plundering its riches, dictating to its rulers, humiliating its people, terrorizing its neighbors, and turning its bases in the Peninsula into a spearhead through which to fight the neighboring Muslim peoples.

If some people have in the past argued about the fact of the occupation, all the people of the Peninsula have now acknowledged it. The best proof of this is the Americans' continuing aggression against the Iraqi people using the Peninsula

"Al-Qaida-Sponsored Attack on the United States, September 11, 2001." Here, United Airlines flight #175 is about to strike the south tower of the World Trade Center, New York. The majority of those involved in the attacks were Saudis with some Egyptians and Yemenis. Nearly all of them were Western educated and had lived in the United States and/or Europe. Although the immediate response of the George W. Bush administration would be to retaliate by attacking al-Qaida and the Taliban government in Afghanistan, the 9/11 attacks would also be used to justify an invasion of Iraq, despite the fact Saddam Hussein and his Sunni followers had no connection to al-Qaida.

as a staging post, even though all its rulers are against their territories being used to that end, but they are helpless. Second, despite the great devastation inflicted on the Iraqi people by the crusader-Zionist alliance, and despite the huge number of those killed, which has exceeded 1 million . . . despite all this, the Americans are once against trying to repeat the horrific massacres, as though they are not content with the protracted blockade imposed after the ferocious war or the fragmentation and devastation. . . .

Third, if the Americans' aims behind these wars are religious and economic, the aim is also to serve the Jews' petty state and divert attention from its occupation of Jerusalem and murder of Muslims there. The best proof of this is their eagerness to destroy Iraq, the strongest neighboring Arab state, and their endeavor to fragment all the states of the region such as Iraq, Saudi Arabia, Egypt, and Sudan into paper statelets and through their disunion and weakness to guarantee Israel's survival and the continuation of the brutal crusade occupation of the Peninsula.

All these crimes and sins committed by the Americans are a clear declaration of war on Allah, his messenger, and Muslims. And ulema have throughout Islamic history unanimously agreed that the jihad is an individual duty if the enemy destroys the Muslim countries. . . . On that basis, and in compliance with Allah's order, we issue the following fatwa to all Muslims:

The ruling to kill the Americans and their allies—civilians and military—is an individual duty [absolute obligation] for every Muslim who can do it in any country in which it is possible to do it, in order to liberate the al-Aqsa Mosque (Jerusalem) and the holy mosque (Mecca) from their grip, and in order for their armies to move out of all the lands of Islam, defeated and unable to threaten any Muslim. This is in accordance with the words of Almighty Allah, "and fight the pagans all together as they fight you all together," and "fight them until there is no more tumult or oppression, and there prevail justice and faith in Allah."

This is in addition to the words of Almighty Allah: "And why should ye not fight in the cause of Allah and of those who, being weak, are ill-treated (and oppressed)?—women and children, whose cry is: 'Our Lord, rescue us from this town, whose people are oppressors; and raise for us from thee one who will help!'"

We—with Allah's help—call on every Muslim who believes in Allah and wishes to be rewarded to comply with Allah's order to kill the Americans and plunder their money wherever and whenever they find it. We also call on Muslim ulema, leaders, youths, and soldiers to launch the raid on Satan's U.S. troops and the devil's supporters allying with them, and to displace those who are behind them so that they may learn a lesson. . . .

Almighty Allah also says: "O ye who believe, what is the matter with you, that when ye are asked to go forth in the cause of Allah, ye cling so heavily to the earth! Do ye prefer the life of this world to the hereafter? But little is the comfort of this life, as compared with the hereafter. Unless ye go forth, He will punish you with a grievous penalty, and put others in your place; but Him ye would not harm in the least. For Allah hath power over all things."

In the aftermath of the 9/11 terrorist attacks on the United States, American forces immediately attacked Afghanistan and ousted the Taliban government from Kabul. But the Taliban regrouped in mountain passes along the Afghan-Pakistan border with Bin Laden and his forces. Four months later, President George W. Bush (1946–) delivered his State of the Union address to Congress. In it he referred to the "Axis of Evil," North Korea, Iraq, and Iran; Iran until then had quietly cooperated with the United States against al-Qaida in Afghanistan. The speech also signaled a growing administration interest in regime change in Iraq, over a year before the invasion, although Iraq had no links to al-Qaida. Not all security experts agreed with the plan to invade Iraq. In August 2002, Brent Scowcroft (1925–), national security adviser to Presidents Gerald Ford (1913–2006) and George H. W. Bush, wrote an impassioned op-ed in the *Wall Street Journal* pleading with President George W. Bush not to attack Iraq. He argued that it would divert precious resources from the counterterrorism effort then under way, and would likely lead to a lengthy and costly occupation of Iraq.

Office of the Press Secretary, January 29, 2002

The President's State of the Union Address: The United States Capitol

Washington, D.C. 9:15 P.M. EST

THE PRESIDENT: Thank you very much. Mr. Speaker, Vice President Cheney, members of Congress, distinguished guests, fellow citizens: As we gather tonight, our nation is at war, our economy is in recession, and the civilized world faces unprecedented dangers. Yet the state of our Union has never been stronger. We last met in an hour of shock and suffering. In four short months, our nation has comforted the victims, begun to rebuild New York and the Pentagon, rallied a great coalition, captured, arrested, and rid the world of thousands of terrorists, destroyed Afghanistan's terrorist training camps, saved a people from starvation, and freed a country from brutal oppression. The American flag flies again over our embassy in Kabul. Terrorists who once occupied Afghanistan now occupy cells at Guantanamo Bay. And terrorist leaders who urged followers to sacrifice their lives are running for their own. America and Afghanistan are now allies against terror. We'll be partners in rebuilding that country. And this evening we welcome the distinguished interim leader of a liberated Afghanistan: Chairman Hamid Karzai (1957–).

The last time we met in this chamber, the mothers and daughters of Afghanistan were captives in their own homes, forbidden from working or going to school. Today women are free, and are part of Afghanistan's new government. And we welcome the new Minister of Women's Affairs, Doctor Sima Samar (1957–) [awarded the Nobel Peace Prize in 2011] . . . Our cause is just, and it continues. Our discoveries in Afghanistan confirmed our worst fears, and showed us the true scope of the task ahead. . . . our war against terror is only beginning. Most of the 19 men who hijacked planes on September the 11th were trained in Afghanistan's camps, and so were tens of thousands of others. Thousands of dangerous kill-

"Afghan Refugees Outside Kabul." The 2002 attack on Afghanistan in immediate retaliation for the 9/11 al-Qaida attacks displaced hundreds of thousands of civilians as this photo painfully shows. It also led to many innocent persons being imprisoned where they were tortured on suspicion of supporting terrorism. The United States dropped leaflets in Afghanistan promising rewards of $5,000 to anyone handing in a "terrorist." This encouraged many Afghans to denounce local rivals or innocent people who were then imprisoned in Afghanistan or at Guantanamo in Cuba.

ers, schooled in the methods of murder, often supported by outlaw regimes, are now spread throughout the world like ticking time bombs, set to go off without warning. Thanks to the work of our law enforcement officials and coalition partners, hundreds of terrorists have been arrested. Yet, tens of thousands of trained terrorists are still at large. These enemies view the entire world as a battlefield, and we must pursue them wherever they are.

Our nation will continue to be steadfast and patient and persistent in the pursuit of two great objectives. First, we will shut down terrorist camps, disrupt terrorist plans, and bring terrorists to justice. And, second, we must prevent the terrorists and regimes who seek chemical, biological or nuclear weapons from threatening the United States and the world. . . . Camps still exist in at least a dozen countries. A terrorist underworld—including groups like Hamas, Hezbollah, Islamic Jihad, Jaish-i-Mohammed—operates in remote jungles and deserts, and hides in the centers of large cities. . . .

Our second goal is to prevent regimes that sponsor terror from threatening America or our friends and allies with weapons of mass destruction. Some of these regimes have been pretty quiet since September the 11th. But we know their true nature. North Korea is a regime arming with missiles and weapons of mass destruction, while starving its citizens. Iran aggressively pursues these weapons and exports terror, while an unelected few repress the Iranian people's hope for freedom. Iraq continues to flaunt its hostility toward America and to support terror. The Iraqi regime has plotted to develop anthrax, and nerve gas, and nuclear weapons for over a decade. This is a regime that has already used poison gas to murder thousands of its own citizens—leaving the bodies of mothers huddled over their dead children. This is a regime that agreed to international inspections—then kicked out the inspectors. This is a regime that has something to hide from the civilized world.

States like these, and their terrorist allies, constitute an axis of evil, arming to threaten the peace of the world. By seeking weapons of mass destruction, these regimes pose a grave and growing danger. They could provide these arms to terrorists, giving them the means to match their hatred. They could attack our allies or attempt to blackmail the United States. In any of these cases, the price of indifference would be catastrophic. . . . Time is not on our side. I will not wait on events, while dangers gather. I will not stand by, as peril draws closer and closer. . . . History has called America and our allies to action, and it is both our responsibility and our privilege to fight freedom's fight. It costs a lot to fight this war. We have spent more than a billion dollars a month—over $30 million a day—and we must be prepared for future operations. . . . While the price of freedom and security is high, it is never too high. Whatever it costs to defend our country, we will pay. . . . For too long our culture has said, "If it feels good, do it." Now America is embracing a new ethic and a new creed: "Let's roll." In the sacrifice of soldiers, the fierce brotherhood of firefighters, and the bravery and generosity of ordinary citizens, we have glimpsed what a new culture of responsibility could look like. We want to be a nation that serves goals larger than self. We've been offered a unique opportunity, and we must not let this moment pass. . . . We have known freedom's price. We have shown freedom's power. And in this great conflict, my fellow Americans, we will see freedom's victory.

Thank you all. May God bless.

Shirin Ebadi received the Nobel Peace Prize in 2003 for her work on behalf of human rights in Iran, the first Iranian and first Muslim woman to be so honored. She worked in the Department of Justice under the Shah's regime and became the first woman in Iranian history to be appointed a judge. After the 1979 Islamic Revolution, she and other women judges were judged unqualified to be judges and were demoted to clerks. She was not granted a lawyer's license and permitted to practice law until 1992. She incurred the wrath of government officials by defending persons attacked by individuals associated with the Islamic government, and she cofounded the Association for Support of Children's Rights in 1995. In her Nobel Prize acceptance speech, she spoke out on behalf of rights for women in Muslim countries but also criticized the selective application of human rights' principles by the United Nations with respect to the Middle East. Repeatedly harassed by the Ahmedinejad government, she left Iran in 2009 and now lives in London.

In the name of the God of Creation and Wisdom

Your Majesty, Your Royal Highnesses, Honourable Members of the Norwegian Nobel Committee, Excellencies, Ladies and Gentlemen,

I feel extremely honoured that today my voice is reaching the people of the world from this distinguished venue. This great honour has been bestowed upon me by the Norwegian Nobel Committee. I salute the spirit of Alfred Nobel and hail all true followers of his path.

This year, the Nobel Peace Prize has been awarded to a woman from Iran, a Muslim country in the Middle East. Undoubtedly, my selection will be an inspiration to the masses of women who are striving to realize their rights, not only in Iran but throughout the region—rights taken away from them through the passage of history. This selection will make women in Iran, and much further afield, believe in themselves. Women constitute half of the population of every country. To disregard women and bar them from active participation in political, social, economic and cultural life would in fact be tantamount to depriving the entire population of every society of half its capability. The patriarchal culture and the discrimination against women, particularly in the Islamic countries, cannot continue for ever.

Honourable members of the Norwegian Nobel Committee!

As you are aware, the honour and blessing of this prize will have a positive and far-reaching impact on the humanitarian and genuine endeavours of the people of Iran and the region. The magnitude of this blessing will embrace every freedom-loving and peace-seeking individual, whether they are women or men. I thank the Norwegian Nobel Committee for this honour that has been bestowed upon me and for the blessing of this honour for the peace-loving people of my country.

Today coincides with the 55th anniversary of the adoption of the Universal Declaration of Human Rights; a declaration which begins with the recognition of the inherent dignity and the equal and inalienable rights of all members of the human family, as the guarantor of freedom, justice and peace. And it promises a world in which human beings shall enjoy freedom of expression and opinion, and be safeguarded and protected against fear and poverty. Unfortunately, however, this year's report by the United Nations Development Programme (UNDP), as in the previous years, spells out the rise of a disaster which distances mankind from the idealistic world of the authors of the Universal Declaration of Human Rights. In 2002, almost 1.2 billion human beings lived in glaring poverty, earning less than one dollar a day. Over 50 countries were caught up in war or natural disasters. AIDS has so far claimed the lives of 22 million individuals, and turned 13 million children into orphans.

At the same time, in the past two years, some states have violated the universal principles and laws of human rights by using the events of 11 September and the war on international terrorism as a pretext. The United Nations General Assembly Resolution 57/219, of 18 December 2002, the United Nations Security Council Resolution 1456, of 20 January 2003, and the United Nations Commission on Human Rights Resolution 2003/68, of 25 April 2003, set out and underline that all states must ensure that any measures taken to combat terrorism must comply with all their obligations under international law, in particular international human rights and humanitarian law. However, regulations restricting human rights and basic freedoms, special bodies and extraordinary courts, which make fair adjudication difficult and at times impossible, have been justified and given legitimacy under the cloak of the war on terrorism.

The concerns of human rights' advocates increase when they observe that international human rights laws are breached not only by their recognized opponents under the pretext of cultural relativity, but that these principles are also violated in Western democracies, in other words countries which were themselves among the initial codifiers of the United Nations Charter and the Universal Declaration of Human Rights. It is in this framework that, for months, hundreds of individuals who were arrested in the course of military conflicts have been imprisoned in Guantanamo, without the benefit of the rights stipulated under the international Geneva conventions, the Universal Declaration of Human Rights and the [United Nations] International Covenant on Civil and Political Rights.

Moreover, a question which millions of citizens in the international civil society have been asking themselves for the past few years, particularly in recent months, and continue to ask, is this: why is it that some decisions and resolutions of the UN Security Council are binding, while some other resolutions of the council have no binding force? Why is it that in the past 35 years, dozens of UN resolutions concerning the occupation of the Palestinian territories by the state of Israel have not been implemented promptly, yet, in the past 12 years, the state and people of Iraq, once on the recommendation of the Security Council, and the second time, in spite of UN Security Council opposition, were subjected to attack, military assault, economic sanctions, and, ultimately, military occupation?

Ladies and Gentlemen,

Allow me to say a little about my country, region, culture and faith.

I am an Iranian. A descendent of Cyrus The Great. The very emperor who proclaimed at the pinnacle of power 2500 years ago that "... he would not reign over the people if they did not wish it." And [he] promised not to force any person to change his religion and faith and guaranteed freedom for all. The Charter of Cyrus The Great is one of the most important documents that should be studied in the history of human rights. I am a Muslim. In the Koran the Prophet of Islam has been cited as saying: "Thou shalt believe in thine faith and I in my religion". That same divine book sees the mission of all prophets as that of inviting all human beings to uphold justice. Since the advent of Islam, too, Iran's civilization and culture has become imbued and infused with humanitarianism, respect for the life, belief and faith of others, propagation of tolerance and compromise and avoidance of violence, bloodshed and war. The luminaries of Iranian literature, in particular our Gnostic literature, from Hafiz, Mowlavi [better known in the West as Rumi] and Attar to Saadi, Sanaei, Naser Khosrow and Nezami, are emissaries of this humanitarian culture. Their message manifests itself in this poem by Saadi:

> "The sons of Adam are limbs of one another
> Having been created of one essence.
> When the calamity of time afflicts one limb
> The other limbs cannot remain at rest."

The people of Iran have been battling against consecutive conflicts between tradition and modernity for over 100 years. By resorting to ancient traditions, some have tried and are trying to see the world through the eyes of their predecessors and to deal with the problems and difficulties of the existing world by virtue of the values of the ancients. But, many others, while respecting their historical and cultural past and their religion and faith, seek to go forth in step with world developments and not lag behind the caravan of civilization, development and progress. The people of Iran, particularly in the recent years, have shown that they deem participation in public affairs to be their right, and that they want to be masters of their own destiny.

This conflict is observed not merely in Iran, but also in many Muslim states. Some Muslims, under the pretext that democracy and human rights are not compatible with Islamic teachings and the traditional structure of Islamic societies, have justified despotic governments, and continue to do so. In fact, it is not so easy to rule over a people who are aware of their rights, using traditional, patriarchal and paternalistic methods.

Islam is a religion whose first sermon to the Prophet begins with the word "Recite!" The Koran swears by the pen and what it writes. Such a sermon and message cannot be in conflict with awareness, knowledge, wisdom, freedom of opinion and expression and cultural pluralism.

The discriminatory plight of women in Islamic states, too, whether in the sphere of civil law or in the realm of social, political and cultural justice, has its roots in the patriarchal and male-dominated culture prevailing in these societies, not in Islam. This culture does not tolerate freedom and democracy, just as it does not believe in the equal rights of men and women, and the liberation of women from male domination (fathers, husbands, brothers . . .), because it would threaten the historical and traditional position of the rulers and guardians of that culture.

One has to say to those who have mooted the idea of a clash of civilizations, or prescribed war and military intervention for this region, and resorted to social, cultural, economic and political sluggishness of the South in a bid to justify their actions and opinions, that if you consider international human rights laws, including the nations' right to determine their own destinies, to be universal, and if you believe in the priority and superiority of parliamentary democracy over other political systems, then you cannot think only of your own security and comfort, selfishly and contemptuously. A quest for new means and ideas to enable the countries of the South, too, to enjoy human rights and democracy, while maintaining their political independence and territorial integrity of their respective countries, must be given top priority by the United Nations in respect of future developments and international relations.

The decision by the Nobel Peace Committee to award the 2003 prize to me, as the first Iranian and the first woman from a Muslim country, inspires me and millions of Iranians and nationals of Islamic states with the hope that our efforts, endeavours and struggles toward the realization of human rights and the establishment of democracy in our respective countries enjoy the support, backing and solidarity of international civil society. This prize belongs to the people of Iran. It belongs to the people of the Islamic states, and the people of the South for establishing human rights and democracy.

Ladies and Gentlemen

In the introduction to my speech, I spoke of human rights as a guarantor of freedom, justice and peace. If human rights fail to be manifested in codified laws or put into effect by states, then, as rendered in the preamble of the Universal Declaration of Human Rights, human beings will be left with no choice other than staging a "rebellion against tyranny and oppression". A human being divested of all dignity, a human being deprived of human rights, a human being gripped by starvation, a human being beaten by famine, war and illness, a humiliated human being and a plundered human being is not in any position or state to recover the rights he or she has lost.

If the 21st century wishes to free itself from the cycle of violence, acts of terror and war, and avoid repetition of the experience of the 20th century—that most disaster-ridden century of humankind,—there is no other way except by understanding and putting into practice every human right for all mankind, irrespective of race, gender, faith, nationality or social status.

In anticipation of that day.

With much gratitude

Shirin Ebadi

The March 2003 invasion of Iraq succeeded in capturing Saddam Hussein and overthrowing his government, but failed to stabilize the country. The resulting turmoil saw major displacements of Iraqis, both within the country and without, as Shi'i and Sunni militias attacked urban neighborhoods populated by their opposite factions and cleansed them. The external exodus added to the refugees who had fled Saddam Hussein's regime, creating severe problems especially for Syria and Jordan, which are poorly equipped to handle such large numbers of refugees. This Amnesty International report from 2007 documents the difficulties faced both by the Iraqis and the host countries.

1. A spiraling crisis

The humanitarian crisis triggered by the mass exodus of refugees from the on-going and widespread violence in Iraq shows little sign of abating. In fact, recent estimates show this to be the fastest growing displacement crisis in the world with the number of those displaced now having reached 4.2 million, 2.2 million internally displaced within Iraq, and over 2 million outside the country. . . .

The extreme violence and instability propelling people to flee Iraq has resulted in the largest population movement in the Middle East since Palestinians were displaced following the creation of the State of Israel in 1948. Unsurprisingly, such widespread displacement has had a profound impact within Iraq and for the political, economic and social stability of the main countries hosting these populations. . . . Despite this critical situation, the response of many in the international community, including states that participated in the US-led invasion and can be considered to have a particular obligation to address the humanitarian effects of their military action, has been inadequate. . . .

1.2 Situation in Syria and Jordan

The willingness of Syria and Jordan to jointly host around 2 million Iraqi refugees is commendable and stands in contrast to the approach of other countries bordering Iraq, such as Saudi Arabia. The Saudi Arabian authorities have maintained a closed border to people attempting to flee from Iraq and have announced that the Kingdom will build a wall along this border for security reasons. . . . Saudi Arabian security forces are said to be deployed along the border with Iraq from Kuwait to Jordan in order to intercept those seeking to cross. Although Saudi Arabia's interest in maintaining security measures at its borders is acknowledged, such measures must also allow refugees access to the country in line with international law. . . .

1.2.1 Conditions in Syria

Today Syria hosts an estimated 1.4 million Iraqi refugees. The country has long been a place of refuge for Iraqis. During Saddam Hussain's rule, thousands of people opposed to his government went into exile in Syria, including members of the current government of Iraq. While many Iraqis returned home following the US-led invasion in 2003, the number of Iraqis who have taken refuge in Syria has risen dramatically over the past four years. According to a survey by UN agencies, there were about 450,000 Iraqi refugees living in Syria at the end of 2005. Just over a year later, by the first quarter of 2007, there were more than 1 million, an exodus fueled by rising sectarian violence in Iraq, particularly after the February 2006 attack on the Shi'a holy shrine in Samarra. . . . The number of Iraq's non-Muslim religious minorities, such as Christians and people belonging to the Sabean/Mandaean community, continues to be disproportionately high among the refugee population. Over the past 18 months, non-Muslim religious communities have felt themselves particularly vulnerable in Iraq. They have been caught in the sectarian conflict between Sunnis and Shi'as but have been unable to obtain adequate protection from an Iraqi government that can barely function, and do not have armed groups of their own to defend themselves against militant Sunni and Shi'a forces. Scores of Christians and Sabeans/Mandaeans have been taken hostage and killed by armed groups in Iraq. In addition, a number of women from various communities have reportedly fled from Iraq to Syria because they were at risk of becoming victims of so-called honour crimes.

Almost all of the Iraqi refugees interviewed by Amnesty International in Syria in June 2007 were recent victims of serious human rights abuses in Iraq and felt they had been left with no choice but to leave the country. They included Sunni Muslims who had been resident in predominantly Shi'a neighbourhoods in Baghdad or other towns and cities, and Shi'a Muslims who had lived in predominantly Sunni districts. All had been forced to leave their homes when their neighbourhoods were cleared through a process akin to "ethnic cleansing" by members of sectarian armed groups. Several refugees reported that they had left their homes after receiving threats from Sunni or Shi'a armed groups that they would otherwise be killed. . . . A few, both men and women, said that they had been raped—mainly by members of armed groups. . . .

1.2.2 Conditions in Jordan

There are an estimated 500,000 to 750,000 Iraqi refugees in Jordan, although no official statistics are publicly available and there is some confusion about the figures. . . .

During the period of Saddam Hussain's government, thousands of Iraqis took refuge in Jordan for political reasons or due to the economic hardship caused by the international sanctions on Iraq. Today, the majority of Iraqi refugees reside in Amman and its surroundings—many live in the eastern parts of the city where rents are cheaper. An imam and preacher (khateeb) from Baghdad, who was detained and tortured by US forces in 2003 and then by Iraqi forces in 2005 and, on each occasion, subsequently released uncharged, told Amnesty International about the situation and fears of Iraqi refugees in Jordan:

"This is a safe country. But we have no legal status here. Our residence permits have expired; we have exhausted [our savings]. If we have to leave, this could mean that thousands would have to leave and would be sent to the border. The Iraqi government and the militias would take their chance to kill them . . . What we request is a residence [permit] which prohibits us to be deported and financial support to cover living expenses." . . .

Most Iraqis are in an irregular situation in Jordan. Amnesty International was told that many Iraqis have been arrested by Jordanian police and security forces for overstaying and, sometimes, for working illegally. Those arrested, it is alleged, are often forcibly returned to Iraq; in most cases, they are returned to Iraq by land, which is the most dangerous way to travel and places them at risk. . . . In one case, a group of six or seven Iraqi Shi'a from Samawa were said to have been forcibly returned through the Iraq/Jordan border (Treibeel border crossing) in December 2006. In Iraq, their vehicle was reportedly forced to stop near al-Ramadi by insurgents, who then beheaded all but one of the occupants. The beheadings were apparently video-taped. The one passenger left unharmed apparently lied to the assailants and convinced them that he was from al-Adhamiya, a Sunni district in Baghdad. . . .

This 2004 report from Human Rights Watch places American treatment of prisoners in Abu Ghraib and other prisons in Iraq in the context of the war on terror following the 9/11 attacks and the use of Guantanamo, Cuba, and prisons in Afghanistan as holding and interrogation centers. The photos and ensuing publicity became well-known in the Middle East, along with the rendition of certain prisoners to Arab countries such as Syria and Egypt for torture. The estimates following that seventy to ninety percent of Abu Ghraib inmates were there by mistake apply also to Guantanamo prisoners, but all were subjected to such treatments. All U.S. personnel involved had legal immunity from Iraqi laws and only two military guards were court-martialed and imprisoned, including Sergeant Graner mentioned following; both were released within two years. No officers were charged.

Since late April 2004, when the first photographs appeared of U.S. military personnel humiliating, torturing, and otherwise mistreating detainees at Abu Ghraib prison in Iraq, the United States government has repeatedly sought to portray the abuse as an isolated incident, the work of a few "bad apples" acting without orders. On May 4, U.S. Secretary of Defense Donald H. Rumsfeld (1932–), in a formulation that would be used over and over again by U.S. officials, described the abuses at Abu Ghraib as "an exceptional, isolated" case. In a nationally televised address on May 24, President George W. Bush spoke of "disgraceful conduct by a few American troops who dishonored our country and disregarded our values."

In fact, the only exceptional aspect of the abuse at Abu Ghraib may have been that it was photographed. Detainees in U.S. custody in Afghanistan have testified that they experienced treatment similar to what happened in Abu Ghraib—from beatings to prolonged sleep and sensory deprivation to being held naked—as early as 2002. Comparable—and, indeed, more extreme—cases of torture and inhuman treatment have been extensively documented by the International Committee of the Red Cross [ICRS] and by journalists at numerous locations in Iraq outside Abu Ghraib.

. . . [I]n the aftermath of the September 11 attacks on the United States, the Bush administration . . . effectively sought to rewrite the Geneva Conventions of 1949 to eviscerate many of their most important protections. These include the rights of all detainees in an armed conflict to be free from humiliating and degrading treatment, as well as from torture and other forms of coercive interrogation. . . . The United States began to create offshore, off-limits, prisons such as Guantanamo Bay, Cuba, maintained other detainees in "undisclosed locations," and sent terrorism suspects without legal process to countries where information was beaten out of them. . . . Ignoring the deeply rooted U.S. military practice of applying the Geneva Conventions broadly, U.S. Defense Secretary Donald H. Rumsfeld labeled the first detainees to arrive at Guantanamo on January 11, 2002 as "unlawful combatants," automatically denying them possible status as prisoners of war [POWs]. "Unlawful combatants do not have any rights under the Geneva Convention," Mr. Rumsfeld said, overlooking that the Geneva Conventions provide explicit protections to all persons captured in an international armed conflict, even if they are not entitled to POW status. Rumsfeld signaled a casual approach to U.S. compliance with international law by saying that . . . "The reality is the set of facts that exist today with the al-Qaeda and the Taliban were not necessarily the set of facts that were considered when the Geneva Convention was fashioned."

[As a result] the United States began to employ coercive methods designed to "soften up" detainees for interrogation. These methods included holding detainees in painful stress positions, depriving them of sleep and light for prolonged periods, exposing them to extremes of heat, cold, noise and light, hooding, and depriving them of all clothing. News reports describe a case where U.S. personnel with official approval tortured a detainee held in an "undisclosed location" by submerging him in water until he believed he would drown. These techniques, familiar to victims of torture in many of the world's most

"Abu Ghraib Prison, Iraq." Abu Ghraib became notorious for its abuse of prisoners who were deliberately humiliated as well as tortured, often for the amusement of the Americans guarding them. Here are hooded Iraqi men forced to form a pile of their naked bodies. As the accompanying document states, this image was used as a screen saver on a computer in the interrogation room. The abuse began once the commanding officer at Guantanamo prison, General Geoffrey Miller, was assigned to Abu Ghraib to encourage the "softening up" of prisoners before interrogation.

In his first official address after the terrorist attacks of September 11, 2001, President George W. Bush promised ongoing military retaliation and warned nations of the world, "Either you are with us or with the terrorists." But he also appealed to Muslims worldwide and vowed the United States would adhere to core American principles, which, in the context of human rights, were not upheld in treating Muslim prisoners.

I also want to speak tonight directly to Muslims throughout the world. We respect your faith. It's practiced freely by many millions of Americans and by millions more that America counts as friends. Its teachings are good and peaceful and those who commit evil in the name of Allah blaspheme the name of Allah. . . . I ask you [American people] to uphold the values of America, and remember why so many have come here. We are in a fight for our principles and our first responsibility is to live by them. . . .

repressive dictatorships, are forbidden by prohibitions against torture and other cruel, inhuman or degrading treatment not only by the Geneva Conventions, but by other international instruments to which the U.S. is a party and by the U.S. military's own long-standing regulations. . . . Yet . . . Investigations of deaths in custody languished; soldiers and intelligence personnel accused of abuse, including all cases involving the killing of detainees, escaped judicial punishment. When, in the midst of the worst abuses, the International Committee of the Red Cross complained to Coalition forces, Army officials apparently responded by trying to curtail the ICRC's access. . . .

The severest abuses at Abu Ghraib occurred in the immediate aftermath of a decision by Secretary Rumsfeld to step up the hunt for "actionable intelligence" among Iraqi prisoners. The officer who oversaw intelligence gathering at Guantanamo was brought in to overhaul interrogation practices in Iraq, and teams of interrogators from Guantanamo were sent to Abu Ghraib. . . . The captain who oversaw interrogations at the Afghan detention center where two prisoners died in detention posted "Interrogation Rules of Engagement" at Abu Ghraib, authorizing coercive methods (with prior written approval of the military commander) such as the use of military guard dogs to instill fear that violate the Geneva Conventions and the Convention against Torture and Other Cruel, Inhuman Degrading Treatment or Punishment.

Unlike U.S. actions in the global campaign against terrorism, the armed conflict in Iraq was justified in part on bringing democracy and respect for the rule of law to an Iraqi population long-suffering under Saddam Hussein. Abusive treatment used against terrorism suspects after September 11 came to be considered permissible by the United States in an armed conflict [in Iraq] to suppress resistance to a military occupation. . . .

The United States, as an Occupying Power in Iraq under the Geneva Conventions, may deprive civilians in Iraq of their liberty in only two situations: for "imperative reasons of security," or for prosecution. Since President Bush declared the end of major combat in Iraq in May 2003, more than 12,000 Iraqis have been taken into custody by U.S. forces and detained for weeks or months. Until very recently, the U.S. has failed to ensure that so-called security detainees received a proper review of their cases as is required under the Geneva Conventions. In its February 2004 report to Coalition forces, the International Committee of the Red Cross reported that military intelligence officers told the ICRC that 70 to 90 percent of those in custody in Iraq last year had been arrested by mistake.

What is clear is that U.S. military personnel at Abu Ghraib felt empowered to abuse the detainees. The brazenness with which the soldiers at the center of the scandal conducted themselves, snapping photographs and flashing the "thumbs-up" sign as they abused prisoners, suggests they felt they had nothing to hide from their superiors. The abuse was so widely known and accepted that a picture of naked detainees forced into a human pyramid was reportedly used as a screen saver on a computer in the interrogation room. According to Maj. Gen. Taguba, "interrogators actively requested that MP guards set physical and mental conditions for favorable interrogation of witnesses." [The] MP Brigade [was] directed to change facility procedures to "set the conditions" for military intelligence interrogations. Taguba cited the testimony of several military police: "One said the orders were 'Loosen this guy up for us. Make sure he has a bad night. Make sure he gets the treatment.'" Another stated that "the prison wing belongs to [Military Intelligence] and it appeared that MI personnel approved the abuse." That MP also noted that "[t]he MI staffs, to my understanding, have been giving Graner [an MP in charge of night shifts at Abu Ghraib] compliments on the way he has been handling the MI [detainees]. Example being statements like 'Good job, they're breaking down real fast.'"

Dr. Mohamed El Baradei (1942–) was the Director General of the International Atomic Energy Agency (IAEA), an intergovernmental organization within the United Nations. The son of a lawyer who was formerly President of the Egyptian Bar Association, Dr. El Baradei holds a Doctorate in International Law from the New York University School of Law. A former Egyptian diplomat, Dr. El Baradei joined the International Law Program at the United Nations Institute for Training and Research in 1980, and, from 1981 to 1987, he was also an Adjunct Professor of International Law at the New York University School of Law. In 2005, he became the second Egyptian to win a Nobel Prize, the first being the writer Naguib Mahfouz in 1988. He delivered this Nobel lecture in Oslo.

My sister-in-law works for a group that supports orphanages in Cairo. She and her colleagues take care of children left behind by circumstances beyond their control. They feed these children, clothe them and teach them to read. At the International Atomic Energy Agency, my colleagues and I work to keep nuclear materials out of the reach of extremist groups. We inspect nuclear facilities all over the world, to be sure that peaceful nuclear activities are not being used as a cloak for weapons programmes. My sister-in-law and I are working towards the same goal, through different paths: the security of the human family. But why has this security so far eluded us? I believe it is because our security strategies have not yet caught up with the risks we are facing. The globalization that has swept away the barriers to the movement of goods, ideas and people has also swept with it barriers that confined and localized security threats.

A recent United Nations High-Level Panel identified five categories of threats that we face:

1. Poverty, Infectious Disease, and Environmental Degradation;
2. Armed Conflict—both within and among states;
3. Organized Crime;
4. Terrorism; and
5. Weapons of Mass Destruction.

These are all 'threats without borders'—where traditional notions of national security have become obsolete. We cannot respond to these threats by building more walls, developing bigger weapons, or dispatching more troops. Quite to the contrary. By their very nature, these security threats require primarily multinational cooperation. But what is more important is that these are not separate or distinct threats. When we scratch the surface, we find them closely connected and interrelated.

We are 1,000 people here today in this august hall. Imagine for a moment that we represent the world's population. These 200 people on my left would be the wealthy of the world, who consume 80 percent of the available resources. And these 400 people on my right would be living on an income of less than $2 per day. This under-privileged group of people on my right is no less intelligent or less worthy than their fellow human beings on the other side of the aisle. They were simply born into this fate. In the real world, this imbalance in living conditions inevitably leads to inequality of opportunity, and in many cases loss of hope. And what is worse, all too often the plight of the poor is compounded by and results in human rights abuses, a lack of good governance, and a deep sense of injustice. This combination naturally creates a most fertile breeding ground for civil wars, organized crime, and extremism in its different forms.

In regions where conflicts have been left to fester for decades, countries continue to look for ways to offset their insecurities or project their 'power'. In some cases, they may be tempted to seek their own weapons of mass destruction, like others who have preceded them. Fifteen years ago, when the Cold War ended, many of us hoped for a new world order to emerge. . . . But today we are nowhere near that goal. We may have torn down the walls between East and West, but we have yet to build the bridges between North and South—the rich and the poor. Consider our development aid record. Last year, the nations of the world spent over $1 trillion on armaments. But we contributed less than 10 percent of that amount—a mere $80 billion—as official development assistance to the developing parts of the world, where 850 million people suffer from hunger. My friend James Morris heads the World Food Programme, whose task it is to feed the hungry. He recently told me, "If I could have just 1 percent of the money spent on global armaments, no one in this world would go to bed hungry."

It should not be a surprise then that poverty continues to breed conflict. Of the 13 million deaths due to armed conflict in the last ten years, 9 million occurred in sub-Saharan Africa, where the poorest of the poor live. Consider also our approach to the sanctity and value of human life. In the aftermath of the September 2001 terrorist attacks in the United States, we all grieved deeply, and expressed outrage at this heinous crime—and rightly so. But many people today are unaware that, as the result of civil war in the Democratic Republic of the Congo, 3.8 million people have lost their lives since 1998. Are we to conclude that our priorities are skewed, and our approaches uneven? . . . Whether one believes in evolution, intelligent design, or Divine Creation, one thing is certain. Since the beginning of history, human beings have been at war with each other, under the pretext of religion, ideology, ethnicity and other reasons. And no civilization has ever willingly given up its most powerful weapons. We seem to agree today that we can share modern technology, but we still refuse to acknowledge that our values—at their very core— are shared values. I am an Egyptian Muslim, educated in Cairo and New York, and now living in Vienna. My wife and I have spent half our lives in the North, half in the South. And we have experienced first hand the unique nature of the human family and the common values we all share.

Shakespeare speaks of every single member of that family in The Merchant of Venice, when he asks: "If you prick us, do we not bleed? If you tickle us, do we not laugh? If you poison us, do we not die? And if you wrong us, shall we not revenge?" And lest we forget: There is no religion that was founded on intolerance—and no religion that does not value the sanctity of human life. Judaism asks that we value the beauty and joy of human existence. Christianity says we should treat our neighbours as we would be treated. Islam declares that killing one person unjustly is the same as killing all of humanity. Hinduism recognizes the entire universe as one family. Buddhism calls on us to cherish the oneness of all creation. . . .

Some would say that it is too idealistic to believe in a society based on tolerance and the sanctity of human life, where borders, nationalities and ideologies are of marginal importance. To those I say, this is not idealism, but rather realism, because history has taught us that war rarely resolves our differences. Force does not heal old wounds; it opens new ones. Imagine what would happen if the nations of the world spent as much on development as on building the machines of war. Imagine a world where every human being would live in freedom and dignity. Imagine a world in which we would shed the same tears when a child dies in Darfur or Vancouver. Imagine a world where we would settle our differences through diplomacy and dialogue and not through bombs or bullets. Imagine if the only nuclear weapons remaining were the relics in our museums. Imagine the legacy we could leave to our children. Imagine that such a world is within our grasp.

Mohamed El Baradei

Tunisia and Egypt Rebel: Dictatorships and Crony Capitalism

In December 2010, Muhammad Bouazizi, from the town of Sidi Bouzid in the interior of Tunisia, immolated himself when ordered to stop selling vegetables and fruit from his stand because he did not have the money for a vendor's permit. Contrary to earlier reports, Bouazizi was not college educated, but he was apparently the sole support of his widowed mother and seven siblings. His act became a catalyst for popular uprisings not only in Tunisia but throughout MENA thanks to Facebook and other Web sites. The following interview with a Tunisian scholar suggests reasons for the outbursts of fury that led to the downfall of the Ben Ali and Mubarak governments.

[What happened in Tunisia] was a popular uprising . . . lead [sic] by young people who were protesting the prevalence of unemployment in the country. Many of these young unemployed have college degrees. . . . Fifty percent of the Tunisian population is under the age of thirty and forty percent of these young people are unemployed. This is a situation you find throughout the Middle East and North Africa. . . . [with] Tunisia a little special [because] so many of them are educated. Jobs are indeed very scarce and accessible only to the well-connected, the privileged. [In an interview on French radio, a young man said] . . . 'You need to know someone who will give you a job—or you need to pay for it. If you want a job as a primary school teacher, it's $5,000, for a high school teacher position . . . it will cost you between $10,000 and $8,000.' Corruption has basically spread throughout Tunisian society, although it is a relatively new phenomenon, unlike other countries in the MENA region. . . .

(Zine el-Abidine) Ben Ali justified his . . . grip on power with a total absence of political rights for the Tunisian people . . . by the need to fight Islamic terrorism, and was a close ally of France, Europe and the U.S. . . . The targets of his repressive policies [arbitrary arrest and torture of his opponents] were first the Islamic movement activists [although] the Islamists are known in Tunisia to be rather moderate. . . . They want to play by the rules—democratic rules; they do not want to reverse women's rights, which . . . are quite substantial. Ben Ali . . . also cracked down on secular opponents. . . . With regard to the media, they were so stifled that one commentator compared them to the press of North Korea. . . . In the 2010 Press Freedom Index, Tunisia was ranked one hundred sixty-fourth out of one hundred and seventy-eight countries. . . .

However, the Ben Ali regime [building on past president Habib Bourguiba's accomplishments] did produce some notable achievements: building physical infrastructure, expanding the educational system; furthering gender equality. . . . But [these accomplishments and economic growth were] mainly based on tourism and textiles, all requiring a low cost, minimally trained workforce [which] couldn't integrate all these educated workers with college degrees. [Also these] investments benefited the coastal regions . . . [creating a very serious regional imbalance]. One can add that the implementation of what is called the 'Washington Consensus', as requested by international financial organizations, geared at establishing a free market economy, reducing government budget deficit, and inserting Tunisia into the global economy, did also contribute to the widening of the gap between rich and poor. . . .

"Tunisia's Liberation from Ben Ali Regime." This poster, with a male and female figure, is captioned at the top with the saying "Tunis, we [will] die for you." The bottom captions are "June 2011" and "with full determination." The woman's inclusion in the poster suggests the modern gender views of most Tunisians.

[The protests] were basically demanding the instauration [*sic*] of democracy in Tunisia, and an end to a system of wide-ranging corruption headed by Ben Ali, his wife and their respective families and extended families.... They were at the core ... of the corruption system in Tunisia.

This 2009 cable from the U.S. ambassador to Tunis indicates the opulent lifestyle of the extended family of Tunisian President Zine El-Abidine Ben Ali, particularly the relatives of his second wife, one of whom is Sakher El-Materi, mentioned here. The palatial residences of the family members, often built on illegally seized land, were visible to all. After Ben Ali and his relatives fled the country, the large residence in Hammamet mentioned in this cable was destroyed and looted by Hammamet residents.

Monday, 27 July 2009, 16:09

S E C R E T TUNIS 000516

SUBJECT: TUNISIA: DINNER WITH SAKHER EL MATERI

REF: TUNIS 338

Classified By: Ambassador Robert F. Godec for reasons 1.4 (b) and (d)

2. (S) Presidential son-in-law and wealthy businessman Mohamed Sakher El Materi, and his wife, Nesrine Ben Ali El Materi hosted the Ambassador and his wife for dinner at their Hammamet beach residence July 17....

Freedom of Expression 3. (S) Ambassador raised the need for more freedom of expression and association in Tunisia. El Materi agreed. He complained that, as the new owner of Dar Assaba, the largest private newspaper group in the country, he has been getting calls from the Minister of Communications complaining about articles he has been running (Comment: This is doubtful).... 5. (S) El Materi complained at length about Tunisian bureaucracy, saying it is difficult to get things done. He said communication inside the bureaucracy is terrible. He said people often "bring wrong information" to the President implying he had to get involved sometimes to get things corrected....

El-Materi Unplugged: Home/Personal Life

11 (S) El-Materi's house is spacious, and directly above and along the Hammamet public beach. The compound is large and well

guarded by government security. It is close to the center of Hammamet, with a view of the fort and the southern part of the town. The house was recently renovated and includes an infinity pool and a terrace of perhaps 50 meters (approx. 150 feet). While the house is done in a modern style (and largely white), there are ancient artifacts everywhere: Roman columns, frescoes and even a lion's head from which water pours into the pool. El Materi insisted the pieces are real. He hopes to move into his new (and palatial) house in Sidi Bou Said in eight to ten months.

12. (S) The dinner included perhaps a dozen dishes, including fish, steak, turkey, octopus, fish couscous and much more. The quantity was sufficient for a very large number of guests. Before dinner a wide array of small dishes were served, along with three different juices (including Kiwi juice, not normally available here). After dinner, he served ice cream and frozen yoghurt he brought in by plane from Saint Tropez, along with blueberries and raspberries and fresh fruit and chocolate cake. (NB. El Materi and Nesrine had just returned from Saint Tropez on their private jet after two weeks vacation. El Materi was concerned about his American pilot finding a community here. The Ambassador said he would be pleased to invite the pilot to appropriate American community events.)

13. (S) El Materi has a large tiger ("Pasha") on his compound, living in a cage. He acquired it when it was a few weeks old. The tiger consumes four chickens a day. (Comment: The situation reminded the Ambassador of Uday Hussein's [Saddam Hussein's son] lion cage in Baghdad.) El Materi had staff everywhere. There were at least a dozen people, including a butler from Bangladesh and a nanny from South Africa (NB. This is extraordinarily rare in Tunisia, and very expensive.)

17. (S) Throughout the evening, El Materi often struck the Ambassador as demanding, vain and difficult. He is clearly aware of his wealth and power, and his actions reflected little finesse. He repeatedly pointed out the lovely view from his home and frequently corrected his staff, issued orders and barked reprimands. Despite this, El Materi was aware of his affect [*sic*] on the people around him and he showed periodic kindness. He was unusually solicitous and helpful to the Ambassador's wife, who is disabled. . . . As for the dinner itself, it was similar to what one might experience in a Gulf country, and out of the ordinary for Tunisia.

Egypt's Crony Capitalism

Egypt's privatization and structural adjustment programs have led to a brand of crony capitalism. . . . (where) a small; group of people own the lion's share of the assets. Privatization legislation has in effect meant replacing the public monopoly [government control] with a private monopoly. The middle class has been shrinking, while there has been an engagement of the super rich. State owned enterprises have been sold to a minority of rich people. The record of private enterprises creating jobs is very poor. We are not reaping the benefits of an energetic bourgeoisie. What we have created is [a] parasitical comprador class. The consequences will be no less than catastrophic. This society is a candidate for a difficult period of violent social conflict, and the kind of government we have will not do.

19. (S) Most striking of all, however, was the opulence with which El Materi and Nesrine live. Their home in Hammamet was impressive, with the tiger adding to the impression of "over the top." Even more extravagant is their home still under construction in Sidi Bou Said. That residence, from its outward appearance, will be closer to a palace. It dominates the Sidi Bou Said skyline from some vantage points and has been the occasion of many private, critical comments. The opulence with which El Materi and Nesrine live and their behavior make clear why they and other members of Ben Ali's family are disliked and even hated by some Tunisians. The excesses of the Ben Ali family are growing.

The decades since 1950 have witnessed the explosion of huge cities in MENA as immigrants from the overpopulated countryside flocked to urban centers. Today Cairo's population is officially under eight million but with the suburbs is estimated at seventeen million.

This article by the Egyptian paper *Al-Ahram Weekly Online* correspondent Mohamed El-Sayed on Egypt in 2008 refers to the "bread riots" of January 1977 when President Anwar al-Sadat raised the price of bread and cooking oil by one piaster (approx. one U.S. cent) to try to cut food subsidies. The ensuing attacks not only on government buildings but on nightclubs frequented by wealthy Persian Gulf Arabs, and the rage of people mired in poverty while surrounded by symbols of wealth, forced Sadat to rescind the cuts.

Though relatively unnoticed in the Western press, the Egyptian upheavals of 2008 discussed here foreshadowed the upheaval of 2011 that ousted President Husni Mubarak.

Memories of 1977

. . . Egyptians are generally not rebellious people though when their stomachs are empty the government should beware. . . . Demonstrations . . . hit the streets of Cairo, Port Said and Mahalla . . . [last] week when the public finally began to protest against increases in the price of basic commodities. Memories of the bread riots that broke out when President Anwar El-Sadat attempted to cut subsidies on a range of basic foodstuffs [January 1977] were never far away. . . . Last Thursday, the Egyptian Movement for Change (Kifaya, i.e. 'Enough!') attempted to stage the first demonstration in Cairo's Sayeda Zeinab Square. Security forces arrested around 50 Kifaya members along with a number of journalists covering the event. . . . The heavy-handed approach adopted by the police towards the protesters prompted the Washington-based Human Rights Watch to criticise the Egyptian authorities. "Egyptian authorities are taking every opportunity to signal to citizens that when it comes to peaceful criticism of government policies forget about exercising your rights," said Joe Stork, deputy director of Human Rights Watch's Middle East division.

On Saturday, the Ghad ('Tomorrow') Party organised a demonstration in the Mediterranean city of Port Said, about 220 kilometres north east of Cairo. Blaming the government for the increase in prices of basic foodstuffs they carried bread and cooking oil bottles and warned the government against removing subsidies on basic commodities. A day later 5,000 people attended a demonstration in the industrial city of Mahalla, Gharbiya governorate, 123 kilometres north of Cairo, organised by Wafd, the Nasserist Arab, Ghad and the frozen Labour parties and the Muslim Brotherhood. . . . They warned government officials that another bread uprising could be in the offing. The same governorate was the site of another demonstration by 300 people protesting a shortage of flour at the only bakery in the village of Kafr Hassaan. "The government is scared of another hungry riot," argued Kifaya general coordinator Abdel-Wahab Elmessiri, . . . The prevention of peaceful demonstrations calling for a reduction in basic commodity prices, Elmessiri continued, could lead to "a populist uprising in the form of catharsis that could destroy everything." He had hoped that the government would be more rational in its response to such protests and work on reducing basic commodity prices. "This [rebellion], if it happens, will not be to the benefit of any party, the people, the government or the opposition." . . . Elmessiri [cited] the series of labour strikes that hit the country last year. "Even [Egyptian] pilgrims organised sit-in strikes during the pilgrimage season in Mecca, and strikes have been organised by civil servants, unheard of in Egypt's modern history."

While opposition leaders are using an alarmist tone, Mohamed Kamal, member of the ruling National Democratic Party's Policies Committee, told *Al-Ahram Weekly* that the warnings against potential riots are exaggerated. "Egyptian society is going through a

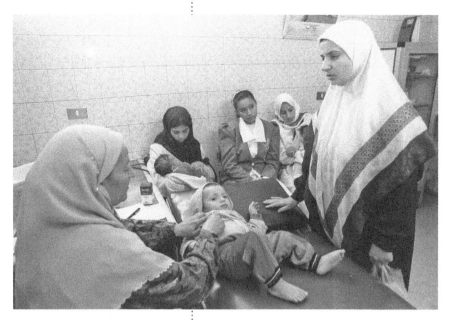

"Muslim-Sponsored Health Care for the Poor, Cairo, c. 1995." A basic reason for the popularity of groups such as the Muslim Brotherhood is their focus on social services and welfare, including providing clinics for health care in impoverished city neighborhoods or in villages, far from the major urban areas. Where the Egyptian state has failed to provide for its citizens, Muslim social welfare associations have stepped into the breach.

period of political and economic mobility. Our society is witnessing an unprecedented degree of freedom of expression, and it's normal for societies in a state of transition to experience what's happening in Egypt." . . .

". . . There is no confidence in the government," Ammar Ali Hassan, director of the Middle East Studies and Research Centre, told the *Weekly*. "The desire to protest has overwhelmed a large sector of society." . . .

As this *Forbes Magazine* interview with Kalle Lasn, publisher and editor of *Adbusters* magazine, suggests, the populist movement in the United States and elsewhere in Europe was inspired by the Arab Spring, especially events in Tunisia. Globalization may no longer signify only the impact of Western policies on the non-Western world, but the opposite as well.

The Brains Behind "Occupy Wall Street"

Meet the second most evilest man in the world (after George Soros). This isn't the 60s. And it isn't the pre-Iraq War protests either. Occupy Wall Street, supposedly, is different. It has no leader. It has no political action committee behind it. One can argue that the protests against Wall Street this month really started in Tunisia. That's where the idea came from. But the guys who took that Arab movement and ran with it are based in Vancouver.

Kalle Lasn, 69, is their quasi leader. He's the publisher and editor of *Adbusters* magazine. It's a small, non-influential critical and artsy magazine with a decent following of around 90,000 who call themselves "culture jammers." Occupy Wall Street began in the conference rooms at that Vancouver mag. I spoke with Lasn in July, right after the new edition of *Adbusters* hit the news stands with the now famous image of a ballerina balancing on the Wall Street bull. Above her head read the Twitter hashtag #OccupyWallStreet. Lasn didn't know what this movement would become. Just two and a half short months later, it's the talk on *The Talk*, *The View* and every major news channel. I spoke with him again this afternoon about this weekend's European wide protest, the G-20 and a worldwide Robin Hood tax.

Kenneth R: *The Washington Post* calls you the leader of Occupy Wall Street. What do you make of that?

Kalle L: This is a leaderless movement. But the founding of the idea came out of lots of brainstorming here among our staff editors, photographers, freelancers and people on our list-serve. Back in the summer we were all talking about what we were going to do next with the magazine and we were all inspired by what happened in Tunisia and thought that America was ripe for this type of rage. We put feelers out on our forums. So it was relatively recent, in June, when we came up with this idea and launched the hashtag in mid-July with the magazine and then it just took off. Once that issue was published, we started putting out tactical briefings to our list serve. Kalle is a man of the world, so it is no surprise to him or his network of culture jammers, that a Wall Street protest was conceived far away in Vancouver, Canada. That's fairly close to the site where another surprising protest in U.S. history took place. The 1995 anti-globalization protests caught everyone by surprise in Seattle during the annual meeting of the World Trade Organization. Back then, the model was to attack corporate control over the public sphere like a pack of wolves. There was an alpha male and those who followed behind in a pack. The new model has evolved from a pack . . . to a swarm. Kalle gets inquiries and emails about Occupy Wall Street from London to Shanghai, but he's not ringing his hands and sticking pins in a wall-sized map about where his next diabolical plan against capitalism will take shape.

Kalle was born in Estonia and moved to Australia when he was 7. He hit Canada in his 30s and has been in Vancouver ever since. He traveled to the U.S. for a year, back in the 1960s. We joked a little tongue in cheek. (This is me getting my Fox on.)

KR: Of course, you did. You were a hippy and you were radicalized in San Francisco.

KL: I went to a Jimi Hendrix concert.

KR: See.

KL: But it wasn't the concert that radicalized me. I remember the people there were so alive. The young people in Occupy Wall Street are a lot like that. . . .

Glossary

abu Father

afaqi Literally, those coming from the "horizons" or from the provinces; contrasts with the urbane inhabitants of Tunis, the baldi

'alim/'ulama' (ulema) A religious scholar or savant

aman An assurance of protection or clemency; a pardon

amin Chief, head, or master of a guild

amir/umara' Prince, emir, or tribal chief; also governor of a province

a'yan Notables

bey Prince or governor ruling in the name of the Ottoman sultan

bint Daughter

burnus A hooded wool cloak

dabtiya The urban police

daftir/dafatir A notebook, roster, dossier, or file

dar/bayt House

Dar al-Islam The abode of Islam; the Islamic world

dey Official of the Ottoman Empire

diwan Council, administrative office, chancellery

fallah/fallahin Peasant or farmer

faqih Expert in *fiqh*, a legist or jurisprudent

fatwa An authoritative legal opinion regarding Islamic law

fiqh Islamic jurisprudence

funduq A poor man's urban hostel, normally for those from outside Tunis; also used to designate the spaces in Tunis where the foreigners resided and worked

hadith A Prophetic tradition; narrative relating the deeds and utterances of the Prophet Muhammad and his companions

ha'ik An outer garment usually made of a long piece of white woolen material and covering the head and body

hajj Pilgrimage to Mecca incumbent on all able Muslims at least once in a lifetime

Haramayn The two holy cities, Mecca and Medina

Hijaz The western coast of the Arabian Peninsula on the Red Sea where Mecca and Medina are located

hubus/ahbas In North Africa, a charitable or religious foundation; property of inalienable legal status whose revenue serves pious purposes as known as *waqf* or *awqaf* in the eastern Arab world

hurma Holiness, sacred, sacrosanct

ibn Son

imam A leader in prayer in Sunni Islam; the head of the community in Shi'i Islam that is split into two major religious schools.

jama'a A tribal or village assembly or council of elders

jihad Inner jihad—individual moral striving to do good; outer jihad—religious or holy war

kahiya Government official, roughly governor

katib A writer, scribe, or secretary

khalifa Caliph, historically, successor to the Prophet Muhammad as head of the Islamic community (umma); also a deputy of a ruler or a senior official

khassa The elite, notables, upper class

khaznadar State treasurer; keeper of the state's revenues

kuttab A Quranic school

madrasa A religious school or college, often attached to a mosque

majlis al-shari'a An Islamic court or tribunal

Mashriq The eastern Arab world, including Egypt, as opposed to the Maghrib (North Africa), from Libya to Morocco.

masjid Mosque

milk (mulk) Private property

mufti An expert in Islamic law authorized to issue *fatwa*-s

na'ib A representative, agent, or deputy

Persia The term used to refer to Iran by Western peoples from the Greeks onward, and found in nineteenth and early twentieth-century references. Modern usage is that of 'Iran.'

qadi A Muslim judge or magistrate

qa'id Chief or leader, tribal or provincial administrator, also governor

al-Qa'ida   Popularly known as al-Qaeda, the Islamist organization formed by Osama bin Laden in Afghanistan; term means "the base" or "headquarters."

qasba   Fortress or citadel; often the highest point in the city

qubba   Dome; a domed building or shrine commemorating a saint

ribat   A fortress or fortified place; also one of the two suburbs of Tunis

safsari   A very fine white cloak or mantle often using wool and silk

shari'a   Literally, the "path to be followed"; the holy law of Islam

sharif/shurafa'/ashraf   A descendant or descendants of the Prophet Muhammad or of his lineage; a noble person

shaykh   An elder, chief, head of a tribe, master of a sufi order

shaykh al-madina   A sort of city manager responsible for law and order in urban areas

sufi   An Islamic mystic; a member of a mystical order or brotherhood

sultan   One holding power, usually absolute power, as the Ottoman Sultan

suq   A market, bazaar, or fair

tadhkira/teskere   Permit or license; written authorization

Tanzimat   Reorganizations, meaning specifically the Ottoman state-sponsored reforms of the nineteenth century

umm   Mother

umma   The community of Muslims

'urf   Customary law

zawiya/zawaya: Literally, a "corner": a religious building enclosing a saint's tomb; a small mosque or prayer room; a sufi center often including a mosque, hospice, and educational facilities

Timeline

1453
Ottoman Turks take Constantinople, signaling end of Byzantine Empire and beginning of Ottoman Turkish Empire

1517
Ottomans absorb Egypt into Ottoman Empire; as protector of the Holy Places of Mecca and Medina, Ottoman Sultan takes title of Caliph, claiming right to lead Islamic community

1699
Treaty of Karlowitz; Ottomans cede Hungary to Austrian Empire; first treaty with Christian power where Ottomans gave up territory

1787–1807
Reign of Sultan Selim III; inaugurates Ottoman reform efforts

1798
Napoleon leads French invasion of Egypt

1799
Napoleon abandons Egypt, returns to France

1801
French military forces evacuate Egypt, return to France

1805–1848
Muhammad Ali, Ottoman officer, governs Egypt, fails to establish state independent of Ottomans, but secures recognition of dynastic rule within his family

1830
French invade Algeria; begin colonization effort lasting to 1962

1839
Ottomans declaration of *Hatti Sherif* of Gulhane; begins Ottoman reform era known as Tanzimat

1848–1896
Reign of Shah Nasir al-Din in Persia (also known as Iran and officially decreed as such in 1935).

1853–1856
Crimean War

1856
Ottoman Declaration of *Hatti Humayun*, extending and specifying equal rights of Ottoman subjects

1860
Maronite–Druze hostilities in Lebanon lead to massacre of Christians in Damascus and European intervention

1860–1918
Mt. Lebanon region administered as separate governorate in Ottoman Empire

1869
Opening of the Suez Canal

1875
British government buys shares of Suez Canal owned by Egyptian ruler, Khedive Ismail

1876
Ottomans announce first constitution, parliament opens 1877; constitution and parliament suspended 1878

1878
British take Cyprus from Ottomans

1881
French take Tunisia as reward for British taking Cyprus—will remain to 1956

1882
British invade Egypt responding to nationalist opposition to European control of Egypt's finances; Will remain to 1956. Emergence of Zionist sentiment in Eastern Europe; seven thousand Russian Jews depart for Palestine

1890–91
Violent Iranian protests over government's awarding of concession to Englishman to control tobacco industry; Shia clergy lead mobilizing of opposition; concession revoked

1896
Qajar ruler, Shah Nasir al-Din, assassinated. Theodor Herzl publishes *Der Judenstaat* (The Jewish State), calling for Jewish homeland

1897
World Zionist Organization formed in Basle, Switzerland

1901
William Knox D'Arcy, British subject, awarded concession for developing Iran's oil and natural gas reserves, excepting Russian sphere of influence in the northern sector of the country.

1906
Dinshawai incident in Egypt results in massive Egyptian protests and Lord Cromer's departure in 1907

1906–07
Qajar rulers in Iran accede to demands for issuance of constitution (December 1906) and passing of supplemental laws granting Shii clerics right to review legislation (October 1907)

1907
Anglo-Russian Convention dividing Iran into spheres of influence

1908
Oil discovered by D'Arcy concession in southwest Iran. Young Turk Revolution forces Sultan Abdul Hamid to restore 1876 constitution and call for parliamentary elections

1909

Ottoman army ousts Sultan Abdul Hamid. Anglo-Persian Oil Company takes over D'Arcy oil concession in Iran

1911

Italy invades and annexes Libya, loses control during World War II

1912

France declares protectorate over Morocco, will remain to 1956

1914

British Government acquires majority of shares in Anglo-Persian Oil Company to guarantee supplies to its fleet. Outbreak of World War I; Ottoman Empire enters on side of Germany and Austria-Hungary in November

1915

February—Gallipoli Campaign begins—lasts until Allied withdrawal January 1916. Ottomans begin ouster of Armenians from eastern Anatolia, leading to major atrocities. Hussein-McMahon Correspondence begins in July, ends in January 1916. British fail in attempt to take Baghdad, army captured by Turks

1916

Sykes-Picot Agreement dividing Arab lands between France and Britain. Sharif Hussein of Mecca initiates Arab Revolt

1917

United States enters World War I. British issue Balfour Declaration, November 2. Bolshevik Revolution in Russia, November, leads to Russian withdrawal from war (January 1918)

1918

January. U.S. President Woodrow Wilson declares Fourteen Points. October. British and Arab forces take Damascus, Ottoman Empire surrenders. November. World War I ends

1919

Paris Peace Conference opens in January. March. Egyptian nationalist leader Saad Zaghlul exiled to Malta. Major Egyptian rebellion ensues. British withdraw troops from Syria in November, abandoning attempt to renege on 1916 Sykes-Picot Agreement that awarded Syria to France

1920

March. Syrian National Congress proclaims Syrian independence with Emir Feisal as King of Syria; Turkish National Assembly establishes provisional government against sultan with Mustafa Kemal as president. March–October. Major Iraqi tribal rebellion against British centralized rule; British use poison gas against tribal resistors. July. French invade Syria from Mt. Lebanon, oust Feisal, take over Syria. September. France creates country of Lebanon by taking land from Syria

1921

Cairo Conference where British install Feisal in Iraq, give his brother Emir Abdullah eastern Palestine as new region to be known as Transjordan, separated from Palestine mandate awarded to Britain. Colonel Reza Khan of Persian Cossack Brigade seizes effective power in Iran; establishes new, Pahlavi, dynasty in 1925.

1922

British unilaterally declare Egyptian independence but retain control of major governmental functions. League of Nations officially approves British/French mandates for Iraq, Palestine, Syria, and Lebanon, originally allotted in 1920. Mustafa Kemal abolishes office of sultan in Turkey

1923

Lausanne Treaty recognizes Turkish independence; Ankara declared new Turkish capital; Mustafa Kemal elected Turkish president

1924

Turkish National Assembly abolishes the office of the Caliphate, Ottoman ruling house goes into exile; signals start of Kemal's secular reform project. Abd al-Aziz Ibn Saud takes control of Mecca and Medina, drives Sharif Hussein of Mecca into exile, gains effective control over what will become Saudi Arabia

1928

Hasan al-Banna forms Muslim Brotherhood in Egypt

1929

Zionist-Palestinian clashes over Western Wall access lead to major Palestinian attacks on Jews with serious casualties on both sides, and Jewish evacuation of Hebron

1930

Turkish women granted right to vote

1932

Saudi Arabia declared a kingdom with international recognition under leadership of Ibn Saud who will rule to 1953. Iraqi independence; enters League of Nations

1933

Adolf Hitler assumes power in Germany; racial laws against Jews trigger major Jewish emigration to Palestine

1935

Reza Shah calls for 'Iran' to be used officially instead of 'Persia'; Anglo-Persian Oil Company becomes Anglo-Iranian Oil Company (AIOC)

1936–39

Palestinian Arab Revolt

1936

Anglo-Egyptian treaty grants Egypt greater independence, restricts British forces to Suez Canal Zone; King Farouk assumes the monarchy in Egypt

1937

Peel Commission report recommends partition of Palestine

1938

Turkey's leader, Mustafa Kemal Ataturk dies. First major oil discovery in Saudi Arabia

1939

British White Paper restricting Jewish immigration to Palestine and land purchases. Outbreak of World War II; will last to 1945

1941

Reza Shah forced into exile by Britain and France. Succeeded by his son, Muhammad Reza Shah Pahlavi

1942

Biltmore Conference in New York City mobilizes major political support in the U.S. for a Jewish state in Palestine

1945

United Nations formed

1947

United Nations Special Commission on Palestine recommends its partition into two states, approved by United Nations General Assembly in November; Zionists accept recommendation, Arabs reject it

December 1947–May 1948

Civil war in Palestine

(continued)

1948

Israeli independence declared May 14. Transjordan becomes Hashemite Kingdom of Jordan. May–October. Arab-Israeli wars, Israeli victories lead to truces signed in 1949

1950

Two-party elections in Turkey oust Republican People's Party founded by Ataturk, install Democratic Party

1951

Iranian National Front calls for nationalization of AIOC, subsequently approved by the *majlis* (Iranian parliament); Muhammad Mossadeq elected prime minister. Emir Abdullah of Jordan assassinated

1952

Military officers stage coup in Egypt, overthrowing monarchy of King Farouk; they are led by Colonel Gamal Abd al-Nasser who becomes president in 1954

1953

American-British coup overthrows Iranian Prime Minister Muhammad Mossadeq, restores Muhammad Reza Shah to full power

1954

Nasser signs agreement with Britain for withdrawal of remaining British troops from Suez Canal Zone by 1956; Algerian revolt for independence begins, known as the Battle of Algiers

1955

Iraq joins Western Cold War defense alliance known as Baghdad Pact. Nasser of Egypt signs arms agreement with Czechoslovakia, backed by Soviet Union

1956

France grants independence to Tunisia and Morocco after demonstrations against French control in both countries; does so to concentrate on retaining Algeria. Suez Crisis: Egypt's Nasser nationalizes Suez Canal in July after United States withdraws from promised financing of major dam project; this leads in October to Israeli-British-French assault on Egypt in failed attempt to overthrow him

1958

Iraqi Revolution overthrows Hashemite Kingdom created after World War I; series of military-dominated governments will follow. Egypt and Syria merge to become United Arab Republic; Syria will secede in 1961

1959

Palestinian revolutionary group, Fatah, founded in Kuwait; Yasser Arafat one of its members

1960

OPEC (Organization of Petroleum Exporting Countries) founded; initial members are Saudi Arabia, Iraq, Iran, Kuwait, and Venezuela; later expands to thirteen members. Turkish military, guardian of Mustafa Kemal Ataturk's secular reforms, overthrows Democratic Party, charging electoral violations. Prime Minister Adnan Menderes had campaigned on restoring Muslim practices outlawed by Ataturk; Menderes and two colleagues are put to death

1962

Algeria gains independence from France. Over one million Europeans forced to leave

1964

Iran's parliament passes American-encouraged law granting immunity to American military and civilian advisory personnel; this leads to emergence of Ayatollah Ruhollah Khomeini as leader of those denouncing Iran's concessions to the United States as reminder of the country's subjugation to foreign interests at end of nineteenth century; the shah exiles Khomeini to Turkey from where he goes to Iraq where he stays until 1978. Creation of Palestine Liberation Organization (PLO) in Cairo by Arab League

1967

Six-day Arab-Israeli war (June 5–10); Israel occupies Sinai Peninsula, West Bank, Golan Heights, annexes East Jerusalem to Israel

1969

Yasser Arafat becomes head of PLO

1970

Palestinian-Jordanian clashes lead to PLO offices and cadres moving to Lebanon. Egypt's Nasser dies, succeeded by Vice-President Anwar al-Sadat

1973

Arab (Egypt and Syria)-Israeli October war; leads to Arab oil boycott

1977

Menachem Begin elected Israeli prime minister; represents right-wing ideology seeking to retain West Bank. Egypt's Sadat flies to Jerusalem, addresses Knesset, calling for peace; initiates Egyptian-Israeli peace talks. Conservative Islamist groups gain strength in Egypt, opposed to Sadat's economic policies and his overtures to Israel

1978

Camp David Egyptian-Israeli talks sponsored by U.S. President Jimmy Carter establish basis for Egyptian-Israeli peace treaty, signed March 1979; Israel withdraws fully from Sinai Peninsula by April 1982. Saddam Hussein consolidates his control of Baathist regime in Iraq

1979

Islamic Revolution in Iran; popular demonstrations lead to overthrow of Pahlavi dynasty, to be succeeded by Ayatollah Khomeini who establishes an Islamic regime. Soviet Union invades Afghanistan

1980–1988

Iraq–Iran war, begun by Iraq

1980

Turkish military again intervenes, ousts prime minister suspected of representing Muslim interests; massive arrests result

1981

Israel annexes Golan Heights. Egypt's Anwar al-Sadat assassinated, succeeded by Vice-President Husni al-Mubarak; many in Islamist groups linked to Sadat's assassination are later allowed to leave Egypt, go to Afghanistan to participate in American–Saudi financed *jihad* against Soviet forces there

1982

Israel invades Lebanon; PLO forced to remove headquarters to Tunis

1987

First Palestinian *intifada* erupts as protest against Israeli occupation policies in Gaza and West Bank. Hamas is formed as Muslim Palestinian resistance organization. Tunisian President Habib Bourguiba ousted in coup engineered by minister of interior; had ruled since Tunisia gained independence in 1956.

1988

PLO renounces terrorism in terms acceptable to United States; Reagan administration authorizes talks with PLO officials

1989

Soviet forces withdraw from Afghanistan. Al-Qaeda (the base) formed in Afghanistan, led by Osama bin Laden and Shaykh Ayman al-Zawahiri; Ayatollah al-Khomeini dies

1990

Iraq's Saddam Hussein orders Iraqi forces to invade Kuwait in August

1991

U.S.-led coalition ousts Iraqi forces from Kuwait; United States establishes protected area for Iraq's Kurdish population in northern region of Iraq. Algeria begins process of two-stage elections, cancels second stage after indications that an Islamist party will gain victory; Islamist Salvation Front mobilizes forces, ignites civil war vs. the regime from 1993 onward

1993

Israel and PLO reach accord (Oslo I) on Palestinian autonomy in Palestinian areas of Gaza, and in Jericho on West Bank; in letters of recognition, Arafat as PLO head recognizes Israel's right to exist; Yitzhak Rabin, Israeli prime minister, recognizes PLO as representing the Palestinian people. Taliban take over power

in Afghanistan, ending civil wars that had followed U.S. withdrawal of aid following departure of Soviet forces in 1989

1995

Second Israeli-Palestinian accord (Oslo II) reached, sparks massive right-wing Israeli protests at likelihood of ceding West Bank land; prime minister Rabin assassinated by right-wing opponent of accord

1999

King Hussein of Jordan dies, had ruled since 1953

2000

Israeli-Palestinian peace talks at Camp David, brokered by Clinton administration, fail, lead to second Palestinian intifada following Israeli rightist Ariel Sharon's visit to Temple Mount. Hafiz Al-Asad, president of Syria, dies, had ruled since 1970, succeeded by his son, Bashar. George W. Bush elected president of United States

2001

Al-Qaeda-sponsored terrorist attacks on United States (September 11th) lead to declaration of "war on terror" and invasion of Afghanistan by end of year

2002

Justice and Development Party, representing Muslim values, elected in Turkey, signaling broader acceptance of Islam in Turkish politics

2003

United States invades and occupies Iraq, overthrowing Saddam Hussein regime

2004

Yasser Arafat dies in Paris

2005

Israel withdraws all settlers from Gaza with goal of retaining most of West Bank

2006

Hamas elected to office in Palestinian elections in January; though Hamas participation had been backed by Bush administration, it immediately calls for boycott of new Palestinian government. Israeli-Hizbollah war in southern Lebanon, July–August, ends in stalemate, Israeli withdrawal

2008

Turkish parliament passes law permitting women to wear headscarves at universities, overthrowing eighty-year-old laws banning their use. Major protests in Egypt over unemployment, rising food prices, charges of corrupt government. Israeli assault on Gaza in December, retaliation for rocket attacks on southern Israel by Islamist group, Islamic Jihad

2009

Iranian elections result in President Ahmedinejad's reelection, sparking massive protests in and outside Iran; those inside Iran are brutally crushed. Barack Obama elected

U.S. President; Benjamin Netanyahu elected Israeli Prime Minister; Obama declares opposition to Israeli settlement expansion, Netanyahu vows to continue settlement building

2010–late 2012

"Arab Spring" erupts in December 2010 in Tunisia. Term refers to popular protests against long-standing regimes and lack of popular representation. Protests lead to fall of Tunisian government of Ben Ali in January 2011 and of Mubarak in Egypt in February, the former going into exile, Mubarak under house arrest. Similar uprising in Libya leads to civil war and death of Muammar al-Qaddafi in August 2011, and to change of government in Yemen. Protests in Bahrain, home port of the U.S. Fifth Fleet, are crushed by ruling dynasty, aided by Saudi forces with American acquiescence. In Syria similar calls for greater popular representation met with government military reprisals and eruption of civil war that continues. New governments have been elected in Tunisia and Egypt

2010–2012

Iran's nuclear enrichment program sparks increasing calls from Israel for end to any enrichment, with threats of an Israeli military attack on enrichment sites.

Netanyahu also demands the United States support Israel militarily. The United States imposes an economic sanctions program against Iran to force submission to its negotiating terms, backed by most Western powers

2011

Palestinian Authority President Mahmud Abbas fails in his bid to gain United Nations recognition of Palestinian statehood, blocked by American efforts. United States withdraws all combat forces from Iraq by end of year; estimated 9,000 contractors remain with U.S. Embassy personnel

2012

Palestinian and Israeli Arab populations in Gaza Strip, Israel, and West Bank now exceed Israeli Jewish populations in Israel, West Bank, and Golan Heights. U.S. Special forces assassinate Osama Bin Laden in Pakistan

2011–2012

Saudi Arabia's King Abdullah grants Saudi women the right to vote in municipal elections (2011); two Saudi female athletes are for the first time permitted to participate in the Olympic games, held in London, Summer 2012

Further Reading

Overviews

Amin, Cameron Michael, Benjamin C. Fortna, and Elizabeth Frierson, eds. *The Modern Middle East: A Sourcebook for History*. New York: Oxford University Press, 2006.

Bonine, Michael E., Abbas Amanat, and Michael Gaspar, eds. *Is There a Middle East? The Evolution of a Geopolitical Concept*. Stanford, Calif.: Stanford University Press, 2011.

Brand, Laurie A. *Cittizens Abroad: Emigration and the State in the Middle East and North Africa*. Cambridge: Cambridge University Press, 2006.

Clancy-Smith, Julia. "Mediterranean Historical Migrations: An Overview." In *Encyclopedia of Global Human Migration*, Immanuel Ness, ed. London: Wiley Blackwell, 2012.

Cleveland, William, and Martin Bunton. *A History of the Modern Middle East*. 4th ed. Boulder, CO: Westview Press, 2009.

Davis, Diana K., and Edmund Burke III, eds. *Environmental Imaginaries of the Middle East and North Africa*. Athens, OH: Ohio University Press, 2011.

Dawisha, Adeed. *Arab Nationalism in the Twentieth Century: From Triumph to Despair*. Princeton and Oxford: Princeton University Press, 2003.

Esposito, John L, Senior ed. *The Oxford Encyclopedia of the Islamic World*, revised ed. New York: Oxford University Press, 2009.

Fawaz, L. T., and Bayly, C. A. eds. *Modernity & Culture: From the Mediterranean to the Indian Ocean*. New York: Columbia University Press, 2002.

Findlay, Carter V. *The Turks in World History*. New York: Oxford University Press, 2005.

Gelvin, James. *The Modern Middle East, A History*. New York: Oxford University Press, 2005.

Hourani, Albert. *A History of the Arab Peoples*. Cambridge, Mass.: Belknap Press of Harvard University Press, 1991.

Khater, Akram Fouad. *Sources in the History of the Modern Middle East*. Boston: Houghton Mifflin, 2004.

Louis, William Roger. *The British Empire in the Middle East: Arab Nationalism, the United States, and Postwar Imperialism. 1945–1951*. Oxford: Oxford University Press, 1984.

McNeill, John R. *The Mountains of the Mediterranean World: An Environmental History*. Cambridge: Cambridge University Press, 1992.

Owen, Roger. *The Middle East in the World Economy, 1800–1914*. London and New York: Methuen, 1981.

Owen, Roger, and Sevket Pamuk, eds. *A History of Middle East Economies in the Twentieth Century*. London and New York: I. B. Tauris, 1998.

Rogan, Eugene L. *The Arabs: A History*. New York: Basic Books, 2009.

Schendel, Willem van, and Erik J. Zürcher, eds. *Identity Politics in Central Asia and the Muslim World: Nationalism, Ethnicity, and Labour in the Twentieth Century*. New York: I. B. Tauris, 2001.

Shields, Sarah D. *Fezzes in the River: Identity Politics and European Diplomacy on the Eve of World War Two*. Oxford: Oxford University Press, 2011.

Sluglett, Peter, ed. *The Urban Social History of the Middle East, 1750–1950*. Syracuse, N.Y.: Syracuse University Press, 2008.

Iran

Abrahamian, Ervand. *A History of Modern Iran*. New York: Cambridge University Press, 2008.

Abrahamian, Ervand. *Khomeinism: Essays on the Islamic Republic*. Berkeley: University of California Press, 1993.

Arjomand, Said Amir. *The Shadow of God and the Hidden Imam: Religion, Political Order, and Societal Change in Shi'ite Iran from the Beginning to 1890*. Chicago: University of Chicago Press, 1984.

Arjomand, Said Amir. *The Turban for the Crown: The Islamic Revolution in Iran*. New York: Oxford University Press, 1988.

Keddie, Nikki. *Modern Iran: Roots and Results of Revolution*, updated ed. New Haven, Conn.: Yale University Press, 2006.

Women's Worlds in Qajar Iran: www.qajar .women.org

Ottoman Empire

Boyer, Ebru, and Kate Fleet. *A Social History of Ottoman Istanbul*. New York: Cambridge University Press, 2010.

Hanssen, Jens, Thomas Phillipp, and Stefan Weber, eds. *Arab Provincial Capitals in the Late Ottoman Empire*. Würzburg, Germany: Ergon on Kommosson, 2002.

Inalcik, Halil, and Donald Quartaert, eds. *An Economic and Social History of the Ottoman Empire, 1300–1914*. Cambridge, UK: Cambridge University Press, 1994.

Pamuk, Sevket. *The Ottoman Empire and European Capitalism, 1820–1913: Trade, Investment, and Production*. Cambridge, UK and New York: Cambridge University Press, 1987.

Quartaert, Donald. *The Ottoman Empire, 1700–1922*. Cambridge, UK: Cambridge University Press, 2000.

Sluglett, Peter, ed., with Stefan Weber. *Syria and Bilad al-Sham under Ottoman Rule: Essays in Honor of Abd al-Karim Rafeq*. Boston: Brill, 2010.

Minorities

Braude, Benjamin, and Bernard Lewis, eds. *Christians and Jews in the Ottoman Empire: The Functioning of a Plural*

Society. Two Volumes. New York: Holes & Meier, 1982.

Goldberg, Harvey E., ed. *Sephardi and Middle Eastern Jewries: History and Culture in the Modern Era*. Bloomington: Indiana University Press, 1996.

Miller, Susan G., and Mauro Bertagnin, eds. *The Architecture and Memory of the Minority Quarter in the Muslim Mediterranean City*. Cambridge: Harvard University Press Graduate School of Design, 2010.

Shatzmiller, Maya, ed. *Nationalism and Minority Identities in Islamic Societies*. Montreal: McGill–Queen's University Press, 2005.

North Africa

Clancy-Smith, Julia A. *Mediterraneans: North Africa and Europe in an Age of Migration, c. 1800–1900*. Berkeley: University of California Press, 2011.

Clancy-Smith, Julia, ed. *North Africa, Islam, and the Mediterranean World from the Almoravids to the Algerian War*. London: Frank Cass Publications, 2001.

Coller, Ian. *Arab France: Islam and the Making of Modern Europe, 1789–1831*. Berkeley: University of California Press, 2010.

Davis, Diana K. *Resurrecting the Granary of Rome: Environmental History and French Colonial Expansion in North Africa*. Athens: Ohio University Press, 2007.

Algeria

Zeynep Çelik, Julia Clancy-Smith, and Frances Terpak, eds. *Walls of Algiers: Narratives of the City through Text and Image*. Los Angeles: the Getty Research Institute, and Seattle: University of Washington Press, 2009.

Clancy-Smith, Julia. *Rebel and Saint: Muslim Notables, Populist Protest, Colonial Encounters (Algeria and Tunisia, 1800–1904)*. Berkeley: University of California Press, 1994.

Ruedy, John. *Modern Algeria: The Origins and Development of a Nation*. Bloomington: Indiana University Press, 1992.

Silverstein, Paul. *Algeria in France: Transpolitics, Race, and Nation*. Bloomington: Indiana University Press, 2004.

Egypt

Baron, Beth. *The Woman's Awakening in Egypt: Culture, Society and the Press*. New Haven, Conn.: Yale University Press, 1994.

Beinin, Joel, and Zachary Lockman. *Workers on the Nile: Nationalism, Communism, Islam, and the Egyptian Working Class, 1882–1954*. Princeton: Princeton University Press, 1987.

Daley, M. W., ed. *The Cambridge History of Egypt: Volume 2. Modern Egypt from 1517 to the End of the Twentieth Century*. Cambridge, UK: Cambridge University Press, 1998.

Gershoni, Israel, and James Jankowski. *Egypt, Islam and the Arabs: The Search for Egyptian Nationhood, 1900–1930*. New York: Oxford University Press, 1986.

Jankowski, James. *Egypt: A Short History*. Oxford: Oneworld Press, 2000.

Reid, Donald M. *Whose Pharaohs?: Archaeology, Museums and Egyptian National Identity from Napoleon to World War I*. Berkeley: University of Californian Press, 2002.

Reimer, Michael. *Colonial Bridgehead: Government and Society in Alexandria, 1807–1882*. Cairo: American University in Cairo Press, 1997.

Morocco

Pennell, C. R. *Morocco since 1830: A History*. London: Hurst & Company, 2000.

Miller, Susan. *A History of Morocco, 1800–2000*. Cambridge: Cambridge University Press, 2012.

Palestine/Israel

Bregman, Ahron. *Israel's Wars: A History Since 1947*, 3rd ed. New York: Routledge, 2010.

Bregman, Ahron. *A History of Israel*. New York: Palgrave Macmillan, 2003.

Gerber, Haim. *Remembering and Imagining Palestine: Identity and Nationalism from the Crusades to the Present*. New York: Palgrave MacMillan, 2008.

Khalidi, Rashid I. *Palestinian Identity: The Construction of a Modern National Consciousness*. New York: Columbia University Press, 1997.

Lentin, Ronit, editor. *Thinking Palestine*. New York: Zed Books, 2008.

Lucas, Noah. *The Modern History of Israel*. New York: Praeger, 1975.

Pappé, Ilan. *A History of Modern Palestine: One Land, Two Peoples*, 2nd ed. Cambridge, UK: Cambridge University Press, 2006.

Quandt, William B. *Peace Process: American Diplomacy and the Arab-Israeli Conflict Since 1967*, 3rd ed. Washington, D.C., and Berkeley: Brookings Institution and University of California Press, 2005.

Sayigh, Yazid. *Armed Struggle and the Search for State: The Palestinian National Movement, 1949–1993*. New York: Oxford University Press, 1997.

Schindler, Colin. *A History of Modern Israel*. New York: Cambridge University Press, 2008.

Smith, Charles D. *Palestine and the Arab-Israeli Conflict*, 8th ed. Boston: Bedford St Martins, 2012.

(continued)

Stockdale, Nancy L. *Colonial Encounters Among English and Palestinian Women.* Gainesville: University Press of Florida, 2007.

Syria, Lebanon, Iraq, Jordan

Gualtieri, Sarah M. A. *Between Arab and White: Race and Ethnicity in the Early Syrian American Diaspora.* Berkeley: University of California Press, 2009.

Hanssen, Jens. *Fin de Siècle Beirut: The Making of an Ottoman Provincial Capital.* Oxford: Clarendon Press, 2005.

Khater, Akram F. *Inventing Home: Emigration, Gender, and the Middle Class in Lebanon, 1870–1920.* Berkeley: University of California Press, 2001.

Khuri-Makdisi, Ilham. *The Eastern Mediterranean and the Making of Global Radicalism, 1860–1914.* Berkeley: University of California Press, 2010.

Méouchy, Nadine, and Peter Sluglett, eds., with Gérard Khoury and Geoffrey Schad. *The British and French Mandates in Comparative Perspective.* Boston: Brill, 2004.

Salibi, Kamal. *A House of Many Mansions: The History of Lebanon Reconsidered.* Berkeley and Los Angeles: University of California Press, 1988.

Sluglett, Peter. *Britain in Iraq: Contriving King and Country,* rev. ed. New York: I. B. Tauris, 2007.

Tripp, Charles. *A History of Iraq.* Cambridge, UK: Cambridge University Press, 2000.

Tunisia

Perkins, Kenneth J. *A History of Modern Tunisia.* Cambridge, UK: Cambridge University Press, 2004.

Turkey

Hanioğlu, M. Sükrü. *Atatürk: An Intellectual Biography.* Princeton: Princeton University Press, 2011.

Zürcher, Erik Jan. *Turkey: A Modern History,* 3rd ed. London: I. B. Tauris, 2004.

Zürcher, Erik Jan. *The Young Turk Legacy and Nation Building: From the Ottoman Empire to Ataturk's Turkey.* London: I. B. Tauris, 2010.

Women and Gender

Abu-Lughod, Lila. *Writing Women's Worlds: Bedouin Stories.* Berkeley: University of California Press, 1993.

Amin, Cameron Michael. *The Making of the Modern Iranian Woman: Gender, State Policy, and Popular Culture.* Gainesville: University Press of Florida, 2002.

Baron, Beth. *Egypt as a Woman: Nationalism, Gender and Politics.* Berkeley: University of California Press, 2005.

Booth, Marilyn, ed. *Harem Histories: Envisioning Places and Living Spaces.* Durham, N.C.: Duke University Press, 2010.

Clancy-Smith, Julia. *Exemplary Women and Sacred Journeys: Women and Gender in Judaism, Christianity, and Islam from Late Antiquity to the Eve of Modernity.* Washington, D.C.: The American Historical Association, 2005.

Gabbay, Alyssa, and Julia Clancy-Smith, eds. *Fathers and Daughters in Islam.* Special Issue of the *Journal of Persianate Studies* 4, 1 (2011).

Meriwether, Margaret, and Judith Tucker, eds. *A Social History of Women and Gender in the Middle East.* Boulder, CO: Westview Press, 1999.

Sonbol, Amira. *Women of Jordan: Islam, Labor and the Law.* Syracuse: Syracuse University Press, 2003.

Thompson, Elizabeth. *Colonial Citizens: Republican Rights, Paternal Privilege, and Gender in French Syria and Lebanon.* New York: Columbia University Press, 2000.

Tucker, Judith. *Women in Nineteenth Century Egypt.* Cambridge, UK: Cambridge University Press, 1985.

Industry and Labor

Beinin, Joel. *Workers and Peasants in the Modern Middle East.* Cambridge, UK: Cambridge University Press, 2001.

Goldberg, Ellis Jay. *The Social History of Labor in the Middle East.* Boulder, CO: Westview Press, 1996.

Quataert, Donald. *Ottoman Manufacturing in the Age of the Industrial Revolution.* Cambridge, UK: Cambridge University Press, 1993.

Quataert, Donald, and Erik Jan Zürcher, eds. *Workers and the Working Class in the Ottoman Empire and the Turkish Republic.* London and New York: Tauris Academic Studies with the International Institute of Social History, Amsterdam, 1999.

Literature

Badran, Margot, and Miriam Cooke, eds. *Opening the Gates: A Century of Arab Feminist Writing.* London: Virago Press, 1990.

Booth, Marilyn. *May Her Likes Be Multiplied: Biography and Gender Politics in Egypt.* Berkeley: University of California Press, 2001.

Ostle, Robin, ed. *Modern Literature in the Near and Middle East, 1950–1970.* Routledge/SOAS Contemporary Politics and Culture in the Middle East Series. London: Routledge, 1991.

Education

Ayalon, Ami. *Reading Palestine: Printing and Literacy, 1900–1948.* Austin, Tex.: University of Texas Press, 2004.

Fortna, Benjamin C. *Imperial Classroom: Islam, the State and Education in the Late Ottoman Empire.* Oxford: Oxford University Press, 2002.

Fortna, Benjamin C. *Learning to Read in the Late Ottoman Empire and the Early Turkish Republic.* New York: Palgrave Macmillan, 2011.

Reid, Donald M. *Cairo University and the Making of Modern Egypt.* Cambridge, UK: Cambridge University Press, 1990.

Annotated Websites

Internet History Sourcebook Project

http://www.fordham.edu/halsall

Contains links to research sources for all regions of the world, for example, the Internet Islamic History Sourcebook and the Internet Modern History Sourcebook. The sites either contain documents or information on where they can be located.

Historical Text Archive

http://historicaltextarchive.com

Contains numerous documents on world history, including on MENA.

Clancy-Smith, Julia. "Women and Imperialism in North Africa, 19th–20th centuries."

http://chnm.gmu.edu/wwh

Fourteen documents translated from French and Arabic, with commentary, introductions, and teaching guide for one of the curriculum module in the "Women in World History Project," the Center for History and New Media Project, George Mason University.

World War I Document Archive

http://www.lib.byu.edu/-rdh/wwi

Superb archive on World War I in MENA

United Nations Documents on Israel and Palestine [UNISPAL]

http://domino.un.org/unispal.nsf

Contains all relevant documents and sources such as maps covering period 1945–present.

Foreign Relations of the United States, 1861–1958/60 (375 volumes)

http://www.digicoll.library.wisc.edu/FRUS/

This is the online record of the Foreign Relations of the United States produced by the State Department's Office of the Historian; printed volumes are available from the Government Printing Office. FRUS began with the Lincoln administration. There are two cumulative indexes covering 1861–1899 and 1900–1918. Those for 1918–1920 contain records for the Paris Peace Conference following World War I.

Foreign Relations for the United States, 1948–1976

http://www.state.gov/r/pa/ho/frus

Like the previous citation, these records are also available in printed volumes at the Government Printing Office. Although these volumes date from the Truman administration, sources are limited to the Cold War for that period; more extensive coverage can be found in the previous citation. Volumes for the Eisenhower administration are not as numerous as that found for the Kennedy administration (25 volumes), Johnson administration (34 volumes), and the Nixon and Ford administrations, where fifty-four volumes will be published when the series is completed; many volumes now available, including that for the Nixon administration, cover Middle Eastern issues.

Middle East Studies Association [MESA]

http://www.mesa.arizona.edu

MESA is the major professional organization for scholars of the Middle East in North America. Its Website contains links connecting to other search engines as well as to research institutions and scholarly organizations in the United States and abroad, including regional organizations such as the American Institute for Maghrib Studies and the Syrian Studies Association.

American Institute for Maghreb Studies [AIMS]

http://www.h-net.org/~maghrib

AIMS is the leading scholarly association for North African Studies. H-Maghrib is a list serve dedicated to scholarly research on North Africa for all historical periods, disciplines, and topics.

Association for Middle East Women's Studies [AMEWS]

http://www.amews.org

The association specializes in women's studies for the Middle East. Its Website also contains links to other organizations and groups.

http://www.Qajarwomen.com

A virtual archive of documents, photos, and images of Iranian women's worlds during the Qajar Dynasty.

History-NET Websites for scholarly discussion, access to sources, free subscription

Turkish and Ottoman History and Culture
H-TURK@H-NET.MSU.EDU

Gender in the Middle East
H-GENDER-MIDEAST@H-NET.MSU.EDU

Contemporary Middle Eastern affairs, including modern history
H-MIDEAST-POLITICS@H-NETMSU.EDU

Text Credits

Main Text

23–27: *Napoleon in Egypt: al-Jabarti's Chronicle of the French Occupation, 1798.* (Princeton: Markus Weiner Publishers, 1997), trans Shmuel Moreh, introduction by Robert L. Tignor, 136, 24–31, 109–10.

27–29: Ibid.

29–30: Gouvernor Général d'Algérie, *Bulletin Officiel des Actes du Gouvernment* (Paris: Imprimerie Royal, 1834–1854), I, 9, trans. in John Ruedy, *Land Policy in Colonial Algeria* (Berkeley and Los Angeles: University of California Press, 1967), 39–40. Republished in Robert Landen, *The Emergence of the Modern Middle East: Selected Readings.* (New York: Van Nostrand Reinhold, 1970), 150–51.

30–31: Alf Andrew Heggoy, *The French Conquest of Algiers, 1830: An Algerian Oral Tradition.* (Athens, Ohio: Ohio University Center for International Studies, 1986), 20.

31–32: Capitaine Carette, *Algérie*, in *L'Univers pittoresque. Histoire et description de tous les peuples, de leurs religions, moeurs, coutumes, industrie.* (Paris: Firmin Didot, 1850, 30–31 trans. Julia Clancy-Smith.

32–34: Statutes of the United States—© 1996–2007. The Avalon Project at Yale Law School. The Lillian Goldman Law Library in Memory of Sol Goldman. 127 Wall Street, New Haven, Connecticut 06520. http://avalon.law.yale.edu/19th_century/ot1862.asp.7

34–35: John Pudney, *Suez: De Lesseps' Canal* (New York: Praeger Publishers, 1970), 102–103.

35–37: Joseph Hendershot Park. *British Prime Ministers of the Nineteenth Century: Policies and Speeches.* (New York: New York University Press, 1916), 237–44.

37–39: Rondo Cameron, ed., *Civilization Since Waterloo: A Book of Source Readings.* (F. E. Peacock Publ., Itasca, Ill., 1971), 264–65.

39–41: Jules François Camille Ferry, "Speech Before the French Chamber of Deputies, March 28, 1884," *Discours et Opinions de Jules Ferry*, Paul Robiquet, ed. (Paris: Armand Colin & Cie., 1897), 199–201, 210–11, 215–18., trans. Julia Clancy-Smith.

41–43: The Earl of Cromer, *Modern Egypt*, 2 vols. (London: Macmillan, 1908) 2: 326–30.

43–44: *The Zionist Idea: A Historical Analysis and Reader.* Arthur Hertzberg, ed. (New York: Meridian Books Inc., 1960): 204–9, 215–23.

45: Samuel M. Zwemer, D. D., and Arthur J. Brown, D.D., *The Nearer and Farther East.* (New York: The MacMillan Company, 1908), 70, 85–6.

46–47: Julia Clancy-Smith, "A Woman Without Her Distaff: Gender, Work, and Handicraft Production in Colonial North Africa," in Margaret Meriwether and Judith Tucker, eds., *A Social History of Women and the Family in the Middle East,*. (Boulder, CO: Westview Press, 1999). Documents from the Bibliotheque de la Ville de Paris, Fonds Bougle, Manuscrits Hubertine Auclert, La Presse et le Feminisme, 1880–1914, carton no. 2. Trans. by Julia Clancy-Smith. Women in World

History is a project of the Center for History and New Media, George Mason University, and part of World History Matters, with support from the National Endowment for the Humanities, ©2004–2006 Center for History and New Media.

47–48: Julia Clancy-Smith, "Imperialism in North Africa, "in Women in World History is a project of the Center for History and New Media, George Mason University, and part of World History Matters, with support from the National Endowment for the Humanities, © 2004–2006 Center for History and New Media. Coriat's 1902 report was originally published in Akram F. Khater, *Sources in the History of the Modern Middle East.* (Boston: Houghton Mifflin, 2004), 87–88.

49: Zeynep Çelik, *Displaying the Orient: Architecture of Islam at Nineteenth-Century World's Fairs,* (Berkeley and Los Angeles: University of California Press, 1992), 18.

49–51: Karl Baedeker, *Egypt and the Sudan: Handbook for Travellers.* Sixth Remodelled Edition (Leipzig: Karl Baedeker Publishers, 1908), xxiii–xxiv, 120.

51–53: Wilfred Scawen Blunt, *My Diaries: 1888–1914.* (London: Martin Secker, 1932), 212–213, 299, 375–77.

53: Ibid., 560–61.

53–54: Ziad Fahmy, *Ordinary Egyptians: Creating the Modern Nation Through Popular Culture,* (Stanford: Stanford University Press, 2011), 108.

54–56: J. C. Hurewitz, ed., *The Middle East and North Africa in World Politics: A Documentary Record,* 2 volumes. *European Expansion, 1535–1914,* 2nd ed. (New Haven: Yale University Press, 1975), I, 482–4.

56–57: Source: Great Britain, *Parliamentary Papers,* London, 1908, Vol CXXV, Cmd. 3750. © 1996–2007 The Avalon Project at Yale Law School. The Lillian Goldman Law Library in Memory of Sol Goldman. 127 Wall Street New Haven, Connecticut 06520. http://avalon.law.yale.edu/20th_century/angrusen.asp

57–59: Source: Jamal al-Din al-Afghani, *Al-'Urwa al-Wuthqa* (The Indissoluble Bond), August 28, 1884, trans. in Nikki R. Keddie, *An Islamic Response to Imperialism: Political and Religious Writings of Sayyid Jamal al-Din al-Afghani.* (Berkeley and Los Angeles: University of California Press, 1968), 175–80.

65–67: C. R. Pennell, National University of Singapore from Chronicles of al-Jabarti—cAbd al-Rahman al-Jabarti *cajaib al-athar f-il-tarajim w-al-akhbar,* Cairo 1297/1879 IV, 93–94,141–142, 154, 183, 208–209). © 1990–2008 Donald J. Mabry / The Historical Text Archive: http://historicaltextarchive.com.

67–68: Camron Michael Amin, Benjamin C. Fortna, and Elizabeth Frierson, eds., *The Modern Middle East: A Sourcebook for History.* (New York: Oxford University Press, 2006), 40–41.

69: Ibid., 40.

70: Ibid., 41–42.

70–71: Ibid., 402–03.

71–74: "Hatti Sherif of Gülhane: The Rose Garden Decree." J .C. Hurewitz, ed. *Diplomacy in the Near and Middle East: A Documentary Record,* 2 volumes, *1535–1914* (Princeton: D Van Nostrand Company, 1956), I, 113–15.

74–75: Susan Gilson Miller, ed. and trans., *Disorienting Encounters: Travels of a Moroccan Scholar in France, 1845–1846* (Berkeley: University of California Press, 1992), 123, 124, 125, 126, 131.

75–76: Julia Clancy-Smith, "A Visit to a Tunisian Harem." In *Journal of Maghrebi Studies* 1–2, 1 (Spring 1993): 43–49. Taken from a manuscript entitled "On the Tunisian Harem," based on three different eye-witness accounts by European women furnished to the English traveler in Tunisia, James Richardson, and included in his "An Account of the Present State of Tunis," 1845, Public Record Office, London, Foreign Office Records, Tunisia, 102/29.

76–77: Khayr al-Din, *The Surest Path to Knowledge Concerning the Condition of States.* L. Carl Brown, ed., trans., and introduction, *The Surest Path: The Political Treatise of a Nineteenth-Century Muslim Statesman* (Cambridge, MA: Harvard University Press, 1967) 71–73.

78–82: Edward G. Browne, *A Brief Narrative of Recent Events in Persia, followed by a Translation of "The Four Pillars of the Persian Constitution."* (London: Luzac & Co., January 1909), 65–101.

82–84: Proclamation for the Ottoman Empire. Rondo Cameron, ed., *Civilization since Waterloo: A Book of Source Readings.* (Itasca, Ill.: F. E. Peacocks, 1971), 244–46.

84–85: Mervet Hatem, " 'Aisha Taymur's Tears and the Critique of the Modernist and Feminist Discourse on Nineteenth-Century Egypt," in Lila Abu-Lughod, ed., *Remaking Women: Feminism and Modernity in the Middle East.* (Princeton: Princeton University Press, 1998), 76–77.

85: Ziad Fahmy, *Ordinary Egyptians: Creating the Modern Nation Through Popular Culture.* (Stanford: Stanford University Press, 2011), 81.

86–88: Source: Qasim Amin, *Al-Mar'ah al Jadidah* (The New Woman) (Cairo, 1900), in Qasim Amin, *The Liberation of Women, The New Woman: Two Documents in the History of Egyptian Feminism,* Trans. by Samiha Sidhom Pederson (Cairo: American University in Cairo Press, 2001), 130–34.

88–93: Bahithat al-Badiya 1909 lecture. *Oxford Islamic Studies Online,* http:www.oxfordislamic studies .com.exproxy2.library.arizona.edu/article/book/islam-9780195154672/islam-9780195154672-chapter-5.

93–94: Fahmy, *Ordinary Egyptians,* 82.

95: 1889 letter from Yusuf Bey, Ottoman consul, Barcelona, in Roberto Marín-Guzmán and Zidane Zéraoui, *Arab Immigration to Mexico in the Nineteenth and Twentieth Centuries: Assimilation and Arab Heritage* (Austin, TX: Morgan Printing, 2003), 28.

95: Letter from Nuam Pasha, governor of Mount Lebanon, to the Ottoman Minister of the Interior, 1895 in Ibid.,31.

100–2: Charles F. Horne, ed., *Source Records of the Great War.* 7 volumes. (Indianapolis: The American Legion Press, 1931): II, *1914*, 398–400.

102–4: Halide Edib Adivar, *The Memoirs of Halide Edib* (New York and London: The Century Co., 1926): 450–51, 468.

104–5: Sapper H. P. Bonser, Royal Engineers (Signals), February 1916 to July 1919. Foreign Service units: 74th Divisional Signal Company, Egypt, Southern Palestine; Detached Duty, Fayoum Area; U.U. Cable Section. Royal Engineers, Egypt, Palestine, Syria. C. B. Purdom, editor. *Everyman at War.* (London: 1930), republished with introduction by Jon E. Lewis. (Guilford, CT: Globe Pequot Press, 2005): 311–18.

105–7: Horne, ed., *Source Records*, III, *1915*. 263–67.

107–9: Ellis Ashmead-Bartlett's Private Letter to Prime Minister Asquith, 8 September 1915. www.nla.gov.au/gallipolidespatches/2-2-3-ashmead.html; National Library of Australia

109–13: "The Armenian Massacres," By Dr. Martin Niepage (1886–1953), 1915. Horne, ed., *Source Records*, III, 1915, 161–72.

113–16: "The Hussein-McMahon Correspondence, July 1915–January 1916," George Antonius, *The Arab Awakening* (New York: Capricorn Books, 1965), 414–20.

117: "The Sykes-Picot Agreement, 1916." Ibid.,: 428–30.

118: "The Balfour Declaration, 1917." *Palestine Royal Commission Report.* Presented by the Secretary of State for Colonies to Parliament by Command of His Majesty, July 1937. Cmd. 5479. (London: His Majesty's Stationery Office, 1937): 16–17.

119–20: "Woodrow Wilson's 'Fourteen Points' Speech, 8 January 1918." Horne, ed., *Source Records*. VI. *1918*. 3–6.

120–22: "Article 22 of the Covenant of the League of Nations." *The League of Nations Covenant.* (London: the League of Nations Union, 1919).

122–25: "Resolutions of the General Syrian Congress, Damascus, July 2, 1919." Antonius, *The Arab Awakening*, 440–42.

125–27: The Gertrude Bell Archive, "The Diaries," The Robinson Library, Newcastle University: www.gerty.ncl.ac.uk

127–29: Huda Shaarawi, *Harem Years: The Memoirs of an Egyptian Feminist*, trans., ed., and introduced by Margot Badran. (New York: Feminist Press of the City University of New York, 1987), 112–17.

130: Ziad Fahmy, *Ordinary Egyptians: Creating the Modern Nation Through Popular Culture.* (Stanford: Stanford University Press, 2011): 134.

131–33: "The Anglo-Persian Treaty of August 1919." United States Department of State, *Foreign Relations of the United States, 1919.* 2 volumes, II, 698–704. Downloaded from http://digicoll.library.wisc.edu/FRUS.

133–35: "A Report on Mesopotamia by Ex.-Lieut.-Col. T. E. Lawrence," *The Sunday Times*, 2 August 1920.

157–58: Bernard Lewis, *The Emergence of Modern Turkey.* 2nd ed.. (London: Oxford University Press, 1968), 268–69, 271, 278.

158: "Turks Will Adopt New Name System: Find that Family Designation Necessary to Needs of Modern State," *The New York Times*, January 21, 1934.

158–59: www.turkishdailynews.com.tr/archives.php?id=22473]

159–60: Halide Edib, "Dictatorship and Reforms in Turkey," *Yale Review*, XIX (September 1929), 27–44.

161: Camron Michael Amin, *Making the Modern Iranian Woman: Gender, State Policy and Popular Culture, 1865–1946* (Gainesville: University Press of Florida, 2002), 83.

162–64: Etel Adnan, "Growing Up to be a Woman Writer in Lebanon," keynote address delivered to Association of Middle Eastern Women's Studies meeting, Boston, 1986. In Margot Badran and Miriam Cooke, eds,., *Opening the Gates: A Century of Arab Feminist Writing* (Bloomington: Indiana University Press, 1990), 5–20.

165–66: *Egypt, Tourist Guide: General Information on Travelling* (Cairo: Egyptian State Tourist Administration, 1937): 5–7, 15–42, 45–46.

166–68: Taha Hussein, *The Future of Culture in Egypt* (Cairo, 1938), trans. by Sidney Glazer. (American Council of Learned Societies Near Eastern Translation Program, Number Nine. Washington, D.C., 1954), 1–4, 7–8, 15, 17–18, 21–22.

169–70: Naguib Mahfouz, *Midaq Alley*, 1947, trans. by Trevor Le Gassick. (Washington, D.C.: Three Continents Press, 1977): 1–2, 53, 127, 190–91, 243–45.

171–73: "Between Yesterday and Today," by Hassan al-Banna. *Five Tracts of Hasan al-Banna 1946–1949: A Selection from the 'Majmu'at Rasa'il al-Imam al-Shahid Hasan al-Banna'*, trans. and annotated by Charles Wendell. (Berkeley and Los Angeles: University of California Press, Publications in Near Eastern Studies, Volume 20, 1978): 13–39.

173–74: Anna and Pierre Cachia, *Landlocked Islands: Two Alien Lives in Egypt* (Cairo: The American University in Cairo Press, 1999), 132–33.

174–75: Albert Memmi, *The Pillar of Salt*, trans. by Edouard Rodith. (Chicago: J. Philip O'Hara, 1975), 99–101.

175–77: Perdita Huston, *Motherhood by Choice: Pioneers in Women's Health and Family Planning* (New York: The Feminist Press, 1992), 96–98. Biography from Julia Clancy-Smith, "Women in World History," Center for History and New Media, George Mason University. © 2004–2006 Center for History and New Media.

178–79: "Program of l'Etoile Nord-Africaine, 1933," trans by Mitch Abidor from *Messali Hadj par les Textes;*

textes choisis et presentés par Jacques Simon (Paris: Editions Bouchéne, 2000), http://www.marxists.org/archive/messali-hadj.

179–81: "Habib Bourguiba's Note to Pierre Vienot, the Popular Front Undersecretary for French Foreign Affairs, 28 August 1936;" from Habib Bourguiba, *L'Action Tunisienne*, 23 December 1936, reprinted in J. C. Hurewitz, *The Middle East and Africa in World Politics*, 2 volumes, (New Haven: Yale University Press, 1979), II, 496–99

182–84: "The Mandate for Palestine (July 24, 1922), the League of Nations." The Royal Institute for International Affairs, Information Department Papers No. 22A, *Great Britain and Palestine, 1915–1939*, The Edition of January 1937 Revised and Enlarged. (London: Oxford University Press, July 1939): Appendix II, 119–23.

184–87: "British White Paper of June 1922 On European Jewish Immigration to Palestine" Ibid., Appendix III, 123–126.

187–90: "British White Paper of Palestine of 1939." Ibid., Appendix VI, 134–40.

190–91: "Statement of President Harry S Truman (1884–1972)," October 4, 1946. *A Decade of American Foreign Policy: Basic Documents 1941–1949* (revised edition). Department of State Publications 9443; Department and Foreign Service Series 415. (Washington, D.C., U.S. Government Printing Office, Office of the Historian, 1985): 692–93.

192–93: T. G. Fraser, *The Middle East, 1914–1979* (New York: St. Martin's Press, 1980), 66–67.

194–96: Nissim Rejwan. *The Last Jews of Baghdad: Remembering a Lost Homeland.* (Austin: the University of Texas Press, 2004): 126–32.

196–97:. Nadje Sadig al-Ali, *Iraqi Women: Untold Stories from 1948 to the Present* (London and New York: Zed Books, 2007), 24–25.

197–98: Department of State, *American Foreign Policy, 1941–1949*, 718–19.

198–201: "The International Petroleum Cartel," Staff Report to the Federal Trade Commission, released through Subcommittee on Monopoly of Select Committee on Small Business, U.S. Senate, 83d Cong., 2nd sess (Washington, D.C., 1952), Chapter 5, "Other Common Ownerships in the Middle East," 113–136.

207–8: Ministry of Foreign Affairs, Israel, Law of Return 5710-1950. Passed by the Knesset on the 20th Tammuz, 5710 (5th July, 1950). www.mfa.gov.il

208–9: Nadje Sadig al-Ali, *Iraqi Women: Untold Stories from 1948 to the Present.* (New York: Zed Books, 2007): 26–27.

209–10: *Identity Card* by Mahmoud Darwish 1964. By courtesy & © 2000 Barghouti.com Copyright © 2000 Media Monitors Network.

211–12: Premier Gamal Abdul Nasser, *Egypt's Liberation: The Philosophy of the Revolution*. Introduction by Dorothy Thompson. (Washington, D.C.: Public Affairs Press, 1955): 19, 27–8, 31–6, 39–40.

213: The Eisenhower Doctrine, January 5, 1957. *The Department of State Bulletin*, XXXVI, No. 917 (January 21, 1957): 83–7.

213–14: Dwight D. Eisenhower, *The White House Years: Waging Peace, 1956–1961*. (Garden City, N.Y.: Doubleday, 1965): 266, 289, 291.

214–15: Marvin E. Gettelman & Stuart Schaar, editors, *The Middle East and Islamic World Reader*. (New York, Grove Press, 2003): 254–55.

215–16: George McGhee, *On the Frontline in the Cold War: An Ambassador Reports*. (Westport, Conn.: Praeger, 1997): 144.

216–18: Donald J. Mabry / The Historical Text Archive: Electronic History Resources, 1990–2007, http://historicaltextarchive.com

218–20: Henri Alleg, *The Question*, trans. by John Calder, Preface by Jean-Paul Sartre. (London: John Calder Publishers, 1958): 45–50, 56–8, 95–6.

220–21: C. L Sulzberger, *The Last of the Giants*. (New York: Macmillian Company, 1970), 548–49.

221–22: Perdita Huston, *Motherhood by Choice: Pioneers in Women's Health and Family Planning*. (New York: The Feminist Press of the City of New York, 1992): 99–101.

222–24: Sources: Leila Abouzeid, *Women Return to Childhood: The Memoir of a Modern Moroccan* (Austin, Texas: The Center for Middle Eastern Studies, 1998), 3, 36–37; and Julia Clancy-Smith, "Imperialism in North Africa, 18th–20th Centuries," the Center for History and New Media Project, George Mason University, "Women in World History." http://chnm.gmu.edu/wwh.

224: Quoted in Amira Sonbol, *Women of Jordan: Islam, Labor, and the Law* (Syracuse: Syracuse University Press, 2003), 93–94.

225–26: Security Council Resolution 242. *Foreign Relations of the United States, 1964–1968*. Vol. XIX, *Arab-Israeli Crisis and War 1967*. Harriet Daschiell Schwar, ed.. (Washington, D.C.: U.S. Government Printing Office, 2004): 1062–63.

226–27: Naomi Shermer, "Jerusalem the Gold." Israeli Ministry of Foreign Affairs, www.gov.il

228: Mona Takieddine Amyuni. In Lamia Rustum Shehadeh, ed., *Women and War in Lebanon* (Gainesville: University Press of Florida, 1999), 89.

229–33: Qaddafi's *Green Book*. http://www .mathaba.net/gci/theory/gb.htm, accessed via Council on Foreign Relations: http://www.cfr.org/libya/ libya-al-qaddafis-green-book/p20282

234–35: Sayyid Qutb, *Milestones* (Beirut: The Holy Koran Publishing House, 1978): 14–17, 32–34, 104–5, 113.

235–37: Marvin E. Gettelman and Stuart Schaar, editors, *The Middle East and Islamic World Reader*. (New York: Grove Press, 2003): 255–57.

237: Lyrics: Ahmed Shafik; music: Mohamed Abdel Wehab; from *Enta Omri*—English lyrics and short mp3 excerpts of original recording of one of Umm Kulthum's best known songs. Translation by the late Hani Guirguis of Toronto, Canada. Translation provided courtesy of Yasmina Ramzy of Arabesque Academy of Toronto, Canada.

238–39: David McMurray, "Haddou: A Moroccan Migrant Worker," in Edmund Burke III, editor, *Struggle and Survival in the Modern Middle East* (Berkeley and Los Angeles: University of California Press, 1993), 378–80.

247–49: Annette Grossbongardt in Istanbul; © SPIEGEL ONLINE 2007. All Rights Reserved; reproduction only allowed with the permission of SPIEGELnet GmbH Der Spiegel online: www.spiegel .de/international/world/0,1518,477158,00.html April 13, 2007 for all four articles. Translated from the German by Christopher Sultan.

249–50: Parliamentary Assembly, Council of Europe Doc. 10358 rev. 25 November 2004; http:// assembly/coe.int/Documents/WorkingDocs/Doc04/ EDOC10358.htm.

249–50: Nicholas Kulish ," Euro 2008 Germany, Turkey and Jumbled Loyalties," ; Steffen Scholz contributed reporting. : New York Times June 25, 2008,; Copyright 2008 The New York Times Company.

250–51: Julia Clancy-Smith, "Women in World History," © 2004–2006 Center for History and New Media, George Mason University. From the recording entitled "Amina: Wa di Yé," Mega Studio, Paris, 1992. Trans.Julia Clancy-Smith. Radio France Internationale (RFI), July 2001, www.rfimusique.com/siteEn/ biographie, "Amina."; and www.beurfm.net/article.

251–53: "France: Headscarf Ban Violates Religious Freedom: By Disproportionately Affecting Muslim Girls, Proposed Law Is Discriminatory," New York, February 27, 2004. http://hrw.org/english/ docs/2004/02/26/france7666.htm. © Copyright 2003, Human Rights Watch 350 Fifth Avenue, 34th Floor, New York, NY 10118 3299, USA.

253–56: Katrin Bennhold, "French Muslims Find Haven in Catholic Schools," New York Times, September 25, 2008.

256–58: Zehra Ayman and Ellen Knickmeyer, "Ban on Head Scarves Voted Out in Turkey: Parliament Lifts 80-Year-Old Restriction on University Attire." Washington Post, February 10, 2008; A17.

258–59: Sadeeka Arebi, Women and Words in Saudi Arabia: The Politics of Literary Discourse (New York, Columbia University Press 1994), 279–80, quoted in Guity Nashat and Judith Tucker, eds., Women in the Middle East and North Africa, 2 vols. (Bloomington: Indiana University Press, 1998) 2: 124.

259–62: Unofficial English translation of the 2004 Moroccan Family Law (Moudawana) prepared by a team of English and Arabic speaking lawyers and a professional Arabic English Moroccan translator at the Global Rights Head Office in Washington and their Field Office in Morocco. Sherifyan Dahir (Royal Edict) n° 1.04.22 issued on 12 Dou Al Hijja 1424. Translation copyright 2005 by Global Rights. www.globalrights.org/morocco

263–64: www.mfa.gov.il/MFA/Peace+Process

264–66: Likud: Walter Laqueur and Barry Rubin, eds., The Israel-Arab Reader: A Documentary History of the Middle East Conflict. (New York: Penguin Books, 1984): 591–2. Hamas: Shaul Mishal and Avraham Sela, The Palestinian Hamas: Vision, Violence and Coexistence. (New York: Columbia University Press, 2006), 176–83.

267–68: Posted at globalresearch.ca 15 October 2001. Translated from the French by Bill Blum. The URL of this article is: http://www.globalresearch.ca/articles/ BRZ110A.html. Copyright, Le Nouvel Observateur and Bill Blum. In Marvin E. Gettelman and Stuart Schaar, eds., The Middle East and Islamic World Reader. (New York: Grove Press, 2003): 273–74.

268–72: Nadje Sadig Al-Ali, Iraqi Women: Untold Stories from 1948 to the Present. (London: Zed Books, 2007), 49–50, 117–18, 128, 163, 165–66, 181, 210.

272–75: Federation of American Scientists. World Islamic Front Statement February 23, 1998. www.fas .org/irp/world/para/docs/980223-fatwa-htm.

275–78: President Bush's State of the Union Address 2002 www.whitehouse.gov/news/ releases/2002/01/20020129-11.html.

278–83: "Shirin Ebadi—Nobel Peace Prize Lecture." . http://www.nobelprize.org/nobel_prizes/peace/ laureates/2003/ebadi-lecture.html. Copyright © The Nobel Foundation 2003.

283–86: "Iraq: Millions in flight: the Iraqi refugee crisis," Amnesty International, September 24, 2007. www.amnesty.org/en/library/info/MDE14/041/2007

286–89: "The Road to Abu Ghraib," Human Rights Watch. http://www.hrw.org/reports/2004/06/08/ road-abu-ghraib.

289–92: "Dr. Mohamed El Baradei—Nobel Peace Prize Lecture 2005," http://www.nobelprize.org/ nobel_prizes/peace/laureates/2005/elbaradei-lecture .html. Copyright © Nobel Web AB 2008.

292–94: Nejib Ayachi, "Remarks on the Unfolding of Events and the Nature of Tunisia's Political Regime." Transcripts of the Maghreb Center Conference on the Breakdown of Autocracy in Tunisia. February 9, 2011. www.maghrebcenter.org

294–96: guardian.co.uk, Tuesday 7 December 2010 16.29 EST http://www.guardian.co.uk/world/ us-embassy-cables-documents/2183.

296–98: "Memories of 1977," Al-Ahram Weekly Online, weekly.ahram.org.eg/2008/881/eg5.htm

298–99: Ken Rapoza, "The Brains behind Occupy Wall Street and where Its Heading," http://www .forbes.com/sites/kenrapoza/2011/10/14/ the-brains-behind-occupy-wall-street-and-where -its-heading.

Sidebars

20: J. C. Hurewitz, ed. *Diplomacy in the Near and Middle East*. 2 volumes. *A Documentary Record, 1535–1914*. (New York: D. Van Nostrand Company, 1956): I, 109–10.

20: The Hon Evelyn Ashley, M. P. *The Life of Henry John Temple, VISCOUNT PALMERSTON, 1846–1865, with Selections from his Speeches and Correspondence*. 2 volumes, second edition. (London: Richard Bentley & Son, 1876): II, 41–2.

22: Quoted in Roger Owen, *Lord Cromer: Victorian Imperialist, Edwardian Proconsul*. (Oxford: Oxford University Press, 2004): 169.

22: Ashley, *VISCOUNT PALMERSTON*, II, 308.

31: Zeynep Çelik, *The Remaking of Istanbul: Portrait of an Ottoman City in the Nineteenth Century*. (Berkeley: University of California Press, 1993), 33:

37: George Douin, *Histoire du règne du khedive Ismail*. (Rome, 1934): 2:10, quoted in Zeynep Çelik, *Displaying the Orient: Architecture of Islam at Nineteenth-Century World's Fairs*. (Berkeley and Los Angeles: University of California Press, 1992): 13.

41: Sir Mortimer Durand, *Life of the Right Hon. Sir Alfred Comyn Lyall*. (Edinburgh and London: William Blackwood and Sons, 1913): 426–7.

43: Theodor Herzl, *Zionist Writings: Essays and Addresses*. Volume 1. *January 1896–June 1898*, trans. by Harry Zohn. (New York: Herzl Press, 1973): 211–15.

45: Quote in Ussama Makdisi, *The Culture of Sectarianism: Community, History, and Violence in Nineteenth-Century Ottoman Lebanon*. (Berkeley: University of California Press, 2000): 92.

49: Roger Allen, *A Period of Time: A Study and Translation of Muhammad al-Muwaylihi's 'Hadith Isa Ibn Hisham*. (St. Antony's College, Oxford: Ithaca Press, 1992): 314–15.

53: George Bernard Shaw, "The Dinshawai Horror," taken from Shaw, *John Bull's Other Island, 1907*, quoted in Owen, *Lord Cromer*, p. 339.

58: I. *Arab Nationalism: An Anthology*. Sylvia G. Haim, editor. (Berkeley: University of California Press, 1964): 81–82. II. Neville J. Mandel, *The Arabs and Zionism before World War I*. (Berkeley: University of California Press, 1976): 52.

71: Camron Michael Amin, Benjamin C. Fortna, and Elizabeth Frierson, eds, *The Modern Middle East: A Sourcebook for History*. (New York: Oxford University Press, 2006), 405.

77: Allen Christelow, "Intellectual History in a Culture Under Siege: Algerian Thought in the Last Half of the Nineteenth Century." *Middle Eastern Studies* 18, 4 (1982), 392.

84: Jasamin Rostam-Kolayi, "Origins of Iran's Modern Girls' Schools: From a Private/National to Public/State," in *Journal of Middle East Women's Studies* 4, 3 (2008), 59.

94: Akram Fouad Khater, *Inventing Home: Emigration, Gender, and the Middle Class in Lebanon, 1870–1920* (Berkeley: University of California Press, 2001), 1.

102: Liman von Sanders, *Five Years in Turkey* (Annapolis: U.S. Naval Institute, 1927), 131.

116: Public Record Office, Great Britain. FO 371/2486/163832 October 26, 1915.

118: Leonard Stein, *The Balfour Declaration*. (London: Vallentine Mitchell, 1961): 664.

123: *Palestine Papers 1917–1922: Seeds of Conflict*. Compiled and Annotated by Doreen Ingrams. (London: John Murray,1972): 73.

125: Ibid.

130: Elizabeth Monroe, *Britain's Moment in the Middle East, 1914–1956*. (London: Allen & Unwin, 1963): 56.

161: Harry A. Franck, *The Fringe of the Moslem World*, (New York: The Century Co., 1928), 171.

173: Elizabeth Thompson, *Colonial Citizens: Republican Rights, Paternal Privilege, and Gender in French Syria and Lebanon* (New York: Columbia University Press, 2000), 204.

177: Eqbal Ahmed and Stuart Schaar, "M'hamed Ali: Labor Organizer." In Edmund Burke III, ed., *Struggle and Survival in the Modern Middle East* (Berkeley and Los Angeles: University of California Press, 1993), 201.

179: Rick Atkinson, *An Army at Dawn: The War in North Africa, 1942–1943*. 2 volumes. I., *The Liberation Trilogy*. (New York: Henry Holt and Company, 2002): 34.

182: Chaim Weizmann, *Trial and Error: The Autobiography of Chaim Weizmann*. (New York: Schocken Books, 1966): 279–80.

206: Albert Memmi, Memmi, *Decolonisation and the Decolonized*, trans. by Robert Bononni. (Minneapolis: University of Minnesota Press, 2006): 3–4.

211: Lawrence James, *The Illustrated Rise and Fall of the British Empire*. Abridged by Helen Lownie (New York: St. Martin's Press, 1999), 316.

213: Wilbur Crane Eveland, *Ropes of Sand: America's Failure in the Middle East*. (New York: W.W. Norton, 1980): 252.

214: Kermit Roosevelt, *Countercoup: The Struggle for the Control of Iran*. (New York: McGraw-Hill Book Company, 1979): 8.

224: Amira Sonbol, *Women of Jordan: Islam, Labor, and the Law* (Syracuse: Syracuse University Press, 2003), 87.

225: *Papers of Lyndon Baines Johnson, President 1963–1969*, President's Appointment File (Diary Backup), Box 67. Lyndon Baines Johnson Presidential Library [LBJL].

226: *Foreign Relations of the United States, 1964–1968*. Volume 19, Harriet Dashiell Schwar, editor. *Arab-Israeli Crisis and War, 1967*. (Washington: U.S. Government Printing Office, 2004): #269, 444–47, 12 June 1967.

235: Asadollah Alam, *The Shah and I: The Confidential Diary of Iran's Royal Court, 1969–1977*. Introduced and ed. by Alinaghi Alikhani; trans. by Alinaghi Alikhani and Nicholas Vincent. (New York: St. Martin's Press, 1992), 158–159.

236: Ibid.,114–115.

239: Homa Hoodfar, "Survival Strategies and the Political Economy of Low-Income Households in Cairo," in *Development, Change, and Gender in Cairo: A View from the Household*, eds. Diane Singerman and Homa Hoodfar (Bloomington: Indiana University Press, 1996), 115.

245: Orhan Pamuk, *Istanbul: Memories and the City*, trans. by Mauren Freely. (New York: Alfred A. Knopf, 2005), 47.

248: Germaine Tillon, *France and Algeria: Complementary Enemies*, trans. by Richard Howard. (New York: Alfred A. Knopf, 1961): 119.

265: Rabin: David Makovsky and Michal Yudelman, "PM: Oslo II is 'Blow to Greater Israel.'" *Jerusalem Post International Edition*, August 26, 1995.; Netanyahu: Sarah Honig, "Opposition stages its own signing, declares loyalty to Land of Israel." Ibid. October 7, 1995; Amir: Raanan Ben-Zur, www.ynet .com May 4, 2012.

267: Samuel P. Huntington, *The Clash of Civilizations and the Remaking of World Order*. (New York: Simon and Schuster, 1996), 51.

288: http://georgewbush-whitehouse.archives.gov .news/releases/2001/09

296: Nader Ferghany, lead author of the *Arab Human Development Report* (Cairo, 2002), quoted in Stephen King, "Remarks on the Socio-Economic Causes of the [Tunisian] Uprising." *Transcripts of the Maghreb Center Conference on the Breakdown of Autocracy in Tunisia*. February 9, 2011. www.maghrebcenter.org

Picture Credits

Acknowledgments

The authors wish to acknowledge the effort and care taken by Sandra J. Kimball in preparing the index, as well as the reviewers, in particular, L. Carl Brown.

Index

References to illustrations and their captions are indicated by page numbers in **bold**. Surnames beginning with *al-* or *el-* are alphabetized by the remaining portion of name. "MENA" in all instances refers to Middle East and North Africa.